T0250512

# Ethical Reasoning
## —————— *in the*
# Mental Health Professions

Gary George Ford

**CRC Press**
**Boca Raton   London   New York   Washington, D.C.**

## Library of Congress Cataloging-in-Publication Data

Ford, Gary George
    Ethical reasoning in the mental health professions / Gary George Ford.
       p. cm.
    Includes bibliographical references and index.
    ISBN 0-8493-2077-1 (alk. paper)
    1. Mental health personnel--Professional ethics. 2. Psychiatric ethics. I. Title.

RC455.2.E8 F67 2000
174′.2—dc21
                                                                  00-058556

**Visit the CRC Press Web site at www.crcpress.com**

© 2001 by CRC Press LLC

No claim to original U.S. Government works
International Standard Book Number 0-8493-2077-1
Library of Congress Card Number 00-058556
Printed in the United States of America 2 3 4 5 6 7 8 9 0
Printed on acid-free paper

*To my daughters, Lynette Jeanne and Caroline Ruth,
and my wife, Angela Mae, the loves of my life.*

# Preface

This book is, first and foremost, a treatise in applied ethics. Most ethics texts explain the duties of professionals that are outlined in the profession's ethical code. This book is designed to assist the mental health professional in developing the ability to reason ethically, a skill that is an extraordinarily important component of professionalism in any field, but one that is grossly underdeveloped in many professionals. The greatest challenges to ethical professional practice are the novel situations that arise involving conflicts between two ethical principles. Readers will learn how to resolve these conflicts in a rational manner by understanding the philosophical sources of professional ethical duties and applying that knowledge to practical problems using a new model of ethical decision making.

As readers immerse themselves in ethical issues pertaining to therapy, assessment, teaching, and research in later chapters, they will have ample opportunity to practice their ethical reasoning skills in their consideration of the complex and thought-provoking case examples provided in each chapter. Each of these chapters also concludes with an ethical dilemma that readers can work to resolve using the model of ethical decision making.

This book is also unusual in that the ethical codes of both psychology and counseling receive extensive treatment. Understanding both the similarities and differences in the points of emphasis in these codes will enrich professionals' understanding of the range of ethical considerations relevant to the practice of a mental health profession. Second, consultation between psychologists and counselors will be facilitated by understanding the similarities and differences in the ethical concerns of the two professions. Finally, many professionals who receive graduate training in psychology go on to be licensed as counselors. Likewise, master's-level counselors often enroll later in a doctoral program in clinical or counseling psychology. Understanding the ethical codes of both professions will make these transitions easier and avoid potential ethical difficulties resulting from confusion between the roles of psychologist and counselor.

The purpose of this book is to provide mental health professionals with formal training in ethical reasoning. Four tasks that are fundamental to ethical professional practice will be emphasized. The first task is to become familiar with the ethical code of their profession. An overview of psychology's "Ethical Principles of Psychologists and Code of Conduct" (APA, 1992) will be presented in Chapter 2, and counseling's *Code of Ethics and Standards of Practice* (ACA, 1997) will be discussed in Chapter 3.

The second task is to develop a greater knowledge of how the validity of ethical beliefs can be supported by rational arguments. In Chapter 4, the major Western philosophical theories of ethical obligation will be presented to provide a context readers can use in their efforts to develop a rational philosophical grounding for the values that will guide their ethical conduct as professionals. The models presented will also enable readers to develop a clearer understanding of the philosophical underpinnings of the ethical codes of the mental health professions.

As readers become increasingly sensitive to the presence of ethical issues and more sophisticated in their understanding of the variety of ethical considerations that can arise in clinical, teaching, and research settings, they will become aware of a fundamental problem that has perpetually plagued ethical theorists in philosophy as well as mental health professionals who seek to apply ethical principles in their work. In many situations, philosophically sound ethical values appear to conflict with one another. For example, a student asks a clinical psychology professor, whose class he had taken the previous semester, for an appointment to see her as a client in her part-time psychotherapy practice. The student is a psychology major, so the professor explains that having a psychotherapy client who is also a student in her department constitutes a dual relationship. However, the student says that she is the only person he can talk to about his problems and that he will leave school if necessary to be treated by her. This situation does involve a dual relationship, but the welfare of the individual is also an important consideration.

What is the ethically appropriate response in this situation? Unfortunately, there is not a set of simplistic behavioral rules available that will inform professionals regarding the ethically appropriate course of action in each novel situation they encounter. Even the ethical code of a profession provides only general guidelines for appropriate conduct, leaving considerable ambiguity regarding what professionals should do within such circumstances. To address these complex problems effectively, professionals must develop the ability to *reason* ethically, a skill that will enable them to resolve practical ethical problems by weighing the relative importance of competing ethical considerations. Learning to reason ethically is the third and most important task readers will undertake in this book. Ethical reasoning skills will allow professionals to resolve ethical conflicts, which is the most difficult challenge in the endeavor to behave as an ethical professional.

Several of the most promising methods proposed by moral philosophers to resolve conflicts between ethical principles, or *ethical dilemmas,* will be described in Chapter 5. Then, a model for ethical decision making will be presented in Chapter 6 to assist professionals in structuring their ethical deliberations in a manner that will make it possible for them to resolve ethical conflicts rationally. In each subsequent chapter, a special case scenario will be presented to provide readers with an opportunity to practice using the model and further develop their ability to resolve ethical conflicts. In addition, numerous case examples involving multiple, competing ethical considerations are distributed throughout each chapter of the book. In the early chapters, they can serve as brain teasers, but as readers develop their skills, I hope that they will revisit those cases and attempt to resolve them.

The fourth important task, which is based on mastery of the first three tasks, is to develop an increased awareness of both the obvious and subtle ethical and legal issues that arise in the daily practice of a mental health profession. The only way that professionals can be confident of behaving in an ethical manner is to develop an exquisite sensitivity to the presence of such issues in their everyday professional behavior. Both obvious and subtle ethical and legal issues pertaining to the various activities in which mental health professionals are involved (e.g., psychotherapy, assessment, teaching, research) and the organizations in which they work are discussed in greater detail in Chapters 7 through 11. Legal issues and applications in the practice of mental health professions are presented in Chapters 12 and 13. I selected the issues to be addressed in this book based on their importance to mental health professionals and because the students in my ethics classes have always found them to be intriguing. It is my hope that this book will provide readers with the tools they will need to conduct themselves in an ethically effective manner throughout their professional careers.

I would like to thank the many graduate students who have taken my ethics course and provided feedback on manuscript chapters. I would also like to thank Stephen F. Austin State University for the Faculty Development leave that enabled me to complete the project. In addition, I would like to express my sincere appreciation to Barbara Norwitz and Carol Hollander of CRC Press for their patience, assistance, and encouragement in bringing this work to fruition. I am very grateful to Beverly Hughes of Stephen F. Austin State University for her assistance in preparing the appendices for publication and for her enthusiasm for the project. I would also like to thank Angie Lopez for her help in proofreading the appendices. Most of all, I would like to thank my wife, Angela, for all of her support and invaluable editorial assistance at each stage of this long process.

# Table of Contents

# 1 Introduction

This chapter introduces the field of ethics and a number of the issues that will be addressed throughout the book, including the role of personal values in professional behavior and the relationship between law and ethics. The ethical code of each of the mental health professions will also be introduced. Finally, the importance of developing ethical reasoning skills in order to become a competent mental health professional will be demonstrated.

## WHAT IS ETHICS?

The field of ethics is a philosophical discipline concerned with the morality of human behavior, with right and wrong. Some ethical theories present arguments about what is most valuable in life. This type of theory, called a *theory of value,* is considered an ethical theory because whatever is valued most highly in human life, based on its own intrinsic worth, is argued to be the greatest "good" in life. A second type of ethical theory presents arguments that particular behaviors are morally wrong (i.e., unethical) while certain other behaviors are right and *ought* to be performed under specified circumstances. These theories are referred to as *theories of obligation.* The morally prescribed behavior (i.e., the "right" thing to do) would be said to constitute a person's ethical *duty* in that situation; he has a moral obligation to perform that behavior in such circumstances. For example, one might argue that when a person sees someone about to step off the curb into oncoming traffic, she ought to attempt to warn the person. Warning a person, whenever possible, to prevent him from being harmed would be her moral duty. A theory of obligation is a *normative ethical theory* because it stipulates moral duties that apply to everyone. Similarly, professional ethical codes state the normative ethical expectations for all members of a profession.

Theories of obligation also attempt to provide a philosophical (i.e., rational) justification for the existence of ethical duties and for the particular duties being advocated by the theory. The question of how ethical propositions can be justified rationally is a *metaethical* issue. Generally, theories of obligation possess both normative and metaethical components. In other words, the theories describe *what* behaviors represent specific ethical duties for everyone and provide an explanation of *why* those behaviors constitute legitimate ethical duties.

The relation of ethical (normative) and metaethical considerations is illustrated by the distinction between the specific ethical duties presented in the ethical code of a mental health profession and the underlying ethical principles that provide the philosophical justification for those specific duties. If someone were to ask why confidentiality is such an important professional ethical duty, he would be inquiring about the rational justification of such a duty. A professional's response, which might be a brief explanation of the Kantian principle of respect for persons, would constitute a metaethical justification of the specific professional ethical duty of preserving clients' confidentiality.

---

**Case Example 1.1**

*A psychologist is working with a female client who is very upset about deciding whether to sign a Do-Not-Resuscitate (DNR) order for her terminally ill father. She is unsure whether such an action is morally consistent with the tenets of her religion. On the other hand, she cannot afford the cost of continued medical treatment. She asks her psychologist for advice. He tells her to sign the order; she has more than fulfilled her duty toward her father.*

*When the psychologist mentions the situation to a colleague, the colleague says that it was inappropriate for the psychologist to tell the client what to do because it showed a lack of respect for her personal autonomy. The psychologist replied that he felt it would show a lack of regard for his client as a person if he had ignored her request for help in resolving the painful dilemma. The colleague responds that the psychologist does not understand what respect for autonomy really means.*

*Does he?*

---

## ETHICS AND PERSONAL VALUES

Each person possesses *ethical beliefs,* which are guidelines that provide moral direction and organization for her conduct. Her beliefs provide her with a sense of what is the right thing to do in a particular situation. Underlying these beliefs are the *ethical values* she ascribes to, the general principles that constitute her sense of what is right and what is wrong, what is good and what is evil. These values are acquired from many sources: parents and family, culture, formal ethics training, and her own rational analysis of ethical issues.

People do not normally think about why they hold the ethical values they do. The problem of providing a rational justification for their ethical values generally only arises when they are confronted by a person or culture that possesses particular values that are contrary to theirs. Their attempts to argue that their values are "better" or more "ethical" require a metaethical theory that will enable them to evaluate the two sets of values against a mutually agreed upon set of rational criteria. Chapters 4 and 5 discuss a few of the more significant ethical theories that have been advanced by philosophers over the centuries and the metaethical support the theories have provided for the existence of genuine ethical duties.

## THE ROLE OF VALUES IN THE PRACTICE OF A MENTAL HEALTH PROFESSION

Ethical values are not the only sort of *personal values* people hold that are important to their professional activities. Their personal likes and dislikes, along with their attitudes and beliefs about a multitude of issues in life, are also values that influence their perception of people and situations. For example, if a counselor prefers quiet people and considers them "nicer" than more talkative, outgoing individuals, this personal preference constitutes a value judgment. In general, people tend to be relatively unaware of the role their subjective values play in their daily lives. However, awareness of one's personal value system is an important component of being an ethical professional because the clinical, teaching, and research activities professionals engage in are all an expression of their values. To act on the basis of personal biases and preferences in their professional activities, rather than being guided by objective, well-reasoned principles, would be to behave arbitrarily rather than scientifically and would involve a very significant risk of acting unethically (R. F. Kitchener, 1980).

A professional's personal values influence his viewpoint on human motivation and human behavior, thereby affecting his choice of theoretical orientation. In clinical work, his values influence his beliefs regarding the nature of psychopathology, the appropriate goals of treatment, and the most efficacious methods for accomplishing those goals (R. F. Kitchener, 1980, 1991). For example, a humanistic psychotherapist has a very different viewpoint regarding the nature of behavior change than an operant behavior therapist.[1] Furthermore, the personal values of therapists (e.g., regarding religious belief) may differ from those of their clients (Bergin, 1980, 1991). Clinicians must be sensitive to the danger of imposing their values on their clients. Obviously, they can only address this threat to their ethical obligation to respect the dignity and autonomy of their clients effectively if they are aware of their personal values and the role of values in psychotherapy.

In teaching, an instructor's values play a role in determining what topics she chooses to include in a course and which of the potential explanations of a phenomenon she emphasizes in her class presentation. As was the case with therapists, the professor is an important figure of authority. Thus, the potential for her personal values to unduly influence her students' thinking is a matter to be considered seriously in deciding what to say in class. Similarly, a researcher's particular areas of interest and the projects he undertakes are also a reflection of his values. In fact, every judgment a mental health professional makes is, at least in part, a value judgment. Increased awareness of personal values through critical self-assessment is the best method for a professional to develop a clearer understanding of the role her values play in her professional activities and the best safeguard against arbitrarily imposing her values on the people she serves.

---

**Case Example 1.2**

*A counselor is contacted by a couple who wants him to work with their 17-year-old daughter. The daughter is sexually active, and the parents want her to stop engaging in that behavior. During an intake interview, the young woman reports that she is careful about contraception and practices "safe sex." She says that she enjoys sex and experiences no guilt about her sexual behavior. In spite of her parents' objections, she has no intention of stopping her sexual activity. How should the counselor proceed?*

## ETHICS AND LAW

A third important component of professional practice, along with an understanding of moral principles and personal values, is knowledge of the law. Some people believe that morality and law are basically the same thing. This belief is true in some instances. For example, it is morally wrong for a psychologist to murder a participant in her research study and, of course, there are laws forbidding such behavior. Although illegal acts are also generally regarded as unethical, there are some acts that would be regarded as unethical but legal. For example, having a consensual sexual relationship with an adult psychotherapy client is unethical for a psychologist, but it is not necessarily illegal. Thus, morality is distinct from law, but both should serve the same basic purpose: facilitation of the satisfaction of individual needs in a manner that does not conflict with the needs of others or the stability of the society as a whole. Both laws and ethics are designed to provide standards that facilitate harmonious social existence.

In some situations, the law might require a professional to do something she considers to be unethical. For example, a state statute might require a clinician to provide her client's psychotherapy records to the court if the client becomes involved in a custody battle in the context of his divorce and the records are subpoenaed as evidence relevant to the client's fitness as a parent. Legally, the clinician is required to turn over the records to the court. However, if the client were involved in psychotherapy to deal with issues pertaining to the divorce and had explored his homosexual fantasies in the course of the therapy, the clinician might feel that her client's case for custody could be unfairly biased by having this information taken out of context. As a result, she might argue that turning over her records constitutes an unethical breach of the client's confidentiality. However, if she resists the subpoena, claiming that such disclosure is a violation of her professional ethics, she could be held in contempt of the court order.

The interaction of the legal system with professional and ethical issues in the mental health professions, as in the previous example regarding the legal limits of client confidentiality, is a compelling reason for becoming familiar with state laws concerning the practice of mental health professions. Another important legal aspect of mental health practice involves state licensing boards. All states regulate the use of certain protected titles (e.g., "psychologist"). Many states' licensing laws also specify services (e.g., personality assessment utilizing projective tests) that only members of particular professions (e.g., psychologists, psychiatrists), by virtue of their specialized training, are deemed legally competent to provide. State boards also regulate professional conduct and misconduct of those licensed to practice the profession through means such as investigating and adjudicating complaints concerning any sort of illegal or unprofessional conduct by a licensed member of the profession. The legal aspects of professional practice, including the functioning of state licensing boards and the procedures for dealing with ethical complaints against mental health professionals, are discussed in Chapters 12 and 13.

---

**Case Example 1.3**

*A counselor is treating a male client for an anxiety problem. The client is a lawyer trying to earn a junior partnership in a firm, so he works long hours and is under considerable stress. He tells the counselor that he occasionally takes his frustrations out on his 10-year-old son. He gives an example of having come home from work the previous week to find that his son had not mowed the lawn as he was supposed to. The client relates that he "lost it" and began hitting the boy with the buckle end of his belt all over his body. He said that he always feels "awful" after these episodes.*

*The counselor informs him that his behavior qualifies as physical abuse of a child and that she is legally required to report his behavior to Child Protective Services. The client responds that she had told him that everything they discussed was confidential. He says that if she violates his confidentiality by reporting him, he will sue her for malpractice.*

*What should the counselor do?*

---

## WHY DO PROFESSIONS DEVELOP ETHICAL STANDARDS?

The ethical standards for a profession are generally codified by the dominant professional organization. For example, the American Bar Association established the ethical code for the legal profession, the American Medical Association for the practice of medicine, the American Counseling Association (ACA) for counseling, and the American Psychological Association (APA) for the practice of psychology. Each of the mental health professions (i.e., psychology, counseling, psychiatry, and social work) has developed its own ethical code.

The creation of an ethical code can be viewed as part of the process of development that occurs in a profession. As the profession begins to establish itself as a viable contributor to society, practitioners experience an increasing need to clarify their sense of professional identity by distinguishing themselves from those practicing other professions and occupations. The establishment of an ethical code is one way of communicating to students and practitioners of the profession the basic principles, ideals, and subject matter of the profession. Also, as a profession becomes larger, with more practitioners operating in increasingly diverse employment contexts, the frequency of questions and problems relating to ethical matters is very likely to increase. The ethical code addresses this issue by establishing standards of professional conduct that provide some specific behavioral guidelines and serve to sensitize all members of the profession to ethical issues involved in the practice of the profession.

The publication of a professional ethical code also serves a number of other purposes, such as influencing the public's perception of a profession. The code provides the public with information regarding the nature of the profession and the special talents and qualifications of those practicing it. An ethical code generally addresses both the rights (e.g., freedom of inquiry) and responsibilities of those practicing the profession. The ethical code also informs the public that members of the profession are obligated to uphold specific ethical standards of behavior in their dealings with consumers. For example, the public is assured in the ethical codes of the various mental health professions that professionals maintain confidentiality regarding their interactions with clients and limit their practice to areas of demonstrated competence. This assurance of the "professionalism" of psychologists, psychiatrists, counselors, and social workers is quite different from what people can reasonably expect in most business dealings. Generally, people operate at their own risk in purchasing goods or services. However, a professional ethical code informs the public that the notion of *caveat emptor* ("Let the buyer beware!") does not apply when dealing with members of that profession. Thus, publishing a code of ethics enhances the respectability and prestige of a profession in the eyes of the public by assuring the public that the professional organization is concerned with regulating and monitoring the conduct of its members.

Presenting a public statement emphasizing the willingness of the profession to uphold high ethical standards through self-regulation of the behavior of its members may be intended to impress more than just the general public. The creation of an ethical code also sends a clear message to state and federal legislators that no regulation of the profession is needed; the profession is demonstrating the capability of regulating itself and protecting the interests of consumers. In addition to reassuring governmental agencies that the profession poses no potential danger to the public, the ethical code, by extolling the benefits of the profession to society, also represents a significant step in the process of creating a unique niche for the profession. The culmination of the establishment of the identity of a profession comes about when state governments enact licensing laws, which specify that only members of a given profession are uniquely qualified to provide certain sorts of services to the public and are permitted to use a protected professional title.

## THE HISTORY OF ETHICS IN PSYCHOLOGY

Psychology was the first mental health profession to establish an ethical code. The code served as a model for those developed by the other mental health professions. The APA first established a Committee on Scientific and Professional Ethics in 1938 to consider the possibility of developing an ethical code (Golann, 1970). The committee, which determined that publishing a code at that point would be premature, nevertheless became a standing committee of APA "to deal with charges of unethical behavior of psychologists" (APA, 1952, p. 426). In 1947, the committee recommended that psychology develop a formal ethical code, and the Committee on Ethical Standards for Psychology was created for this task. The Committee on Ethical Standards believed that psychology's ethical code should be developed in an empirical manner, as befitted an empirical science. The committee proposed that the content of the code be determined inductively, by soliciting input from all APA members regarding ethical issues they had encountered in their practice of psychology. The committee viewed this approach as being consistent with social psychology research, which indicated that a code would be followed more closely and viewed as more authoritative by psychologists if they had been given the opportunity to have a role in developing it.

In 1948, the committee contacted all of the members of APA and asked them to submit a synopsis of a situation in which they had made a decision having ethical implications and to indicate what they believed to have been the ethical issue involved. More than 1000 case scenarios were provided by the APA membership. The committee sorted the submissions into six general categories: public responsibility, client relationships, teaching, research, writing and publishing, and professional relationships (Golann, 1970). Following extensive discussion within the field, the first ethical code for psychology, *Ethical Standards of Psychologists*, was published in 1953 (APA, 1953).

The original *Ethical Standards* "provided a comprehensive and detailed code" covering ethical and professional issues (Golann, 1970, p. 400). In fact, the code was 171 pages in length, with a total of 106 principles under the six category sections, including many specific case examples. Critics argued that many of the principles overlapped, that issues of professional courtesy were given equal status to serious ethical issues, and that the code placed too little emphasis on ethical issues pertaining to nonclinical areas of psychological practice (APA Committee on Ethical Standards of Psychologists, 1958).

The committee that had created the first code had assumed that the code would certainly need to be revised periodically in light of future experience and developments in the field. The first major revision of the *Ethical Standards* took place in 1958 (APA, 1958). The 1958 version consisted of 18 general principles and was only four pages in length. The principles were quite broad in scope, with fewer specific behavioral requirements and prohibitions. The committee believed that this approach was appropriate, given the increasing complexity of the issues facing psychologists. Specific examples of ethical issues, like those included in the 1953 code, were eliminated. Because of the widely divergent environments in which psychologists practiced their profession, it was thought that specific case scenarios would be of limited relevance to most psychologists and would likely be more frustrating than helpful.

During the next decade, two relatively minor revisions of the *Ethical Standards* were adopted, in 1963 and 1968 (APA, 1963, 1968). These versions of the ethical code consisted of 19 principles and a few moderately specific behavioral standards concerning certain aspects of psychological practice (e.g., advertising one's professional services). The 1968 version was in place for a decade, followed by two rapid-fire revisions of the code (APA, 1979, 1981a). The 1981 version consisted of 10 principles: responsibility, competence, moral and legal standards, public statements, confidentiality, welfare of the consumer, professional relationships, assessment techniques, research with human participants, and care and use of animals. (The final principle was added in the 1981 revision to the nine principles of the 1979 code.) The title of the ethical code was also changed in 1981 to "Ethical Principles of Psychologists." Minor amendments to the 1981 "Ethical Principles" were adopted in 1989 (APA, 1990), reflecting APA's attempt to mollify the Federal Trade Commission, which was dissatisfied with the constraints that the "Ethical Principles" placed on psychologists' right to advertise their services to the public.[2]

## "ETHICAL PRINCIPLES OF PSYCHOLOGISTS AND CODE OF CONDUCT"

The current version of psychology's ethical code, adopted in 1992, represents another substantial structural reworking of the code (APA, 1992). It consists of an introduction, preamble, six general principles, and a much longer section of specific ethical standards grouped under eight broad headings. The current version of the "Ethical Principles" is presented in Appendix A. The content of the code is detailed in Chapter 2. No doubt the "Ethical Principles," like the ethical codes of the other mental health professions, will require further revision as the ethical challenges faced by psychologists continue to evolve and the professional activities of psychologists become even more complex.

## COUNSELING: *CODE OF ETHICS AND STANDARDS OF PRACTICE*

The American Counseling Association (ACA) first published an ethical code in 1961. The code has undergone four revisions during the past 35 years. The current version of the *Code of Ethics* is presented in Appendix B. The format of the current version (ACA, 1997) is quite similar to that of psychology's ethical code, presenting a code of ethics followed by more specific standards of practice. Though also quite similar to the "Ethical Principles of Psychologists and Code of Conduct" (APA, 1992) in its points of emphasis, counseling's ethical code provides much more specific guidance regarding a host of pragmatic ethical concerns, including respecting diversity, dual relationships, record keeping, group work, termination and referral, and computer technology. For example, a subsection of Section B (Confidentiality) addresses specifically the issue of client access to records. Counselors are encouraged to provide clients with access to their records, though a paternalistic exception of withholding any aspect of the record that might be "detrimental to the client" is included (ACA, 1997, B.4.d). The standards of practice, which provide very specific statements regarding behaviors that are required or proscribed, are organized by the same section headings as the code of ethics. The content of counseling's ethical code is discussed in detail in Chapter 3.

## PSYCHIATRY: *THE PRINCIPLES OF MEDICAL ETHICS, WITH ANNOTATIONS ESPECIALLY APPLICABLE TO PSYCHIATRY*

The professional ethical code for psychiatry was first published by the American Psychiatric Association as a special supplement to the American Medical Association's *Principles of Medical Ethics* in 1973. Prior to that, psychiatrists, like other physicians, subscribed to *The Principles of Medical Ethics,* the general ethical code for all physicians. The present version of psychiatry's ethical code, adopted in 1993, consists of *The Principles of Medical Ethics* along with extensive annotations addressing specific areas of relevance of each of its seven sections to the practice of psychiatry

(American Psychiatric Association, 1993). It differs from the "Ethical Principles of Psychologists and Code of Conduct" in its focus on general principles to guide the professional conduct of psychiatrists and fewer specific behavioral prohibitions. Psychiatry's code is similar in structure and style to previous versions of the "Ethical Principles" (e.g., APA, 1990).

Psychiatry's ethical code addresses many of the same issues as the ethical codes of psychology and counseling. Respect for each client's human dignity is said to underlie the psychiatrist's commitment to protecting clients' confidentiality, developing professional competence (which is to be maintained through continuing education), refusing to tolerate discriminatory policies or practices, upholding standards of professionalism in dealings with other professionals, and addressing unethical behavior by other psychiatrists.

One area in which psychiatry's ethical code is actually more specific (and more stringent) than the "Ethical Principles" (APA, 1992) and *Code of Ethics* (ACA, 1997) is dual relationships with clients. Section 2 states that "sexual activity with a current or former patient is unethical" (American Psychiatric Association, 1993, p. 4). Also, Section 4 states that sexual relationships with students and trainees "often [take] advantage of inequalities in the working relationship and may be unethical" (American Psychiatric Association, 1993, p. 7) because of the negative impact on the teacher–student relationship and/or the trainee's treatment of clients in cases being supervised by the psychiatrist. Teacher–student relationships are not, however, strictly forbidden.

Psychiatry is currently the only mental health profession that must also deal with ethical issues pertaining to the use of medication in the treatment of clients' problems (e.g., medicating hospitalized clients against their will). A longstanding ethical concern for psychiatrists is the conflict between their respect for the human dignity of their clients and the use of invasive treatment procedures without clients' consent (e.g., Jellinek & Parmelee, 1977). This issue is not addressed directly in psychiatry's ethical code, except in statements that psychiatrists will always act in a manner that is consistent with mental health laws and regulations.

## SOCIAL WORK: *CODE OF ETHICS OF THE NATIONAL ASSOCIATION OF SOCIAL WORKERS*

The National Association of Social Workers (NASW) adopted its first ethical code in 1979. It has been revised twice since that time, in 1990 and 1993 (NASW, 1993). As stated in the preamble, the fundamental values of the social work profession are regard for "the worth, dignity, and uniqueness of all persons" and respect for people's "rights and opportunities" (NASW, 1993, p. v). The social work code covers the same general areas as the ethical codes of the other mental health professions.

The code of ethics consists of six major principles. The first principle provides guidelines regarding the professional behavior of social workers. The issues covered include competence, dealing responsibly with personal problems that might affect professional performance, integrity, and the duty to protect the welfare of research participants. The second principle concerns social workers' duties to clients. The

interests of clients are always the primary consideration for social work professionals, which entails that social workers not exploit clients in any manner and that social
workers foster autonomy by respecting the confidentiality of clients and by empower-
ing clients to exercise their capacity for self-determination. Social workers' responsibilities to other social workers and to members of other professions are addressed
in the third principle. The fourth principle concerns social workers' responsibilities
to their employers and the organizations in which they are employed. Social
workers work "to prevent and eliminate discrimination" in any organization with
which they are associated (NASW, 1993, p. 8). The final two principles address
social workers' duties to their profession and to the promotion of the general
welfare of society.

The ethical code is not intended to provide specific rules governing social workers'
behavior. "Rather, it offers general principles to guide conduct, and the judicious
appraisal of conduct, in situations that have ethical implications" (NASW, 1993, p. v).
However, the code of ethics is supplemented by no less than 15 specific sets of
standards designed to provide additional direction in particular areas (e.g., clinical
social work) and issues (e.g., continuing education) of concern to the profession
(e.g., NASW, 1982, 1989).

## THE LIMITATIONS OF ETHICAL CODES

The ethical codes of the mental health professions present ethical considerations one
at a time. This approach may tend to foster the misleading impression that ethical
considerations (e.g., confidentiality, competence) are independent of one another.
Nothing could be further from the truth. Consequently, trying to follow a profession's
ethical code and standards of conduct in a rote manner will not enable a professional
to function ethically. Situations arise in the daily practice of a mental health profession that involve multiple ethical considerations. The most difficult situations are
*ethical dilemmas*, in which ethical considerations actually conflict with one another
(K. S. Kitchener, 1984). For example, counseling's *Code of Ethics* discusses the
critical importance of obtaining informed consent from research participants (ACA,
1997, G.2.a). This section is followed immediately by a discussion of the conditions
under which deceiving research participants is permissible (ACA, 1997, G.2.b).
Nevertheless, counseling's ethical code makes no mention of the potential for ethical
principles to conflict. In the section concerning professional responsibility, counselors are instructed only "to consult with other counselors or related professionals
when they have questions regarding their ethical obligations or professional practice"
(ACA, 1997, C.2.e).

One of the primary goals of this book is to make certain that mental health
professionals are well prepared to identify complex ethical situations and to resolve
them in an ethical, rational manner. The next two chapters provide a comprehensive
introduction to the ethical codes of psychology and counseling, respectively.
Chapters 4 through 6 provide the tools necessary for professionals to identify and
resolve complex ethical situations that arise in their professional activity in a
rational manner.

> **Case Example 1.4**
>
> *A neuropsychologist conducts an evaluation of a 75-year-old man at the request of his daughter. He has been experiencing memory problems. Although he is still quite aware and able to function fairly well, the results of the neuropsychological testing and some additional medical tests conducted by colleagues indicate that the man is in the early stages of Alzheimer's disease. His daughter meets with the neuropsychologist and pleads with her not to tell her father about the diagnosis. She says that her father has always said that he would commit suicide if he was diagnosed with any form of dementia so that his family would not be saddled with him as he declined physically and mentally.*
>
> *The neuropsychologist feels an obligation to respect the client's right to know his diagnosis, but she does not want to harm the client and his family.*
> *What should the neuropsychologist do?*

## SUMMARY

This chapter introduced the field of ethics, a philosophical discipline concerned with the morality of human behavior. The two main types of ethical theories are theories of value and theories of obligation. The former identify what is valued most highly in life (i.e., the "greatest good"), while the latter actually prescribe what one ought to do in a given situation. The ethical practice of a mental health profession requires the professional to develop a greater awareness of her ethical beliefs and values because her clinical, research, and teaching activities all reflect her personal value system. As a mental health professional, she should always strive to avoid acting solely on the basis of personal biases and preferences. Rather, professional judgments should be grounded in well-reasoned, objective principles. In addition to awareness of moral principles and personal values, practicing a mental health profession in an ethical manner requires knowledge of the law. Morality and law are two distinct sets of guidelines and do not always coincide, although they serve the same purpose: to provide standards of conduct that promote harmonious social existence.

Professions develop ethical standards for several reasons. Usually, the dominant professional organization establishes the ethical code of the profession. The American Psychological Association established the first ethical code for psychology in 1953. The code has undergone several revisions since then. The current version of the ethical code, "Ethical Principles of Psychologists and Code of Conduct," was adopted in 1992. Counseling created its *Code of Ethics and Standards of Practice* in 1961. Psychiatry established its own ethical code, distinct from that of the other medical professions, in 1973. The code consists of *The Principles of Medical Ethics* and extensive annotations specific to the field of psychiatry. Finally, social work adopted the *Code of Ethics of the National Association of Social Workers* in 1979.

# 2 "Ethical Principles of Psychologists and Code of Conduct"

This chapter describes the essential features of psychology's ethical code (APA, 1992). Historically, it was the first ethical code established by a mental health profession and has served as the model for the ethical codes developed by counseling, psychiatry, and social work. This chapter will provide an opportunity for readers to assess how their values relate to the ethical code of the profession of psychology.

The most recently published revision of the "Ethical Principles" (APA, 1992) consists of six general principles and a separate set of ethical standards. The new format reflects a shift in emphasis toward greater specificity in the ethical code regarding behaviors that are clearly unethical and unprofessional. In this chapter, each of the general principles will be presented, along with examples of ethical issues and ethical standards relevant to each principle. General principles and ethical standards pertaining to specific areas of practice in psychology (e.g., psychotherapy, assessment, teaching, and research) will be discussed in greater detail in later chapters.

## INTRODUCTION

The introduction to the "Ethical Principles" describes the preamble and general principles as *"aspirational goals"* of psychologists (APA, 1992). The ethical standards, on the other hand, are a set of enforceable rules of varying specificity that govern the professional activities of psychologists. Obviously, the standards do not provide an exhaustive set of rules. Rather, they are designed to address some of the most common areas of complaint about psychologists' behavior.

The "Ethical Principles" does not apply only to members of APA. Licensed or certified psychologists are bound by the code if it has been adopted by their state board (as is the case in most states). Many graduate programs in psychology also require that students admitted to the program behave in accordance with the "Ethical Principles." In addition, the "Ethical Principles" is employed by the APA Ethics Committee and review committees of any other organization that adopts these principles, in addition to its own rules and standards, to judge the ethicality of a psychologist's actions in the event of a complaint. It is the duty of every psychologist to be informed regarding the content of the "Ethical Principles" (APA, 1992, 8.01). Ignorance of the code is no excuse for professional misconduct.

The "Ethical Principles" applies to the professional activities of psychologists. The ethical code is not intended to apply to the private lives of psychologists. However, any aspect of psychologists' private lives that relates to their professional activities (e.g., personal relationships with students or clients) *is* subject to the ethical standards of the profession. The point is that the personal activities of a psychologist, such as her personal political convictions, for example, are her private business and not a matter of professional concern, unless she were to make public statements *as a psychologist* that suggest that her political stance is the position a psychologist would take based on scientific evidence.

There may also be instances in which the "Ethical Principles" prohibits psychologists from engaging in activities that are permitted by law. For example, though in some states it is now a felony for a psychotherapist to engage in a sexual relationship with a current client (McMahon, 1997), the constraints put on psychologists' personal relationships with people they are involved with professionally are not generally reflected in legal statutes. In such cases, "psychologists must meet the higher ethical standard" of psychology's ethical code (APA, 1992). In other instances, psychologists might encounter a situation that is not covered by law or by the "Ethical Principles." In such situations, they are directed to consult the specialty guidelines and standards that supplement the "Ethical Principles" (e.g., APA, 1981b, 1987, 1993a); professional colleagues; and "the dictates of their own conscience" (APA, 1992). This instruction reinforces the view that functioning as an ethical professional requires psychologists to develop a clear understanding of their own ethical values and the philosophical basis of those values.

Any concerns regarding unethical or unprofessional behavior on the part of a psychologist can be investigated and punished by APA and/or the state board that has licensed the psychologist. Psychologists are ethically obligated to cooperate with ethics committees investigating a complaint (APA, 1992, 8.06). The functions of ethics committees and state boards of psychology, as well as the procedures followed in investigating alleged ethical violations, are discussed in Chapter 13.

---

**Case Example 2.1**

*A psychology faculty member frequently presents his viewpoint in his classes that the U.S. government has been guilty of immoral acts against its citizens and should be overthrown, by force if necessary. A student makes a complaint to the APA Ethics Committee stating that the faculty member is behaving inappropriately in presenting these subversive ideas in class instead of teaching his students about psychology. The psychologist responds to the complaint by saying that his right to express his political opinions is protected by the First Amendment and that APA is intruding into his private behavior.*

*Is the psychologist's behavior ethically appropriate?*

## PREAMBLE

The previous version of the "Ethical Principles" preamble (APA, 1990) began with a statement affirming psychologists' respect for "the dignity and worth of the individual" (APA, 1990, p. 390). In the current version of the preamble, this issue is not addressed until the second paragraph, in a statement regarding psychologists' social responsibility, which expresses a more paternalistic concern for the welfare and protection of the people psychologists serve. The primary focus of the preamble has shifted to an assertive statement concerning the roles psychologists perform and the contributions they make to society. For example, one of the services psychology is said to provide is "to help the public in developing informed judgments and choices concerning human behavior" (APA, 1992).[3] Essentially, the preamble serves the purpose of enhancing the public image of psychology.

In closing, the preamble reiterates the point that behaving ethically as a psychologist "requires a personal commitment to a lifelong effort to act ethically" (APA, 1992). To apply the principles and standards appropriately and to resolve reasonably issues not addressed in the "Ethical Principles," psychologists must commit themselves to developing ethical competence.

## GENERAL PRINCIPLES

### PRINCIPLE A: COMPETENCE

The principle of competence is intended to insure that the services mental health professionals provide to the public are of the highest possible quality and that professionals do not go beyond the limits of their expertise in determining the range of services they are able to provide (Cottone & Tarvydas, 1998). Competence encompasses two fundamental ethical principles: *beneficence,* which means doing good for others, and *nonmaleficence,* which means doing no harm to others.

Psychology's specialty guidelines and standards were designed to provide additional information on the issue of competence for various service delivery specialties within the profession. "Guidelines" are recommended procedures and are not intended to be binding in the same sense that published "standards" or "ethical principles" are. Published guidelines related to specific areas of competence include the following: "General Guidelines for Providers of Psychological Services" (APA, 1987), "Specialty Guidelines for the Delivery of Services by Clinical Psychologists, Counseling Psychologists, Industrial/Organizational Psychologists, and School Psychologists" (APA, 1981b), "Guidelines for Providers of Psychological Services to Ethnic, Linguistic, and Culturally Diverse Populations" (APA, 1993a), *Standards for Educational and Psychological Testing* (American Educational Research Association, American Psychological Association, & National Council on Measurement in Education, 1999), *Ethical Principles in the Conduct of Research with Human Participants* (APA Committee for the Protection of Human Participants in Research, 1982), and *Guidelines for Ethical Conduct in the Care and Use of Animals* (APA, 1993b). The *Publication Manual of the American Psychological*

*Association* (APA, 1994b) also includes information regarding ethical issues in conducting and reporting research.

The proliferation of specialty guidelines reflects the dramatic increase in the specialized activities in which psychologists are involved. With so many specialties and subspecialties in psychology, it has become extremely difficult to produce general ethical guidelines that address the very different sorts of complex issues that arise in the dissimilar contexts in which psychologists practice their profession. Moreover, psychology has become such a technical and complex field that it is difficult to keep abreast of developments in one specialty area, let alone several. Thus, the principle of competence is intended to direct psychologists to stick closely to their area of training and expertise in delivering professional services as practitioners, teachers, or researchers.

Competence involves psychologists' recognition of their professional limitations and weaknesses, as well as their strengths and skills. This ethical issue is extremely important because a professional's blindness to areas of weakness as well as his unrealistic appraisal of his strengths constitutes a major risk to the welfare of those served by the professional and erodes public trust in the profession. The fundamental ethical principle of nonmaleficence is violated when professionals provide services outside their area of expertise (APA, 1992, 1.14). Although psychologists may not always be able to benefit those they serve, they must take every measure to make certain that they do not hurt anyone. Failure to recognize their limitations is a major source of ethical complaints and malpractice suits. Ensuring the public that psychological services are provided by competent professionals is the ethical basis for procedures such as quality assurance reviews and peer review programs.

The professional performance of otherwise competent mental health professionals can be impaired by personal problems (e.g., marital conflict, substance abuse) that interfere with their ability to perform their duties (APA, 1992, 1.13). The principle of nonmaleficence requires that professionals curtail the services they offer when they are impaired. For example, a marital therapist going through a divorce in his own life may have difficulty viewing the marital difficulties of his clients objectively. His anger about his personal situation could result in a negative, hostile countertransference toward the women in the couples he treats. In such a circumstance, the principle of competence requires that the therapist stop working with couples until his personal problems have been resolved. An even more extreme potential negative effect of impairment was revealed in the finding that male professionals' emotional distress and substance abuse are associated with increased risk of sexual boundary violations with clients and students (Thoreson, Shaughnessy, Heppner, & Cook, 1993).

A related threat to professional competence is the phenomenon of "burnout" (Skorupa & Agresti, 1993). A professional experiencing burnout feels overwhelmed by the demands of her work and ineffective in her professional efforts. She typically feels underappreciated by her students or clients and disappointed in their lack of achievement. Burnout certainly impairs a professional's competence because she is not able to muster any enthusiasm for her work or to empathize with the people she interacts with professionally. As a result, she may withdraw from the clients or students she serves and develop a cynical attitude toward them (Mills & Huebner, 1998). A professional experiencing burnout or some other form of personal impairment has an obligation to seek assistance with her problems and to make certain that the people she serves are not impacted adversely by her impairment (e.g., by referring clients to other professionals). The issue of therapist impairment is addressed in Chapter 7.

---

**Case Example 2.2**

*A female clinical psychologist and a male social worker are co-leaders of a therapy group for inpatient substance abusers. They had an excellent professional rapport, which led to a social relationship in which they dated and seriously considered marriage. The psychologist broke off the relationship, but they decided to continue their professional collaboration in the group. However, she feels that the social worker has started to undercut her authority in the group by frequently disagreeing with her comments to group members. She spoke to him about it, and he accused her of trying to cover up her professional incompetence by silencing him. He insisted that his comments are always made in the best interests of group members.*

---

Another major issue related to the principle of competence is what constitutes sufficient training or experience to claim "competence" in an area of psychology. Is the granting of a legal license to provide a service sufficient? Is it necessary that a psychologist receive training in an APA-approved program? With regard to claims of competence in a specialized therapeutic technique, is a psychologist competent to provide a specialized service (e.g., hypnosis) after reading a book on the subject? After reading two books? After attending a weekend workshop? Or is it necessary to complete an accredited certification program in the technique, including supervised experience in a clinical setting, to establish competence? A clinician may have had only limited academic exposure to a particular therapeutic orientation and yet still consider it appropriate to utilize certain techniques, such as Rational-Emotive Therapy or Person-Centered Therapy, in clinical practice. Similarly, clinicians of many different theoretical orientations might have very little understanding of current theory and research concerning psychological defense and yet feel comfortable interpreting their clients' behavior as defensive (Bridwell & Ford, 1996). Yet another related concern is how a clinician could be competent to treat children, adolescents, and adults (three very different areas of specialization). If you check the yellow pages listings in any major city, you will find that many practitioners advertise such varied expertise.

---

**Case Example 2.3**

*A counseling psychologist in a small town is asked to provide assessment services for the local elementary school. The school psychologist who had been at the school moved to a larger city, and there is no one else in town available to conduct the special education evaluations that are desperately needed to provide children with proper educational placement. The counseling psychologist has spent his entire career working with adult clients.*
*What should he do?*

The recent debate in psychology over whether clinical psychologists should be able to prescribe psychotropic medications for their clients has focused considerable attention on the extent of academic and experiential training necessary to develop competence to provide a particular type of service. Proponents of this initiative have argued that allowing psychologists to obtain prescription privileges would provide greater continuity of care for clients and would enable clients to obtain psychotherapeutic *and* psychopharmacological treatment more economically. In 1990, the APA established an ad hoc task force on psychopharmacology to make recommendations regarding appropriate training requirements for prescribing psychologists (Smyer et al., 1993). These recommendations were followed by suggested models for the undergraduate and graduate training of prescribing psychologists that would require considerably more background in the natural sciences, neuroscience, and pharmacology (e.g., Chafetz & Buelow, 1994).

Critics of this initiative have argued that to be truly competent to dispense psychotropic medications, prescribing psychologists would need to meet all of the requirements that physicians do. In spite of the fact that psychologists would only prescribe medications for the treatment of mental disorders, the psychologists would need to have a thorough understanding of drug interaction effects, which could only be gained by achieving the level of mastery of biology and chemistry possessed by physicians. Critics have also argued that any graduate training curriculum adequate to produce psychologists competent to prescribe psychotropic drugs would, for reasons of length and expense, negatively impact students' exposure to the science of psychology and to training in psychotherapy. In 1995, the American Association of Applied and Preventive Psychology passed a resolution opposing prescription privileges for psychologists; they have since been joined by several other psychology organizations ("AAAPP Declares Its Own 'War on Drugs,'" 1995). They argue that prescription privileges would be detrimental to the profession of psychology because clinical psychology would become more like the profession of psychiatry and that consumers would suffer as a result of psychologists becoming less proficient at the practice of psychotherapy in order to provide a service that is already provided by medical practitioners. This debate will likely continue for many years to come.

Once a professional has developed expertise in an area of specialization, the issue of what sorts of effort are adequate for maintaining that level of scientific and professional competence arises (APA, 1992, 1.05). Psychologists are ethically obligated to base their judgments "on scientifically and professionally derived knowledge" (APA, 1992, 1.06). This requirement cannot be fulfilled unless a psychologist is familiar with the current professional literature. Twenty-five years ago, Dubin (1972) estimated that the half-life (i.e., the length of time before half of the information one learned in training is outdated) of a doctoral degree in psychology was 10 to 12 years. It is certainly shorter now.

The issue of maintaining competence is not unique to the mental health professions. Medicine, for example, experiences dramatic advances in theory and technique quite frequently. Professions have addressed this issue by requiring continuing education of professionals for annual renewal of their license to practice. Most state boards of psychology now have mandatory continuing education requirements. However, no profession has yet taken the step of requiring practicing professionals to be reexamined (i.e., to pass the current version of the state licensing examination) for license renewal.

---

**Case Example 2.4**

*A licensed clinical psychologist specializes in neuropsychological assessment at the hospital where he has worked for many years. Needing money to pay for his child's college education, he decides to start a private practice to increase his income. Since there is not much demand in his community for neuropsychological testing, he decides to offer psychotherapy services, after attending a workshop to brush up on the therapy skills he learned as a graduate student.*
    *Is the psychologist's behavior ethically appropriate?*

---

Another issue relating to competence that was quite controversial for many years involves the retraining requirements for psychologists who want to change their specialty to that of a provider of clinical services. For example, suppose someone who was trained in graduate school as a social psychologist obtained a license as a doctoral-level psychologist and now wishes to provide psychotherapy services. What sorts of additional training experiences will be necessary for this individual to be deemed competent to engage in clinical work? APA published the "Policy on Training for Psychologists Wishing to Change Their Specialty" in 1976. This policy states that "psychologists taking such training must meet all requirements of doctoral training in the new psychological specialty" (Conger, 1976, p. 424). Some universities offer one- or two-year respecialization programs for this purpose.

A final issue related to competence is the status of master's-level psychologists, particularly those in clinical practice. Arnhoff and Jenkins (1969) reported that the National Science Foundation's survey of APA members revealed that fully one-third of the psychologists responding possessed subdoctoral training. Though the profession of psychology has long recognized that the social need for psychologists cannot be met by the number of doctoral-level psychologists being produced (APA Committee on Subdoctoral Education, Education and Training Board, 1955), APA has nevertheless always regarded the doctoral degree as the basic professional credential in the field (Robiner, Arbisi, & Edwall, 1994).

Relatively little research has addressed the relationship between degree level and professional competence. Stevens, Yock, and Perlman (1979) found that master's-level clinicians function quite competently in the community mental health center system. Similarly, Hargrove (1991) asserted that available evidence indicates that master's-level practitioners can capably address the mental health needs of rural populations in the absence of adequate numbers of doctoral-level psychologists. In fact, Hargrove argues that master's-level psychologists need to be granted the autonomy under licensure laws to provide treatment without the direct supervision of a doctoral-level psychologist. In a number of states, master's-level practitioners are being granted greater autonomy. Nevertheless, in some states, a master's-level psychologist with 20 years of clinical experience could be supervised by a Ph.D. psychologist who has been practicing for only a year.

## Principle B: Integrity

This principle stresses that psychologists are honest and forthright in all professional activities. The integrity of mental health professionals requires that they keep their promises and follow through on the professional commitments they make to clients, students, employers, and research participants. In addition, professional integrity incorporates the fundamental ethical principle of justice. Mental health professionals treat people justly by giving the needs of each individual affected by a situation due consideration.

The most important and controversial issue pertaining to integrity is multiple relationships (APA, 1992, 1.17). Once a psychologist has developed a professional relationship with a client, student, or research participant, is it appropriate to engage in any other sort of relationship with that person? For example, is it appropriate for a clinical psychologist to have as a client a student currently enrolled at the institution where the psychologist teaches? Does it make a difference whether or not the client is a psychology major? Is it in any way inappropriate to teach classes taken by a *former* psychotherapy client? Is it ethically appropriate to employ a student to do yard work or babysit, since such an arrangement does constitute a dual relationship (i.e., as teacher and employer)? The concern is that factors in the first relationship (e.g., teacher-student) might affect one or both persons' conduct in the second (e.g., employer-worker). For example, a student might feel that she needs to accept a lower rate of pay from a professor for babysitting because refusing the job might affect her grade adversely. It is also possible that other students might view her as the "teacher's pet" because of her extracurricular relationship with the professor through the babysitting and believe that her high grades are a function of preferential treatment. Psychologists are advised to always "be sensitive" to the potential implications of such relationships, particularly to the possibility that a conflict of interest may exist and/or that a student, client, or research participant could be harmed or exploited (APA, 1992, 1.17[a]).

The guidelines regarding sexual relationships with students and clients are much more explicit (APA, 1992, 1.19). Psychologists should never engage in a sexual relationship if they have any "evaluative or direct authority" over a student, which covers much more territory than having the student in a class. With regard to psychotherapy clients, sexual relationships with current clients are strictly forbidden (APA, 1992, 4.05). Psychologists should also never accept a former sexual partner as a therapy client (APA, 1992, 4.06).

Historically, the major area of controversy has been the issue of sexual relationships with *former* therapy clients. The "Ethical Principles" state that at least two years must have passed since the appropriate termination of the therapy before such a relationship could possibly be ethically appropriate and that, even then, such relationships are to be avoided "except in the most unusual circumstances" (APA, 1992, 4.07). Some states (e.g., Florida) have statutes or state board rules forbidding such relationships for much longer periods, if not forever. One might well question whether such a relationship could ever be ethically appropriate, an issue that will be discussed in the chapter concerning ethical issues in psychotherapy. The issue of multiple relationships is addressed in greater detail in Chapters 7 (therapy clients) and 10 (students and supervisees).

---

**Case Example 2.5**

*A clinical psychologist working in an inpatient facility is conducting research on risk factors for suicide. He recruits participants from all of the psychiatric wards in the hospital, but finds that most of the clients who agree to participate are from his ward, and even more specifically, from his treatment team.*

---

The principle of integrity also relates to the issues of making public statements as a professional and to advertising professional services (APA, 1992, 3.0). Psychologists are not only responsible for their own public statements, they are also obligated to prevent a publisher, workshop sponsor, newspaper, or other source from misrepresenting their credentials or services (APA, 1992, 3.01). In other words, psychologists have an obligation to educate, if necessary, those they work with in order to avoid such misrepresentation.

Psychologists are permitted to advertise their services on television and radio, as well as in the newspaper and telephone directory. In advertising psychological services, psychologists must avoid any statement that could potentially confuse the public or be subject to misinterpretation. Therefore, a psychologist should list his degree (e.g., Ph.D.), rather than referring to himself as "Doctor" or "Dr.," which could be misinterpreted as a medical credential. Psychologists can only list degrees they have earned (e.g., cannot list themselves as Ph.D. candidates). Also, it would be misleading to list Ph.D.s after their names if they had obtained Ph.D.s in history prior to earning M.A.s in psychology. Essentially, psychologists may include in their advertisements any information that is not deceptive or misleading and that is of potential interest to consumers.[4]

Advertising a free consultation is considered an inappropriate "bait and switch" tactic because the client is encouraged to initiate a relationship with the therapist for free, but then is required to pay after having invested considerable emotional energy in the initial free session. Similarly, if a psychologist does not necessarily provide treatment herself for those responding to advertisements for her psychological practice, the credentials of those who will be providing treatment should be listed in the advertisement. In fact, when clients call to arrange an appointment, they should be told the professional credentials of the person they will see. Psychologists should also be very careful about listing professional affiliations so that there is no suggestion of sponsorship or endorsement of their services by the organization. For example, a clinical psychologist in private practice who is also a university professor should not list the university affiliation on his practice stationery.

---

**Case Example 2.6**

*A psychologist distributed a leaflet advertising her private practice. The leaflet had a picture of her license issued by "The University of The State of New York" and listed a variety of specialties (e.g., Adult, Adolescent, Child, Individual, Group) as if they were listed on the license.*
*Is the psychologist's advertisement ethically appropriate?*

---

## PRINCIPLE C: PROFESSIONAL AND SCIENTIFIC RESPONSIBILITY

Psychologists are obligated at all times to behave in a professional, responsible manner toward all consumers of psychological services (e.g., students, clients, research participants). As a consequence, psychologists can never justify inappropriate behavior by stating that they were following their employer's instructions. Psychologists always have a professional obligation to look out for the interests of the consumer, even if no one else will. This responsibility may at times require psychologists to educate their organizational employers regarding the ethical principles of the profession (APA, 1992, 8.03). Issues arising from practicing psychology in different organizational settings are discussed in Chapter 8.

A second issue pertaining to the principle of professional and scientific responsibility is psychologists' sensitivity to the importance of referring people receiving psychological services to other professionals (e.g., psychiatrist) for treatment or consultation whenever such services are in the best interest of the consumer. Appropriate referral to other professionals is the hallmark of psychologists' respect for the expertise of those professionals (APA, 1992, 1.20). Another of the criticisms that can be made against the initiative to allow psychologists to prescribe psychotropic medications is that such an enterprise shows a lack of respect for the unique expertise of medical practitioners.

---

**Case Example 2.7**

*A client seen as an outpatient by a clinical psychologist is admitted involuntarily to a psychiatric hospital following a suicide attempt. The psychologist visits her client and finds that he is being treated with a major tranquilizer (i.e., an antipsychotic medication), in spite of his diagnosis of major depression. She finds him to be sleepy and unresponsive. Her client tells her that he hates how the medication makes him feel. The psychologist consults with the psychiatrist responsible for the client's inpatient treatment. The psychiatrist feels that the medication he has prescribed is appropriate and tells the psychologist that she is exceeding the boundaries of her professional competence in questioning the client's medication.*

*The psychologist is concerned about her client's well-being and tells him that even though he has been committed to the hospital, he still has the right to refuse treatment that he thinks is not in his best interest. The psychiatrist is furious that a fellow professional has subverted his authority with a client in this manner.*

*Did the psychologist behave inappropriately?*

---

As was stated earlier, the "Ethical Principles" is intended to govern the *professional* activities of psychologists. Psychologists retain the same freedom as any other individual to choose the values that will guide their personal lives. However, psychologists are obligated to behave, even in their private lives, in such a way that they do not "compromise their professional responsibilities or reduce the public's trust in psychology and psychologists" (APA, 1992, Principle C). Thus, psychologists behaving in an illegal or antisocial manner in their private affairs risk ethical censure as professionals and loss of licensing privileges.

## Principle D: Respect for People's Rights and Dignity

This principle begins with a statement regarding psychologists' respect for the dignity and worth of all people, as well as the rights of people to self-determination and autonomy. The principle of autonomy underlies the respect mental health professionals have for people's rights to make their own decisions about how to lead their lives.

---

**Case Example 2.8**

*A client consults a qualified sex therapist for treatment of an erectile dysfunction. In the course of the intake interview, he reveals that he is HIV positive and has been counseled regarding "safe" sexual practices.*
*Should this revelation impact the treatment plan?*

---

Respect for people is also the ethical foundation for the duty of confidentiality (APA, 1992, 5.0). Privacy is a constitutional right, protected in the Fourth Amendment. One's right to privacy can be violated only under certain specified conditions (e.g., when one is suspected of illegal acts, resulting in the issuance of a search warrant). Confidentiality, on the other hand, is a standard of professional conduct that implies an explicit contract not to reveal anything about a client, except under certain agreed upon circumstances (Koocher & Keith-Spiegel, 1998). The confidentiality of information disclosed by psychotherapy clients may also be guaranteed in the mental health laws of a particular state.

Ethical issues that can arise pertaining to confidentiality include the following: (a) the circumstances under which confidentiality may be violated; (b) the confidentiality of clients under the age of 18 who are brought in for treatment by a parent or guardian; (c) which staff members at a university, clinic, or hospital should have access to confidential information; and (d) the proper procedures for maintaining and disposing of confidential records. Confidentiality issues pertaining to therapy (Chapters 7 and 8), assessment (Chapter 9), and research (Chapter 11) are discussed in greater detail later.

An interesting related issue is whether clients should have access to their own mental health records. If there is not a state statute pertaining to client access to institutional (school, hospital, clinic) mental health records, individual institutions generally set their own policies covering their records. In contrast, there is frequently not a statute or clear policy regarding the records compiled by private practitioners. Clients' access to their mental health records is a matter of institutional and professional policy because legally the records are not the property of clients; records belong to the professional or institution that creates them. In general, clients, or their representatives, can obtain access to their institutional records by making

---

**Case Example 2.9**

*A client with a history of Schizophrenia, Paranoid Type is being treated by a clinical psychologist at a community mental health center. The client is concerned about the possibility of losing his job because his behavior is, at times, experienced by others as "strange." He tells the psychologist that his employer knows that he is receiving treatment at the center and discusses his sense that he is being singled out for criticism at work. The next day, the client's employer calls the psychologist out of concern to let her know that her client's symptoms seem to be worsening. The employer informs her of the client's behavior at work, and the psychologist encourages the employer to call again if there is any change in the client's behavior.*

*Did the psychologist behave appropriately?*

---

**Case Example 2.10**

*A psychologist is employed as a behavioral medicine specialist in a medical-surgical hospital. She receives a consultation to evaluate a patient for depression. The patient is terminally ill and in great pain. He confides to her, in the strictest confidence, that his spouse is going to bring him a poison substance so that he will be able to commit suicide without intervention by the medical staff.*

*What should the psychologist do?*

---

a formal written request. Respect for clients' autonomy and right to know the facts about their treatment and condition is an important ethical argument in support of providing them access to their mental health records. In addition, one might well question how clients can provide truly informed consent (as required by Ethical Standard 5.05[b]) for the release of their record to some third party if they do not know what the record contains.

The limitations placed on client access have centered on two major areas of clinical and ethical concern. The first is that the client's emotional state could be harmed by information in the record. Clinicians often perceive a conflict to exist between their ethical duty to respect the autonomy of the client and the ethical principle of beneficence, which is the desire to do only good for the client. The result has traditionally been a policy of *paternalism*, literally behaving like a father toward clients. Acting paternalistically involves making judgments of what is in the best interest of clients, based on the assumption that clients' judgment might be impaired by their fragile emotional state. Some have argued that if a client were to be upset by something disturbing in his record, it could, in some instances, involve an additional risk of physical harm to himself or someone else, such as a staff member (McShane & Rowe, 1994). This concern adds the additional ethical issue of the clinician's duty to consider the welfare of all individuals potentially affected directly by the situation.

The second major consideration is that the record could contain information provided by, or pertaining to, some third party. The client's autonomy may conflict here with the duty to protect the confidentiality of a third party. This consideration could be deemed a sufficient reason to deny the client access to that portion of the record (McShane & Rowe, 1994).

Research on the subject of providing clients access to their records has indicated primarily positive effects of client access with clinical supervision (e.g., Houghkirk, 1977; Parrott, Strathdee, & Brown, 1988; Roth, Wolford, & Meisel, 1980; Stein, Furedy, Simonton, & Neuffer, 1979). Issues that arise when clients are permitted or denied access to their records, and other matters pertaining to record keeping (e.g., record retention) in mental health, are addressed in Chapter 7.

The principle of respect for people's rights and dignity is also an important motivation for psychologists to be sensitive to cultural, individual, and gender differences that might influence the value and effectiveness of their professional activities involving various individuals and groups. In addition to issues of competence in providing services or instruction to individuals of different backgrounds and/or lifestyles, the issue of respect for the personal, cultural, and religious *values* of students, clients, and research participants is extremely important. For example, Bergin (1991) has argued for many years that the religious values of psychotherapists and their clients frequently differ, with psychotherapists generally being less religious than their clients. When a therapist's values, which are inevitably an aspect of the therapy, influence the client either overtly or covertly, a serious lack of respect for the dignity of the client is shown.[5] A similar concern arises about the potential influence of the values of professors on students. The ethical point being made in the principle regarding respect for people's dignity is that psychologists need to be sensitive to these differences and to their own value biases in order to avoid even subtle forms of value imposition or discrimination against people operating from a different value orientation (Grimm, 1994; Schwehn & Schau, 1990). The ethical issue of values and psychotherapy is discussed in greater detail in Chapter 7.

---

**Case Example 2.11**

*A therapist is treating two female clients for depression. The first is of Iranian heritage. The second is a fifth-generation American, born and raised in New York. Both are rather passive in their marital relationships, deferring consistently to their husbands. The therapist recognizes the possible cultural basis of the Iranian client's behavior and is careful not to impose his values by identifying her passivity in the marital relationship as a symptom or problem. He does, however, believe that the passivity of the American client is a potential source of feelings of powerlessness and diminished self-esteem. He plans to address the issue of her marital relationship and suggest that she might feel better if she asserted herself more in her marriage.*

---

Finally, the fundamental ethical value of respect for the dignity and autonomy of each person espoused by all mental health professionals places them in a very

---

**Case Example 2.12**

*A client in individual therapy is involved in a very unhappy, unsatisfying marriage. She reveals that she has had a long-term extramarital affair as a means of obtaining the affection she needs because she does not want to end her marriage and break up her family.*

---

difficult position when a client wishes to end her own life. On the one hand, a mental health professional would want to promote the autonomy of the client by respecting her decisions regarding the conduct of her life. On the other hand, concern for the client's well-being frequently results in paternalistic behavior toward a suicidal individual, such as depriving her of her civil liberties by hospitalizing her involuntarily to preserve her life. Paternalistic actions taken to protect the client also generally involve violating the confidentiality of the client by informing legal authorities and/or hospital personnel of her stated intention to kill herself. This type of ethical dilemma becomes even more pronounced in cases of "rational" suicide, in which an apparently competent person makes the decision that she would prefer to end her life (Battin, 1999). The ethical complexities associated with suicide prevention are discussed in Chapter 12.

## PRINCIPLE E: CONCERN FOR OTHERS' WELFARE

This principle incorporates the fundamental ethical duties of autonomy, justice, beneficence, and nonmaleficence. Concern for others is said to be expressed when psychologists "weigh the welfare and rights" of any consumer of psychological services or other person affected by the actions of the psychologist (APA, 1992, Principle E). This statement strongly suggests that concern for the welfare of the consumer is always an important issue, but one that sometimes must be weighed or balanced against one or more other considerations. However, the additional potential considerations are not stated explicitly.

One type of situation that requires psychologists to weigh very carefully the welfare of each individual affected is a potential "duty to warn" scenario. This classic ethical-legal dilemma in clinical practice occurs when, in the context of a "special relationship" like a psychotherapeutic relationship, a client threatens to harm a specific person. The most notable legal case to address this type of ethical dilemma is *Tarasoff v. Board of Regents of the University of California* (1974/1976). The case involved a lawsuit in which the parents of Tatiana (Tanya) Tarasoff sued the University of California after their daughter was stabbed to death by Prosenjit Poddar, a graduate student from India attending the University of California (VandeCreek & Knapp, 1993).

The events that led to the death of Tanya Tarasoff were essentially as follows: Tanya had befriended Poddar when they met at a campus activity, and he became deeply infatuated with her. When Tanya made it clear to him that she did not feel the same way about him, he became extremely upset. Poddar initiated outpatient psychotherapy with Dr. Lawrence Moore, a psychologist at a facility affiliated with the university, to deal with his anger and hurt. In the course of his treatment, Poddar confided to Dr. Moore that he intended to kill Tanya Tarasoff when she returned from her summer vacation in Brazil. After consulting with his colleagues, who agreed with Dr. Moore that Poddar was psychotic and required involuntary commitment to an inpatient facility, Dr. Moore asked the campus police to take Poddar into custody and initiate commitment procedures. The campus police interviewed Poddar, but found him rational and did not commit him when he promised to stay away from Tanya (VandeCreek & Knapp, 1993). Tanya was not contacted by the police or by any of the mental health professionals who had been involved in Poddar's treatment. (He terminated treatment after the police interview.) In fact, "Dr. Harvey Powelson, the director of the department of psychiatry, … requested that the police chief return Moore's letters, ordered Moore to destroy his therapy notes, and requested that no further attempts be made to commit Poddar" (VandeCreek & Knapp, 1993, pp. 3–4). Shortly thereafter, Poddar killed Tanya at her home after she refused to speak with him.[6]

In such a case, an ethical respect for persons would result in the psychologist experiencing a conflict between the obligation to protect the confidentiality of a client and not reduce the client's willingness to continue psychotherapy to deal with dangerous impulses versus the obligation to ensure the physical well-being of the potential victim. In the *Tarasoff* case, the California Supreme Court ruled in 1976 that a mental health professional involved in a psychotherapeutic relationship can, under certain circumstances, incur an obligation to "protect others from harm, or to warn them of potential harm" (VandeCreek & Knapp, 1993, p. 5). The case represented a landmark decision because it extended the duty to warn to outpatient treatment settings. Previous rulings had only concerned the obligation of a psychiatric facility to warn potential victims when an inpatient who had threatened them directly was being released. The circumstances under which mental health professionals are obligated to violate a client's confidentiality, and the implications of such decisions for psychotherapy, are discussed in Chapter 7.

---

**Case Example 2.13**

*An adult client being treated for depression by a clinical psychologist reveals during a session that she has thought about killing herself. When the psychologist asks her whether she has decided how she would commit suicide, she says that she would take an overdose of her mother's sleeping medication. She then says that she really has no intention of harming herself. The psychologist, who once had a client commit suicide, calls the client's mother and tells her that her daughter is at risk for suicide and needs to be watched. When the client finds out what he did, she is very upset that he violated her confidentiality. He tells her that her life is more important than any rule about privacy.*
*Did the psychologist act appropriately?*

---

A different set of conflicts regarding concern for others' welfare occurs very commonly in psychologists' research activities, such as when psychologists utilize deception to keep research participants from discovering the hypothesis being tested

and then debrief participants and disclose the true nature of the study. The fundamental ethical conflict involved in the use of deception in research is between the
principles of concern for the welfare of participants (i.e., the duty to obtain fully
informed consent) versus the potential benefit to society of research requiring deception. Furthermore, the psychologist's regard for the welfare of research participants
would suggest that whenever deception is used in research, debriefing should be
done immediately after the individual has participated in the study. However, if the
study is to be conducted over a period of several weeks with different groups of
participants from the same population (e.g., undergraduate students), researchers
may decide to delay debriefing participants until all data have been collected. Such
a delay is deemed justifiable because of the possibility that debriefed participants
might discuss the study with individuals who have not yet participated. Disclosure
of the nature of the study prior to participation would represent a significant threat
to the internal validity of the study.

When debriefing is postponed, the researcher is making a choice to further
compromise the duty to protect the welfare of participants in favor of the potential
of the research project to benefit society. Postponing debriefing, though inconsistent
with the welfare of the client (whose right to informed consent has already been
violated), is nevertheless permitted under some circumstances. The use of deception
"must be explained to participants as early as is feasible, preferably at the conclusion
of their participation, but no later than at the conclusion of the research" (APA, 1992,
6.15[c]). These examples illustrate the potential for conflict between ethical considerations that are each recognized as important in the "Ethical Principles." The ability
to resolve such conflicts in a reasonable manner is an important aspect of practicing
psychology as an ethical professional. Ethical considerations in the use of deception
are discussed further in Chapter 11.

---

### Case Example 2.14

*During the fall semester, a psychology researcher conducts a study involving
deceptive feedback about the results of a "personality test." One group of student
participants receives positive feedback; the other receives negative feedback.
The dependent variable is how much time they spend reading their "results"
on a computer screen. The psychologist plans to conduct a follow-up study
during the spring semester, and he fears that next semester's participants could
learn about the deception from fellow students if he debriefs fall participants
now. Consequently, he decides to hold off debriefing the participants until all
the spring semester data have been collected.*

*Is the psychologist's debriefing plan ethically acceptable?*

---

## PRINCIPLE F: SOCIAL RESPONSIBILITY

This principle begins with a presentation of some ways in which psychology benefits
society. For example, psychological research produces scientific advances that
improve human welfare. Psychologists also develop methods through their research
and practice that are intended to reduce human suffering.

As was discussed above in relation to the principle of integrity, psychologists are responsible for making certain that public statements made by others do not mislead the public in interpreting psychologists' work and its significance. Psychological assessment data are particularly vulnerable to misinterpretation and misuse if their dissemination is not managed responsibly by psychologists. For example, raw data from psychological assessments may be released only to competent professionals (APA, 1992, 2.02[b]). Clients, who are generally not qualified to interpret test data, should be provided with a comprehensive explanation of the results of their testing in nontechnical language to avoid misinterpretation on their part (APA, 1992, 2.09). Issues pertaining to assessment and testing are discussed in greater detail in Chapter 9.

In all professional activities, psychologists are obligated to comply with the law. Although stating that psychologists ought to obey the law seems incredibly obvious, there certainly are instances in which a psychologist might experience conflict between legal requirements and competing ethical considerations. Chapter 1 included a discussion of the conflict that might arise if confidential therapy records were to be subpoenaed for review during child custody proceedings. Information presented from the records without the appropriate therapeutic context might well be misinterpreted and unfairly bias the court against the client.

Some psychologists have also pointed out that mandated reporting laws, like the blanket legal requirement that suspected child abuse be reported to the appropriate child welfare authorities, could in some cases conflict with the best interests of the child and other parties involved. Mandated reporting laws generally stipulate that if the professional *suspects* abuse, he or she is obligated to report it to the appropriate authorities, even in the absence of any direct evidence that abuse has occurred. Failure to report abuse can result in criminal penalties against the professional (VandeCreek & Knapp, 1993).

Suppose, however, that a psychologist is treating a man who has a long history of problems with assertiveness and internalization of a great deal of anger. Occasionally, when the client does express anger about some situation, he experiences difficulty in controlling himself adequately; he yells and curses and has even grabbed and hit his children. He reports that he feels very badly about these incidents later and wants help in managing his anger more effectively. If the psychologist suspects that her client might have grabbed or struck one of his children in an abusive manner during one or more of these episodes, she is legally required to report her suspicions. However, she might believe very strongly that her client does not represent a threat to his children at present and that reporting the matter will only reduce the likelihood that he will continue to be open and honest in therapy so that the situation can be resolved.

Critics of mandatory reporting laws believe that clinicians should be given greater latitude to use their judgment in deciding when reporting of abuse is necessary and appropriate. Those who advocate mandatory reporting with a very low threshold for reporting (i.e., *suspicion* of abuse) argue that a child's well-being should not hinge on the accuracy of a clinician's judgment of a very complex set of circumstances. Advocates of mandatory reporting also point out that confronting an abusive parent with the magnitude of his act by reporting it to legal authorities should only enhance his motivation to resolve the issues that resulted in his abusive behavior. The issue of child abuse is discussed in greater detail in Chapter 8.

The principle of social responsibility also states that psychologists should try to influence the legislative process to "encourage the development of law and social policy that serve the interests of their patients and clients and the public" (APA, 1992, Principle F). The APA has been very active in trying to influence legislative bodies addressing such issues as abortion and health care reform. Critics of the APA's political stances (e.g., on abortion rights, see footnote 3) argue that the organization is involving itself inappropriately in political issues under the guise of providing an objective, scientific viewpoint. The health care lobbying efforts of the APA have been criticized as serving the financial interests of psychologists, rather than reflecting a genuine concern for the social issue of prioritizing the expenditure of limited health care resources in the most reasonable manner.

The concluding sentence of the principle of social responsibility states that psychologists "are encouraged to contribute a portion of their professional time for little or no personal advantage" (APA, 1992, Principle F). A professional might fulfill this obligation by offering a sliding scale that will enable people with fewer financial resources to obtain psychological services or by donating her professional services to charitable work (e.g., volunteering to assist at a shelter for battered women). However, at present, there is no requirement that psychologists engage in charitable activity.

---

### Case Example 2.15

*Two psychologists, one a college professor and one a clinician in private practice, are discussing their work. The professor mentions that he volunteers one afternoon a week at the local shelter for abused women, playing with the children staying there and helping them with their homework. He says that he thinks psychologists, like everyone else, have a duty to "give something back." The clinician says that he feels the same way, so he uses a sliding scale in his practice that allows clients with lower incomes to pay as little as $40 per session, instead of his full fee of $90.*

*Is the behavior of both of these psychologists consistent with the spirit of the principle of social responsibility?*

---

## SUMMARY

This chapter presented a detailed overview of the American Psychological Association's "Ethical Principles of Psychologists and Code of Conduct." The philosophical underpinnings of psychology's ethical code were highlighted in the discussion of the preamble and introduction to the code. Each of the six general principles was described in detail. Particular issues and ethical standards pertaining to each general principle illustrated the practical applications of the principles in teaching, research, and clinical activities.

# 3 Counseling's *Code of Ethics and Standards of Practice*

This chapter concerns the ethical code of the profession of counseling, ACA's *Code of Ethics and Standards of Practice* (ACA, 1997). Counseling's *Code of Ethics* is similar in many ways to psychology's "Ethical Principles," discussed in the previous chapter (APA, 1992). This similarity is not surprising given the considerable overlap in the concerns and roles of the two groups of professionals. However, the two codes are structured quite differently, and there are notable differences in points of emphasis of the two codes.

The most recent revision of the *Code of Ethics* (ACA, 1997) consists of eight sections, representing different areas and aspects of professional practice, and a separate set of Standards of Practice. The eight sections include much more concrete detail regarding ethical and professional practice than the General Principles of psychology's ethical code do. The eight sections really combine the abstract General Principles and more specific Ethical Standards of psychology's ethical code (APA, 1992). The Standards of Practice, at the end of counseling's ethical code, are a very concise set of even more specific minimal standards governing the professional behavior of counselors.

## PREAMBLE

The counseling profession is identified with the goal of enhancing "human development throughout the life-span" (ACA, 1997). This goal is pursued through a recognition and appreciation of diversity, both within and across cultures. Respect for diversity is grounded in the regard for the "worth, dignity, potential, and uniqueness of each individual" (ACA, 1997). The counseling code begins by emphasizing its role in supporting people in their lives, a quite different emphasis from psychology's focus on its altruistic task of delivering the benefits of science for the betterment of humanity.

## CODE OF ETHICS

### SECTION A: THE COUNSELING RELATIONSHIP

The profession's applied, service emphasis is reinforced strongly in its choice to have the first section of the ethical code detail aspects of counselor-client relationships. The section begins with a restatement of counseling's respect for the dignity of clients. Counselors strive to promote the positive growth and development of clients (ACA, 1997, A.1.b). This emphasis is different than the emphasis on treating mental illness that dominates the mental health scene today. Counselors are less focused on diagnosis and "cure" than they are on helping clients to develop their ability to adapt better and cope more effectively with the challenges of modern life. Nevertheless, mental health counselors, like clinical and counseling psychologists, are prepared to work effectively with severely disturbed clients (Cottone & Tarvydas, 1998).

Promoting client welfare and positive growth requires counselors to "avoid fostering dependent counseling relationships" (ACA, 1997, A.1.b). Mental health practitioners, particularly those working in private practice settings, face difficult challenges in maintaining an adequate caseload of clients. As a result, it can be difficult to terminate relationships with clients who are still willing to attend sessions, even when the clinician should be able to recognize that the meetings are no longer of substantive benefit to the client. Clients sometimes remain in therapy for years, though it is evident that most therapeutic gains are made within the first 6 to 12 months of treatment (Howard, Kopta, Krause, & Orlinsky, 1986). When economic self-interest becomes an issue for therapists, a conflict of interest can be said to exist because the best interest of the client should be the only relevant consideration in this matter.

---

**Case Example 3.1**

*A male counselor has been working with a female client for ten months on grief and adjustment issues following the death of her husband. The counselor recently began to notice clear indications that the client has developed an erotic transference toward him. He interprets this transference as a sign of her increasing dependence on him and decides to terminate counseling with her to avoid fostering a dependency relationship.*

*Is the counselor's proposed course of action ethically appropriate?*

---

The subsection concerning career counseling taps another traditional component of counseling practice (ACA, 1997, A.1.e). Prior to becoming involved in the treatment of individuals suffering from psychopathology, counselors historically focused on vocational, rehabilitation, and adjustment issues. This career counseling focus overlaps substantially with the personnel component of industrial/organizational (I/O) psychology. Career counselors provide information, testing, and support to individuals seeking to choose a vocational path. They also work in business and industry to identify the best candidates for available positions, matching applicants' skills with the requirements of the position. Furthermore, they assist employees in adapting more effectively to workplace conditions and challenges and are often associated with today's Employee Assistance Programs (EAPs), where they address personal problems experienced by employees that are impairing occupational performance (Cottone & Tarvydas, 1998). Issues pertaining to counselors providing services in organizational settings are discussed in Chapter 8.

---

**Case Example 3.2**

*A counselor working in the Career Services Office of a university has a client who requests information about the job opportunities and training requirements for a career as a mortician. The client explains his interest by saying that he does not really get along with people well and has always been fascinated by dead things.*

---

Counselors, like all mental health professionals, have an ethical obligation to respect diversity and individual differences (ACA, 1997, A.2). This theme is addressed repeatedly in the *Code of Ethics,* as it was in psychology's "Ethical Principles." As discussed in Chapter 2, mental health professionals should not engage in or condone discriminatory practices. A fundamental tenet of all mental health disciplines is that each individual is unique. Individuals are influenced by cultural factors, their present environment, and myriad experiential and biological developmental events. Mental health professionals' fundamental respect for the autonomy and uniqueness of each individual requires that they strive to understand the cultural and personal perspectives of the people they serve. Mental health professionals also recognize that value differences will inevitably exist between them and the people they serve. They must be careful not to impose their personal values on the people they interact with as professionals. The role of values in counseling and psychotherapy is discussed further in Chapter 7.

---

**Case Example 3.3**

*A white counselor in a small Southern town is acquainted with a fellow counselor who is an African American. The African American counselor is a private practitioner with an excellent reputation and very impressive clinical skills. Nevertheless, the white counselor is more likely to refer clients to other counselors who, though competent, are arguably not as skilled as the African American counselor, because she knows from experience that the townspeople have enormous difficulty relating to a therapist of a different ethnic group. Each of the five people she has referred to the African American clinician either declined to pursue treatment or requested another referral. The counselor does not want to decrease the probability that people referred will pursue the counseling treatment they need.*

*Is the counselor's behavior ethically appropriate?*

---

The *Code of Ethics* also addresses the important issue of informed consent in therapy and counseling (ACA, 1997, A.3). Clinicians have an ethical duty to provide clients with information such as the fee for therapy, the frequency and duration of sessions, any risks associated with the process, the confidential nature of therapy, and the limits of confidentiality. In addition, the clinician and client should discuss and agree on the goals of the therapy and the methods that will be used to attain those goals. The duty of informed consent is grounded in the clinician's respect for the autonomy and welfare of clients. Clients can only make a meaningful choice regarding participation in counseling or psychotherapy if they understand the issues that are important to consider in making that choice. The issue of informed consent in counseling and psychotherapy is discussed further in Chapter 7.

---

**Case Example 3.4**

*A counselor is contacted by an individual who tells her that he has been in counseling "for years" because he suffers from Obsessive-Compulsive Disorder. When they meet, the counselor dispenses with most of her usual informed consent procedure because the client seems very familiar with the therapy process and she does not want to appear patronizing.*

---

The *Code of Ethics* also points out the importance of clinicians not allowing their personal problems and needs to spill over into the counseling relationship, as well as the dangers of multiple relationships. Moreover, the same clear language is used in both the *Code of Ethics* and the "Ethical Principles" in forbidding sexual relationships with clients and former clients.

An interesting issue addressed in this section of the *Code of Ethics* that is not dealt with explicitly in the "Ethical Principles" is the complications introduced into the counseling relationship by treatment contexts involving multiple clients (i.e., marital, group, and family therapy). Counselors are obligated to clarify their relationship with each of the parties involved during the process of obtaining informed consent and to consider carefully whether a group setting is appropriate for each client's needs. Confidentiality issues unique to multiple client contexts, discussed in Section B of the *Code of Ethics,* also need to be addressed before treatment begins.

---

**Case Example 3.5**

*A client diagnosed with Avoidant Personality Disorder is encouraged by her counselor to participate in a group he conducts, in addition to her individual therapy. The counselor tells her that the group experience will enable her to work gradually on developing her interpersonal skills. When she attends her first group session, she learns that it is a psychodrama group, and she is asked to "act out" her interpersonal anxiety in front of the group. She excuses herself and flees the building.*

---

Two other important issues pertaining to the counseling relationship that are addressed in Section A of the code are referral and termination. In some cases, clinicians decide that it is in the best interest of a client to work with a different professional. Many factors can contribute to such a decision, but the overriding consideration should be the counselor's belief that a professional colleague will be better able to assist the client (ACA, 1997, A.11.b). Sometimes, issues in the therapeutic relationship (e.g., transference, countertransference) or additional treatment issues outside the counselor's range of competence (e.g., serious substance abuse) might cause her to consider referring a client to another counseling professional. In other cases, a therapist might believe that a client's needs will be better served by involving another type of professional (e.g., psychiatrist, clinical psychologist, social worker) in the treatment. Generally, such a decision is preceded by a consultation with the colleague she is considering making the referral to, as well as careful deliberation regarding the potential effect of the referral on the client. The counselor making the referral is responsible for ensuring that her client understands the reasons for the referral and does not feel abandoned by her (ACA, 1997, A.11.a). It is unethical to accept payment from another professional for referring a client (ACA, 1997, D.3.b).

The overriding issue in referral is the welfare of the client. Therapists should not be motivated by the desire to protect their professional "turf" by proving that their competence extends as far as that of any other professional. Clinicians should not fail to make an appropriate referral because they want to avoid acknowledging an area of professional weakness. As discussed in Chapter 2, competence involves a professional's understanding of both her strengths *and* limitations.

---

**Case Example 3.6**

*A client suffering from depression contacts a counselor about pursuing therapy. When they meet, the client discusses her history, which involves periodic episodes of depression, and they set up a treatment plan. The counselor asks if she is taking any medication, and the client indicates that she is not. The counselor wonders whether antidepressant medication would be helpful to the client, but assumes that she does not wish to be medicated because she chose to pursue treatment with a counselor rather than a psychiatrist.*

---

Termination of the counseling relationship is appropriate when the clinician believes that the client is no longer benefiting from treatment or has achieved the agreed upon treatment goals. The clinician should raise the issue of termination during a session to learn how the client perceives the situation. Ideally, the client will agree that termination is appropriate. If not, the counselor should state his reasons for raising the issue, supplementing his points with illustrations from the process of the counseling sessions. If the client raises cogent objections to termination (e.g., an additional, reasonable therapeutic goal she would like to pursue), the clinician can certainly postpone any action, though he should reflect carefully on whether his client's desire to continue the relationship is motivated by dependency on him. As discussed earlier, clinicians should increase a client's sense of personal autonomy and capacity for self-determination. Dependency issues should be addressed as an important reason to work toward terminating the therapeutic relationship (ACA, 1997, A.1.b).

## SECTION B: CONFIDENTIALITY

Counseling devotes a separate section of its ethical code to the issue of confidentiality, as does psychology (APA, 1992, 5.0). Both professions acknowledge that the confidential nature of the counseling or therapy relationship constitutes the most basic ethical duty of mental health professionals. Without the assurance of confidentiality, therapy and counseling could not succeed because clients would not be willing to share their innermost thoughts and feelings with the clinician. As discussed in Chapter 2, the ethical duty to protect a client's confidentiality is based on mental health professionals' respect for the client as a person. Clinicians respect a client's right to privacy just as they would want to have their own right to privacy respected. Failure to preserve a client's confidentiality is one of the most serious ethical violations a mental health professional can commit because it threatens to diminish public confidence in the professionalism of clinicians. Breaches of confidentiality violate the trust clients place in mental health professionals. A mental health facility or practice can be ruined by even a single substantiated case of a clinician revealing information about a client inappropriately.

---

**Case Example 3.7**

*A counselor is treating a woman who reports that she had recently been kidnapped and sexually assaulted. She reported the crime to the police. However, due to her history of emotional instability (she qualifies for a diagnosis of Borderline Personality Disorder) and her limited ability to provide details regarding the location of the attack and her attacker (she was tied up and blindfolded throughout the incident), the police did not take the complaint very seriously. Another of the counselor's clients, a male diagnosed as Antisocial Personality Disorder, after posing a string of questions regarding confidentiality, describes having kidnapped and raped a woman, and the counselor realizes it was her other client he had attacked.*

*What, if anything, should the counselor do?*

---

A potential limitation on confidentiality that is discussed in this section of the code concerns "Contagious, Fatal Diseases" (ACA, 1997, B.1.d). Over the past 20 years, there has been considerable controversy regarding whether mental health professionals have a duty to warn an HIV-positive client's spouse or lover if the client indicates that she does not plan to inform her partner of her condition and plans to engage in sexual relations with her partner. Although this issue is not addressed explicitly in psychology's "Ethical Principles," counseling's *Code of Ethics* states that counselors are "justified in disclosing information to an identifiable third party" if the client has not already informed the individual and "is not intending to inform the third party in the immediate future" (ACA, 1997, B.1.d).

The justification for violating a client's confidentiality under these circumstances is the counselor's "duty to warn" the third party whose life could be threatened directly by the client's behavior, similar to the Tarasoff case discussed in Chapter 2.

The ethical dilemma, as in that case, is the client's right to confidentiality versus the counselor's obligation to protect the welfare of the third party. It is important to attend carefully to several points that could complicate a counselor's decision about whether to act on the basis of Section B.1.d. First, some states have specific regulations or statutes regarding the confidentiality of an individual's HIV status; in those states, counselors might be engaging in an illegal act if they were to disclose the information. Second, the section states that a counselor "is *justified*" in disclosing the information under the appropriate circumstances. This wording suggests that disclosure is permitted, but not required. An interesting recent ruling by the Texas Supreme Court rejected the general notion of a "duty to warn," stating that disclosures to medical or law enforcement personnel were *permitted*, but not *mandated* (*Thapar v. Zezulka*, 1999). Third, it would be extremely difficult to know for certain that a client "is not intending to inform the third party in the immediate future" (ACA, 1997, B.1.d). For example, when a counselor informs his client that he intends to disclose the information to the third party, which would be the ethically appropriate procedure (in accordance with Section B.1.f), the client is very likely to respond that she will inform the person herself. She is stating an intention, but does the counselor believe that her sudden change of heart is real? If he decides to violate her confidentiality, his action is certainly open to question based on her stated intention to inform the third party.

---

**Case Example 3.8**

*A counselor is conducting marital therapy with a couple. The husband contacts the counselor privately and reveals that he has had two homosexual affairs during the past six months. He does not want to tell his wife about the affairs, which he attributes to his wife's lack of interest in sexual relations. He reports that he simply needed a sexual outlet. He says he decided to tell the counselor because he thinks she should know everything about the problems in the marriage. The counselor discovers that both affairs involved incidents of unprotected oral and anal sex. He has not had an HIV test, and he has never been diagnosed with a sexually transmitted disease.*

*The counselor wonders whether she should tell the client's wife about the affairs because he could quite possibly be putting her at risk when they are intimate, but is unwilling to tell her.*

*What should the counselor do?*

---

A number of additional confidentiality considerations arise in multiple client treatment settings, such as marital, family, and group therapy (ACA, 1997, B.2). There are two major areas of concern that should be addressed: (a) whether information conveyed individually to the clinician outside the treatment setting will be regarded as confidential, and (b) whether group members are expected to maintain confidentiality concerning what other clients disclose during the sessions, as the clinician does. It is extremely important for clinicians to discuss these matters before beginning treatment so that everyone involved is aware of and agrees to abide by the ground rules established, thereby enabling clients to make their own informed decision regarding how much they wish to self-disclose in the group context.

A good approach for clinicians to use regarding individual interactions with marital, family, or group therapy clients is to let them know that individual disclosures outside of the treatment sessions can potentially complicate and subvert the treatment process. Therefore, clients are urged to discuss matters during the session, rather than contacting the therapist at other times. The clinician can also inform clients that when individuals do disclose information to her outside of the sessions, she will reserve the right to report the information at the next meeting, if she deems it appropriate and important for the other client(s) to know the information. This approach will allow the clinician to judge on a case-by-case basis whether she wants to report the information.

Clinicians should never guarantee that other clients will maintain confidentiality regarding disclosures made during the sessions. Clients are not trained as clinicians are to preserve confidentiality, and they do not have an ethical obligation to preserve the confidentiality of other clients. It is possible, however, that a client whose confidentiality was violated by another group member could pursue legal recourse against that group member (Roback, Moore, Bloch, & Shelton, 1996). Even if the members of a group were to support a ground rule to maintain the confidentiality of other group members, the clinician should not adopt it as a formal rule for the group because of the risk of "setting up" a client by making a commitment she cannot necessarily keep. Confidentiality matters in counseling and psychotherapy are discussed further in Chapter 7.

---

**Case Example 3.9**

*A group therapy client reveals that she is not really in love with her husband anymore and that her primary attachment is to her children. She expresses concern about what will happen to her marriage when the children grow up and leave home. A member of the group meets her husband at a business seminar and comments that some "rekindling" might be needed if he expects to hold on to his marriage. The husband questions his wife about this odd comment, and she tells him what she had discussed in the group. Her husband, feeling hurt and humiliated, files for divorce. The woman sues her group therapist because of the damage that was done to her life as a result of her participation in the group.*

---

The confidentiality of children or incompetent clients is limited under most circumstances (ACA, 1997, B.3). Parents generally have the right to know what is happening in their child's treatment because it is the parent who provides legal consent for the child to participate in treatment. It is important that children realize their privacy is limited so dramatically. Child clients can then make an informed decision regarding what they wish to disclose to their counselor (and, possibly thereby, to their parents). Interestingly, many parents are far more interested in getting help for their child, or improving their child's behavior, than they are in knowing what their child is disclosing to the therapist. Of course, a clinician is obligated under any circumstances to inform parents of any behavior that would put their child at risk of being harmed.

Many states do permit children and adolescents to self-consent to treatment under certain specified circumstances, thereby eliminating their parents' right to know the details of the treatment. These special circumstances generally include treatment for physical and/or sexual abuse, substance abuse, or suicide risk. The purpose of these statutes is to encourage children to pursue treatment for these serious problems without being inhibited by fear of parental retribution. Issues pertaining to confidentiality in the treatment of children and adolescents are discussed in greater detail in Chapter 7.

---

**Case Example 3.10**

*A woman contacts a child counselor and requests that he work with her 8-year-old son, who is having severe difficulty following rules at home and at school. During the intake interview, the counselor informs the mother of the legal limits on the confidentiality of children and of the fact that her son may not be very willing to open up to the counselor, knowing that what he discloses can be shared with his parents. The mother says, "I'll tell him that you won't tell us about anything that he tells you. We just want you to fix him!"*

---

Record keeping and the issue of client access to records were discussed in Chapter 2. Counseling's ethical code recognizes that it is generally in the interest of clients to permit them access to their clinical records (ACA, 1997, B.4.d). However, clients should not be provided with portions of records that "may be misleading and detrimental" to them or will compromise the confidentiality of another client, as in the case of group therapy records. Although the *Code of Ethics* retains elements of the paternalistic concern about client access to records that has characterized medicine and psychology, counseling is considerably more receptive to providing clients direct access to their mental health records. This issue is discussed further in Chapter 7.

An issue pertaining to both confidentiality and the ethical duty of informed consent is the requirement that counselors obtain clients' permission prior to video- or audiotaping sessions. This ethical duty is also covered in the "Ethical Principles" (APA, 1992, 5.01[c]). Counseling and psychotherapy sessions are routinely audiotaped in many treatment and training settings, but the clinician must obtain a client's written permission to audio- and/or videotape sessions prior to turning on any recording device. Generally, this permission is obtained prior to the first session in a statement that covers all subsequent meetings. The permission form should also explain what use will be made of the recording (e.g., supervision), how long the recordings will be retained, and how they will be disposed of or erased.

Occasionally, a client will object to being recorded. In many treatment settings, the clinician's concern for the client's comfort and willingness to participate would take precedence and no recording would be done. In training clinics, however, electronic recording and/or observation of sessions is necessary for adequate supervision of trainees. In such a circumstance, the clinician needs to explain to the client that recording is a necessary condition for being treated in a training facility. The client should be informed of the procedures in place to safeguard his confidentiality (e.g., storing recordings in a securely locked cabinet). If the client is still uncomfortable with the idea of being taped, an appropriate referral should be arranged to enable the client to obtain treatment in a more suitable setting.

---

**Case Example 3.11**

*Prior to his initial session with a new client, a counseling practicum student informs the client that he will need to audiotape the sessions so that he can review them during his weekly meetings with his supervisor. The client says she will consent to being taped if the tapes are turned over to her when they are no longer needed for the therapist's supervision. She thinks she would benefit from listening to the sessions again to reinforce the things she learns in the counseling.*
*What should the practicum student do?*

---

A final issue pertaining to confidentiality is consultation with other agencies and professionals (ACA, 1997, B.6). Counselors and psychologists consult on a case only when it is in the client's interest (APA, 1992, 5.02, 5.06). They do not gossip among themselves about clients, even though fellow professionals would be obligated to keep the information confidential. Any communication of information about a client, even to other mental health professionals, is an invasion of the client's privacy. For example, it is inappropriate for counseling or psychology graduate practicum students to discuss their clients with each other outside of case conference and supervision settings. Avoiding the use of names is not sufficient. Apart from supervision, keeping information confidential means not discussing it with *anyone*.

Consultation is very common among members of a treatment team in a psychiatric facility or between rehabilitation counselors and medical personnel involved in the rehabilitation of a physically disabled client. When consultation is appropriate, clinicians generally inform clients in advance of the need for consultation and sharing of information among different treatment providers. In consultations, clinicians limit their sharing of confidential material to information that is directly germane to the issue requiring consultation. When consulting about a case with professionals not directly involved in a client's treatment, clinicians endeavor to avoid revealing the client's identity or any identifying information. Finally, clinicians always obtain the written consent of clients before transferring any records or reports to other mental health professionals as part of a consultation or referral.

When a mental health professional takes on the role of conducting a consultation with a client, she should never assume that the referring agency or clinician has informed the client regarding the purpose, procedure, and anticipated outcome of the consultation. A consultant should always discuss these issues with the client at the outset of the consultation and present the results of the consultation to the client prior to obtaining the client's informed consent to provide a report of the consultation to the referring agency or clinician (ACA, 1997, D.2.c).

---

**Case Example 3.12**

*A counselor finds it helpful to "decompress" at night by talking to his wife about some of his clients. She understands the importance of never sharing these conversations with anyone else and she often gives him a different perspective on his interactions with clients.*
    *Is the counselor's behavior ethically acceptable?*

---

## SECTION C: PROFESSIONAL RESPONSIBILITY

This section begins with a statement regarding the obligation of counselors to learn and abide by the *Code of Ethics* (ACA, 1997, C.1). Next, the issue of professional competence, discussed extensively in Chapter 2, is presented. The limits of competence, the training required to claim competence, and the importance of continuing education for maintaining competence are addressed. An interesting additional point included in the *Code of Ethics* is that counselors are ethically required to monitor and evaluate their professional effectiveness on an ongoing basis as a means of self-improvement (ACA, 1997, C.2.d). Although methods of conducting this evaluation are not specified, private practitioners are strongly encouraged to make arrangements with peers to obtain supervision for their cases. Clearly, claims of professional competence in any field cannot reasonably be made in the absence of evaluations of the effectiveness of one's professional performance. Many professionals welcome the end of supervision requirements after they qualify for licensure, not appreciating the importance of supervision to their ongoing professional development. Although supervision can be personally threatening at times because of anxiety about the possibility of a negative evaluation, it is the ethical duty of licensed mental health professionals to continue to strive to improve their effectiveness in serving the needs of their clients.

Another aspect of professional responsibility concerns the public statements (e.g., advertisements of services) made by counselors (ACA, 1997, C.3). The *Code of Ethics* gives counselors a great deal of latitude in determining what is appropriate to include in advertisements of their professional services, provided that the information is accurate. In doing so, ACA avoids potential complaints from the Federal Trade Commission like those experienced by APA (see footnote 4).

Mental health professionals also have responsibilities to other professionals (ACA, 1997, C.6). The *Code of Ethics* points out the importance of respecting the different models and approaches used by different groups of mental health professionals in working with clients. For example, it is generally unethical for a counselor to question, during a counseling session, the value of a pharmacological treatment for depression that a client is receiving from a psychiatrist. First, such behavior shows a lack of respect for the expertise and competence of the psychiatrist, a fellow professional. Second, hearing such a criticism from her counselor could be harmful to the client, who might begin to distrust her psychiatrist or even decide to discontinue the medication. If the counselor is concerned about the efficacy of the medication, a consultation with the psychiatrist would be appropriate. Two treatment providers working with the same client should consult periodically anyway to make certain that they are not working at cross-purposes (with the client's consent, of course).

Professionals are also respectful of different theoretical models and treatment approaches of others in their own field. For example, counselors utilizing a psychodynamic approach should be careful not to denigrate the behavioral or person-centered models employed by fellow counselors. These attacks are generally the result of professional jealousies; they confuse clients and students, who tend to assume that an authoritative professional would not make such a statement unless it were grounded in fact. Unprofessional squabbling of this sort also diminishes the public's perception of the counseling field.

---

**Case Example 3.13**

*A counselor working in a university counseling center has had several clients who had been referred by, or had previously received treatment from, the health clinic on campus, which also provides mental health services. Three of these clients said that they were treated by a particular social worker at the health clinic. Each of them complained about her limited understanding of their problems and ineffectiveness as a counselor, which resulted in them seeking treatment at the counseling center. The counselor is concerned about the quality of service provided by the social worker. The reports of the three clients strongly suggest that the person has inadequate clinical skills to provide effective mental health services. However, the counselor knows that he has an ethical duty to respect the expertise of other professionals. The only data he has are the reports of the three clients about what transpired in their interactions with the social worker. He is unsure about whether to take any action and, if so, what sort of action would be appropriate.*

*What should the counselor do?*

---

## Section D: Relationships with Other Professionals

The first subsection deals primarily with ethical issues that arise when counselors are employees of an organization (ACA, 1997, D.1). Mental health professionals are unlike most other employees in that they not only have obligations and duties as employees of the organization, but they are also obligated to abide by the ethical code and guidelines of their profession. These two sets of obligations can conflict at times. For example, a counselor working in an Employee Assistance Program (EAP) interviews a client who discloses that he was told he would be fired if he did not complete treatment successfully. The counselor has a professional obligation to discuss with her supervisors the negative implications of coercing an employee into undergoing treatment and to assert the viewpoint of her profession that participation in counseling should be voluntary (ACA, 1997, D.1.c).

The *Code of Ethics* also addresses the obligations of counselors who are employers, rather than employees (ACA, 1997, D.1). Counselors should use nondiscriminatory practices in hiring and be careful to employ people who are competent and trained sufficiently to fulfill their assigned roles successfully (ACA, 1997, D.1.h-i). An employer's competence in personnel selection, training, and communication of goals and expectations benefits employees by creating a less stressful work environment. Counselors should also promote the professional development of their employees through in-service training (ACA, 1997, D.1.e). Finally, counselors should not exploit or harass employees; rather, they should model the professionalism they expect of their employees (ACA, 1997, D.1.k).

No mental health professional knows how best to help every client or how to deal with every situation that arises in the course of her professional activity. It is frequently helpful to consult more experienced colleagues when a clinician is unsure about some aspect of her clinical, teaching, or research activity. Counselors can choose to consult other professionals whenever they deem it to be in the best interest of the people they serve (ACA, 1997, D.2.a). As discussed earlier, they are mindful of keeping identifying information concerning their clients to an absolute minimum in their discussions with consultants.

## Section E: Evaluation, Assessment, and Interpretation

Psychological or educational assessment is undertaken only when it is in the best interest of the client. Testing is not done routinely or in the absence of any client need. For example, clients should not be asked to complete a depression screening instrument that a clinician is developing as part of their treatment. The validation or norming of a test should only involve clients who consent voluntarily to complete it as research participants.

Clinicians must use only well-validated tests, and only for the purposes for which the tests were designed and validated. Furthermore, they should only use tests that they are competent to administer, score, and interpret. The use of computerized test administration, scoring, and/or interpretation software does not diminish the clinician's responsibility for the accuracy of the test scores or the validity of the interpretations included in the assessment report.

In selecting tests, clinicians should be careful to use tests only with the populations represented in the normative sample. If a test must be used with clients who were not represented in the norm group, clinicians must weigh the potential effects of a host of demographic variables that could influence the validity of the test results (ACA, 1997, E.6.b, E.8). The nature and purpose of testing should be explained beforehand to clients to obtain their informed consent to the assessment procedure. Feedback concerning the results of the assessment should also be provided to clients so that they can make an informed decision regarding who they want to receive the results.

A final issue pertaining to assessment is the dramatic increase in the use of computer technology in mental health practice during the past three decades. Clients not only complete assessments on computers, but also diagnostic interview procedures. There are even computer-assisted therapy software programs. Clinicians need to be extremely sensitive to the fact that some clients, particularly older people, are inexperienced and, as a result, uncomfortable with computers (ACA, 1997, A.12.a). When computers are used in assessment and/or treatment, clinicians are responsible for making sure that clients receive adequate training in the use of the software programs and that assistance is available to them as they complete a computerized task. In addition, alternative procedures that do not involve a computer should be available for clients who express discomfort about using a computer or have difficulty mastering the computer task. Computers can increase the efficiency of a mental health practice, but this benefit would never outweigh the consideration of the welfare of a client. Ethical issues related to assessment are discussed in detail in Chapter 9.

---

### Case Example 3.14

*A counselor operating a large practice asks clients suffering from depression to complete a Beck Depression Inventory each week when they come in for a session, so he can monitor their progress. An elderly male client, fearing that his test results could be obtained by "hackers" via the Internet, always understates his depressive symptoms on the test.*

---

## SECTION F: TEACHING, TRAINING, AND SUPERVISION

Counselors involved in educational programs should be skilled both as teachers and practitioners (ACA, 1997, F.1.a). The *Code of Ethics* places considerably greater emphasis on the supervisory duties of faculty than the "Ethical Principles" does. Because supervisory relationships tend to be less formal and involve more self-disclosure than faculty-student interaction in the context of an organized class, supervisors must be particularly careful to avoid forming multiple relationships with supervisees and maintain the professional boundaries that preclude inappropriate sexual relationships with supervisees (ACA, 1997, F.1.b, F.1.c). Supervision of counseling practica is recognized as a separate area of professional competence that faculty must develop (ACA, 1997, F.1.f). Supervisors are also responsible for insuring that the services delivered by trainees are of professional quality (ACA, 1997, F.1.g).

A difficult issue for all graduate training programs in mental health disciplines is how best to address concerns regarding a student's personal fitness for a career as a mental health professional. Some students are clearly too shy to engage clients effectively in counseling; in other cases, students might suffer from psychopathology that would impair their ability to relate well with clients and maintain appropriate professional boundaries. Training programs have an ethical duty to both their students and the clients their students serve to confront these issues and attempt to remedy them (ACA, 1997, F.3.a). After all, mental health professionals express a strong belief in the value of therapeutic counseling to stimulate behavior change and personal growth. It would be hypocritical not to encourage students with these sorts of personal limitations to pursue personal growth experiences in order to achieve their career goal of becoming mental health professionals. It would also be unethical to permit a student to work with clients if the graduate training faculty did not believe the student could provide effective treatment.

**Case Example 3.15**

*A clinical psychology graduate student suffering from Bipolar Disorder stopped taking her medication during a very hectic part of the semester. Two weeks later, she had to be hospitalized for stabilization. When she returned to school, she was encouraged to switch to a nonclinical program of study and was told that she would not be permitted to take a practicum class because the clinical faculty had an obligation to protect the welfare of clients treated in the training clinic.*

*What ethical considerations are relevant to this situation? Was the action of the clinical faculty ethically appropriate?*

Nevertheless, confronting students with concerns about their capabilities is generally extremely uncomfortable for everyone involved. Furthermore, the judgment that a student may not be ready to engage in a practicum experience is a clinical judgment of the graduate training faculty that is based on data less straightforward than course grades or GRE scores. There are no clear criteria for making such decisions. Another complicating factor is the Americans with Disabilities Act (ADA), passed by the United States Congress in 1990. ADA prohibits discrimination against the disabled, including both the physically disabled and people with mental or psychological disorders. Some universities, citing ADA, question whether a student who has met the academic prerequisites can legally be refused admission to a practicum course on the grounds that she is emotionally unfit. As a result, programs sometimes allow such a student to continue, arguing that everyone should be given a chance to show what she is capable of.

There are several problems with this approach. First, practicum supervisors are not fulfilling their professional ethical obligation to insure that clients treated by practicum students receive professional quality treatment. Second, by failing to address the problem proactively, supervisors are putting clients at risk of possibly being harmed by their counseling experience. Third, if the practicum is uneventful, they are passing on the problem to future supervisors or the state licensing board, rather than dealing with the issues in real time and attempting to remediate them.

To manage this type of situation in an ethical, professional manner, graduate training programs must establish criteria for admission to practicum that include the graduate training committee's assessment that a student possesses the emotional fitness to work effectively with clients. These policies must be applied in a nondiscriminatory manner to all students in the program. ADA is not incompatible with such a policy; it simply requires that employers and universities provide people with mental impairments "reasonable accommodations" that would permit them to engage in productive work. However, there are no reasonable accommodations that would make it possible for an emotionally unfit student (or employee) to work effectively with clients. If a university policy were inconsistent with the graduate training program policy, the clinicians of the graduate training committee would make it clear to the university that their primary obligation is to the ethical code of their profession and the welfare of clients. Students in training are also obligated to place the welfare of clients first because students must also abide by the *Code of Ethics* (ACA, 1997, F.3.e). Of course, students receiving a negative evaluation of their ability to progress in the graduate program must be given the right to appeal the ruling (ACA, 1997, F.3.a).

When it is necessary to deny a student admission to a practicum course, remediation of the student's emotional problems should certainly be the focus of the process. Counseling or psychotherapy should be recommended, when appropriate. The clinician providing such services should, with the client's permission, make important contributions to subsequent reviews of the student's situation. Additional ethical issues pertaining to teaching and supervision are addressed in Chapter 10.

## SECTION G: RESEARCH AND PUBLICATION

This section focuses on ethical issues concerning the use of human participants in research, such as the duty to obtain informed consent. As discussed in Chapter 2, mental health professionals are permitted to deceive research participants about the true nature of a study when "alternative procedures are not feasible and the prospective value of the research justifies the deception" (ACA, 1997, G.2.b). The *Code of Ethics* distinguishes between research methodology involving "concealment" and "deception." A large proportion of personality and social psychology studies involve concealing the true purpose of the study by not fully informing participants regarding the purpose and procedures of the study (e.g., what the questionnaires are specifically designed to measure); a smaller proportion involve deception. This distinction is important because even though concealment does not involve actively deceiving participants, it nevertheless represents a failure to fully carry out the researcher's duty to obtain the informed consent of participants prior to conducting the study. The issue of deception in research is addressed in greater detail in Chapter 11.

In reporting the results of research studies in professional presentations and publications, mental health professionals are obligated to present their results accurately and not withhold results that are inconsistent with hypotheses or desired outcomes. For example, in conducting an outcome evaluation of a day treatment program for psychiatric clients, a researcher found that clients participating in the program socialized more, were more compliant with their prescribed medication regimen, and experienced fewer symptoms than a matched group of clients that did not participate in the program. The researcher was surprised to find that day treatment program participants also consumed significantly more alcohol than the matched control group participants, perhaps because they socialized with the other clients in the evening as well.

The researcher might worry that presenting the last finding would create a negative impression of the day treatment program in people's minds. Instead of focusing on the benefits of the program for clients, people might conclude that the program causes clients to be influenced by the substance abuse behavior of a few participants. Nevertheless, it would be unethical to suppress such a result. The researcher can certainly offer his interpretation of the meaning of the finding, but it must be reported. The recipients of the research report will draw their own conclusions regarding the result, which might include the feeling that the difference in alcohol consumption was a preexisting difference between the two groups. Suppressing research results is always unethical, even when done from benevolent motives.

One of the limitations of scientific research in recent decades has been the decline in the frequency of replication studies, which are studies designed to reproduce the conditions of a previous study to see whether similar results are obtained with a different group of research participants. The replication of significant research findings reduces the likelihood that a statistically significant result obtained by chance will be mistakenly viewed as a genuine phenomenon. Replications also serve to protect research disciplines against academic dishonesty on the part of researchers. Replication studies are conducted less frequently today because they are unlikely to be publishable, based on the notion that they do not contribute new information to the field. More frequently, researchers will conduct a study similar to one that was published, with the addition of a new variable or measure to carry the line of research a step further. When planning such a study, the researchers will typically contact the authors of the original study to obtain information regarding their methodology, measures and scoring procedures, and the like. Researchers conducting meta-analyses might also request information, including raw data, from other researchers in order to select studies for inclusion in their sample and to conduct their analyses. Researchers are ethically obligated to comply with such requests (ACA, 1997, G.3.e).

Another research-related issue is plagiarism, or presenting the work of another as one's own. The possibility of plagiarism can be avoided in research presentations, articles, and books by citing the sources of previous research findings and ideas. Through this procedure, the author gives credit to the original source of the information being presented, making a clear distinction between her original data and ideas and those borrowed from other sources (ACA, 1997, G.4.a). Material taken word-for-word from another source is indicated by the use of quotation marks, followed by the citation of the original source (APA, 1994).

Finally, the issue of authorship in research studies has been a somewhat contentious one in the mental health professions. The *Code of Ethics* is not very specific regarding methods for determining authorship or the order in which authors should be listed, with the exception of student research. It is stated that students should be the first author of articles "substantially based on a student's dissertation or thesis" (ACA, 1997, G.4.c). Most faculty members agree that this principle should apply to doctoral students' dissertation research. On the other hand, many students complete their master's thesis requirement by assisting a faculty member with research that has already been developed by the faculty member as part of his research program. In cases of this sort, a student is not ethically entitled to claim first authorship for the project merely because it was her thesis (Shadish, 1994). Authorship order should be determined based on the relative contributions of each author to the project (APA, 1994). Their status as student or faculty member is irrelevant to this determination (Thompson, 1994).

## SECTION H: RESOLVING ETHICAL ISSUES

Counselors, like other mental health professionals, are responsible for studying the ethical code of their profession (ACA, 1997, H.1). If questions arise regarding the

---

**Case Example 3.16**

*Two counseling faculty members and a graduate student collaborate on a research project. They agree that the senior faculty member should be listed as first author, even though she did not contribute as much to the study as the other two. She has a national reputation, and they figure that their article is more likely to be accepted by a prominent journal if she is first author.*
    *Is their plan ethically appropriate?*

---

ethical propriety of a counselor's professional activity, ignorance of his ethical duty would never constitute an excusing condition. The appropriate method for dealing with suspected ethical violations and the process used by state boards and ethics committees to investigate and resolve formal ethics complaints are addressed in Chapter 13.

## THE EXISTENCE OF ETHICAL CONFLICT

The ethical codes of the mental health professions discuss ethical duties one at a time, as if each ethical consideration (e.g., confidentiality, competence) were independent of the others. As noted repeatedly in the last two chapters, they are not. None of the ethical codes of the mental health professions effectively address the issue of how to resolve conflicts between ethical principles. For example, in cases of ethical conflict, psychologists are instructed to supplement the information provided in the "Ethical Principles" with "guidance drawn from personal values, culture, and experience" (APA, 1992, Preamble). The problem with appealing to the personal values of professionals, as K. S. Kitchener (1984) has pointed out, is that "acting ethically involves professionals in difficult decision-making for which they are poorly prepared" (p. 43).

As discussed in Chapter 1, one of the primary goals of this book is to prepare mental health professionals to identify complex ethical situations and to resolve them in an ethical, rational manner. To this end, the major philosophical approaches to ethical reasoning are described in Chapter 4. The chapter is intended to provide an understanding of the fundamental philosophical principles underlying the ethical codes of the mental health professions. Chapter 5 presents the viewpoints of moral philosophers regarding the best methods of resolving ethical dilemmas, and Chapter 6 introduces a model of ethical decision making based on the most promising philosophical methods for resolving ethical dilemmas. This model will provide a framework that mental health professionals can use to resolve complex ethical situations that arise in any aspect of their professional activity.

## SUMMARY

This chapter presented ACA's *Code of Ethics and Standards of Practice* (ACA, 1997), which governs the professional behavior of counselors. The code consists of a preamble, eight general sections addressing different aspects of professional practice (e.g., the counseling relationship; evaluation, assessment, and interpretation; teaching, training, and supervision), and a set of specific standards for counselors to follow. The tone of the *Code of Ethics* communicates counselors' respect for each individual and their desire to help individuals grow and cope more effectively with the challenges of life. Although the code overlaps considerably with psychology's "Ethical Principles," ACA's ethical code differs from that of the APA in several ways. For example, ACA's code devotes greater attention to multiple client treatment contexts (i.e., group, marital, and family counseling), the benefits of providing clients access to their treatment records, ethical issues pertaining to the administration of graduate training programs, and the ethical obligations of practicum and internship supervisors. The chapter concluded with a brief discussion of the potential for ethical principles to conflict in some instances, an important limitation of ethical codes.

# 4 Models of Ethical Reasoning

Consider the following situation: A psychologist decides that the best method of helping his client overcome her fear of intimacy is to become involved in a sexual relationship with her. She trusts him implicitly, and he feels very strongly that the experience will be a positive one for her.

## THE PHILOSOPHICAL BASIS OF ETHICAL JUDGMENTS

Is this type of intimate relationship ethically appropriate for a psychologist to pursue? Hopefully, mental health students and practitioners would respond universally with a resounding "No!" However, in order to establish rules of conduct for mental health professionals that all professionals are obligated to obey, the committee that creates the ethical code of a profession must be able to go beyond simply stating which behaviors are required and prohibited by developing a rational justification for the professional ethical principles and standards of conduct they propose. In other words, a rationally compelling explanation of *why* a particular behavior is acceptable or unacceptable must be possible. These explanations, though not generally stated in the ethical code, constitute the philosophical grounding of the ethical perspective of the profession.

Why is it wrong for the psychologist to engage in a sexual relationship with his client if he believes that such a relationship will be of benefit to her? The fact that there are rules prohibiting such behavior is not an adequate explanation of *why* the behavior is inappropriate. The validity of the rule must be demonstrated rationally in order to assert that the psychologist in question is *obligated* (i.e., has an ethical *duty*) to obey that rule.

This chapter will examine the ability of the major ethical theories of Western philosophy to provide the philosophical grounding for the ethical standards of a mental health profession. The merits of each theory will be evaluated critically and its relevance to the mental health professions will be emphasized.

## ETHICAL RELATIVISM

Ethical relativism, the viewpoint that there are no universally valid ethical principles, has become a rather imprecise term because it has been used in a variety of ways by different people. It is often presented roughly as the view that a particular action (e.g., not paying for food provided by someone else) may be ethically appropriate in one circumstance (e.g., when a guest at someone's home) and inappropriate in another (e.g., when eating at a restaurant). By this definition, everyone would qualify as a relativist, but this is not the true, technical meaning of the term (Brandt, 1959).

Genuine ethical relativism involves the assumption that the ethical values of different individuals sometimes conflict in fundamental ways. In a fundamental conflict, two parties do not simply disagree regarding matters of fact, as would be the case if two people disagreed about the appropriate criteria for a valid diagnosis of Schizophrenia, Paranoid Type. Rather, the two parties agree on the facts of the matter (e.g., both acknowledge the same set of diagnostic criteria for paranoid schizophrenia), but disagree regarding the morality of making such a diagnosis.

A second assumption that is characteristic of most forms of ethical relativism is that these fundamental disagreements cannot, at least in some cases, be resolved rationally. In other words, there is not always one demonstrably "correct" moral evaluation of an act, so two conflicting moral viewpoints may be argued to be equally correct. When this assumption is added, the position is referred to as *metaethical relativism*. The metaethical relativist would assert that either no effective method exists for resolving such moral dilemmas (such a position is referred to as *methodological metaethical relativism*), or if a method exists for resolving ethical conflicts, it is effective in only a limited number of cases (*nonmethodological metaethical relativism;* Brandt, 1959). With regard to the vignette at the beginning of the chapter, a metaethical relativist might argue that establishing whether the psychologist's actions are ethical or not by rationally comparing the validity of values supporting such a practice and those condemning it is impossible.

Two forms of ethical relativism that have become quite popular in American culture, and particularly in the social sciences, are cultural relativism and personal relativism. *Cultural relativism* is the viewpoint that fundamental disagreements regarding ethical matters often occur between members of different cultural groups. Cultural relativism is based on the assumptions that people acquire most of their personal values from their culture and that values and normative behavioral expectations vary from one culture to another. Some formulations of cultural relativism add the component that members of a particular culture are ethically obligated to abide by the moral standards of their culture, in which case the viewpoint is a form of *normative cultural relativism*. Normative cultural relativists differ on the question of whether people should always obey the values of their own culture or whether they should conform their behavior to the values of the culture they are currently in (e.g., when in Rome, do as the Romans do).

The perspective of *personal relativism* involves a position like the following: If someone genuinely believes that it is right (or wrong) to do A in circumstance C, then it *is* right (or wrong) for him to do A in C. For example, personal relativists would consider the actions of the psychologist in the vignette at the beginning of the chapter appropriate because he genuinely believes that initiating a sexual relationship with his client will benefit her. According to personal relativism, if a person believes that his action is appropriate, his action cannot be criticized on ethical grounds by others. This idea is consistent with the viewpoint that a person's affective sincerity (rather than any question of the objective "rightness" or "wrongness" of his actions) is what makes his behavior ethical.

## CRITICAL EVALUATION OF ETHICAL RELATIVISM

Ethical relativism, in its various forms, asserts that reason does not provide an adequate means of evaluating the ethical status of an action in some, most, or perhaps even in all cases. However, the viewpoint that ethical positions conflict in fundamental, irresolvable ways does not entail that either position is correct or that either is incorrect. In fact, if you follow through with the implications of ethical relativism, you wind up with *ethical skepticism,* the viewpoint that no ethical belief can be proven to be universally valid; therefore, all that remains are ethical attitudes or opinions.

Cultural relativism involves the additional problem of determining what culture to refer to in determining the appropriateness of a person's actions (e.g., American society, her ethnic subculture, her local community?). In the case of incarcerated prisoners, is their behavior to be evaluated by reference to the normative expectations within the prison? Clearly not, if the goal is to rehabilitate the prisoners so that they can become productive members of the larger society. Another problem with cultural relativism, which is obvious to most people, is that the ethical status of an action does not hinge on its social acceptability. Thus, cultural relativism, in equating morals with *mores* (i.e., the habits or manners of a particular culture or group), is really a rejection of the possibility of any objective ethical standard for judging actions.

Finally, formulations of personal relativism do not generally assert any conditions under which an action is morally inappropriate. The viewpoint that a person always acts morally if she acts in accordance with her true feelings does not necessarily entail that she acts immorally if she fails to act on the basis of her feelings. Any meaningful ethical perspective must, at a minimum, specify conditions under which actions are to be regarded as ethically appropriate *and* inappropriate.

## RELEVANCE OF ETHICAL RELATIVISM TO
## THE MENTAL HEALTH PROFESSIONS

As R. F. Kitchener (1991) has pointed out, ethical relativism is an untenable position for any mental health professional to espouse. If there are to be any standards of professional behavior, mental health professionals must be able to provide a rational justification for the ethicality and unethicality of particular actions. Failure to do so leads to *ethical nihilism* (i.e., the position that since ethical distinctions possess no meaning or validity, arguing about ethical matters is utterly pointless). If a rational justification for a profession's ethical requirements cannot be produced, then professionals cannot reasonably be compelled to obey such requirements. Therefore, although the rational justification of ethical propositions is not an easy task, especially when there are conflicting moral considerations in a situation, a mental health profession cannot abandon the task of developing such a groundwork without abandoning all hope of establishing and enforcing standards of acceptable professional behavior.

The intuitive, "seat-of-the-pants" ethical opinions provided by personal relativism are not adequate as ethical justification in a mental health profession (or any other profession). If behaving in a manner that one sincerely believes to be appropriate constitutes ethical practice, then any sort of unprofessional behavior (like that of the psychologist in the vignette) could be argued to be permissible. Professionals cannot be permitted to "just wing it" in deciding ethically appropriate methods of treatment, teaching, and conducting research without significantly diminishing public confidence in the standard of behavior within the profession.

The other major variant of ethical relativism, cultural relativism, is clearly opposed to the fundamental principles underlying the ethical codes of the mental health professions. For example, if a mental health profession were to espouse cultural relativism, there would be no justification for supporting the autonomy of a person if personal autonomy were not valued by the culture, or simply if personal autonomy could be argued to reduce the likelihood that an individual would adopt each of the values of the dominant culture. In clinical practice, there is often a degree of conflict between the interests of the culture and the individual. If a client is experiencing ambivalence about her homosexual impulses in a cultural context that is strongly heterosexual, there is a question as to whether the role of the therapist is to make the individual a better "fit" in the culture by encouraging her to behave in a manner consistent with the values of the dominant culture or to explore her feelings and determine her own course in life in an autonomous manner. Normative cultural relativism would encourage therapists, teachers, and researchers to impose their values (i.e., the values of the dominant culture) on clients, students, and research participants.

Finally, the unacceptability of cultural relativism is further illustrated when you consider the additional difficulties introduced by the presence of subcultures within a dominant cultural context. If therapists, researchers, and teachers were ethically obligated to adopt the values of the dominant culture, how would they resolve conflicts with the values of their native culture or subculture? Furthermore, how would they be expected to deal with the multicultural issues posed by clients, research participants, and students who identify themselves with other cultures or subcultures?

Clearly, ethical relativism has little to offer as a source of ethical justification for the mental health professions other than illustrating the negative consequences of the failure on the part of professionals to provide adequate rational justification for their ethical judgments. The search for sources of support for the ethical principles of mental health professionals must continue.

---

**Case Example 4.1**

*A client in a substance abuse treatment facility tells a psychologist about the activities (e.g., drug-dealing, assault) he was involved in prior to entering court-ordered treatment. When the psychologist asks him how he feels about having committed those crimes, he responds, "That was no crime. Everyone was doing that stuff. You just don't understand how it works on the street."*

---

## ETHICAL HEDONISM

Ethical hedonism is a theory of value. Hedonism comes from the Greek word *hedone,* which means "pleasure." The Greek philosopher Epicurus (ca. 342–270 B.C.), an early adherent of the hedonistic perspective, asserted that the greatest good is that which is intrinsically desirable (i.e., desired for itself, not as a means to some further end) and that the only thing that is truly intrinsically desirable in life is pleasure (Russell, 1945). By pleasure, Epicurus meant that which is enjoyable. Thus, the goal of hedonism is to always enjoy oneself. "Pleasure is the beginning and end of the blessed life" (quoted in Russell, 1945, p. 243). Pain is the only thing that is intrinsically undesirable.

In his original formulation of the hedonistic position, Epicurus did not propose an unbridled pursuit of sensual (i.e., "dynamic") pleasures. Rather, he advocated a simple life of philosophical reflection (i.e., "static" pleasure) as the most pleasurable, or good, life (Russell, 1945). Because Epicurus viewed pleasure as the absence of discomfort, he preferred a life without surging bodily passions. Though such passions are perhaps pleasurable for a brief period, they tend to be followed by discomfort when the intense pleasure ends. For example, the psychologist and his client might experience considerable pleasure from their sexual passion, but sexual activity can result in great discomfort later if their sexual desires are not satisfied completely or if one or both of the people experience regret about the relationship. Epicurus believed that mental activity that enabled a person to achieve a clearer understanding of himself and his world was highly pleasurable and that it avoided the discomfort that tended to follow intense physical pleasure.

A long line of distinguished thinkers (e.g., Thomas Hobbes, Jeremy Bentham, James Mill, John Stuart Mill, Henry Sidgwick, and Sigmund Freud) have advanced and refined the hedonistic theory of value since the time of Epicurus, although the definitions of pleasure presented by these thinkers varied. Today, the general hedonistic viewpoint is that a person is experiencing genuine pleasure if and only if, at the time that she is engaging in an activity, the experience or activity is enjoyed *for itself;* that is, the person would not wish to change the activity and would prefer that it not be changed by anyone else either. Although hedonism has been used as the foundation of the theory of obligation known as utilitarianism, ethical hedonism is not a proposal about what is morally right; it is simply a statement of what is *intrinsically* desirable. Many things, such as money, are desirable *instrumentally* (i.e., for the desirable consequences they produce), but only pleasure is desired as an end in itself.

## CRITICAL EVALUATION OF ETHICAL HEDONISM

The first problem with the hedonistic position is that hedonists attempt to argue from facts to value. Even if it is true that pleasure is intrinsically desirable, that does not make pleasure "good" in an ethical sense. In fact, the argument that pleasure is the only thing that is intrinsically desirable can itself be disputed. One could argue that to obtain pleasure, a person must want something other than pleasure for its own sake. For example, for the attainment of knowledge to be pleasurable, the person must have had an intrinsic desire to attain knowledge. Joseph Butler (1692–1752) argued that the ethical hedonist fails to recognize that there must be "particular passions" that enable people to obtain pleasure (1726/1950, p. 14).

Ethical hedonism also does not account for the obvious fact that people are motivated by factors that do not depend on the belief that the future event will be pleasant for them personally (e.g., being thought well of after their death). People will even risk personal loss rather than violate their moral principles. Of course, the hedonist will argue that, under such circumstances, behaving in accordance with their values must be pleasurable. However, what is intrinsically desirable in this case is behaving in a manner consistent with their personal morality. The behavior is not simply a means to some other end (i.e., the attainment of pleasure).

## RELEVANCE OF ETHICAL HEDONISM TO THE MENTAL HEALTH PROFESSIONS

As a theory of value, ethical hedonism is not intended to inform mental health professionals of their ethical duties. However, hedonism becomes a theory of obligation when it is combined with utilitarianism, the next theory to be presented. Nevertheless, the hedonistic perspective has been utilized by a number of psychological theorists (e.g., Freud, 1923/1961; Thorndike, 1911, 1940) attempting to understand the fundamental principles accounting for human motivation. These motivational theories are referred to as *psychological hedonism*. In such a model, the goal of life is the pursuit of pleasure. Therefore, the motivation underlying a person's preference for one state of affairs over another is that the preferred one is expected to provide more pleasure. For example, E. L. Thorndike presented the "law of effect" in his behavioral theory, which postulates that if a behavior is followed by a "satisfying state of affairs," the association of the behavior with the situation will be strengthened, whereas if a behavior is followed by an "annoying state of affairs," the association will be weakened (Thorndike, 1911, p. 245). Similarly, Freud (1923/1961) viewed human behavior as dominated by the "pleasure principle"; human beings seek to satisfy their instinctual drives, which are experienced as pleasurable, while avoiding a buildup of instinctual tension, which is painful.

Psychological hedonism, as a theory of motivation, raises an interesting question regarding the role that self-interest plays in human behavior. If the motivation underlying all behavior is the pursuit of pleasure, does it follow that people always behave selfishly? Though all hedonists do not necessarily adopt this view, which is referred to as *psychological egoism,* a hedonist would certainly argue that human beings always act in accordance with their self-interest. Even if people behave in an altruistic manner (i.e., engage in a behavior that involves some degree of self-sacrifice out of concern for another), behaving in such a manner must be consistent with their self-interest in order to be pleasurable (e.g., they might find it very pleasurable to be regarded as charitable).

But, is this behavior selfish? Clearly not. Two obviously different senses of self-interest must be distinguished in ethical hedonism. What might reasonably be called selfish behavior involves a disregard for the interests of others; selfish people think only of themselves when determining their course of action. On the other hand, when people brush their teeth, the behavior shows a clear regard for the individuals' own interests, but does not necessarily involve a disregard for the interests of others. Although an ethical hedonist might justifiably argue that people never act against their own interests, even in altruistic behavior, it does not follow that all behavior is selfish, as psychological egoism would maintain (Butler, 1726/1950).

---

**Case Example 4.2**

*A counselor attempts to encourage a depressed client to take advantage of opportunities to become involved with people by pointing out that her loneliness has made her miserable. He tells her that, although there is no guarantee that people will respond positively to her, at least taking the risk of reaching out to others has the potential to bring her happiness. "And after all," he says, "isn't that what we're all looking for in life: happiness?"*

---

## UTILITARIANISM

Utilitarianism is one of the two major theories of ethical obligation in modern Western thought. For the utilitarian, the ethical rightness of wrongness of an action depends on the goodness or badness of its consequences. Because of its focus on the ends achieved by an action, utilitarianism is characterized as a *teleological* theory of obligation (from the Greek word *telos,* meaning "ultimate end"). The notion of "the good" in most utilitarian conceptions is borrowed from ethical hedonism: pleasure or happiness is the good. However, some formulations of utilitarianism, such as that of G. E. Moore (1962), assert that certain mental experiences (e.g., the acquisition of knowledge) possess intrinsic value independent of the pleasure that may be associated with them. This viewpoint has been referred to as *ideal utilitarianism* (Smart & Williams, 1973, p. 13).

Jeremy Bentham (1748–1832) was an important figure in the development of utilitarianism. His formulation of the *principle of utility,* which underlies all utilitarian ideas, states that an action is ethical if it brings about the greatest positive balance of pleasure over pain because pleasure is good, and people are obligated to bring the good into existence (Bentham, 1789/1948). If all available options will produce some degree of suffering, the ethically appropriate alternative involves the least negative balance of pain. Utilitarianism boils down to this one principle, which serves as the standard for judging the morality of any proposed action. It is certainly appealing to believe that one reasonably quantifiable consideration can solve all moral questions and dilemmas.

There have been several different formulations of the utilitarian perspective. One distinction utilitarians have made is whether the principle of utility should be applied to particular acts or to general classes of acts (i.e., rules). In *act utilitarianism,* the pleasure criterion is applied to each particular action; therefore, a person judges the ethical status of each action by its consequences. On the other hand, in *rule utilitarianism,* the ethical status of general rules of conduct is evaluated by judging the likely consequences if everyone were obligated to behave in a similar manner (Smart & Williams, 1973). A rule will be adopted as an ethical duty (e.g., people should keep their promises) if the general consequences of behaving in accordance with this rule produce greater pleasure than those achieved by adopting an alternative rule. Act utilitarianism is generally regarded as being more flexible than rule utilitarianism because the act utilitarian is sensitive to potential changes in the ethical status of an act performed in different circumstances.

Another issue for utilitarians is whose pleasure is to be taken into account when applying the principle of utility — the individual's or that of the community? For the proponent of *egoistic utilitarianism,* an action's goodness depends on its consequences for the particular person engaging in the action. Conversely, an advocate of *universalistic utilitarianism* would assert that the ethical status of an action is a function of its consequences for everyone (usually within some specified community) affected by the action. Everyone ought to act so as to support the general happiness of the community to the highest degree, with each person regarding his personal happiness as being of equal importance to the happiness of every other member of the community (Smart & Williams, 1973).[7] Bentham (1789/1948) asserted that the interest of the community should not conflict with the interest of individuals. "The interest of the community then is, what? — the sum of the interests of the several members who compose it" (p. 126).

An example of the application of universalistic utilitarian principles is the Oregon Health Plan, a health care reform initiative implemented by the state of Oregon in 1994. In response to escalating health care costs, the Oregon state legislature created a Health Services Commission to develop a plan to ration health care to those receiving health insurance from the state (e.g., Medicaid recipients). The plan expanded Medicaid enrollment by 50%, including working people with incomes below the federal poverty line, while controlling the cost of medical coverage (Cutler, McFarland, & Winthrop, 1998). The commission developed a prioritized list of medical and mental health problems after considering the benefits of treatment to the individual and society versus the cost to society of providing or withholding treatment, the chronicity of the condition, the risk of death associated with the condition and the probability that treatment would extend life, and the effectiveness of treatment in restoring "the individual to a level of function at or close to the premorbid level" (Pollack, McFarland, George, & Angell, 1994, p. 526). The state legislature determined that sufficient funds existed to cover the top 616 diagnostic categories, which included the majority of mental health conditions. Among the mental health conditions excluded from coverage in the Oregon Health Plan were Conversion Disorder (in adults), Hypochondriasis, and a number of personality disorders, including Antisocial, Paranoid, Dependent, Avoidant, Schizoid, Obsessive-Compulsive, Histrionic, and Narcissistic (Pollack et al., 1994).

Those who prioritized the disorders recognized that conditions excluded from coverage are serious and painful for those suffering from them. However, the commission's concern was to use the limited health care dollars available to the state to provide health coverage for as many people as possible and to benefit the most people to the greatest possible extent. These considerations outweighed the suffering of the people whose diagnoses were not covered. Such utilitarian considerations are compelling to many people, particularly taxpayers, who are aware that there is a limit to the financial resources a state can invest in health care. In practice, the prioritized list has not been used extensively to deny people needed mental health services. Instead, cost containment has been achieved by forcing Medicaid recipients into managed care programs that may provide less extensive treatment (Bodenheimer, 1997). Nevertheless, if medical costs increase, the prioritized list remains a legally acceptable means of rationing health care in Oregon.

## CRITICAL EVALUATION OF UTILITARIANISM

Because the theory of value underlying utilitarianism is hedonism, utilitarians have been confronted with many of the same criticisms as proponents of hedonism. For example, the issue of arguing from facts to values is even more pressing for the utilitarian. Even if a person were to accept the argument that pleasure is that which is most desired in life, he still cannot establish that pleasure is good, in an ethical sense. Utilitarians must be able to do so in order to argue that people are ethically obligated to act only in ways that maximize pleasure.

An even greater problem for universalistic utilitarians, like Bentham (1789/1948) and Mill (1863/1910), is demonstrating that it would follow from the goodness of an individual's own pleasure that he is obligated to promote "the general happiness" of his community. Why could a person not say, "Yes, the general happiness is good, but I am interested only in my own happiness?" Indeed, it appears that most people actually are far more invested in their personal interests than in the interests of other people and do not exhibit the general attitude of "benevolence" that utilitarians assume characterizes human beings (Smart & Williams, 1973). The tendency of people's individual interests to conflict is precisely why issues concerning ethical behavior draw so much attention in the first place (Russell, 1945).

Another issue that universalistic utilitarians have not addressed sufficiently is the question of how the good (i.e., pleasure) ought to be distributed across the community. For example, what if a particular action would produce a great deal of pleasure for a small group of people, whereas another course of action would benefit more people, but produce a smaller total quantity of pleasure? An extreme example of the important issue of the distribution of the good is that a rule utilitarian could present an argument defending the ethicality of slavery on the basis that it is economically advantageous to the society *as a whole* (i.e., that it produces greater total happiness). However, an ethical theory that is compatible with slavery is preposterous because of its utter incompatibility with theories of justice.[8]

Utilitarianism's focus on the consequences of acts raises other issues. For example, Williams pointed out that since it is the existence of pleasurable and painful states of affairs in the world that matters to a utilitarian, regardless of how those states of affairs come to be, the individual would appear to bear equal responsibility for states of affairs that she produces by means of her own acts and those states of affairs that she does not prevent from existing (Smart & Williams, 1973). It would appear that her responsibility for her own acts is no different than her responsibility for the acts of other people that produce desirable or undesirable states of affairs. Williams referred to this issue as the "negative responsibility" entailed by the utilitarian perspective (Smart & Williams, 1973, p. 95).

Of course, critics of utilitarianism could question the meaningfulness of ever holding an individual directly responsible for states of affairs in the world, particularly remote consequences of an individual's own acts. For example, suppose a psychotherapist discharges a client prematurely from a treatment program because of countertransferential issues. While attempting to hitchhike home, the client meets a man with whom she establishes an extremely positive relationship and goes on to live happily ever after. Can the psychotherapist be meaningfully said to have acted in an ethically appropriate manner because the long-term effect of his action had been an increase in the happiness of the client and her mate? Remember that, for the utilitarian, the individual's intention in performing the act should not matter, for it is states of affairs (i.e., consequences) that are ultimately valued. The direct and indirect consequences of an individual's act are the sole determinants of ethical responsibility.

Williams also pointed out that the exclusive emphasis given to consequences in the utilitarian perspective makes the individual's own moral feelings unimportant. "Utilitarianism alienates one from one's moral feelings; … more basically, it alienates one from one's actions as well" (Smart & Williams, 1973, p. 104). The utilitarian's confused, impersonal conceptions of responsibility ignore the following commonsense ethical notions: (a) the limits of personal responsibility, (b) the difference between intentional and unintentional consequences, and (c) the essential ethical difference between acts *I* perform and those performed by others.

A final problem confronting utilitarians is how a person can be expected to calculate the potential consequences of her response options in situations involving conscious moral decision making. When an action would produce a mixed effect of pleasure and pain, as is frequently the case, how is she to compare the pleasure accruing to one person with the pain accruing to another? Furthermore, is she supposed to consider only the immediate consequences of the act or the potential long-term effects — what J. J. C. Smart calls "the 'ripples on the pond' postulate" (Smart & Williams, 1973, p. 33)? What if the short-term effects are positive (e.g., increasing a hospitalized client's sense of personal autonomy by agreeing to discharge him to live independently), but the long-term effects could be quite negative (e.g., his potential noncompliance with his medication regimen possibly resulting in his becoming dangerous to himself or others)? How much reflection is necessary prior to acting to insure adequate consideration of the likely short-term and long-term consequences? What appeared initially to be a very pragmatic, quantifiable approach to making ethical judgments actually turns out to be a model that is all but impossible to apply successfully.

## RELEVANCE OF UTILITARIANISM TO THE MENTAL HEALTH PROFESSIONS

The justification provided in professional ethical codes for the use of deception in research (discussed in the previous chapter) is primarily utilitarian in nature. Researchers are permitted to deceive participants, thereby violating the duty to obtain informed consent, if "they have determined that the use of deceptive techniques is justified by the study's prospective scientific, educational, or applied value" (APA, 1992, 6.15). Under certain circumstances then, a researcher's obligation to individual participants may be outweighed, at least to a limited extent, by his interest in promoting the welfare of society in general.

The utilitarian notion that people ought to promote the happiness of others affected by their actions is also quite consistent with the spirit of the ethical codes of the mental health professions. In fact, this is the ethical duty of beneficence, which underlies the concern that mental health professionals show for the welfare of clients, students, research participants, and others affected by their actions (Cohen & Cohen, 1999).

Professionals have an ethical duty to strive to bring about good, positive consequences for the people they serve. In a situation that cannot result in pleasurable consequences for the people involved, mental health professionals have an ethical duty to minimize the harm or pain suffered by those involved. This is the ethical duty of nonmaleficence, which also clearly has its roots in utilitarian reasoning. However, although utilitarian considerations can explain professionals' concern about the consequences of their actions, such considerations cannot account for why professionals care about the consequences for other people. Utilitarian theory does not explain the respect of mental health professionals for the autonomy, or personhood, of the people they serve.

Indeed, the major shortcoming of utilitarianism as a potential philosophical foundation for ethical decision making in the mental health professions is that the needs of a particular individual have very little significance from a utilitarian perspective, especially when those needs are inconsistent with the needs of the society in general. In contrast, the ethical codes of the mental health professions attach great importance to respecting "the rights of individuals to privacy, confidentiality, self-determination, and autonomy" (APA, 1992, Principle D). Thus, there is a definite tension in the "Ethical Principles" (APA, 1992) and *Code of Ethics* (ACA, 1997) between the strongly avowed regard for personal autonomy and the utilitarian justifications for limiting adherence to those values, such as when people are deceived as research participants. The value placed on the autonomy and dignity of the individual by mental health professionals has its ethical roots in the other major theory of ethical obligation, Kant's formalist ethical theory, which is presented next.

---

**Case Example 4.3**

*A counseling psychologist working in a community mental health center receives a telephone call from the mother of a client. The client, who suffers from Schizophrenia, Undifferentiated Type has stopped taking his medication, and his family is very upset. The psychologist explains that her son stops taking his medication because of the extremely unpleasant side effects it produces (e.g., tremors, muscle rigidity, constipation). His mother says that she understands her son's discomfort with the medication, but that having him on the medication makes life much easier for everyone else in the family and the neighborhood. She tells the psychologist that he has an obligation to convince her son to go back on his medication.*

*What should the psychologist do?*

---

## KANT'S FORMALIST ETHICAL THEORY

Immanuel Kant (1724–1804), as a *rationalist* philosopher, believed that truth or knowledge could be discovered only through the principles of logic and reason. Consistent with this view, Kant asserted in his ethical theory that moral truth is determined by assessing whether the principle guiding an action is consistent with the laws of reason. Since all people are rational beings, they are all capable of recognizing the universal validity of rational moral principles (Kant, 1788/1956). Kant's ethical theory is an example of ethical *formalism,* in that the morality of an act is determined formally, by virtue of the rational validity of the maxim involved, rather than by any reference to circumstances or practical consequences of the act.[9]

The principles of morality revealed by reason are known to be *necessarily* true (i.e., could not possibly be false). Also, these principles are known to be true independent of experience (i.e., *a priori*). Just as everyone knows that $2 + 2 = 4$ without having to constantly check the fact by putting two things together with two more, everyone knows that it is wrong to steal. That, according to Kant, is why a moral *maxim* (i.e., description of the principle embodied in an act) is always expressed in the form of a universal command, such as "Thou shalt not steal" (Kant, 1797/1964b). People do not need to establish the validity of this principle through experience (i.e., by gathering data about the effects of stealing). It is obvious to anyone that stealing is wrong, though human beings do not always act in accordance with moral (i.e., rational) principles. People "are unholy enough to be influenced by pleasure to transgress the moral law, although they recognize its authority" (Kant, 1797/1964b, p. 36).

Clearly, Kant makes no reference to the consequences of an act in assessing its ethical status, although Kant certainly believed that operating on the basis of reason benefited both the individual and others. His point was that the rationality of an action is a sufficient justification of its moral status. Also, Kant was not arguing that a person's motivation in behaving morally need always be the rationality of the act. People may act in accordance with the law of reason, but be motivated by a sense of justice, personal affection, or the like.

But how does a person know whether the maxim expressed in a particular act is reasonable (i.e., ethical)? Kant presented his "tests" of the rationality of a maxim in *Groundwork of the Metaphysic of Morals* (1785/1964a). These tests are referred to collectively as the *categorical imperative.* The first test of the categorical imperative is whether the maxim can be expressed meaningfully as an *a priori* universal law of reason. That is, does the maxim make logical sense when expressed as a universal moral law?

For example, suppose a client diagnosed as suffering from Schizophrenia, Paranoid Type asks her therapist to promise her that he will never discuss with anyone else the things she reveals in therapy. The therapist believes that if he refuses to promise and attempts to explain the importance of his documenting the course of her psychotherapy in the hospital records and of discussing aspects of her case with the rest of the treatment team, she will become very agitated and will refuse to participate actively in the therapy. Therefore, he promises her not to reveal anything to anyone, knowing that, although he will follow all ethical guidelines regarding confidentiality, he has no intention of actually keeping the literal promise he is making to her. He justifies lying to her on the basis that it is in her best interest. The nature of his act is expressed in this maxim: "It is permissible to make a promise one has no intention to keep." Is this type of act, which Kant called a "false promise" (Kant, 1785/1964a, p. 70), ethically appropriate? Kant argued that it is not appropriate because if it were universalized, the maxim would entail that everyone make promises with no intention of keeping them. Such behavior would make the notion of a promise meaningless.

By definition, a promise entails that the person sincerely intend to keep the vow made to another. Therefore, such a maxim is obviously unreasonable.

On the other hand, suppose a counseling professor is running late as she tries to get across campus for an important meeting with her dean regarding the status of her application for tenure. As she hurries toward the dean's office, a student who had participated in her research study the previous day stops her to discuss some serious misgivings he has had about the study. The student is obviously quite upset. The professor wants to stop and discuss the matter because the student is apparently in great distress, but decides not to because she does not want to be late for the meeting, which is extremely important to her. She tells him to stop by her office the next morning. Kant would assert that the maxim expressed in this act would be something like, "I am not obligated to assist another who is in distress." Interestingly, when we express this maxim as a universal moral law, it involves no logical contradiction or inconsistency. One can indeed imagine a world where no one provides assistance to another in distress.

However, the fact that a maxim can be universalized without contradiction is not sufficient to declare it ethically appropriate. Kant (1785/1964a) asserted that for a maxim to be demonstrably moral, a rational being would also have to be able to *will* that the maxim be universal law. This requirement constitutes the second component of the categorical imperative. In the example, the professor, as a rational being, could not will that the maxim "One is not obligated to assist another who is in distress" become universal moral law because the maxim would entail that no one would be obligated to assist her if she were in distress herself. A rational being would not act in a manner that directly opposes her own interests. Thus, this maxim fails the second test of the categorical imperative.

The morality of actions is discovered in this negative way for Kant. The tests of the categorical imperative enable people to discover those acts they should not engage in. Acts that are not eliminated by this process are ethically appropriate. According to Kant, when people act immorally, they do so in spite of the fact that they know the act is wrong or that the moral law they are violating is valid universally. In general, they decide hypocritically that their situation constitutes an exception to the general principle involved. Kant allowed for no exceptions to moral duty as it is revealed to human beings by reason.

The tests of the reasonableness of maxims associated with the categorical imperative do not represent a complete explanation of the origin of people's duties toward themselves and others, however. Kant (1785/1964a) explained that when people act in accordance with reason, they act autonomously and freely, that is, in a manner consistent with their nature as rational beings. Such acts are self-caused because the only laws reflected in them are the laws of reason, which are the foundation of human being. Therefore, when people act reasonably, they also act in accordance with the nature of every other human being. They never impose their will on another human being when acting in a reasonable, ethical manner because what one rational being would will is the same thing that any other rational being would. Kant described this harmonious blending of autonomous human rational wills as a "kingdom of ends."

Kant (1785/1964a) argued that there is a fundamental difference between a *thing* and a *person*. The difference is that only rational beings are regarded as persons. People's regard for themselves is based upon their recognition that they possess reason and, thereby, knowledge, which differentiates them from nonrational objects or beings (e.g., nonhuman animals). "Things" have "only a relative value as means" (Kant, 1785/1964a, p. 96). In other words, everything in nature exists as a means to some end, with the exception of human beings. Rational beings "are called *persons* because their nature already marks them out as ends in themselves — that is, as something which ought not to be used merely as a means" (Kant, 1785/1964a, p. 96). Thus, for Kant, all persons possess intrinsic value and are worthy of respect as ends in themselves. Therefore, it follows logically that people should "act in such a way that [they] always treat humanity, whether in [their] own person or in the person of any other, never simply as a means, but always at the same time as an end" (Kant, 1785/1964a, p. 96).

This doctrine of the *kingdom of ends* is simply another implication of the rational basis for morality provided by the categorical imperative. If people act only under maxims that can reasonably be willed to be universal moral law, they will act toward others only in ways that those others, as rational beings, would endorse as ethically appropriate. In doing so, people always show respect for others as ends in themselves (i.e., as autonomous human beings), treating them only as they would will that they themselves be treated. By the same token, this doctrine, which has a strong "golden rule" aspect to it (i.e., "Do unto others as you would have them do unto you"), is very appealing when people consider its implications for how *they* will be treated by others: They can be confident that they will be treated only in ways that they would want to be treated (i.e., in a just and respectful manner).

Morality, for Kant, involves not only an individual's duties to others, but to himself as well. Kant drew a distinction between a person's "perfect" and "imperfect" duties to himself and others (Kant, 1797/1964b). Maxims representing *perfect duties* specify actions that are clearly immoral. For example, the prohibition against stealing constitutes a perfect duty toward others. Stealing from a client by not pointing out his mistake in overpaying for a session is unethical because it shows a lack of regard for the humanity (i.e., personhood) of that individual. An individual's perfect duties toward himself prohibit any action that would compromise his value as a person. For example, smoking cigarettes is contrary to a person's duty to treasure and preserve his own life.

*Imperfect duties,* on the other hand, do not identify specific actions. Rather, they represent ethically appropriate, rational ends that ought to motivate a person's behavior toward himself and others. A person's imperfect duties toward others involve promoting the welfare and happiness of others. For example, a mental health professional has an imperfect duty to promote the welfare of his clients, students, research participants, or anyone else to whom he provides services. Imperfect duties state the goal or end to be sought, but do not specify the acts that are appropriate to bring about those ends (i.e., the duty does not include specific information regarding *how* a mental health professional would achieve the end of promoting the welfare and happiness of those he encounters in his professional activities). A person's imperfect duties toward himself involve striving to perfect his human talents through "the cultivation of his capacities (or natural endowments)" (Kant, 1797/1964b, p. 44).

The differences between Kant's ethical theory and utilitarianism can be illustrated by reconsidering the Oregon Health Plan from a Kantian perspective. The plan had a fundamentally utilitarian rationale: The limited pool of health care funding provided by taxpayers should be used to provide health coverage for as many people as possible by covering only those conditions that would benefit the most people to the greatest possible extent. In discussing criticisms of the plan when the proposal was being debated, Pollack and his colleagues (1994) reported that "some have suggested (only half in jest) that legislators should try the experiment on themselves (or perhaps all state employees) before changing Medicaid" (Pollack et al., 1994, p. 535). This criticism makes the Kantian point that people are obligated to treat other persons only in a manner that they would will to be treated themselves. Picking and choosing which people will be helped could never be willed by rational beings to be universal moral law because people would never wish to cut themselves off from receiving help if they were to suffer from a low priority disorder in the future.

## CRITICAL EVALUATION OF KANT'S FORMALIST ETHICAL THEORY

Kant's categorical imperative is initially quite appealing as a means of testing the reasonableness of maxims. However, the categorical imperative has a deceptive simplicity. Consider the effect of modifying particular features of a maxim on the moral evaluation of that maxim. For example, Kant would argue that it is unethical for a therapist to initiate treatment with a client when she knows there is no room in her present schedule to see the person on a regular basis. However, what would be the ethical status of the maxim if the therapist initiated a therapeutic relationship with a client knowing she could not see the client again the *next day?* Could a person not introduce complex situational factors that would make the application of the categorical imperative confusing, if not impossible?

Second, when maxims are formulated as less complicated general rules of conduct (e.g., one should never tell a lie), the model becomes extremely rigid and insensitive to contextual factors that complicate the situation. For example, most reasonable people agree that there are situations in which telling a lie to spare someone's feelings (e.g., when asked, "How do you like my haircut?") is ethically appropriate. However, such behavior could not be justified under Kant's model.

## RELEVANCE OF KANT'S FORMALIST ETHICAL THEORY TO THE MENTAL HEALTH PROFESSIONS

Kant's emphasis on the respect that should be shown for the autonomy of persons in the kingdom of ends discussion is strongly represented in the ethical codes of the mental health professions. Avoiding exploitative relationships, maintaining confidentiality, providing competent services, avoiding and correcting discriminatory practices, and respecting the rights of research participants are all reflections of the Kantian emphasis on the intrinsic value and importance of the individual. Kant's respect for persons is very similar to Rogers's (1961) attitude of unconditional positive regard for clients; both reflect a complete acceptance of and respect for the freedom, autonomy, and personhood of each individual.

However, in both APA's "Ethical Principles" and ACA's *Code of Ethics,* there is a degree of tension between the ultimate importance of the individual's rights and the desire to promote the scientific goals of the profession through research. Although informed consent is an important value in psychology and counseling, this ethical duty can be compromised through the use of deception in research. This utilitarian justification is curiously incompatible with the Kantian emphasis on respecting "the worth, dignity, potential, and uniqueness of each individual" (ACA, 1997, Preamble).

---

**Case Example 4.4**

*A clinical psychologist is the treatment coordinator for a voluntary inpatient on a ward providing assessment and rehabilitation for clients suffering from a variety of organic brain disorders. The client is a 33-year-old, married, white male suffering from encephalitis, productive aphasia, and AIDS. He is considered demented, but does not communicate with staff, so it's difficult to determine this for certain. He is clearly alert and is generally pleasant and cooperative.*

*The problem is that he is incontinent of urine and stool, and at times masturbates publicly on the ward. Staff members are concerned that his bodily fluids pose a potential hazard for the other clients, many of whom are themselves demented and might be liable to handle or ingest the patient's bodily fluids or fecal material. The staff decides that he must be locked in his room to protect the other clients, although this action will restrict his physical freedom and access to ward activities (e.g., television) tremendously.*

*Is this decision ethically appropriate?*

---

## SUMMARY

Mental health professionals must be able to demonstrate a rational basis for their ethical judgments. This chapter introduced the major Western philosophical approaches to ethical reasoning that can potentially provide an ethical justification for professional judgments.

Ethical relativism takes the position that different individuals (personal relativism) or cultures (cultural relativism) may have different conceptions of what is most valuable in life and of what action is ethically appropriate in a given context. The ethical relativist believes that these fundamental differences cannot be resolved in all cases, so there are no universally valid standards of ethical behavior. Ethical relativism was argued to lead inevitably to ethical skepticism.

Theories of value attempt to establish what is valued most highly in human life. The ethical significance of making such a determination is that what is valued most in human life constitutes the greatest good in life. Ethical hedonism is a theory of value that asserts that pleasure is the only thing valued intrinsically (i.e., as an end in itself) by human beings.

Theories of ethical obligation describe the principles that reveal how people ought to behave (i.e., the principles that constitute their ethical duty). There are two major theories of ethical obligation in Western philosophy. The first is utilitarianism. A utilitarian's ethical duty is stated in the principle of utility: an act is ethically appropriate if it maximizes the positive balance of pleasure over pain. In Kant's formalist theory, the second important theory of obligation, a person's ethical duty is revealed by reason. Using the categorical imperative, a maxim can be tested to determine whether it constitutes a universal moral law consistent with the laws of reason. In his discussion of the kingdom of ends, Kant argued that when people act in accordance with reason, they always treat others in a manner consistent with the way that others (as rational beings) would want to be treated. By acting in this ethical manner, people never impose their will on others because their rational will is the same as everyone else's. All humanity should be treated as an end in itself, never as a means to a person's own irrational, self-centered end.

The relevance of each ethical viewpoint to the mental health professions was presented, along with the major criticisms of each theory. For example, utilitarianism is reflected in the "Ethical Principles" (APA, 1992) in such provisions as the acceptability of using deception in research in certain circumstances. Kant's ethical theory is the basis of many of the ethical concerns emphasized in the ethical codes of psychology and counseling as well, including respect for personal autonomy and concern for the welfare of those affected by a professional's activities.

The discussion of ethical theories in this chapter revealed that while they represent different approaches to ethical justification, no one approach is clearly superior as a basis for professional ethical judgments. Furthermore, in each theory, there is the potential for ethical principles to conflict with one another in some circumstances. The mix of utilitarian and Kantian justifications in the ethical codes of the mental health professions produces significant additional potential for conflict between principles. It is extremely important that an ethical professional be capable of resolving conflicts that arise in situations involving competing ethical considerations. In the next chapter, the viewpoints of various ethical theories regarding such conflicts are presented. Based on the information presented in Chapter 5, a model that professionals can employ to resolve conflicts between competing ethical considerations is presented in Chapter 6.

# 5 Models of Ethical Reasoning in Resolving Ethical Conflicts

The ethical code of each mental health profession is designed to acquaint professionals with the principles, or values, that should guide their behavior. However, the previous chapters demonstrated that the principles that presumably reveal a professional's ethical duty in any situation can sometimes conflict. That is, mental health professionals encounter situations in which it is difficult to determine a course of action that will enable them to fulfill each apparently relevant ethical duty as they would normally strive to do. For example, suppose a client expresses suicidal ideation in a session. She has a plan and the means to carry it out. The clinician regards the client as being in imminent danger. Nevertheless, the client refuses to seek help from family or friends or to admit herself to a hospital. In such a situation, the clinician has, as always, a duty to preserve the client's confidentiality. However, the clinician is also obligated to preserve the life of the client, presumably by having her admitted to a hospital where she will be prevented from harming herself. In this example, two prima facie ethical duties appear to conflict.

An ethically responsible professional must be able to resolve these conflicts in an appropriate manner. But how? In this chapter, the methods of resolving ethical conflicts proposed by the major philosophical models of ethical reasoning described in Chapter 4 will be examined. Two additional models that are designed specifically to address such ethical dilemmas will also be presented. Both of these models, Fletcher's (1966) *situation ethics* and Wallace's (1988) formulation of *ethical contextualism,* emphasize the importance of taking contextual (i.e., situational) factors into account in attempting to resolve apparent conflicts between ethical duties.

## SITUATIONS REQUIRING ETHICAL PROBLEM-SOLVING SKILLS

Due to the potential for ethical duties to conflict in some situations, a professional's adherence to a particular model of ethical reasoning, even when combined with careful attention to the ethical code of her profession, is not sufficient to ensure ethical professional practice. For, although these models and professional codes provide considerable guidance regarding ethical issues, ethical competence also requires that a professional attend carefully to the potential presence of ethical considerations in each situation encountered. If a professional is not *thinking* ethically, there is a distinct possibility that she might overlook subtle, but important ethical considerations.[10] Furthermore, in situations in which ethical considerations appear to conflict, ethical competence requires that she be capable of resolving such conflicts through the use of her practical (i.e., ethical) reasoning ability. Practical reasoning involves adapting general ethical principles to the ever-changing contexts of life in a rationally defensible manner (Wallace, 1988).

Ethical reasoning is a type of problem solving, and the most difficult ethical problems are confronted in situations that involve an apparent conflict between two (or more) fundamental principles. In the example of the Oregon health care reform proposal (Pollack et al., 1994) discussed in Chapter 4, what makes the plan so controversial is that the situation involves not only a prima facie duty to ameliorate the suffering of each person, but also a duty to make certain that the limited available health care resources are distributed in a just and reasonable manner, and a third duty to avoid creating an onerous tax burden for the residents of the state by controlling health care expenditures.[11] It is extremely difficult, and some might argue impossible, to formulate a plan of action that gives due consideration to each of these important, conflicting ethical duties. Ethical dilemmas like this one represent the ultimate test of the viability of an ethical theory.

---

**Case Example 5.1**

*A counselor receives a call from his neighbor asking him to provide counseling for her 8-year-old son. The boy returned recently from summer camp and has exhibited some disturbing behavior changes. His mother says that he has become sullen and aggressive, is wetting his bed, and refuses to talk about his experiences at camp. His parents told him that they wanted him to meet with a counselor. His mother said she is calling the counselor because her son refuses to talk to anyone except him. The counselor knows that the situation involves potentially problematic multiple relationships, but he also feels it is very important that the boy talk with a professional.*

*What should the counselor do?*

---

The major models of ethical reasoning presented in Chapter 4 can each be evaluated further in terms of their efficacy in enabling mental health professionals to resolve apparent ethical conflicts.

## ETHICAL RELATIVISM

Ethical relativism is based on the assumptions that the ethical values of different individuals often conflict in fundamental ways and that there is no method available to resolve all such disagreements (Brandt, 1959). For the ethical relativist, there is *no* effective rational means of resolving conflicts between ethical principles. As discussed in Chapter 4, the assumptions underlying ethical relativism lead invariably to ethical skepticism. The inability to resolve conflicts in a rational manner undermines the rational validity of the ethical values themselves; ethical relativists are incapable of establishing the validity (or invalidity) of any ethical proposition. The utilitarian and Kantian theories are far less pessimistic about the potential to resolve apparent ethical conflicts.

## UTILITARIANISM

Both rule and act utilitarians would argue that genuine ethical dilemmas do not exist because, in all circumstances involving apparent conflict between principles, the only truly relevant ethical consideration is that of maximizing utility (i.e., the balance of pleasure over pain). If applying two different rules (rule utilitarian) or engaging in two different acts (act utilitarian) will produce equal amounts of pleasure, the decision of which rule to apply or which action to perform is of no moral significance because either will produce equally "good" consequences.

## Critical Evaluation of the Utilitarian Viewpoint Regarding Ethical Conflict

In spite of utilitarians' protests to the contrary, the possibility of conflict between competing ethical considerations does exist within both the rule and act utilitarian perspectives. Because rule utilitarians recognize the existence of more than one ethically appropriate rule of conduct, it is always possible for conflicts to arise regarding which rule takes precedence in a given situation. For act utilitarians, ethical conflict can occur because maximizing utility is not the *only* relevant ethical consideration. Specifically, when attempting to discuss the issue of justice, utilitarians must address how the good (i.e., pleasure) ought to be distributed, a criticism presented in Chapter 4.

   Though a utilitarian could argue successfully that the goal of maximizing the sum total of pleasure in a community is accomplished effectively in a capitalist economy like that of the United States, few would agree that the distribution of resources is a just one, with medical and mental health treatment frequently unaffordable for the poor while other segments of the population enjoy enormous wealth. A utilitarian, such as Smart, who is interested in avoiding this criticism of injustice, would argue that the attitude of human beings toward others is (or should be) one of "generalized benevolence, that is, the disposition to seek happiness, or at any rate, in some sense or other, good consequences, for all mankind" (Smart & Williams, 1973, p. 7). He would conclude, then, that such injustices are inconsistent with the utilitarian model in spite of the fact that they appear to maximize utility.

   Clearly, this addition of the principle of benevolence makes ethical conflict quite possible for an act utilitarian because now there are *multiple* relevant ethical considerations (i.e., maximizing utility *and* acting in a benevolent manner) that must be taken into account in a given situation and that might suggest different courses of action (Wallace, 1988). Thus, even utilitarians cannot avoid the need to devise a reasonable method of resolving conflicts between principles, though they offer no such method because they continue to insist that conflict is impossible.

## KANT'S FORMALIST ETHICAL THEORY

Kant's formalist model proposes that there is a rational solution for every ethical question and that the acceptability of any ethical maxim can be established beyond any doubt purely by rational deduction (Kant, 1788/1956). Thus, the Kantian approach also denies the existence of genuine ethical conflicts (Wallace, 1988). For Kant, two maxims cannot both represent reasonable courses of action and yet conflict with one another. Kant (1797/1964b) also asserted that no conflict can occur between "perfect" and "imperfect" duties because perfect duties always take precedence. Apparent ethical conflicts are the result of inadequate analysis and reasoning. Wallace (1988) describes this type of moral theory as requiring a "passive" attitude toward rules; people are simply to accept the dictates of *a priori* universal reason (Kant, 1788/1956). There are no situations in which it would be necessary to reason further about the relevance of a rule to a particular context, relative to other rules which might also apply.

## Critical Evaluation of the Kantian Viewpoint Regarding Ethical Conflict

Kant's passive conception of morality is illustrated in the Chapter 4 example of the "white lie" that is told to spare the feelings of another. For Kant, telling a lie is *wrong* under any circumstances. Most people would argue that this rule applies generally, but with some exceptions, for in real life, conflicts between principles do occur. For example, suppose a would-be murderer approaches a counselor and asks her whether her colleague (who just happens to be his former therapist and intended victim) is in the office today. She knows that if she discloses the fact that her colleague is indeed working in his office, this individual will go in and commit murder. Her practical reasoning power is not tested seriously in coming up with the answer that she should not disclose the truth, on the basis that the principle of preserving life is more important in this situation than the principle of honesty. This example may seem simplistic or extreme, yet Kant uses a similar example in his essay "On a Supposed Right to Tell Lies from Benevolent Motives" (1797/1909). However, Kant's analysis concludes that it would be wrong to lie to the would-be murderer to save the life of the potential victim because the counselor would be violating the universal ethical principle of honesty.[12] "Truth in utterances that cannot be avoided is the formal duty of a man to everyone, however great the disadvantage that may arise from it to him or any other" (Kant, 1797/1909, p. 362). For Kant, the consequences of an act within a specific set of circumstances are irrelevant to the determination of the ethical status of the general ethical principle expressed in the act. To lie is wrong, according to Kant. Period.

However, Kant's analysis does not correspond to how people resolve actual moral problems. People apply rules in an active manner, judging the relevance of each competing consideration to a given situation and actively attempting to work through conflicts between principles. People neither ignore the existence of ethical conflict nor do they throw up their hands and give up when they encounter it. Rather, they try to reason things out. Kant, in his insistence that reason always reveals people's moral duty, evidently did not consider the possibility that reason might inform them of a conflict between two ethical principles (e.g., honesty and respect for life). Kant's unwillingness to recognize the reality of conflicting ethical duties (i.e., moral dilemmas) presents a major problem when people attempt to apply Kantian principles to complex, real-life moral issues.

In the mental health professions, the Kantian position that there is never a genuine conflict between ethical principles has been seemingly supported by arguments that certain ethical considerations are *always* more fundamental than others. For example, there are mental health professionals who have asserted that the ethical principle of nonmaleficence (i.e., "Do no harm") is the most fundamental ethical consideration in psychological assessment (e.g., Brown, 1982) and psychotherapy (e.g., Rosenbaum, 1982). Endorsement of such a scheme would significantly reduce the problems inherent in trying to determine which consideration is most important in a given situation. However, to apply such a guideline as a universal principle of practice again ignores the real possibility of ethical conflict. For example, when a hospitalized client is behaving in a violent manner toward other clients and the treatment staff, whom is the clinician obligated not to harm? If the violent client is restrained physically, the client is harmed, if not physically, then at least in the sense of having his civil liberties curtailed. However, failure to restrain the client would likely result in harm to another client or a staff member. The clinician cannot avoid harming someone, so obviously avoidance of harm cannot be her sole consideration in such a case. Additional considerations (e.g., the desire to benefit the other clients by reducing the level of stress in their environment) are also relevant to her decision. If the clinician seeks instead to minimize harm relative to benefit, it sounds as if she has returned to a utilitarian perspective in which she would need to quantify harm and benefit in a manner that would allow the two to be compared directly, an impossible task.

---

**Case Example 5.2**

*A professor states in the syllabus for her Theories of Personality class that she does not give makeup exams. Each student's lowest score on the four exams given during the semester will be dropped (i.e., not included in the calculation of the student's course grade), so if an exam is missed, the score for that exam will be dropped. A student in her class does poorly on the first exam, but earns an A on each of the next two. His father dies suddenly the day before the fourth exam. He notifies the professor and asks if he can make up the exam when he returns to school after the funeral. The professor says that he need not worry about the exam; it will simply be the one dropped. The student points out that he intended to drop the first exam grade and was counting on earning an A for the course on the fourth exam.*

*The professor says that she understands the student's predicament, but it would not be fair if she changed the class rules for one student.*

*Is the professor treating the student fairly?*

---

## FLETCHER'S SITUATION ETHICS

Situation ethics is a theologically based contextualist approach to ethical decision making presented by Joseph Fletcher (1966). In general, religious perspectives on ethics constitute formalist models like that of Kant; that is, they are ethics based on *rules* governing moral conduct. However, unlike Kant's theory, no appeal to reason is made as the basis of people's obligation to obey the moral laws or commandments of a religion. Rather, the rules are regarded as the revealed will of God, which people are obligated to obey. Theistic theories, therefore, assume a belief in God; only those who share the beliefs of a particular religion will consider themselves obligated to obey its moral laws.

Fletcher acknowledged that Christian ethical principles do appear to conflict at times. However, he argued that apparent conflicts between principles are the result of people's mistaken belief that such principles are universally valid (i.e., valid in every situation at all times). According to Fletcher, the only universally valid moral principle is that of Christian love, or *agape,* which obligates a person to seek always what is best for his neighbor. "There is only one thing that is always good and right, intrinsically good regardless of the context, and that one thing is love" (Fletcher, 1966, p. 60). Because there is only one fundamental rule guiding ethical behavior, Fletcher believed that ethical conflict is impossible.

Fletcher's model is called "situation ethics" because the appropriate application of the principle of love will vary from one situation, or context, to another. Situation ethics is often misconstrued as a form of egoistic utilitarianism or personal relativism, but it is neither. It is pragmatic in that it addresses the consequences of particular acts within specific situations, as does utilitarianism, and it is relativistic only in the limited sense that no specific moral rules are viewed as being valid in every context at all times (i.e., as being universally valid). Christian love is the only universally valid moral consideration.

Fletcher describes situation ethics as a "Christological ethic" because the fundamental ethical principle is that of Christian love modeled on the perfect love of Jesus Christ. When a rule would obligate a person to act in a way that is contrary to love, that rule is not appropriate to the situation. In the earlier example of telling a lie to avoid hurting another's feelings (e.g., if a therapy client asked her therapist his opinion of her new hairstyle, which he did not particularly care for), the situationist would argue that to lie out of love for the other is ethically appropriate. "It is not excusably evil, it is positively good" (Fletcher, 1966, p. 65). All "rules" of morality, such as "It is wrong to tell a lie," are contingent, useful only to the extent that they serve the purpose of love in any situation. "Love's method is to judge by particularity" (Fletcher, 1966, p. 133). "We follow law, *if at all,* for love's sake; we do not follow love for law's sake" (Fletcher, 1966, p. 70).

Although Fletcher did not believe that there are ethical rules that represent the morally correct response to *every* situation at all times, a person's knowledge of rules and ethical precedents is important. "The situationist enters into every decision-making situation fully armed with the ethical maxims of his community and its heritage, and he treats them with respect as illuminators of his problems" (Fletcher, 1966, p. 26). However, moral rules are not followed rigidly or dogmatically. The situationist believes that principles cease to be useful and actually become a hindrance to ethical behavior when they "are hardened into laws" (Fletcher, 1966, p. 32). Careful consideration is required to determine which act will best serve the principle of Christian love in a given context. Fletcher pointed out that while virtue never goes out of style, it is not represented by continuing the same old practices in rote fashion because situations change.

Fletcher (1966) identified four considerations that are important to the process of applying the principle of love in a given situation. A person must identify the end sought, the means required to obtain it, the motive behind the act, and any other probable consequences of the act besides the end sought. Situation ethics has a definite link to utilitarianism in its concern for consequences. However, the goal is not to maximize pleasure, but to choose an action that produces "the greatest amount of neighbor welfare for the largest number of neighbors possible" (Fletcher, 1966, p. 95). According to Fletcher, an act can only be evaluated meaningfully based on the effect it produces, and the motives underlying it, in that particular set of circumstances. "For us, whether it is good or evil, right or wrong, is not *in* the deed but *by* its circumstances" (Fletcher, 1966, p. 133). For example, Fletcher argued that although there are strong religious and ethical arguments against abortion being available on demand, abortion might be an ethically appropriate course of action under certain circumstances. Suppose an unmarried woman suffering from Bipolar Disorder, who is in no condition to deal with a pregnancy or a child, is raped by another psychiatric client and becomes pregnant. A situationist would assert that in this particular set of circumstances, an abortion would arguably best serve the welfare of the woman and should not be rejected out of hand as an option simply because abortion is regarded as immoral in other contexts.

## CRITICAL EVALUATION OF SITUATION ETHICS

Fletcher's view is that ethical judgments are not justifiable through reason; rather, the ultimate source of a person's ethical duty is God's commandment to love his neighbor as himself. The validity of this commandment is assumed, based on Christian faith. Therefore, since Christian love is modeled after the goodness and love of God, it would appear redundant to assert that to act out of love is to do the good. It is like saying, "Go and do what Jesus would do" as a response to moral questions. A person could not go wrong if he followed this advice effectively, but how is he to know what Jesus would do? Fletcher has not helped substantially in the task of identifying what the good (i.e., the loving act) is in complex ethical circumstances because his position is that a person would have to be *in* the circumstance to be able to make a meaningful judgment. Nor would there be any conclusive way, either before or after the fact, to evaluate rationally the ethicality of the chosen course of action. Thus, there would be no rational method of evaluating the adequacy of the subjective conception of Christian love that might motivate a person suffering from Schizophrenia, Undifferentiated Type to kill her children in order to spare them from suffering the pain of living, although no reasonable ethicist would condone such an act.

Because there is but one important ethical consideration for the situationist (i.e., the expression of Christian love in one's actions), no genuine ethical conflict can exist. A person need only judge which option in a situation represents the greatest amount of love for the largest possible group of neighbors. However, to quantify such a matter, which clearly touches on intent as well as consequences, is every bit as impossible (if not more so) than the utilitarian calculus discussed earlier.

Furthermore, a situationist cannot determine in advance how she should act because the importance of situational factors is too great, except to say that she will always act out of Christian love. This conceptualization of ethical behavior is very demanding. It suggests that every situation is a difficult call requiring a careful appraisal of how love can best be served within the circumstances presented. In reality, relatively few situations arise that cannot be managed adequately by referring to the rules of conventional morality. In those difficult cases (each of the examples presented by Fletcher involves an ethical dilemma) requiring reflective ethical decision making, the application of Christian love is arguably reducible to the person's *sentiment* regarding what the best course of action would be. No further justification is needed or is indeed possible. Therefore, situation ethics does not represent a method for resolving ethical dilemmas on a rational basis. Mental health professionals are obligated to be able to cite sound *reasons* in support of the ethical judgments they make. Acting out of benevolence and concern is certainly important, but these considerations are extremely abstract and imprecise. Just as parents and children frequently have very different perceptions of the love associated with corporal punishment, a person's subjective perspective would be of critical importance to his perception of the role of Christian love in any proposed act within a given set of circumstances. Similarly, perspective was important to the precise formulation of a maxim to be evaluated with Kant's categorical imperative.

Finally, although Christian love is an extremely broad concept, it cannot disguise the fact that people encounter situations involving multiple ethical considerations. To claim that all considerations (e.g., confidentiality, concern for the welfare of others, respect for personal autonomy, social responsibility) are subsumed under this general principle has the effect of making ethical problem solving more ambiguous and complicated rather than clearer and easier. The single principle of love becomes so complex that it becomes virtually impossible to compare and quantify the potential implications for love represented by the alternatives in a genuine ethical dilemma.

---

**Case Example 5.3**

A clinical psychologist in a small town is aware of an individual who has terrorized many of the townspeople for several years. He has harassed women and committed a number of crimes against people and their property, but there has never been sufficient evidence to indict him for a crime. Recently, a 12-year-old girl was raped and murdered. Although evidence points strongly to the same man, he has not been arrested.

In an apparent attempt to protect himself in case he is arrested, the man comes to the community mental health center, complaining of a long history of "hearing voices." The psychologist performs an evaluation that indicates the man is malingering, although he does qualify for a diagnosis of Antisocial Personality Disorder. However, in order to protect the community from this "evil" person, the psychologist prepares a report documenting that the client is mentally ill (as he pretends to be) and extremely dangerous to others. Furthermore, the psychologist contacts legal authorities and reports that his evaluation indicates that the man should be committed to a state psychiatric facility.

What ethical considerations are involved in this situation? Is the psychologist behaving in an ethical manner?

## WALLACE'S ETHICAL CONTEXTUALISM

As a contextualist, James Wallace (1988) acknowledged that conflicts do occur between competing ethical principles and that no principle is valid in every conceivable context (i.e., there are no universally valid ethical principles). Wallace pointed out that the existence of ethical conflict is not surprising; rather, it is curious that ethicists have frequently assumed that a deductive system of ethical rules (e.g., Kant's formalist theory), derived independently of experience, could effectively address what people ought to do in the ever-changing contexts of actual human life. "How could a set of principles anticipate the continual and extensive changes in the human condition" (Wallace, 1988, p. 17)? Wallace credited John Dewey with having recognized the importance of changing contexts to ethical decision making and to people's evolving understanding of ethical issues. Dewey (1930) had said, "In quality, the good is never twice alike. It never copies itself. It is new every morning, fresh every evening. It is unique in its every presentation" (Dewey, 1930, p. 197).

How are people capable of adapting their ethical understanding to new and continually changing circumstances? According to Wallace, the moral education people receive as children involves more than the learning of rules. People gradually acquire an increasingly sophisticated understanding of how particular rules apply or do not apply to solving practical moral problems in different sorts of contexts. In other words, people learn that considerations of morality and justice sometimes require that rules be adapted to fit unusual circumstances. "The marvelous plasticity of response of which human beings are capable involves the ability to adapt old routines to new circumstances. Intelligence and understanding are exhibited in such adaptation" (Wallace, 1988, p. 58). This process of adapting the application of rules in deciding what the ethical course of action is in a particular set of circumstances encountered in life is what ethicists call *practical reasoning* (Cohen & Cohen, 1999). Practical reasoning is an area of human inquiry that is evolving continuously as ethical principles are applied in new situations involving new combinations of moral considerations.

As adults, people are not generally even conscious of the need to adapt their moral reasoning to variations in context. Wallace (1988) explained that the moral education people receive provides them with a considerable stockpile of contextually sensitive ethical guidelines, which represent the accumulated practical wisdom of their community and culture. Although most people may not be able to articulate the principles involved, they are nevertheless able to employ this storehouse of practical wisdom with considerable ease to make judgments regarding the relevance of apparently competing ethical rules or to determine which ethical considerations take precedence in a situation. People become aware of the need for practical reasoning only in those difficult cases (i.e., ethical dilemmas) in which it initially appears that whatever option they choose involves ignoring another, equally important ethical consideration. Individuals' practical reasoning capability is employed in such cases to devise creative solutions that best serve each of the relevant considerations in a situation. Therefore, rather than denying the existence of potential conflict between ethical principles and feeling threatened by such a possibility, the ethical contextualist recognizes that human experience has always involved such dilemmas and that the practical reasoning capability of people has generally proven adequate to address these situations reasonably and effectively.

Like Fletcher (1966), Wallace (1988) believed that the ethical principles people have been taught are extremely important to ethical behavior. Kant demonstrated that these ethical principles reveal to people the considerations that ought to be expressed in their acts. Nevertheless, rules alone are not sufficient to guarantee ethical conduct in the changing circumstances of life in which two ethical duties might conflict. To say that "rules are rules" and that circumstances have no bearing on the ethical status of an act is a naive view that does not reflect the manner in which reasonable people actually make ethical judgments. "To be critical, in an important sense of this term, is to be good at seeing how what one already knows can be changed so that it can be brought to bear upon unprecedented situations" (Wallace, 1988, p. 58).

Wallace argued that there are two fundamental types of problems that reveal the insufficiency of ethical rules: issues of relevance and genuine ethical conflicts. First, in cases involving an apparent conflict between principles, rather than applying one or the other rule in a passive, irrational manner, reasoning people assess whether each consideration is truly *relevant* to the context. For example, suppose a student in a statistics class tells his instructor in casual conversation a rumor regarding the behavior of another instructor in the department. Because the student says nothing about keeping the conversation confidential, the instructor repeats the story to the other faculty member (out of concern for the colleague's welfare). The colleague realizes which student must have reported the rumor and confronts the student about it. The student then accuses the statistics instructor of having violated his confidentiality. Although this situation might initially appear to have involved competing ethical considerations, the statistics instructor's knowledge of the "Ethical Principles" enables him to recognize that the purpose of the ethical duty regarding confidentiality is not relevant to this circumstance because neither his relationship with the student nor the nature of the information communicated meets the conditions necessary to establish a duty to maintain confidentiality.

Second, ethical rules are also insufficient when people are confronted with a situation in which two or more relevant ethical principles do genuinely *conflict*. An example of an ethical dilemma would be if a clinician were treating another mental health professional in therapy and she revealed to him in the context of the therapy that she was having a sexual relationship with a current client. In this case, the confidentiality of the client is a relevant ethical consideration, as is the clinician's obligation to protect the welfare of his client and to address unethical behavior on the part of another professional. He would be faced with a conflict between relevant ethical duties which at first glance appears irresolvable (K. S. Kitchener, 1984).

Resolving situations that appear to involve multiple ethical considerations (issues of relevance) or that genuinely do represent conflicts between ethical principles (ethical dilemmas) requires understanding *why* people hold the values they do. In other words, why are the ethical principles involved in the situation important to people? Wallace (1988) asserted that the reason people hold certain values dear is that those values promote human life and human activity in some important way. The key to resolving apparent conflicts between values is to understand the *point* or function of each value and determine how important that consideration is to the situation at hand. These metaethical reflections require a clear understanding of the sources of ethical values, which is the reason so much attention was devoted to the analysis of ethical theories in Chapter 4.

The following example illustrates the application of Wallace's ethical contextualism. A psychology department operates a clinic for the purpose of providing practicum training for clinical graduate students. The clinic provides assessment and psychotherapy services to university students and the local community. The clinic is open only during weekday afternoons. Due to the limited availability of space in the psychology department, several clinical and nonclinical faculty ask if the clinic space could be used to conduct research during the morning and on weekends, justifying their request by citing student need for research space to complete thesis projects and the potential scientific value of both student and faculty research. Some members of the clinical faculty argue that the request should be rejected because the confidentiality of clients could be compromised, noting that client records are kept in the clinic and that clients leave telephone messages on an answering machine in the clinic during nonclinic hours.

Clearly, there are multiple, apparently conflicting ethical considerations cited by the two parties in this case. In attempting to resolve potential ethical conflicts in a rational manner, practical reasoning, according to Wallace, first involves an assessment of the relevance of each of the considerations to the situation. As Aristotle (trans. 1947) pointed out, practical wisdom involves giving each competing consideration the weight it deserves. Obviously, an irrelevant consideration does not deserve the same weight as a relevant one. The obligation to provide sufficient space and resources for students to complete their thesis work is certainly relevant to a fundamental purpose of an academic department. The potential scientific value of faculty research projects is difficult to determine, but conducting research is part of an academic psychologist's job description and the department is certainly obliged to facilitate faculty members' ability to do their jobs.

The issue of ensuring client confidentiality is obviously important to any clinic offering psychological services, but it is unclear how nonclinic personnel's use of the clinic when it is closed would compromise the confidentiality of clients. If client records were not locked away in filing cabinets or were easily accessible without passwords on a computer, an ethical concern would certainly be justified. However, in such an instance, the confidentiality of clients would already be at risk because custodial personnel or anyone else with a key to the clinic door would have access to the material. On the other hand, if practicum students and supervisors are diligent in their duties of putting away notes, files, computer disks, and other confidential material in locked cabinets at the close of clinic hours; making sure that computer records cannot be accessed without well-protected passwords; and keeping the telephone answering machine in a secure, private area, a breach of confidentiality should not be a potential risk.

Thus, it could be argued that the ethical consideration of protecting the confidentiality of clinic clients is being applied inappropriately to the question of how the clinic space can be used when the clinic is closed. Clinical faculty members' sensitivity to the issue of confidentiality is admirable, but the issue is not demonstrably of strong relevance to the context under consideration. If the clinical faculty were to respond that confidentiality is always the primary ethical consideration in *any* context involving the clinic, their position would be revealed to be grounded on the assumptions that there are inviolable ethical rules and that sensitivity to contextual factors is not an important part of practical reasoning. These positions were found to be untenable in the consideration of Kant's formalist theory earlier in this chapter. Thus, there does not appear to be a reasonable ethical objection in this case to using the clinic space for research purposes during nonclinic hours, provided that adequate safeguards are in place to insure client confidentiality.

A genuine ethical dilemma, on the other hand, involves multiple, competing ethical considerations that are each demonstrably relevant to the context. The following example is an ethical dilemma based on the issue of providing clients access to their mental health records. A 23-year-old client who had been hospitalized for an episode of depression requests permission to review her treatment record prior to being discharged. Her therapist is concerned because the section of the record concerning the history of the client's problems states that her first episode of depression occurred when she was 16, shortly after her parents died. Her aunt had told the admitting psychiatrist at that time that the client's father had killed her mother and had subsequently killed himself. The aunt provided a copy of a newspaper account of the events, which was included in the client's record. The therapist is aware that his client was told that her parents had died in an automobile accident; she apparently does not know the true story of her parents' deaths.

Respect for his client's autonomy suggests that she has a right to know what her treatment record contains, including the truth about her family and her own past. On the other hand, the therapist's concern for the welfare of his client is that she could be traumatized by this information. Both of these competing ethical considerations are clearly relevant to the situation. Wallace (1988) argued that to resolve such a dilemma in a reasonable manner, the therapist must try to interpret the meaning and *purpose* of the principles involved "in ways that are faithful to the rules themselves and to the activities the rules are designed to facilitate" (Wallace, 1988, p. 10).

Respect for the autonomy of the client to make decisions about her own life is grounded in people's respect for other persons. People do not believe that it is appropriate for someone else to make important decisions about their lives without their knowledge and consent. People also believe that it is inappropriate to lie to another person because such behavior displays a lack of respect for the individual's personhood. Furthermore, respect for autonomy reflects people's belief in the potential of human beings for growth and self-understanding. One cannot then be truly autonomous without knowledge of relevant aspects of one's past, knowledge that had been denied to this young woman through the deception perpetrated by paternalistic relatives. At the time, she was a minor, but apparently no one had informed her of the truth as an adult either. To deny her access to the information contained in her record about her family is to collude in this ongoing pattern of disregard for her autonomy.

Concern for her welfare was undoubtedly a major consideration in her family's ongoing decision not to tell her the true circumstances of her parents' deaths, for her difficulties with depression have persisted episodically into adulthood. The principle of concern for others' welfare is grounded in mental health professionals' respect and regard for persons, as is the competing principle of respect for a person's autonomy. Not only do clinicians have an obligation never to harm another person intentionally, they also have a duty to try to protect others from harm whenever possible.

The fundamental issue here is whether the therapist is justified in protecting his client from harm by acting paternalistically and denying her access to potentially upsetting information. Denying her access to the information might serve the purpose of protecting her from harm, but only at the expense of ignoring the obligation to respect her autonomy as an individual. The therapist realizes that one could argue that a client is, in fact, "harmed" whenever others interfere with her autonomous functioning. It is rather difficult to justify harming an individual (by denying her autonomy) in order to protect her from harm. Infantilizing someone, as has been done in this woman's case, communicates a profound disrespect for her personhood. Alternatively, providing her with supervised access to the record so that she can learn the truth about her past and work through the implications of these revelations with her therapist would demonstrate respect for her personal autonomy and also address his concern about her psychological welfare. This strategy would also eliminate the possibility that she might learn the truth about her parents sometime after her discharge when she might not have any support available to help her deal with the painful discovery.

This resolution might have occurred to many readers spontaneously as they thought about the case. However, other people might have had different responses to the scenario. The important point is that the process of practical reasoning described above resulted in a solution that is supported by good reasons and is consistent with the purposes of the ethical considerations relevant to the situation, rather than an arbitrarily determined course of action that could be viewed as reflecting the personal ethical biases of the professional involved.

For the ethical contextualist, intelligent moral behavior is always based on an understanding of how ethical principles have been applied in the past and the ends that have been served by those applications (Wallace, 1988). The ethical contextualist demonstrates an understanding of the "ways of life" that represent the accumulated practical wisdom of a society (or in this case, of the mental health professions). The contextualist recognizes that practical reasoning requires that people adapt these ways to novel situations. Ethical problem solving is, therefore, a creative enterprise. Resolving an ethical dilemma seldom involves simply choosing one principle over another; rather, it requires devising a solution that is consistent with the purpose of all principles involved (Wallace, 1988). The ethical contextualist strives to make decisions that reflect the considerations people value most (i.e., that have proven most important and useful to their ways of life), while modifying or excluding what people value less.

## CRITICAL EVALUATION OF ETHICAL CONTEXTUALISM

Wallace (1988) contended that people's everyday experience provides considerable evidence in support of the view that the practical reasoning ability of human beings is effective in meeting the ethical challenges presented by the ever-changing contexts of modern life. Although contextualist theory appears to provide a very promising means of resolving ethical conflict through the use of practical reason, successful application of Wallace's method seems to require considerable metaethical sophistication on the part of a mental health professional. It is necessary that professionals be familiar not only with the values and ethical principles that are to guide their conduct, but the metaethical justifications for those principles as well. Otherwise, they will not be in a position to understand the function of the ethical considerations involved in a situation, which is necessary in order to recognize the points of connection between the considerations and to prioritize the principles in a reasonable way.

The fact that behaving ethically is a difficult challenge is not an indictment of ethical contextualism. It is simply a reality with which the ethical professional must struggle. Exercising practical reasoning in order to behave ethically is not an easy task; however, as Wallace (1988) has pointed out, it is not impossible either. The attention devoted to the ethical principles of mental health professionals in Chapters 2 and 3 and to models of ethical reasoning and sources of metaethical justification in Chapter 4 represents the initial step in developing competence in practical reasoning. This process continues in the next chapter. A model of ethical decision making based on Wallace's ethical contextualism will be presented. This model was created to provide guidance and structure for the ethical deliberations of mental health professionals that will enable them to resolve ethically complex situations in a rationally defensible manner.

## SUMMARY

The ethical codes of the mental health professions do not always provide sufficient information regarding how professionals can resolve ethical conflicts. In this chapter, five models of resolving ethical conflicts were examined and evaluated: ethical relativism, utilitarianism, Kant's formalist theory, Fletcher's situation ethics, and Wallace's ethical contextualist theory. The latter two theories are specifically designed to address ethical dilemmas.

Ethical relativism asserts that ethical dilemmas cannot be resolved rationally. Both utilitarianism and Kant's formalist theory deny the existence of ethical dilemmas, though further analysis of the theories demonstrates that ethical conflict is indeed possible within the frameworks of these theories, but is irresolvable.

In his situation ethics, Fletcher argues that dilemmas are not possible when one acts in accordance with Christian love, which is the one true universal moral principle. Even though Fletcher's theory has the merit of being sensitive to changing contexts, analysis of this theory does not eliminate the possibility of ethical conflicts and the fact that it fails to provide us with a rational and effective means for resolving such conflicts.

Wallace's ethical contextualist theory also emphasizes the importance of adapting ethical guidelines to situational factors. However, Wallace argued that ethical conflict can be resolved and that a rational justification can be provided for ethical decision making. He asserted that people are able to resolve ethical conflicts by drawing on a store of practical wisdom communicated to them by their culture and community. When confronted with a genuine ethical dilemma, people can practice effective practical reasoning by engaging in metaethical deliberations regarding the functions of the relevant ethical considerations. These deliberations involve reflecting on how each consideration contributes to people's ways of life (i.e., in what way the ethical value is *valuable* in human life) in order to devise a solution that is consistent with the purpose of each ethical principle involved in the situation. One shortcoming of Wallace's theory of practical reasoning is that he underestimates the difficulty of attaining the level of metaethical sophistication a professional would need in order to deal effectively with competing ethical considerations. The challenge of reasoning and behaving ethically is difficult, but not impossible. A model to assist professionals in ethical decision making is presented in the next chapter.

# 6 A Model of the Ethical Decision-Making Process

Professional ethical codes have two major shortcomings. First, professional codes are necessarily vague. They offer general principles to guide professional conduct, along with some specific standards and prohibitions, but ethical codes cannot provide direction regarding all of the different circumstances that arise in the practice of a mental health profession. Second, mental health professionals occasionally encounter situations in which two or more ethical principles appear to conflict (e.g., the principles of confidentiality and concern for the welfare of others). The ethical codes of the mental health professions do not provide a method for resolving such ethical dilemmas. As a result, professionals have little guidance other than their personal ethical values to refer to in deciding what to do. They are often uncomfortable with the course of action they select because it is inconsistent with one of the ethical principles involved in the situation (Smith, McGuire, Abbott, & Blau, 1991). Professionals need a rational method of determining an ethically acceptable course of action in such complex circumstances.

Chapter 5 examined the ways in which the major models of ethical reasoning have addressed the issue of resolving ethical dilemmas. This chapter will introduce a new model that professionals can use to reason more effectively when confronted with complex ethical problems and to provide a rational justification for their ethical judgments.

## THE PURPOSE OF THE MODEL

The model to be presented provides a method professionals can use to organize their thinking regarding ethical considerations that will ensure the comprehensiveness of their deliberations in attempting to identify and resolve ethical dilemmas. Also, employing the model will serve to increase their awareness of the ethical complexity associated with their professional activity. Being mindful of the *potential* for ethical complications in a situation will enable professionals to avoid the development of conflicts in many cases. Ethical dilemmas often have a way of "sneaking up" on people when they fail to recognize or appreciate the complex implications of seemingly minor decisions and commitments (MacKay & O'Neill, 1992). For example, suppose a psychotherapy client asks his therapist about her religious beliefs. What ethical consideration(s) should be taken into account in choosing a response to this query? On the other hand, being continually obsessed about the possibility that there are important ethical considerations that may not have been detected (e.g., in the decision of whether or not to offer a student or research participant a cup of coffee) would be nearly as counterproductive to a professional's efficiency as would gross insensitivity to ethical issues.

The purpose of the model is (a) to enable professionals to differentiate contexts involving multiple, or competing, ethical considerations from those that are less ethically complex and (b) to provide a template of steps they can take to resolve complex ethical issues in a rational manner. The model does *not* provide answers to ethical problems, only a framework that will enable professionals to arrive at their own well-informed, rationally based decisions regarding what to do in a particular set of circumstances. The model is designed to apply to ethical issues that might arise in any area of the practice of a mental health profession (e.g., teaching, research, clinical work).

## THE MODEL

A number of others interested in ethics training in the mental health professions have recognized the value of providing students and practitioners with a template outlining the appropriate steps to take in addressing complex ethical questions and in resolving ethical conflicts (e.g., K. S. Kitchener, 1984; Koocher & Keith-Spiegel, 1998; Treppa, 1998; Tymchuk, 1981, 1986). The model presented here borrows extensively from their work, but adds the important insights of Wallace's ethical contextualist theory, presented in Chapter 5.

The fundamental principle underlying this model is that the ethical complexity of a situation must be assessed initially, then continually reassessed in the light of new information obtained and the progress of the professional's practical reasoning. Additional ethical considerations are often identified in the course of these deliberations. Whenever the professional is satisfied that she has addressed the ethical complexity of the situation adequately and a viable option for ethically appropriate action (or nonaction) is available, she can make a decision and conclude her deliberations. An outline of the model is presented in Table 6.1.

In situations involving apparently conflicting ethical considerations, an ethical professional must attempt to resolve the apparent conflict in a rational manner. To do so, she will need to apply her understanding of the sources of moral duties from Chapters 4 and 5 because it is not the ethical principles of the profession, but the moral duties underlying those principles, that are the fundamental source of her ethical obligations. Allegiance to a professional ethical principle (e.g., confidentiality) should be superseded only by another *ethical* consideration that a professional determines to be a more powerful and fundamental ethical obligation in a particular circumstance. "When we do override a moral principle, it should only be done for good moral reasons" (K. S. Kitchener, 1984, p. 53).

A professional's failure to strive to resolve ethical conflicts in a reasonable manner represents an unprofessional attitude of indifference toward her profession and the people she serves (e.g., students, clients, research participants). The preamble of psychology's ethical code states that the effectiveness of ethical standards "requires a personal commitment to a lifelong effort to act ethically" (APA, 1992, Preamble). The development of practical reasoning skills is an essential aspect of this commitment because a professional must be capable of providing a rational moral justification for her decisions in cases involving an apparent ethical conflict.

**TABLE 6.1**
**A Model of the Ethical Decision-Making Process**

1. Initial Appraisal of Ethical Considerations Involved
   a. If no conflict ────────────────────────────→ Make a Decision
   b. If a conflict apparently exists
      ↓
2. Gather Information (facts specific to the case, pertinent ethical and
   legal guidelines, consultation with colleagues and experts)
      ↓
3. Secondary Appraisal of Ethical Considerations Involved
   a. If conflict has been resolved ──────────────────→ Make a Decision
   b. If a conflict still apparently exists
      ↓
4. Metaethical Deliberations Regarding the Relevance of Ethical Considerations
   a. If relevance deliberations resolve conflict ──────────→ Make a Decision
   b. If an ethical dilemma exists
      ↓
5. Metaethical Deliberations Regarding the Resolution of the Ethical Dilemma
      ↓
6. Tertiary Appraisal of Ethical Considerations — Generate Options
      ↓
7. Estimate the Consequences of Each Option
      ↓
8. Make a Decision
      ↓
9. Document Rationale and Decision-Making Process (should be done throughout the process)

## Step 1: Initial Appraisal of Ethical Considerations Involved

This initial step of appraising the presence of potential ethical considerations applies to every sort of occupational situation encountered by a mental health professional (e.g., research, teaching, psychotherapy). An ethical professional must be particularly careful to consider whether, based on the information available, there appear to be any potentially conflicting ethical considerations (i.e., if fulfilling one ethical duty in the situation will lead to the violation of another, equally important duty).

Keep in mind that the task of evaluating the potential presence of ethical considerations is not completed when the professional has identified one principle that appears to be important to the situation. When focusing his attention narrowly on one principle, a professional will frequently overlook, and perhaps violate, other relevant principles. Also, it is important to remember that although the situation may involve a professional relationship with one principal figure (e.g., a psychotherapy client, student), frequently there is more than one person who stands to be affected by the situation (e.g., the client's family, the other students in the class). The professional must consider whether the situation involves a professional responsibility to other parties in addition to the principal party (Koocher & Keith-Spiegel, 1998).

Effective identification of ethical complexity at this initial stage requires that the professional be appropriately sensitive to the presence of ethical considerations. In the example presented earlier of a psychotherapy client asking his therapist about her religious beliefs, it would be important for her to be sensitive to the possibility that her client might view her as an authority on this as well as other matters. The potential for the client to be unduly influenced by her personal values, presented in a professional setting, is an important ethical consideration.[13]

If there are no apparently competing considerations, the professional should terminate his deliberations and act in accordance with the ethical principle(s) and/or legalities involved. It is important for a professional to regard the ethical code of his profession as prima facie valid; that is, the ethical code is a valid guide for professional conduct unless some competing principle or special circumstance is even more compelling (Beauchamp & Childress, 1979).

On the other hand, if the situation does involve apparently competing ethical considerations, the deliberations must continue.

## STEP 2: GATHER INFORMATION

When there are apparently conflicting ethical considerations, the first task is to gather as much information as possible. The specific facts of a situation are enormously important to the fine distinctions that can affect a professional's ethical judgments (K. S. Kitchener, 1984), as was seen in Chapter 5. A professional's ethical decision making is generally only as good as her information.

The second task in the information-gathering process is to review the ethical code of her profession, paying particular attention to principles and standards relevant to the competing ethical considerations she is confronting. In addition, some professions have generated one or more sets of specialty guidelines, such as those published by APA and its divisions (e.g., APA, 1981b, 1987, 1993a). These supplementary guidelines should be consulted if they are relevant to the context in which the conflict has arisen (e.g., research with human participants). Information regarding any legal guidelines that apply is also extremely important insofar as a legal statute might indicate that one of the considerations involved constitutes a legal duty in the situation.[14]

The professional's personal values can certainly bias her perception of a situation and cause her to favor a particular course of action or give undue weight to one of the competing ethical considerations. A mental health professional needs to become consciously aware of her value biases, so she can avoid being unduly influenced by them during the ethical decision-making process.[15]

Another extremely important potential source of information for these deliberations is the opinions of experienced, respected colleagues who have dealt with similar types of situations or of the ethics committee of the professional's state or national organization (e.g., ACA Ethics Committee, 1997a). Consultation with more experienced colleagues could yield information regarding creative solutions that have been developed in response to similar ethical conflicts. Such discussions might also inform a professional of the benefits and drawbacks that others have experienced as a consequence of giving greater priority to one of the ethical considerations involved. As Wallace (1988) pointed out, the practical wisdom of a community (or a profession) is based upon the values of its members and their cumulative experience in applying those values successfully to the ever-changing contexts of community (or professional) life. Effective practical reasoning is always grounded in an understanding of the ways in which similar dilemmas have been resolved in the past. The challenge is to adapt those ways to the present novel context (Wallace, 1988).

## STEP 3: SECONDARY APPRAISAL OF ETHICAL CONSIDERATIONS INVOLVED

If information obtained from any of the sources clearly indicates to the professional that one of the apparently conflicting duties takes priority in a situation like the one he is faced with, the ethical conflict has been resolved and he is ready to make a decision. For example, a client asks to view his treatment record. Although his therapist believes she should respect his autonomy, she is also concerned that in his present condition, he could be harmed emotionally if confronted with his diagnosis. In asking her client about his reasons for requesting to see his records, she learns that he actually saw his diagnosis a week ago while a nurse was updating his record and now simply wishes to better understand his situation. The therapist can simply proceed by allowing the client to see his file because the duties to respect the client's autonomy and protect his welfare are not at odds in this situation. If, on the other hand, the additional information has not resolved the conflict, or has even increased the ethical complexity of the situation (e.g., has introduced additional conflicting considerations), he will next, based on all the information obtained, define the fundamental ethical considerations that appear prima facie relevant to the situation. If any aspect of the situation or the considerations is unclear, he should by all means go back to Step 2 and gather more information. Always remember that the best ethical judgments are the ones based on the best information because situational factors matter a great deal!

## STEP 4: METAETHICAL DELIBERATIONS REGARDING THE RELEVANCE OF ETHICAL CONSIDERATIONS

In situations involving an apparent conflict between ethical duties, a professional must next have a method of determining, on a rational basis, whether each consideration is genuinely *relevant* to the situation. Although all ethical principles are important, they do not all apply to every situation. For example, confidentiality is a vitally important ethical principle, but it is not relevant to a situation in which a mental health professional observes her neighbor abusing his spouse. As discussed in Chapter 5, deliberations regarding relevance involve understanding the *point* of each consideration; that is, the professional must reflect on a metaethical level to determine the reasons that each principle, or value, is taken seriously as an ethical consideration — how the principle contributes to human life (Wallace, 1988). To deliberate effectively, professionals must be able to trace the metaethical origin of any rule of professional conduct. The background in ethical theories provided in Chapters 4 and 5 will assist professionals in this task.

   If the apparent ethical conflict has been addressed on the basis of the deliberations regarding relevance, leaving no further conflict, the professional is in a position to resolve the situation in an ethically appropriate manner. If conflicting, relevant ethical considerations still exist, further deliberations will be necessary in order to rationally resolve the situation, which is now understood to constitute a genuine ethical dilemma.

## STEP 5: METAETHICAL DELIBERATIONS REGARDING THE RESOLUTION OF THE ETHICAL DILEMMA

All of the input obtained thus far should now be applied to the task of analyzing the competing ethical considerations more thoroughly in order to clearly understand the point of each consideration and the weight each one should be given in the specific ethical context being dealt with. Why has such a premium been placed on this value in the past? How does it contribute to the ways of life of a community, or a profession? These metaethical deliberations will generally clarify and simplify a complex ethical problem because the multiplicity of ethical principles stated in a professional code funnels down into a much smaller set of metaethical sources of value. Different ethical principles (e.g., confidentiality and respect for autonomy) that appear to conflict in a given situation are often found to reflect the same fundamental value (i.e., respect for persons is the basis for both the belief that people are entitled to their privacy and that they should be permitted to choose how they wish to conduct their lives). In such a case, resolving the ethical problem is then a matter of devising a solution that best serves the fundamental value that is now recognized as the source of the professional's ethical duty in the situation.

## STEP 6: TERTIARY APPRAISAL OF ETHICAL CONSIDERATIONS — GENERATE OPTIONS

After applying his practical reasoning skills to resolve the ethical dilemma, a professional must again reappraise the situation to evaluate the progress of his deliberations. If he perceives some ambiguity in the situation that is due to the inadequacy of his information, he can always seek additional information. Once he has gathered the new information and has determined the relative importance of each of the competing ethical considerations, he should begin the process of generating behavioral options.

In generating options, the professional returns to the pragmatic level of applying the ethical code to the concrete situation. The best option will be one that is consistent with the purpose of the most fundamental ethical value relevant to the situation, but that does not do harm to any other relevant considerations. Though options reflecting each of the conflicting considerations should be considered, it is extremely important to remember that the solution that best serves the point of each of the competing considerations will generally be a creative solution that represents a departure from options based on the single considerations that usually guide people's thinking. Practical reasoning should be viewed as a highly creative problem-solving activity.

Nevertheless, situations sometimes arise in which none of the options appear ideal. In such circumstances, the principle of nonmaleficence becomes particularly important. For example, if there is no option available that will enable a professional to help everyone involved in the situation, is there at least an option that will enable him to help the person who most needs help and still avoid hurting anyone else? When generating options, he should also always consider the possibility that the most ethically appropriate course is to not take any action. In some circumstances (e.g., a vague threat against another reported to have been made by a research participant), this option may be most consistent with the principle of nonmaleficence.

## Step 7: Estimate the Consequences of Each Option

Once a professional has generated a menu of potential options for action, she should estimate the likely consequences of each option for each person involved, utilizing any evidence available to support such estimates. Though such an estimation is extremely difficult and can never be done with absolute precision (as was discussed earlier with regard to utilitarianism), the probability of particular outcomes is nevertheless an important consideration. Furthermore, given the very careful deliberations involved up to this point in the process, she will likely have a fairly clear sense of the probable consequences of a given option. If she does not, perhaps further information gathering is called for. At the very least, the exercise of estimating the consequences of the solutions she has generated will decrease the probability that she will act impulsively, without giving due consideration to the potential implications of her decision for each person affected. That is to say, while this process may not reveal which option is absolutely the right one, it will make it very unlikely that she will pursue an option that is ethically inappropriate or insensitive.

## Step 8: Make a Decision

Even in the most complex situation, conflicting ethical considerations demand some type of resolution. If time and circumstances permit, a professional might hedge his decision a bit more by proposing his solution to a supervisor or experienced colleague before implementing it. In fact, when faced with a difficult ethical issue, it is always desirable to take as much time as possible to deliberate. Poor judgments are much more likely to occur when a professional is under intense time pressure. Still, in the end, he will need to act. Although he generally will not be certain that he is taking the correct course of action, his degree of comfort in acting will be significantly greater if he has attended carefully to his ethical deliberations and developed a sound, well-informed, rational justification for the action he is taking.

## Step 9: Document Rationale and Decision-Making Process

Whenever a professional takes an action that reflects one or more ethical considerations, even if no ethical conflict was involved, the action taken and the rationale for the decision should be recorded. Documenting the decision and the process of ethical deliberations will be done through whatever form of record keeping is appropriate to the professional context (e.g., client file, research log).

In situations involving an apparent conflict between ethical considerations (i.e., questions of relevance) and in situations representing genuine ethical dilemmas, a professional should keep careful records throughout the process of her deliberations, both to organize her thoughts on the matter and to provide a permanent account of the steps taken in her attempts to resolve the problem. It is essential that she carefully record the rationale for her action. When dealing with a particularly difficult dilemma, it is likely that some people will not agree with the decision she has reached. It is important that she be able to document the care she took in reaching her decision and the fact that she was aware of the relevant considerations, gathered information, consulted with colleagues, etc., so that any reviewer of her decision will recognize that she acted in good faith, that is, based on careful, rational deliberations.

In Chapter 13, the role of professional and governmental review committees is discussed. These committees do not expect professionals to have perfect judgment in difficult ethical matters, but they do expect professionals to demonstrate appropriate care and concern in dealing with ethically problematic situations. It is generally recognized that different individuals, possessing varying degrees of experience, may differ in their ethical opinions (Haas, Malouf, & Mayerson, 1986). Malpractice is not attributed to professionals based simply on a difference of opinion regarding an ethical matter; malpractice involves a judgment that the professional acted capriciously, with apparent disregard for important ethical considerations. Careful ethical deliberations, reflected accurately in official record keeping, will demonstrate appropriate professional behavior.

## A CASE EXAMPLE APPLYING THE MODEL OF ETHICAL DECISION MAKING

Consider the following case, which will illustrate how the decision-making model can be employed to resolve ethically complex situations:

A psychologist is employed on an inpatient substance abuse rehabilitation ward. One of her psychotherapy clients has been told that the medical tests conducted at the time of his admission revealed that he tested positive for the human immunodeficiency virus (HIV). He also has diagnoses of Cocaine Dependence and Antisocial Personality Disorder. He is scheduled to take a weekend pass in 10 days to see his wife and family and to tend to some personal business.

The psychologist has already discussed with her client the importance of telling his wife of his condition and of the need for them to practice "safe sex." He had indicated in response to this information that he would prefer not to tell his wife because she might refuse to have sex with him and would be likely to leave him in the future. He asked if it would be acceptable not to tell his wife about his medical condition if he agreed to use a condom, even though he does not like to use one.

When the psychologist told him that the pass would not be granted under those conditions, he responded, "Okay. Sure, I'll tell her." Her experience with this client leads her to doubt very strongly that he will fulfill his promise to inform his wife of his medical condition when he leaves on his pass.

### STEP 1: INITIAL APPRAISAL OF ETHICAL CONSIDERATIONS INVOLVED

What ethical considerations are involved in this clinical example? First, there is the therapist's regard as a mental health professional for her client's autonomy. Respecting a client's autonomy involves allowing him to manage his own affairs in life, such as determining his own course of behavior on his weekend pass (ACA, 1997, A.1; APA, 1992, Principle D). A second consideration is her concern for the welfare of each individual potentially affected by her actions (APA, 1992, Principle E). There is more than one person potentially affected by this situation: her client, who wants to see his wife and family and tend to personal business; his spouse, who risks contracting the virus if they engage in unprotected sex; and his children, who are likely anxious to see their father as soon as possible and may be affected by whether the personal business is handled. If protecting the welfare of the client's spouse might involve informing her of her husband's medical status, the confidentiality of information pertaining to his treatment is an extremely important consideration (ACA, 1997, B.1.a, B.1.c, B.1.d; APA, 1992, Principle D). There are undoubtedly additional considerations that could be brought out, but, for the purposes of a case example, these are sufficient to establish the existence of a potential conflict between ethical principles.

## STEP 2: GATHER INFORMATION

With regard to the therapist's concern about preserving her client's autonomy, she would meet with him again to discuss his perception of the issues involved in revealing his HIV status to his spouse and of the probable consequences of such a disclosure. She would also want to assess his understanding of, and feelings about, the potential consequences of nondisclosure, under both the conditions of having protected and unprotected sexual relations with his wife.

Concern for the welfare of her client would involve inquiring about the nature of the personal business that he proposes to tend to on the pass. How pressing and important is it? She would also want to consider and discuss with him the potential emotional, social, and legal consequences for him if he were to cause his wife to become infected.

Her concern for the welfare of her client's spouse would focus on the potential danger posed to his wife's health should her client fail to disclose his condition to his wife and engage in unprotected sex. It would be extremely important for the therapist to acquaint herself with the latest medical information regarding the probability that the virus could be transmitted from male to female through unprotected sexual contact.[16] It would be wise to educate her client regarding the danger of transmitting the virus and factors that would increase his spouse's risk of infection, such as the presence of lesions in the female genitalia from previously acquired sexually transmitted diseases (Quinn et al., 1988). She would also want to know whether her client's spouse is aware that he used cocaine intravenously with his substance abusing associates. If so, she should realize that she is engaging in high-risk sexual activity by having unprotected sexual relations with her husband.

Consistent with the therapist's concern about the welfare of her client's spouse, she would also want to review very carefully all available information regarding the client's trustworthiness and the quality of his marital relationship. Both factors could affect the likelihood that he would reveal his status to his spouse.

The client's confidentiality is another extremely important consideration. If the client is uneasy about discussing the matter with his spouse, the therapist might ask whether he would prefer that she inform his spouse or that the three of them meet to deal with the matter therapeutically. If he declines these options, it is clear that any disclosure made by the therapist would constitute a violation of his confidentiality.

As a professional, the therapist would next consult the "Ethical Principles" (APA, 1992) to review Ethical Standard 5 (Privacy and Confidentiality), paying particular attention to Standard 5.01 (Discussing the Limits of Confidentiality) and Standard 5.05 (Disclosures), which describe the circumstances under which confidentiality may be violated. She would also need to review the policies of the institution in which she is working and the laws of the state in which she is practicing regarding confidentiality of medical and mental health information, in addition to checking for state laws regarding specifically the confidentiality of an individual's HIV status. Some states directly prohibit medical professionals from revealing the HIV status of a client to anyone, including identifiable potential victims (VandeCreek & Knapp, 1993). Consulting with the institution's legal counsel and ethics committee would likely be the most efficient method of obtaining information regarding state laws and institutional policies.

The therapist would also need to reflect upon the role her personal values might play in her ethical deliberations. For example, her personal distaste for a man who would place his wife at risk for contracting a deadly disease could cause her to give greater weight to her concern for the welfare of her client's spouse than to her regard for his welfare and confidentiality. The therapist's conscious awareness of her subjective value biases can help her to evaluate her judgments even more critically and thereby minimize the role of her personal feelings in this rational, objective decision-making process.

It would also be prudent for the therapist to consult with colleagues to get their opinions of the situation and to see whether similar issues have arisen in the past. The methods that have been used to deal with complex situations involving confidentiality issues in the past might be helpful to her, as would inquiring about colleagues' level of satisfaction with those solutions.

Suppose the therapist obtained the following information regarding this case: Her client informed her that he is reluctant to tell his wife about his HIV status because he fears that his medical condition, coupled with the fact that he is hospitalized for a substance abuse problem, will cause her to leave him and take the children. He knows that his wife will be expecting him to have sexual relations with her when he goes home on his pass and that, if he brings home condoms, she "will know something is up" because he never uses them. He believes that his spouse would probably assume that he had acquired a sexually transmitted disease as a result of an affair he was having at the hospital (in which case she would also be likely to leave him). Although he reports that his wife is aware of his intravenous use of cocaine, she associates HIV infection with heroin use and has never said anything about his potential exposure to the virus.

The therapist finds that the marriage has been a troubled one, mostly because of his substance abuse. He feels very strongly that his wife and family are "the best thing in [his] life," and he does not want to do anything to jeopardize the relationship further. At present, lying about the situation appears to him to be the only acceptable option.

The client understands the seriousness of the issue of possible infection, but believes it is very unlikely that a woman would be infected by one episode of intercourse. He reported that his wife has never contracted a sexually transmitted disease, so there would be no additional risk factors increasing the probability of her contracting the virus from him. She is using an oral contraceptive, so he is not concerned about her becoming pregnant. He believes that it will be easier to tell her of his condition when he is back at work and living a drug-free life. When the therapist asks the client how his wife will feel then about having been exposed to the virus on this pass, he thinks a moment and replies, "I'll tell her I only just found out about it a few days ago."

The client does not believe that canceling the pass is a viable option because he has been told that he must appear in person to sign important legal papers to insure that his family continues to receive financial support during his rehabilitation.

When the therapist raises the issue of perhaps having his spouse come to the hospital so that they can tell her about his HIV status together, or doing so by telephone, he insists that now is not the time. He inquires about the confidentiality of the information. The therapist replies that although confidential information cannot generally be disclosed without the client's consent, exceptions can be made "to protect the patient or client or others from harm" (APA, 1992, 5.05). He is very disturbed by her statement and says that he would sue her and the hospital if any such disclosure were made.

Though the therapist has difficulty obtaining precise medical information regarding the probability of his spouse acquiring the virus through unprotected sex, the reports she accesses indicate approximately a 1 in 10 infection risk for a single episode of intercourse (Downs & De Vincenzi, 1996). Also, repeated exposure to the virus, even if an individual is already infected, may cause further damage to the individual's immune system (Aronow, 1993).

The therapist is told by the hospital's legal counsel that there is no institutional policy to cover such a situation and no state statutes, beyond those protecting client confidentiality in general, that are related specifically to revealing a client's HIV status. Her colleagues all agree that this case involves an extremely difficult ethical judgment. One colleague points out that the therapist does not know for certain that the client's spouse is not already infected; in fact, he may have acquired the virus from her. (The therapist and the rest of the staff had assumed that he acquired the virus through intravenous drug use involving shared needles.) Another colleague points out that the client has only been hospitalized for two months. Since he was living with his wife prior to entering the hospital, she may well have already contracted the virus from him. (The client subsequently tells her that he and his wife had been having sex only occasionally, approximately twice each month during the six months prior to his entering the rehabilitation program.) The general feeling expressed by the therapist's colleagues is that this is a very complicated issue and that she should continue her attempts to get her client to agree to disclose his HIV status to his spouse. Her colleagues would support a decision to deny the client a weekend pass if he refuses to tell his wife about his medical condition, but they are less certain about whether the circumstances would justify violating the fundamental therapeutic principle of confidentiality if the therapist decided to inform his wife herself without her client's consent.

## STEP 3: SECONDARY APPRAISAL OF ETHICAL CONSIDERATIONS INVOLVED

Based on all of the information obtained in Step 2, the therapist would still have good reason to believe that respect for her client's autonomy is an important ethical consideration. The decision of whether or not to tell his spouse about his condition is a very important and personal one. To deny him a pass or to reveal his HIV status to his wife herself would be extremely paternalistic and clearly inconsistent with Principle D (Respect for People's Rights and Dignity) of the "Ethical Principles" (APA, 1992).

She also agrees with her colleagues that protecting her client's confidentiality is a very important consideration. Violating his confidentiality could have a very negative impact on his family life and personal welfare. It could also interfere significantly with his recovery from substance abuse. If he lost his family, the additional stress resulting from the loss of social support and sense of meaning in his life would certainly increase the risk that he would resume his drug use, perhaps with life-threatening consequences. Also, his anger about being denied a pass or about the consequences of his therapist violating his confidentiality could provide a reason for him to leave treatment and develop a permanent distrust of mental health professionals.

Nevertheless, the therapist is still quite uncomfortable about the threat to his spouse's welfare that will continue to exist if she is not told about his HIV status. In addition, the prospect of potentially having two parents who are HIV-positive would pose a serious threat to the welfare of the client's children. However, her client's statements indicate that he is still unwilling to inform his spouse of his medical condition.

## STEP 4: METAETHICAL DELIBERATIONS REGARDING THE RELEVANCE OF ETHICAL CONSIDERATIONS

First of all, is respect for the autonomy of the client an important ethical consideration in this case? The answer is clearly yes, given that the issues involve whether the client will be permitted to leave the hospital on a pass and be permitted to decide for himself whether he will inform his spouse of his HIV status and, if he does, when he will do so. Respect for the autonomy of clients is fundamental to the regard mental health professionals have for them as *persons*. Denying a client's right to self-determination is contradictory to the Kantian emphasis of the "Ethical Principles."

Concern for the client's welfare is also a relevant consideration because it too is grounded in the professional's respect for clients as persons. Mental health professionals have an obligation to avoid harming a client, or any other person, whenever possible. In this case, it is certainly possible that the client could be harmed if the therapist were to disclose his HIV status to his spouse without his consent.

Concern for the welfare of the client's spouse is also definitely a relevant ethical consideration because her physical well-being is threatened very directly by the combination of her husband's unwillingness to inform her of his HIV status and his refusal to practice safe sex or abstain from sexual contact with her.

Finally, the confidentiality of information pertaining to the client's treatment is also a relevant ethical consideration. Like respect for the client's autonomy, this duty is also based on the professional's regard for her client's personhood and subsequent right to privacy. Although disclosure of confidential material without a client's consent is permitted under certain specified circumstances (APA, 1992, 5.05), it is still unclear whether this case constitutes a legitimate exception to a therapist's obligation to maintain confidentiality.

Since there are multiple relevant, competing considerations in this case, the matter cannot be resolved at this point. A genuine ethical dilemma exists. Further deliberation will be required.

## STEP 5: METAETHICAL DELIBERATIONS REGARDING THE RESOLUTION OF THE ETHICAL DILEMMA

In Step 4, the metaethical significance of each of the competing considerations in this case was discussed to assess whether the fundamental ethical values underlying each consideration were truly relevant to the situation facing the therapist. Since each value was deemed to be relevant, she must now review them again to prioritize the ethical considerations based on their relative importance to this case. This task requires that she understand, on a metaethical level, why each of the considerations is regarded as important by people in general, that is, how each consideration improves the quality of human life.

For example, why is the confidentiality of clients regarded as such a fundamental value by mental health professionals? Confidentiality is valued because of clinicians' regard for clients' personhood, which is generally thought to entail the right to privacy. Also, physicians and mental health professionals have long recognized the importance of confidentiality to successful diagnosis and treatment of human suffering. Clients are only willing to reveal their innermost thoughts and feelings when they are secure in the belief that their therapist will never reveal the information to others inappropriately. Therefore, preserving client confidentiality is fundamental to the practice of psychotherapy, whereas disclosure without the client's consent threatens, to some degree, one of the fundamental precepts that enables psychotherapy to work.

Respect for clients' autonomy (which is also based on the fundamental ethical value of respect for personhood) entails allowing clients to make their own choices in life. For the most part, it is not considered ethically appropriate to interfere with another person's right to choose, even when the choices made are irrational. Many people are hesitant to become involved in psychiatric treatment or psychotherapy because they fear that when they reveal their problems, "They'll lock me up!" Respecting and preserving the autonomy of clients is the only means of counteracting this impression.

The importance placed on respect for a client's personhood also extends naturally to a concern for the welfare of the client, that is, that no harm should come to the client as a consequence of what he or she discusses in a therapy session. Viewed from this perspective, it becomes evident that the principle underlying the therapist's duties to protect her client's confidentiality and to preserve his autonomy is the same regard for personhood that underlies the obligation to be concerned about the welfare of her client *and,* in this case, the welfare of his spouse, as another person affected by the psychologist's actions. When viewed from a metaethical perspective, the three distinct ethical principles of confidentiality, respect for autonomy, and concern for the welfare of others funnel down to one fundamental ethical value: respect for personhood. Although these metaethical deliberations have simplified matters considerably by reducing the multiple ethical considerations to one fundamental ethical value, there is still a conflict between the therapist's regard for the personhood of her client and for the personhood of his spouse. The fact that this situation has such significant potential consequences for his spouse entails that the therapist's obligation to protect her from harm is certainly every bit as important as her duty to protect her client.

Given these considerations, the source of the ethical dilemma in this case is that the therapist cannot adequately serve her ethical duty to both parties in this situation by either disclosing or not disclosing her client's medical condition to his spouse. Either course of action is likely to harm one or both of the people involved. She can protect her client from the negative impact of disclosure, while respecting his autonomy and preserving his confidentiality, but only by putting the physical well-being of his spouse at considerable risk. To sacrifice her well-being to the "higher" duty of preserving the client's confidentiality would be to show a lack of regard for his spouse as an autonomous person. She would be treated as a "thing," a means to the end of protecting the client's confidentiality.

Metaethical reflection reveals that the duty to protect a person's life is clearly more fundamental than the duty to preserve confidentiality, since protecting a person's life is a prerequisite if one is to have any additional duties to value the individual's personhood in other, more specific ways. All available evidence indicates that the threat to the spouse's life is sufficient to override the duty to preserve the client's confidentiality and the therapist's concern about more ambiguous threats to her client's welfare. Her duty to protect the life of her client's spouse represents her most fundamental duty in this situation.

### STEP 6: TERTIARY APPRAISAL OF ETHICAL CONSIDERATIONS — GENERATE OPTIONS

Two options available to the therapist that have already been mentioned are respecting her client's confidentiality by taking no action or informing his spouse of his HIV status if he declines to do so. Taking no action would demonstrate appropriate respect for her client's personal autonomy and confidentiality, but is unacceptable because it totally ignores the consideration of concern for the welfare of his spouse, which was demonstrated in the previous step to be the most fundamental ethical duty in this situation. On the other hand, informing the client's wife of his medical condition without his consent gives priority to the concern for her welfare, but discounts the importance of the client's confidentiality and autonomy. Nevertheless, based on the deliberations in Step 5, this option would appear to be ethically defensible.

Another option is that the therapist could, in consultation with the director of the unit, decide not to allow her client to leave the hospital on a pass. If he does not leave the hospital, he cannot harm his spouse. His confidentiality would not be violated, though such an action would not be consistent with the principle of respect for the client's autonomy.

As was stated earlier, the process of generating options to resolve an ethical dilemma should be viewed as a creative activity, one in which a professional attempts to devise a solution that is consistent with the fundamental ethical duty in the situation (i.e., protecting the life of her client's spouse), but that also reflects, to the greatest extent possible, the other ethical considerations present (i.e., her client's confidentiality, his autonomy, and her concern for his welfare), without totally disregarding any of the relevant considerations.[17] Remember that, as discussed in Chapter 5, practical wisdom is a matter of giving each consideration its due (Wallace, 1988). None of the previous options incorporate each of the conflicting considerations involved in this case.

Is there a way that the therapist can avoid putting her client's spouse at risk without violating his confidentiality or showing a lack of regard for her client's autonomy? He could elect to tell his wife about his HIV status on the telephone prior to leaving the hospital on pass. Alternatively, he could inform her during a marital therapy session with the therapist prior to the pass, so that the implications of his medical condition for the relationship can begin to be addressed therapeutically. Lastly, if the client insists that he is not emotionally prepared to inform his wife of his condition at the present time, he could agree to postpone the pass until he is ready to discuss his condition with her. Any one of these courses of action would protect his spouse from harm while also serving the ethical considerations of preserving his autonomy and confidentiality.

## Step 7: Estimate the Consequences of Each Option

If the therapist informs the client's spouse of his HIV status without his consent, there would no longer be any cause for concern about the spouse's physical well-being. In providing the information, the therapist could also discuss her client's fears about how his spouse would react to the news and provide her with accurate information regarding the implications of his condition for their relationship, possibly reducing the probability of her abandoning the client and the relationship precipitously. However, the therapist will have violated her client's confidentiality and refused to permit him to determine his own course of action in dealing with this highly personal trauma for himself and his family. His wife may still end the relationship. Furthermore, the client may well refuse to continue treatment for his substance abuse disorder with the therapist or any other mental health professional, feeling that therapists cannot be trusted because they will violate his confidentiality.

If the therapist takes no action, respecting her client's confidentiality and right to handle the situation as he sees fit, there is a significant likelihood that she would be placing his wife's health at considerable risk. Although the immediate impact of taking the pass without informing his wife would not likely be negative for the client, he certainly could face problems in the future should his wife test positive for HIV or develop symptoms of AIDS.

The situation is complicated by the client's stated willingness to keep his condition secret from his spouse in spite of the risk of infecting her with the virus. Unfortunately, his behavior is quite consistent with his diagnosis of Antisocial Personality Disorder. His initial willingness to deceive his spouse would cause the therapist to question very seriously the truth of any subsequent statement on his part that he would inform his wife while on pass, prior to engaging in any sexual activity. The client might well make such a statement in order to obtain the pass without having any intention of keeping his promise. Among the diagnostic criteria for Antisocial Personality Disorder in the *DSM-IV* is "deceitfulness, as indicated by repeated lying, ... or conning others for personal profit or pleasure" (American Psychiatric Association, 1994, p. 650). The risk to his spouse that would result from trusting him to tell his spouse of his condition while on pass would make such an option untenable.

If the pass were to be denied, the client would remain at the hospital and would not pose an immediate potential threat to his spouse. In denying the pass, the therapist would protect the well-being of her client's spouse without violating his confidentiality. As stated earlier in this chapter, buying additional time to deliberate about complex ethical situations whenever possible is a sound practice. However, in denying the pass, she would be showing a clear lack of respect for her client's personal autonomy. Also, this action would not necessarily solve the problem. She would need to be prepared to address his likely response of requesting immediate discharge from the hospital. He would not qualify for involuntary commitment, so she would face the same decision all over again, except that now her client's substance abuse treatment would likely be at an end.

If she decided to use the 10 days prior to the scheduled pass to discuss the situation further with her client in the context of psychotherapy, she would show respect for his autonomy by trying to assist him in making an informed, reasonable decision. She would not be compromising his confidentiality. She could express her concern about his welfare by addressing his fears and anxieties relating to both his HIV status and his spouse's possible reaction to learning of his condition. She would also have the opportunity to discuss her ethical concern about ensuring the physical well-being of his spouse. The therapist's emphasis in these sessions would be on her responsibility to protect the well-being of his spouse, just as she has always sought to preserve his. The value and importance he places on his relationship with his spouse suggests that he certainly does not wish to harm her. To harm her would be self-defeating because it would preclude her being able to provide the support he says that he so desperately needs from her. Second, it would be essential that he attempt to look at this situation from his spouse's point of view, as the therapist has done. If he were in his spouse's place and she were the one with the virus, would he not want to be told? The client needs to understand that the respect and concern that he expects from the therapist are also considerations of which his wife is equally deserving. Furthermore, since it is possible that his wife may have already contracted the virus, it is essential to her health that she be informed so that she can be tested and receive information regarding treatment of her condition, just as he has been receiving at the hospital.

The outcome of these discussions might be that he would decide to inform his wife of his condition, which would address the risk to his spouse without impinging on his confidentiality or autonomy. However, the therapist should point out that dealing with such a traumatic, intense issue will be extremely stressful for both of them and should be done in a therapeutic manner. Telling her while on pass would likely produce an emotional confrontation between the two of them that could increase the probability that his spouse would react in an extreme manner, perhaps by leaving him. If this were to occur while he was on pass, it would dramatically increase his susceptibility to resorting to substances to deal with the stress he would experience.

With these considerations in mind, the therapist could suggest that the client arrange for his wife to come to the hospital to meet with both of them so that the matter could be addressed therapeutically. If she were unable to come to the hospital, the issue could be addressed in a three-way conference call or the pass could be postponed until his wife was able to visit the hospital. His decision to inform his spouse regarding his medical condition together with the therapist would address the issues of preserving his autonomy and confidentiality. Also, the therapist would be assured that the spouse's well-being has been protected and would have an opportunity to talk with the spouse about the client's welfare (e.g., his need for his wife's support with his medical difficulties and his substance abuse disorder).

## STEP 8: MAKE A DECISION

Based on the deliberations described above, the therapist must decide on a course of action that she will actually follow. As a result of having worked her way through each step of this decision-making process, she will have acquired adequate information to make an informed decision and will be in a position to document the reasoning behind her decision, as well as the reasons supporting and opposing the options she did not select.

The fundamental ethical consideration in this situation was demonstrated to be the therapist's concern for the physical safety of her client's spouse. However, she also wanted to preserve her client's sense of personal autonomy, his confidentiality, and his welfare and well-being. Consistent with these concerns, she might decide to suggest to her client that the two of them inform his wife of his HIV status together prior to his taking a pass, so that the information can be disclosed and discussed in a therapeutic manner, with the therapist available as an informational resource and source of emotional support for both him and his spouse.

The least desirable outcome would be if her client refused to inform his spouse or insisted that he would handle the matter himself while on pass. As stated earlier, such an option would be ethically unacceptable because the therapist would have no way of verifying that the client had informed his wife and that his wife was not being placed in direct physical danger. The therapist would have to explain to her client the reasons why such a plan would be ethically unacceptable to her. He would need to understand that, while he had several options available regarding how the two of them could inform his wife of his HIV status, the bottom line is that, as a mental health professional, she feels ethically obligated to protect the wife's well-being by making certain that the wife is informed. If he is not ready to tell his wife, the pass would need to be denied. If he insisted on immediate discharge, the therapist would tell him that his wife would need to be informed of his HIV status prior to his discharge. The client would then be free to reevaluate his options.

## Step 9: Document Rationale and Decision-Making Process

The therapist should carefully document the steps she took in addressing this situation to demonstrate her awareness of the issues involved; the information that she used in making a decision, including her contact with the legal representative of the hospital and her consultations with colleagues; the content of her sessions with her client regarding the matter; and the reasoning behind her final decision. The dates and names of the people she had contact with would be an important part of the documentation of the process of her decision making.

Documenting the case carefully at the time will save a considerable amount of trouble later should the decision be reviewed. It is much more difficult to attempt to reconstruct the sequence of events from memory six months later than to document it as it occurs. Furthermore, documentation completed at the time of an event will generally be regarded as a more accurate reflection of what occurred than a reconstruction of events in the face of an inquiry. Finally, the conscientiousness demonstrated by comprehensive documentation provides additional evidence of the sensitivity, attention, and professional competence the therapist displayed in addressing this difficult situation.

## SUMMARY

Two major shortcomings of professional ethical codes are (a) that the codes cannot provide specific guidance regarding the ethically appropriate course of action in every circumstance a professional might confront and (b) that the codes do not provide a method for resolving situations in which two or more codified ethical principles seem to conflict. The model of ethical decision making presented in this chapter provides mental health professionals with a framework for reasoning more effectively when attempting to resolve complex ethical problems. In addition, employing this model will increase professionals' sensitivity to the presence of multiple ethical considerations in situations that arise in the course of their professional activity. Thus, the model will not only help professionals to resolve ethical conflicts, but it will also enable them to foresee and avoid potential conflicts that might otherwise catch them off guard.

The fundamental premise underlying this model is that the ethical complexity of a situation must be assessed initially, then continually reassessed in the light of new information obtained and the progress of decision-making deliberations. Each time the ethical considerations involved in the situation are assessed, the professional must determine whether a conflict exists. If no conflict exists, he should make a decision regarding a course of action. If a conflict exists, he must go through additional steps involving gathering information and conducting metaethical deliberations. This process will enable him to generate viable options, estimate the likely consequences of each option, and arrive at a decision, which he will have documented as being the most rational alternative available in the case. The model for ethical decision making was demonstrated in the example of an inpatient substance abuse client with HIV who requests a weekend pass to visit his family and tend to personal business.

# 7 Ethical Issues in Psychotherapy and Counseling

The relationship between therapists and their clients is extremely complex and intimate. As a result, a host of difficult ethical issues can arise. Because it would be impossible to address all of the potential ethical challenges encountered in psychotherapy, it is vitally important that therapists develop their own ethical reasoning skills to identify and resolve complex ethical situations. In fact, it is difficult to conceive of how a therapist could be professionally competent to deal with all of the complex circumstances that arise inevitably in psychotherapy without having the ability to make sound ethical judgments (Cohen & Cohen, 1999). This chapter will address several of the major ethical considerations that are fundamental to the process of psychotherapy and counseling and provide professionals with opportunities to hone their ethical reasoning skills.

## INFORMED CONSENT

When people first decide to participate in psychotherapy or counseling, they generally have a very limited understanding of what is involved. Their ideas about therapy might be based on depictions on television or in movies. At the outset of treatment, mental health professionals are obligated to provide clients with information that will enable them to make an informed choice regarding whether to pursue therapy. However, perhaps because the therapeutic process is so complex, therapists vary considerably in how specifically they discuss the relevant issues, such as the proposed length of treatment, the nature of the sessions, the treatment plan, confidentiality and its limits, and alternative treatment options. Therapists are generally clearer about the issue of fees with clients, though even in this area, some details may not be addressed adequately.

The fundamental point regarding informed consent is that therapists do not ever want clients to be surprised during the course of treatment by some aspect of the therapeutic arrangement that had not been explained adequately in advance. Although the process of obtaining informed consent can be somewhat time consuming, each component of the treatment agreement must be explained so that the client can grasp it fully. Concepts should be described in language understandable to the client (APA, 1992, 4.02[a]). As in informed consent for research, which will be discussed in Chapter 11, clinicians should avoid providing informed consent explanations and documents that exceed a client's vocabulary level (Hochhauser, 1999). The use of oral explanations, perhaps combined with pictorial representations of key concepts, followed by clients' oral demonstration of their understanding of the concepts involved, can increase clinicians' confidence that they have succeeded in obtaining truly informed client consent (Murphy, O'Keefe, & Kaufman, 1999). If potential clients are legally incompetent, a legally authorized person must provide consent for treatment (APA, 1992, 4.02[b]). In such situations, clients' assent, or agreement, to participate in treatment should still be obtained (APA, 1992, 4.02[c]). Taking the time needed to complete the informed consent process effectively will greatly reduce the possibility of a misunderstanding, and an ethical complaint against the therapist, later.

Therapists should always emphasize the voluntary nature of participation in therapy (ACA, 1997, A.3.b; APA, 1992, 4.02[a]). They should encourage clients to act as consumers (which they are) in making their decision to pursue therapy and in their selection of a therapist. Most people are very careful in selecting the clothing or appliances they buy; they should certainly be just as discriminating in deciding how they want to deal with their life problems and with whom they feel comfortable discussing their innermost feelings. Therapists should emphasize that a client's task during his first meeting with a therapist is to gather as much information about therapy as he wants and to make sure that he is comfortable with the therapist and treatment plan before beginning therapy. A therapist can help a client to feel empowered to focus on these "consumer" considerations by asking him to think about issues such as whether he might prefer a therapist of the other gender.

---

### Case Example 7.1

*A counselor is contacted by an individual who says that she is interested in participating in counseling and wants to interview him to see if she would like to pursue her journey of self-discovery with his assistance. She asks whether there is any charge for a consultation of this type, and he tells her that his usual consultation fee will apply. She haggles with him for a few minutes until he agrees to waive the fee (because he is looking to expand his practice). The consultation goes very well. She appears genuinely interested in working with him. Finally, she asks him what counseling approach he uses. He tells her that he is eclectic, but generally operates from a cognitive-behavioral perspective. She responds that she is interested specifically in a person-centered approach and asks whether he would be comfortable working with her in that fashion.*

---

## FINANCIAL ARRANGEMENTS

Potential clients should be informed about therapy fees and any other financial arrangements (e.g., policy regarding third party payment, sliding scale fee based on family income) when they initially contact the therapist to schedule an appointment. When working in a managed care organization, the therapist should inform the client of the policies affecting both fees and permitted duration of treatment. It is highly desirable for therapists to provide clients with a written copy of their treatment policies at the first appointment.

Consider the following example: A counselor interested in encouraging potential clients to see if counseling would benefit them advertises that anyone can contact him to arrange a free counseling screening appointment. The potential ethical problem with such an arrangement is that clients are encouraged to come in and discuss personal issues with the counselor at no cost, but after going through this difficult process of self-disclosure, they must pay to continue the relationship and obtain any benefit from the process. This situation could be viewed as "setting up" clients by getting them to invest emotional energy in creating a relationship at no cost, then changing the financial terms of the relationship after the client has been "hooked." This procedure is commonly known as a "bait-and-switch" among confidence tricksters.

## Implications of Third Party Payments

Therapists should investigate the outpatient mental health coverage provided for clients who want to obtain health insurance reimbursement for therapy. When clients indicate that they plan to use insurance coverage to pay for therapy sessions, providing informed consent should also involve explaining how the health insurance reimbursement system works. Clients need to be fully informed about their responsibility for deductibles and copayments. In addition, if there is an annual limit for the number of therapy sessions covered by insurance, clients need to know in advance, so they do not become immersed in the process of long-term therapy only to find that their insurance coverage has lapsed after 20 sessions. Furthermore, clients must be informed that the therapist will need to provide a diagnostic code to the insurer. Some clients are very uncomfortable with this process, fearing that their confidentiality may be threatened by the presence of a psychiatric diagnosis in their computerized insurance records. By informing them of the process, therapists allow clients to make an informed choice regarding this issue. Bear in mind that although a therapist can guarantee the confidentiality of her personal records, she cannot *guarantee* that information provided to an insurance company will be protected adequately. A concerned client should be encouraged to contact the insurance company directly to learn more about the security system used to protect the confidentiality of records.

It is also important to inform clients who are interested in marital counseling or treatment for bereavement that health insurers do not necessarily provide reimbursement for treatment of life stressors.[18] Health insurers generally cover illnesses, which means that the client must be suffering from a diagnosable disorder to qualify for reimbursement. Clients can then decide whether to pursue treatment if insurance coverage will not be available.

---

**Case Example 7.2**

*A couple is interested in marital therapy. When the therapist informs them that marital conflict (i.e., Partner Relational Problem) is generally not a diagnosis covered by health insurance plans, the therapy-savvy clients respond that the husband has been very depressed lately as a result of the marital problems. They suggest that he be given a diagnosis of Adjustment Disorder with Depressed Mood, which their insurer will cover.*

*What should the therapist do?*

---

## TREATMENT PLANNING AND GOAL SETTING

Clients should always be involved in treatment planning and the selection of treatment goals as part of the process of providing informed consent for therapy. The therapist should discuss his perception of the client's needs and make appropriate suggestions regarding a treatment plan. To advance the dialogue, the client should be encouraged to provide his ideas, concerns, and questions. The outcome of these discussions should be a clear plan of action understood and agreed to by client and therapist.

In addition to the ethical importance of obtaining informed consent, having clients play an active role in treatment planning and goal setting also makes excellent clinical sense. This process will encourage clients to identify and articulate clearly their reasons for pursuing therapy as well as their hoped-for therapeutic outcomes. Also, clients are likely to be more invested in and motivated to achieve goals that they played a role in formulating than if the goals had been imposed on them by a therapist or some other external authority. Because client motivation has been demonstrated to be a crucial determinant of therapeutic progress, including clients in treatment planning enhances the prospects for therapeutic success (Garfield, 1994).

Finally, in addressing a client's questions about his prognosis (i.e., the likelihood of improvement), a therapist should be careful not to guarantee positive therapeutic results or that a problem can be solved within a specified number of sessions or time period. Offering a guarantee runs the risk of deceiving the client because there are too many variables affecting therapy outcome (e.g., client motivation) to be certain that even a well-validated treatment method will generate the desired results (Garfield, 1994).

---

**Case Example 7.3**

*A man seeks treatment from a sex therapist. He informs the therapist that he is homosexual and is seeking therapy to become heterosexual, in order to reduce his feelings of social alienation and discomfort. He expresses a desire to "fit in better" in society. He has not been able to suppress his homosexual impulses effectively on his own.*

*Are there multiple ethical considerations involved in the therapist's response to the man's request? What response should the therapist make?*

---

## Selection of Treatment Method

Therapists should discuss the methods they intend to use to achieve the agreed upon treatment goals. Some therapists employ a single approach with all of their clients (e.g., psychoanalytic, person-centered), while others take a more eclectic approach based on their perception of the client's characteristics and the treatment issues and goals. In either case, clients should be informed regarding the methods to be used in the therapy and any potential risks associated with those methods. Alternative treatments, even if they do not fall within the therapist's range of competence and would require referral, should be presented as options for the client. In cases in which the therapist is competent in more than one approach to resolving the client's problem, the therapist should present each option, so the client can be involved in the decision-making process.

## Informed Consent to Record or Observe

Therapists and therapists in training frequently find it useful to audiotape or videotape therapy sessions. Training clinics may also be set up to allow supervisors and trainees to observe therapy sessions remotely or behind a two-way mirror. However, therapists are required to obtain the informed consent of clients, preferably in writing, prior to recording or observing sessions (ACA, 1997, B.4.c; APA, 1992, 5.01[c]). Clients should be informed of the purpose of the recording or observation, as well as the protective measures that have been taken to safeguard the clients' confidentiality (e.g., procedures for storage and erasure of recordings).

## Client Access to Records and Diagnostic Information

A final issue regarding informed consent that has proven to be somewhat tricky for mental health professionals is what access clients should have to information pertaining to their diagnosis and treatment. Clients should be informed, before they initiate treatment, as to how their requests to review their therapy records or to know precise diagnostic information will be handled. Clients should also be informed, prior to treatment, about institutional policies and state statutes regarding a client's right to read her treatment record and the possibility that records may be subpoenaed for any court proceedings involving her (Glancy, Regehr, & Bryant, 1998). Clients, or their legal representatives, can generally obtain access to their institutional records by making a formal written request. There are often no statutes governing the records of private practitioners, so these therapists can establish less formal arrangements for clients to review their records.

Simply put, therapists respect the autonomy of their clients, and providing a client with information regarding her condition and treatment is a behavioral indication of this respect (ACA, 1997, B.4.d). However, there is an additional reason for providing clients with access to their treatment records, which involves the issue of informed consent. Clients often sign consent forms to release their records to other professionals (e.g., physicians, health insurance, or managed care utilization reviewers), yet clients can only provide truly informed consent for their records to be shared with other professionals if the clients know what information is being released (ACA, 1997, B.4.e; APA, 1992, 5.05[b]).

Historically, as discussed in Chapter 2, clients were not permitted to read their treatment records because of therapists' paternalistic concern that clients could be harmed emotionally by information in the record. However, the studies that have been conducted to evaluate the effect of providing clients access to their mental health records have indicated very positive results. Although clients can become upset about material in their records, they generally feel "better informed and more involved in their treatment" (Stein et al., 1979, p. 329). Overall, the experience has been regarded as therapeutic and positive by both clients and staff (e.g., McFarlane,

Bowman, & MacInnes, 1980; McShane & Rowe, 1994). It is considered extremely important, however, that professional staff members be present when a client reviews her record to answer questions and discuss any issues that arise (Houghkirk, 1977; Parrott et al., 1988; Roth et al., 1980; Stein et al., 1979).

Nevertheless, there are undoubtedly circumstances in which a therapist might conclude that a client's welfare will be better served by withholding potentially upsetting information, at least temporarily. For example, a therapist might feel that a suicidal client might be harmed by receiving feedback about his recently concluded personality assessment (Cohen & Cohen, 1999). For the most part, though, denying clients access to information about their treatment will only damage their trust and confidence in the therapist. The suicidal client might want feedback about the assessment in order to find out whether the testing picked up on his intense despair. He could, in fact, be reassured by the results that the therapist does indeed understand him and his current state of mind.

Information provided by third parties that is included in a client's record presents a difficult ethical problem. If these informants were promised confidentiality when they provided the information, the therapist is ethically obligated to withhold the information from her client. However, an appropriate informed consent policy for these third parties (e.g., family members) would notify them in advance of the potential limitations (e.g., a court order) on the confidentiality of the information and the possibility that the client could obtain access to her record (McShane & Rowe, 1994).

Finally, the issue of client access to records also has implications for what therapists write in the record. Therapists should always keep in mind that the information they record could be read someday by the client or that it could be subpoenaed for a court proceeding. Therapists should avoid making evaluative or judgmental comments in the record and should think carefully about the potential implications of including information that is not directly germane to the client's treatment, but could prove harmful to the client in another context (e.g., in court). Client records should be regarded as legal documents (Glancy et al., 1998).

---

**Case Example 7.4**

*An acutely manic client in a psychiatric hospital angrily demands to read his treatment record. He says that he is sure the record calls him "mentally ill," when the truth is that he used to be mentally ill but is not anymore. His therapist questions the value of providing him access to his record in his present condition. What are the pros and cons of granting the client's request?*

---

## INFORMED CONSENT TO TREATMENT OF CLIENTS OF DIMINISHED CAPACITY

Competence to provide consent is generally assumed unless there is clear reason to question an individual's capacity to consent (Arthur & Swanson, 1993). Some clients are deemed legally incompetent to manage their own affairs as a function of their psychiatric condition (e.g., some cases of people suffering from one of the schizophrenias or a dementia). These clients cannot legally consent to treatment. In such cases, legal consent for treatment must be obtained from a legally designated guardian.

However, the matter of consent to treatment is not quite that cut-and-dried. A client who has been deemed legally incompetent is still a person worthy of respect. He still has his own preferences and aversions, and his opinions should be respected, provided that he is not endangering himself by virtue of his preferences. Therefore, if an incompetent client does not agree (i.e., provide his assent) to pursue treatment, his wishes should be respected, provided the lack of treatment will not cause him or others substantial harm.

Similarly, legally competent individuals may not always be capable of fully rational decision making. The capacity to make decisions regarding one's treatment is not an all-or-none matter; it is better conceptualized as a continuum (Fellows, 1998). The capacity for rational choice must be assessed based on the client's ability to arrive at a decision through some understanding of the choices involved in a situation and the risks and benefits associated with those choices. For example, even demented clients should be encouraged to choose the foods they prefer and the activities they wish to pursue. As decisions involve greater potential risk, the requirements regarding demonstrated rational capacity should be greater. If the client wishes to overrule the judgment of her treatment providers and her legally authorized guardian, she will need to be capable of providing reasons why the course of treatment is not in her best interest that effectively counter the arguments in favor of providing the treatment.

---

**Case Example 7.5**

*A recently hospitalized client suffering from Schizophrenia, Disorganized Type is experiencing severe psychotic symptoms. He becomes very agitated when approached by staff members or other clients on the unit. The treatment team decides to assign him to a private room to reduce the level of environmental stimulation and to have a staff member stay with him on one-to-one observation at all times. In his present state, the team decides there is no point in explaining the treatment plan to him, so they simply implement it.*
*Is the treatment team's decision ethically appropriate?*

---

## GROUP, MARITAL, AND FAMILY THERAPY

In group, marital, and family therapy contexts, the informed consent of each person participating in the therapy should be obtained. When children are participating in family therapy, parental consent is legally required; the informed assent, or agreement, of children to participate should also be obtained (ACA, 1997, A.8; APA, 1992, 4.03[a]).[19] Similarly, for release of information pertaining to the group process, the consent of all legally competent participants in the group should be obtained. These issues are addressed specifically in the *Code of Ethics of the American Association for Marriage and Family Therapy* (AAMFT, 1991). The AAMFT guidelines are consistent with the APA and ACA ethical codes, though psychology and counseling do not provide as much explicit direction in these matters. Group therapists must also make the nature, goals, and operating procedures of the group very clear to potential clients to insure that the group is consistent with the needs and abilities of clients. In describing the termination procedure for members ready to leave the group, the therapist should also inform group clients that they are free to withdraw from the group if they find the process is not addressing their needs and that the therapist will assist them in selecting an alternative treatment setting. Clients considering joining an existing group should be able to sit in on a group session before deciding whether to join the group as a participant.

Participants in group or family therapy should also be informed of the role the therapist will play in the therapy. For example, if the therapist will function as a facilitator, she should explain that her comments will focus on keeping the group on a track consistent with the group's stated purpose, protecting individual clients from unwarranted attacks or unwanted intrusions into their privacy, and the like. As with all other aspects of informed consent, this procedure will avoid unpleasant surprises for group members and will help them to understand and interpret the therapist's behavior and comments during the group meetings.

---

**Case Example 7.6**

*A group therapist screens each client before the client joins the group. He explains the purpose of the group as an opportunity to discuss problems and issues with other clients and to help each other to deal with life problems. Although he knows that the group can be quite confrontational at times, he does not mention this point during the screening interview because the group rarely confronts new members and he does not want to scare the client about speaking up in the group.*

*Should the therapist act differently?*

---

## CONFIDENTIALITY

Confidentiality is fundamental and essential to effective psychotherapy and counseling. Clients must be confident that their therapist will keep information confidential if they are to feel comfortable revealing intimate information about their lives to the therapist. Unwarranted violations of confidentiality represent the single greatest threat to the practice of mental health treatment. Every aspect of the therapeutic relationship is based on the trust that a client places in her therapist. The ethical duty to preserve clients' confidentiality is grounded in therapists' respect for their clients' intrinsic value as persons.

A client's mere participation in therapy or counseling is confidential information, as is the nature and content of the client-therapist interaction. Under most circumstances, the client must provide his informed consent to the release of any information regarding his treatment. Informed consent in this case would require that the client know specifically what confidential information is being released and to whom. In reference to the issue of the capacity to consent discussed earlier, a client must be competent to provide consent in order for the release to be ethically appropriate.

---

**Case Example 7.7**

*A therapist is employed in a college counseling center. He has been working with a 22-year-old student for six months. She told him that her mother had referred her to the counseling center. His client's mother calls and asks him to give a message to her daughter when she comes in for her appointment that day. What should the therapist say?*

---

A therapist should never discuss a client with anyone not directly involved in the client's treatment. When working in a hospital or clinic, the content of therapy sessions should not be revealed to anyone who does not have a direct need to know. For example, if an inpatient client has expressed suicidal intentions during a session, it would be appropriate to discuss the matter with the supervisor of the nursing staff on the unit, in addition to noting the problem in the client's chart. However, therapists should not be gossips, talking about clients routinely with other staff. Also, it is unethical for a therapist to tell her spouse about her clients, even if her spouse would never reveal the information to anyone else.

Therapists sometimes present case material in public lectures, classes they teach, or publications. They have an ethical duty to make certain that the client being discussed cannot be identified from the information they provide. This goal is generally accomplished by disguising any identifying information (ACA, 1997, B.5.a; APA, 1992, 5.08). Therapists should exercise great care in discussing case material, particularly when it was gathered in their clinical work in a small town, because demographic data (e.g., age, gender, marital status) might be sufficient for some people to identify the client. The therapist should disguise data pertaining to the client so thoroughly that even her family and closest friends are not able to identify her. In the rare instances in which it is appropriate to provide a client's true identity, the client must first review the material to be presented and consent to being identified (ACA, 1997, B.5.b).

In addition to professionals' ethical duty regarding confidentiality, there are legal statutes in many states that address aspects of the confidential nature of therapist-client relationships. Therapists must familiarize themselves with the statutes and regulations of the state in which they practice.

---

**Case Example 7.8**

*A therapist is treating another clinician who reveals that he is having a sexual relationship with one of his clients. She is conflicted about the need to preserve his confidentiality versus her duty to protect the welfare of his client. What should the therapist do?*

---

## Privilege

Confidentiality is a therapist's professional duty, grounded in individuals' legal right to privacy. Privilege is a legal right of clients to prevent a professional from revealing confidential information as a witness in a legal proceeding (e.g., civil court case). Privilege resides in the client, and the professional has an obligation to protect this right, meaning that privileged communications can only be revealed when the client consents to "waive" his right to privilege. The professional should always try to obtain the client's written consent before releasing confidential information (Anderson, 1996). When the client does waive privilege, the professional is generally compelled to reveal the information, even if she does not think it is in the client's best interest. In legal proceedings involving a client, a mental health professional should resist a subpoena if her client does not want her to testify by claiming privilege on behalf of her client.

The existence and scope of legal privilege in communications between mental health professionals and their clients vary from state to state. Some states do not recognize privilege in psychotherapy relationships at all, some acknowledge privilege in civil cases only, and some recognize privilege between therapists and clients in both civil and criminal matters (excluding homicide). Moreover, legal privilege generally does not apply to marital, family, or group therapy because information revealed in a context in which more than two people are present is not considered confidential from a legal standpoint (Anderson, 1996). Specific state statutes may provide exceptions to this general legal principle. However, clients should be informed of the possibility that legal privilege might not exist in a multiple-client therapy context. It is not uncommon for marital therapy clients to wind up as opposing parties in divorce and child custody proceedings. Clients should know that the therapist could be subpoenaed to testify in such a case (Margolin, 1998). It is extremely important that mental health professionals familiarize themselves with the relevant statutes and rules of evidence of the state in which they practice. Interestingly, the United States Supreme Court has recognized psychotherapist-client privilege in civil proceedings in federal courts (*Jaffee v. Redmond,* 1996). Although the case involved a social worker, the ruling referred to "psychotherapists." Therefore, the holding is likely to apply to psychologists and counselors as well (Remley, Herlihy, & Herlihy, 1997).

## Limits of Confidentiality

Although confidentiality is an extremely important ethical duty in psychotherapy and counseling, there are contexts in which legal statutes require or permit disclosure of confidential information by therapists, independent of the consent of their clients. These legal duties, which vary from state to state, constitute limitations on clients' confidentiality. These limitations must be discussed with clients as part of the process of obtaining informed consent for treatment, so that clients will understand any potentially negative consequences of revealing personal information to their therapist (ACA, 1997, B.1.g; APA, 1992, 5.01).

Therapists may, for example, disclose confidential information to protect their clients or others from harm. If a client reveals that he intends to kill his former employer, that he plans to commit suicide, or that he sometimes loses control of his anger and injures his children while punishing them physically, the therapist is ethically (and, generally, legally) obligated to violate the client's confidentiality and inform the proper authorities. The duty to warn was discussed in Chapter 2 in relation to the Tarasoff case. When a therapist is legally permitted or required to disclose confidential information, she should normally discuss the situation with the client prior to making the disclosure, so that the client will understand the justification for her action.

---

**Case Example 7.9**

*A therapist reassures a client at their initial meeting about the confidentiality of their interactions, but fails to inform her about the limits of confidentiality. During the course of the therapy, the client becomes increasingly depressed and suicidal. She calls her therapist to tell him she is going to kill herself and that he should not feel responsible. He asks her to come in for a session; she refuses. He tells her he will need to call the police if she does not agree to let him intervene. She tells him he cannot do that because it would be a violation of her confidentiality. He does notify the authorities, and they intervene before she makes any attempt to harm herself. She then files an ethics complaint against him because he violated her confidentiality.*

*Does she have a case?*

---

Confidential client records stored on a medical insurance company's database may be accessible to law enforcement personnel conducting investigations, without any judicial intervention. Also, the treatment records of individual clients can be requested in the context of investigations of insurance or Medicaid fraud, and there is no clear protection against information concerning criminal behavior in clients' files being used to prosecute them (Perrone, 1997). Professionals have an ethical obligation to resist law enforcement requests for their financial or treatment records with identifying client information, even though their efforts may prove ineffective if a court order is issued to relinquish the records.

## CONFIDENTIALITY ISSUES IN MARITAL AND FAMILY THERAPY

In marital and family therapy, therapists must inform clients of the possibility that information discussed in the therapy sessions could be discoverable in divorce or child custody proceedings (Margolin, 1998). Therapists must also consider how they will handle individual interactions with clients that occur outside of the therapy sessions. For example, suppose a woman participating in marital therapy calls the therapist between sessions and reveals that her lack of effort in marital therapy is due to the fact that she has formed a new romantic attachment, about which her spouse knows nothing. She asks the therapist to keep this information confidential, since he is her therapist. The therapist believes that this information is extremely important for the husband to know, but feels constrained from telling him by his duty to preserve his other client's confidentiality.[20]

A marital or family therapist might deal with the matter of confidentiality proactively by suggesting to the participants that it is undesirable for them to hide anything from each other because honesty and open communication is vital to improving their relationship. Therefore, any conversations one of them has with the therapist must be brought up at the beginning of the following session (ACA, 1997, B.2.b; APA, 1992, 5.01[a]).

---

**Case Example 7.10**

*During a session, a marital therapist is discussing a series of violent confrontations in a marriage in which the husband "went off" on his wife in a jealous rage, with no apparent provocation. The couple is separated currently and the wife has indicated that she is ready to file for divorce. The therapist strongly suspects that the husband's violent outbursts are the result of cocaine abuse. She wonders whether she should bring this matter up in a marital therapy session or speak to him privately. She fears that his wife might file for divorce immediately if the therapist raised the possibility that the husband was a substance abuser.*

*What should the therapist do?*

---

## CONFIDENTIALITY ISSUES IN GROUP THERAPY

Therapy modalities involving multiple, unrelated clients raise additional issues concerning confidentiality. Although the therapist's duty not to disclose confidential information to persons not involved in the treatment does not change, a question arises regarding the duties of clients to one another. For example, if a client in group therapy discusses a personal issue during a session, are other members of the group free to reveal the information to family and acquaintances after the session has ended? Are members of the group permitted to discuss what went on during the session in smaller groups if they go out for coffee following the session?

These issues, like all complex ethical matters, are best dealt with proactively, before they arise. The therapist should discuss the kinds of situations that can arise in group therapy settings when the group begins, so that ground rules can be established regarding how such matters will be handled (ACA, 1997, B.2.a; APA, 1992, 5.01[a]). For example, the therapist might recommend that all members of a therapy group agree not to discuss the content of the sessions with anyone outside the group. However, the therapist cannot guarantee to clients that group members will actually maintain confidentiality, so clients must be warned that information they reveal in the group could be disclosed to people outside the group by other group members. Group members can also be encouraged not to reveal each other's secrets by informing them that they could be expelled from the group for violating agreed-upon confidentiality rules or could potentially be sued by another group member (Roback et al., 1996).

The confidentiality of group members should also be protected by maintaining individual treatment records for each client in the group. Therapists should avoid identifying or discussing any other group members in a client's record because the other clients would not be involved in consenting to the release of the client's record. Generally, interactions in group therapy settings are not considered privileged communications, since other people were present and heard the interaction. Thus, therapists could be compelled to testify about the content of group therapy sessions.

When group therapy clients are concurrently involved in individual therapy with the same therapist, the ground rules regarding the confidentiality of interactions in the two contexts should be clarified in advance. The client should be assured that the therapist will never reveal anything discussed in individual therapy sessions to other members of the group, but that the client is free to do so, if he wishes. Of course, the possibility always exists that the therapist could mistakenly reveal something about the client in group therapy, thinking the client had discussed it previously in that setting. When a group member is participating in individual therapy with another therapist, both therapists are obligated to maintain confidentiality unless the client provides written consent for the two therapists to consult with each other regarding his treatment.

Future therapists might have a negative reaction to these suggestions about disclosing the limits of confidentiality to clients, thinking that such policies might inhibit clients from being completely honest with their therapist. Keep in mind that a therapist has an ethical duty to fully inform clients in advance about the guidelines concerning confidentiality so that *they* can make an informed decision regarding what they do and do not wish to reveal to the therapist. This duty is consistent with the therapist's respect for his client's autonomy and right to self-determination. The therapist, once again, wants to avoid "setting up" a client in any way to experience a negative surprise. In addition, this proactive approach prevents any negative surprises for the therapist, like the marital therapy client's unanticipated disclosure, which, without previous discussion of confidentiality limits, the therapist is obligated not to reveal to the husband (ACA, 1997, B.2.b).

## CONFIDENTIALITY ISSUES IN THE MAINTENANCE AND DISPOSAL OF RECORDS

Therapists are required to maintain confidential records concerning their clients' treatment (ACA, 1997, B.4; APA, 1992, 5.04). Keeping careful records promotes the efficiency of treatment by facilitating review of the progress of treatment and jogging the therapist's memory of the content of previous meetings prior to the next session. Records are also an important means of communicating information about the client to other professionals from whom she might seek treatment.

---

**Case Example 7.11**

*A 26-year-old client is brought to a psychiatric hospital by his parents. His mother meets with the psychologist on the unit, while his father helps him to get settled. The mother tells the psychologist that her son suffers from schizophrenia and that he has become totally unmanageable at home. He has assaulted her husband and threatened her. She says that he cannot return to their home because they are worried about having him in the house with their 14-year-old daughter. The mother asks the psychologist to keep all this information confidential. The psychologist agrees and says that they will work on a plan to discharge her son to a community care facility when he is ready.*

*Two weeks later, his client is doing much better. The psychologist meets with him to discuss a discharge placement. They discuss his progress and medication regimen, as documented in his medical record. The psychologist leaves the room to get a list of community care facilities. When he returns to his office, the client is very agitated and says he does not want to talk anymore. Thirty minutes later, the psychologist receives a call from the client's mother. She says he called home and cursed her for saying he would rape his sister. His mother accuses the psychologist of violating her confidentiality. The psychologist tells her that he revealed nothing of their conversation.*

*How did the client find out what his mother had told the psychologist? Is the psychologist at fault?*

---

Clinicians are responsible for maintaining client records for a number of years after treatment has been completed. Although the length of time that private practice records must be maintained is not usually addressed specifically in state statutes, each state has statutes governing the length of time that *medical* records must be maintained. It is prudent for clinicians to at least abide by the time requirement for medical records in their state. In addition, many states require that medical records for minor clients be maintained for the specified time period *after* the clients achieve the age of majority (e.g., 18) specified by that state. In the absence of other regulations, APA recommends that complete records be retained for seven years, which exceeds the time requirement of any current state statute (APA Committee on Professional Practice and Standards, 1993).

Two additional issues that clinicians must address related to maintaining records are what to do about outdated information in a client's record and how to dispose of records without compromising clients' confidentiality. A clinician is obligated to protect his clients' welfare by keeping records that could potentially benefit their future treatment. Conversely, client welfare considerations require that a clinician protect his clients against the risk of being harmed by outdated or unneeded data in their records (APA Committee on Professional Practice and Standards, 1993). Outdated material most often pertains to assessment data that is no longer relevant to a client's present functioning. However, clinicians should reflect carefully before removing any information from a client's record. With regard to the disposal of records, when the legally appropriate time period has passed, clinicians are responsible for disposing of records in a manner that preserves the confidentiality of clients. Shredding of paper records prior to disposing of them is common practice.

Today, many client records are kept in the form of computer files. The use of computerized records does not diminish clinicians' responsibility regarding the preservation of client confidentiality. Clinicians have a duty to limit access to client records to professionals involved in the individual's treatment. When working in a clinic, hospital, or other organizational setting, clinicians have a duty to make certain that the organization has developed an effective security policy to protect computerized records. Coding records, rather than putting clients' names in the computer file, and setting passwords for access to confidential records are useful means of protecting clients' confidentiality.

Finally, though it is not a pleasant thought, every clinician, especially a private practitioner, should make arrangements for someone to take charge of his client records in the event of his death or severe incapacitation (APA, 1992, 5.09). Failure to do so could compromise clients' confidentiality or harm them by preventing access to those records by professionals who treat them in the future.

## MULTIPLE RELATIONSHIPS

A multiple relationship exists whenever a clinician engages in a social or professional relationship with a client prior to initiating therapy, during the course of therapy, or subsequent to the termination of the therapy relationship (ACA, 1997, A.6; APA, 1992, 1.17). A therapist who provides treatment for a neighbor, hires a current client to repair her roof,[21] provides both individual and group therapy for a client, or has her tax return prepared by a former client is engaging in a multiple relationship. Such relationships, particularly sexual relationships, are a major source of ethics complaints and malpractice suits against therapists (APA Ethics Committee, 1994; Strom-Gottfried, 1999).

Multiple relationships, no matter their nature (e.g., sexual or social), are potentially ethically problematic because they can affect a therapist's professional judgment and thereby the welfare of the client. Conflicts of interest occur in multiple relationships when the therapist's interest is no longer solely the welfare of the client in the therapeutic relationship. In other words, the clinician is no longer a disinterested party; he has a direct interest in some aspect of the client's life outside of therapy (Pope, 1991). For example, if a psychologist were treating a neighbor, he might be less comfortable allowing her to explore her dissatisfaction with her husband during the session due to his friendship with the client's husband. The complications introduced by a multiple relationship are also one of the reasons mental health professionals are encouraged to avoid bartering arrangements. If a client agrees to repair a therapist's roof in exchange for receiving therapy, the therapist might be reluctant to report to the appropriate authorities that the client seems to be abusing his children, until the client has completed the repairs to her roof (ACA, 1997, A.10.c; APA, 1992, 1.18). Once again, the welfare of the client and his family is no longer the sole relevant interest of the therapist. Multiple relationships can also compromise a client's independence of judgment and action. In the example just discussed, even if the client in the bartering arrangement was dissatisfied with the progress he was making in therapy, he might feel that he could not change therapists because he had already started the roofing job on his current therapist's residence.

Therapists who are also college or university faculty members need to avoid mixing these two professional roles because of the potential influence of one relationship on the professional's ability to function effectively in the other. Therapists should not provide treatment for their students, the families of their students, the intimates (e.g., friends, romantic partners) of their students, people likely to become their students (e.g., nonpsychology majors at the same institution), or fellow college or university employees.

Therapists sometimes provide individual therapy to clients they are seeing concurrently in marital or group therapy. Although these are both professional relationships (and, in that sense, do not technically involve multiple roles), seeing a client in two settings does introduce potential ethical complications. A group therapy client might feel compelled to accept the therapist's offer of individual therapy, rather than providing truly voluntary informed consent. Also, clients will tend to develop a stronger, more intense transference to a therapist they see in two settings (Glass, 1998). Moreover, a therapist might relate differently to a client in group therapy if she also sees him for individual therapy because she knows him more intimately. This dynamic can negatively impact the group process. Also, the therapist might unwittingly violate a client's confidentiality by mistakenly mentioning an issue that had been raised in individual therapy. For all of these reasons, and a number of others, it is generally ethically undesirable to form multiple therapeutic relationships with a client. If a group therapy client could benefit from individual therapy, an appropriate referral should be made. In any case, recruiting group therapy clients for individual therapy, or vice versa, certainly *appears* to involve a conflict of interest: specifically, the therapist's desire to expand her income by filling additional client hours (Glass, 1998).

Multiple relationships cannot always be avoided, particularly by a clinician practicing in a small town (Catalano, 1997). Some relationships develop purely out of coincidence, as when the checkout clerk at the grocery store happens to be a client (Pearson & Piazza, 1997). The "Ethical Principles" recognizes this pragmatic reality, but emphasizes nevertheless that such relationships are to be avoided or handled in a professional, therapeutic manner because of their potential for harming clients.

Consider the following example: A counselor in private practice in a small town advertises a receptionist position in the local newspaper. A former client, who completed treatment two years earlier, calls her about applying for the job. The counselor knows that her former client is an extremely capable person. She also believes that the woman's experience as a client would make her particularly sensitive to the feelings and needs of clients she would encounter in the office. She invites the woman for an interview and, following a frank discussion of the potential difficulties of working as employer-employee after having been in a therapist-client relationship, decides to hire her for the position because the benefits seem to outweigh the potential risks.

There are many reasons why a former client would want to work for her therapist, but it is clear that the relationship would be quite different from a normal employer-employee situation. There would be considerable potential for the former therapy relationship to affect the employment relationship. The former client might want to talk about current issues in her life with her employer. She might even feel that now there would be nothing wrong with having a social relationship with the counselor because employees and employers are often friends. Furthermore, the counselor might take advantage of the new relationship to pay her former client less than she would pay another receptionist of equal ability, knowing that her former client will not insist on being paid more. The bottom line is that therapists should avoid multiple relationships because of the possible harm that can result for clients. Even in a small town, the counselor can find another receptionist.

---

**Case Example 7.12**

*A well-known counselor in a small city is shopping at the local Wal-Mart with her husband. She sees a client in the store and, knowing that he is very shy, realizes that he is unlikely to approach them in public. However, she also knows that if she does not greet him, he will feel ignored and think that she is embarrassed to associate with him publicly. She is unsure whether her husband and other people in the store who know her will realize, if she speaks to him, that he is a client of hers.*
*What should she do?*

---

## SEXUAL RELATIONSHIPS WITH CLIENTS

Erotic contact between a therapist and client includes any behavior that is primarily intended to arouse or satisfy sexual desires (Holroyd & Brodsky, 1977). It is obvious to any mental health professional that engaging in such behavior with a client is unprofessional and unethical, yet ethics books and professional codes devote considerable attention to the problem. There are two major reasons why the issue is given such attention. First, a number of studies have suggested that sexual involvement between a therapist and client is extremely likely to harm the client (e.g., Luepker, 1999; Pope & Bouhoutsos, 1986; Somer & Saadon, 1999). Some researchers have labeled the harmful effects on clients "therapist-patient sex syndrome," consisting of a set of symptoms overlapping components of both posttraumatic stress disorder and borderline personality disorder (Pope, 1989).[22] There is also evidence that people who were sexually abused as children might be somewhat more likely to become involved in sexual relationships with their therapists, resulting in another experience of victimization (Luepker, 1999; Pope & Bouhoutsos, 1986). Second, although it is difficult to obtain accurate data concerning the prevalence of this problem, indications suggest that sexual intimacies between therapists and clients, though rare, still occur (Thoreson, Shaughnessy, & Frazier, 1995; Thoreson et al., 1993; Williams, 1992). Male therapists are much more likely to report having had sexual contact with clients than female therapists (Thoreson et al., 1995). The typical offender is a reputable male therapist working alone in a private practice (Somer & Saadon, 1999).

The only way to reduce unethical sexual behavior between therapists and clients is to provide therapists with better training in methods of preventing such incidents from developing (Hoffman, 1995; Plaut, 1997). The context of individual psychotherapy or counseling is extremely intimate and commonly arouses romantic feelings, both on the part of the client (transference) and the therapist (countertransference). Therapists need to acknowledge such feelings to themselves when they occur. Feelings are not the problem; inappropriate behavior is. When strong countertransferential feelings are present, the therapist should consult a supervisor or colleague for assistance in resolving them. The fact that sexual boundary violations are more likely to occur in private practice, where therapists are working alone, means that private practitioners should take the initiative to seek out collegial supervisory relationships in order to have a forum to discuss issues of this sort.

---

### Case Example 7.13

*A recently divorced clinical psychologist in private practice is treating a 25-year-old woman for depression. She is very active sexually, and he finds himself encouraging her to talk more and more in their sessions about her sexual trysts. He rationalizes the discussion of her sexual behavior as an opportunity to address her self-esteem issues. He is also very stimulated by her detailed descriptions of sexual encounters.*

*She is aware of his divorce and offers to cook him dinner some night because he must miss having home-cooked meals.*

*How should the psychologist handle this situation?*

---

Like most ethical problems, the violation of sexual boundaries occurs gradually, so timely action on the part of a therapist who acknowledges a boundary issue with a client can prevent a sexual relationship from developing. Therapists are much more likely to violate professional boundaries when they are experiencing personal problems, particularly in their own intimate relationships. The resolution of boundary problems might involve the therapist seeking therapy for himself. In some instances, referring the client to another therapist might be in the client's best interests, but this decision should be made professionally, based on what is best for the client's welfare, after due consideration of all of the issues involved. Clients should be informed of the reasons for the termination and the ethical rationale for taking that course of action.

In some cases, a client's romantic transference can be the starting point for an inappropriate sexual relationship between therapist and client (Somer & Saadon, 1999). For example, a female client reflects on the fact that she is able to relate the most intimate and embarrassing details of her life to her therapist and realizes that she has never been able to communicate so openly and freely with her husband, or any other man in her life. She feels that her therapist cares deeply for her because he listens attentively and never reacts in a judgmental manner to her disclosures. She is extremely impressed by her therapist: he is intelligent, attractive, sensitive, and has a great sense of humor. She thinks about how wonderful it would be to be with him all the time, rather than just for one hour each week. She begins to fantasize about such a relationship and suspects that he is also interested romantically in her. After all, she figures he must experience this relationship as very special also; being so sensitive, he must be able to feel the chemistry between them. She decides to test her hypothesis by making a few flattering comments about him and making casual physical contact with him to see how he responds.

Therapists must handle a situation like this very carefully. Unfortunately, they generally receive very little instruction regarding such situations in their training. First, therapists should be careful about non-erotic physical contact with clients, as these gestures can be misinterpreted as a desire on the therapist's part for greater physical intimacy. Second, therapists should be sensitive to the possibility that clients can, and often do, form a romantic attachment to their therapist. Third, when a client expresses a romantic interest in the therapist, the therapist should express that he feels flattered, but should firmly explain that such a relationship could never occur for professional and ethical reasons, based on the potential harm that could result for the client. Fourth, it is useful to explain to the client that it is natural for her to experience such feelings in therapy; after all, it is a very intimate situation. The therapist can point out that the client is not responding to him as an individual so much as to his professionalism and his concern for her as her therapist. Fifth, the therapist should be aware that a client's attraction to him can be symptomatic of emotional issues that have also been acted out in other relationships in her life. Often, there is considerable therapeutic value in exploring the reasons she began experiencing such feelings in the process of therapy. Finally, the therapist should make it clear that the client is responding to his professional demeanor; she should not expect the communications she has in relationships outside of therapy to involve the same level of selfless concern that he expresses toward his clients. He might point out that he behaves quite differently when he is not conducting therapy, focusing on *his* interests rather than solely on the concerns of his clients.

Always remember that engaging in a sexual relationship with a client is a profound violation of the professional trust that exists between therapists and clients, like violating a client's confidentiality. Sexual involvement with a client can result in great harm to the client and can destroy a therapist's career. Clients who have been sexually exploited by a therapist will find it difficult to ever form a therapeutic alliance again, which can prevent them from ever dealing effectively with the problems that originally brought them to therapy, not to mention the additional damage done by the exploitative therapist (Luepker, 1999; Wohlberg & Reid, 1996). The professionals who interact with victims of therapist sexual exploitation have an ethical obligation to encourage the victims to pursue ethical and/or legal action against the unethical therapist. Therapists must avoid the desire to protect their colleagues from harm by covering up unethical behavior (Quadrio, 1994). Incredibly, in one study, 18% of the victims of therapist sexual misconduct were subsequently revictimized by another professional (Luepker, 1999).

It is *never* permissible to exploit a client. Also, no matter what the client might do to encourage such a relationship, the therapist will virtually always be held responsible when ethics complaints or malpractice suits are filed; there are no excuses. More than 15 states have created statutes that make the sexual exploitation of a client by a therapist a form of criminal sexual misconduct (McMahon, 1997).

## RELATIONSHIPS WITH FORMER CLIENTS

Multiple relationships with former clients should also be avoided because of the inequality inherent in such relationships due to the individuals' former roles as therapist and client. Such relationships have the potential to harm former clients and to become exploitative. In addition, such a relationship can be harmful by precluding the possibility of resuming the therapeutic relationship at some future date if the client desires additional treatment. In spite of these potential pitfalls, some professionals do develop friendships with former clients (Salisbury & Kinnier, 1996). Additional research is needed to assess the circumstances and consequences of these relationships.

Sexual relationships with former clients are much more common than with clients currently in treatment. In one survey, 7% of male counselors acknowledged sexual contact with former clients (Thoreson et al., 1993). These relationships are forbidden under any circumstances for a minimum of two years following the termination of the therapeutic relationship (ACA, 1997, A.7.b; APA, 1992, 4.07). It seems curious that the ethical codes of psychology and counseling do not forbid these relationships without exception because it is difficult to conceive of a circumstance under which this type of relationship would not be inappropriate forever (Gabbard, 1994). Perhaps there could be unusual circumstances in which a blanket prohibition against relationships with former clients might seem unreasonably restrictive. For example, suppose a client who participated in two sessions of group therapy with a therapist meets him years later after she has completed her own clinical training. Would a relationship between the two of them necessarily be inappropriate because she had once been his client? Remember, though, that even in such unusual circumstances, the burden of proof would always be on the therapist to demonstrate that the relationship was in no way harmful to the former client, exploitative, or indicative of unprofessional conduct during the prior therapy. Therapists are well-served to never entertain the possibility of becoming involved sexually with a former client. The APA Ethics Code Task Force, which is currently preparing a draft of a revision of the "Ethical Principles," intends to recommend that sexual relationships with former clients be prohibited absolutely, no matter how much time has elapsed since the therapeutic relationship ended (Martin, 1999).

## MULTIPLE RELATIONSHIPS IN GROUP THERAPY

As discussed earlier, some therapists conduct individual therapy with clients for whom they are also providing group, marital, or family therapy. Multiple relationships of this type (although both involve a professional, therapeutic relationship) are often ill-advised, complicating the therapist's role in each therapy setting. Therapists should only engage in this type of multiple relationship when there is a very strong rationale for their decision; the desire to fill more client hours or the fact that the client is already comfortable with the therapist is not adequate justification. Therapists should have sufficient confidence in their fellow professionals to recognize that the client will very likely benefit from another therapeutic perspective on her issues.

Group therapy clients sometimes form multiple relationships by developing friendships, or even romantic attachments, with other group members. The issues involved in client-client multiple relationships should be discussed at the beginning of the group. The therapist should point out that outside relationships between group members can complicate the group process as much as a therapist-client multiple relationship. Two group members might develop a tendency to "gang up" on a group member they feel is critical of one of them. They might defend each other against being confronted by group members or the therapist, rather than focusing on making sure they each work on their personal issues in the group. These dyadic relationships, which can play out in many different ways in the group, tend to be extremely harmful to the group process. Therefore, group members might be encouraged to agree not to form outside relationships for the duration of the therapy group.

---

**Case Example 7.14**

*Following a group therapy session, the therapist is invited to go out for coffee with the members of the group. She decides to go, feeling that it will enhance her rapport with the group members. When they meet at a local diner, she realizes that three of the group members are not there. She asks about them, and someone says that they had left before the idea was suggested. The therapist immediately begins to feel uncomfortable, fearing that the other three group members will feel they were excluded. She wishes she had not accepted the invitation.*

---

## COMPETENCE

Mental health professionals have an ethical obligation to promote the welfare of their clients by providing them with the highest quality of professional services possible. In Chapter 2, the principle of competence was said to involve a professional's understanding of her strengths and limitations, both of which are extremely important to the practice of psychotherapy. A therapist's strengths (i.e., areas of professional competence) enable her to help clients with problems that fall within her area(s) of expertise, while her awareness of her limitations prevents her from potentially harming clients by attempting to work with populations or problems outside the range of her professional training and experience. Competent professionals act in accordance with two fundamental ethical principles: beneficence, which entails professionals striving to do only good for their clients, and nonmaleficence, which emphasizes the premium professionals place on making certain that clients are never harmed. In this section, ethical considerations in achieving and assessing one's level of competence will be presented along with the issue of therapist impairment, one of the most significant threats to competent practice.

The minimum standards for competence as a psychotherapist or counselor are based on academic training and supervised experience resulting in professional licensure. A mental health professional's license does not specify what types of clients (e.g., adults, children, adolescents, families, couples) she is qualified to serve, the types of problems she is competent to treat (e.g., adjustment disorders, personality disorders, mood disorders), or the specific interventions (e.g., behavioral, psychodynamic) she is competent to use. A therapist is ethically obligated to restrict her practice to the client populations and intervention techniques with which she is qualified to practice based on her academic background and supervised clinical experience (ACA, 1997, C.2.a; APA, 1992, 1.04[a]). In other words, the matter of determining her competence to work with particular types of clients dealing with specific sorts of problems is left largely to the ethical and professional integrity of the individual professional.

## COMPETENCE WITH DIVERSE CLIENT POPULATIONS

The issues and challenges involved in treating diverse populations vary considerably. Working with children and adults, Hispanics and African Americans, or male and female clients clearly involves different competencies. Therapists need to develop an awareness of, and sensitivity to, diversity issues arising from the different backgrounds of clients (ACA, 1997, A.2.b; APA, 1992, 1.08). Competent therapists recognize and value diversity. They respect individual differences based on age, gender, education, socioeconomic status, group identifications, nationality, ethnicity, religion, and disability. While most people recognize that it is wrong to view women within a cultural context as inferior, it is equally wrong to view everyone in terms of white, male, American cultural values. Therapists develop a better understanding of diversity issues through their training, supervised experience, and later through continuing education and consultation with colleagues. When gender, race, ethnicity, age, religion, sexual orientation, disability, language, socioeconomic status, or other diversity issues cause a therapist to question her ability to competently serve a client's needs, she should seek consultation and, if appropriate, refer the client to a more competent colleague (ACA, 1997, A.11.b; APA, 1992, 1.08). For instance, if a therapist's supervised experience has been limited primarily to the treatment of white college student and adult populations, it is inappropriate for him to offer services for ethnically diverse groups until he obtains diversity training.

---

**Case Example 7.15**

An African American woman, raised in a rural Southern community, consults a counselor about her children's behavioral problems. When asked about her methods of disciplining the children, she says that she does what her mother and grandmother had done. If a child disobeys an important moral or safety rule, she sends him out to cut her a switch and uses it to give him a good spanking. She tells the therapist that if you spare the rod, you spoil the child. The therapist tells her that hitting children with a stick is a form of child abuse and that she will need to learn new methods of discipline, emphasizing rewarding children for good behavior, rather than punishing misbehavior.

Was the therapist's statement ethically appropriate?

---

## COMPETENCE WITH TREATMENT MODELS AND INTERVENTIONS FOR CLIENT PROBLEMS

There is considerable variation among therapists regarding the types of interventions they are competent to provide to assist clients in resolving their problems. Some therapists use one treatment technique (e.g., psychoanalysis, cognitive therapy) for all of their clients, adapting the application of the technique to best address the client's concerns. Other therapists describe themselves as "eclectic"; they use different treatment approaches (e.g., person-centered, behavioral, RET) with different clients based on their assessment of the client and the presenting problem. The key ethical issue in the choice of treatment orientation and intervention techniques is that the therapist must have developed competence in any treatment method he uses through academic training and supervised experience. When the therapist has not established the competencies required to treat the problem a client presents (e.g., parent-child conflict requiring family therapy), the therapist is ethically obligated to refer the client to a colleague competent in that mode of therapy.

Lazarus (1995) raises an interesting issue pertaining to competence in his distinction between technical and theoretical eclecticism. Technical eclecticism involves the selection of specific intervention techniques (e.g., systematic desensitization) that are documented to be among the most efficient methods of helping clients resolve specific problems (e.g., phobias). Theoretical eclecticism involves using different theoretical models, or conceptualizations of human behavior, in working with different clients. For example, a therapist who conceptualizes a male client's anxiety problem as a manifestation of an Oedipal fixation and another client's anxiety as an existential difficulty with confronting the reality of death is practicing theoretical eclecticism.

Lazarus (1995) argues that technical eclecticism, assuming that it is based on adequate training and experience, is a particularly effective method of helping clients. The technically eclectic therapist will be able to adapt his interventions to provide each client with the methods that have been demonstrated to be the most effective means of solving the client's problems. Theoretical eclecticism, on the other hand, is criticized by Lazarus as leading to confused, incompetent therapy practice. To practice competently, therapists need to develop a stable, internally consistent model for conceptualizing human behavior that can guide their approach to clients and selection of techniques to address specific problems.

---

**Case Example 7.16**

*A psychologist in a small town is treating a woman for depression. It becomes apparent that a major issue in the client's depression is her lack of interest in her sexual relationship with her husband. For several years, she has not been able to become aroused sexually, and it has caused her to feel that she is letting her husband down. She consulted her gynecologist, who told her that the problem is psychological and recommended therapy for her sexual dysfunction. The psychologist wants to refer her to a competent sex therapist, but there are no therapists with this specialization within driving distance.*

*Should he attempt to treat her sexual dysfunction?*

---

## DEVELOPING NEW AREAS OF COMPETENCE

Over time, therapists will frequently expand the range of populations they serve and the services they provide by obtaining additional education, training (e.g., continuing education workshops), and supervised experience in new therapy methods and techniques (ACA, 1997, C.2.b; APA, 1992, 1.04[b]). For example, a therapist who provides individual therapy for adults might decide she would like to be able to offer marital therapy or conduct group therapy. Developing a new area of competence is not unlike training in a new area of specialization (Conger, 1976). Therapists should not offer new treatment services without first obtaining adequate training. The primary concern of therapists is always the best interests of their clients. Therefore, "on the job" training without adequate supervision in a new area of expertise is never ethically acceptable because it would involve a risk of providing less than competent services to a client.

## MAINTAINING COMPETENCE

Mental health professionals are also required to maintain an appropriate level of professional competence (ACA, 1997, C.2.f; APA, 1992, 1.05). Therapists are expected to keep abreast of current information by reading the professional literature relevant to their practice and by participating in continuing education activities. Nearly all state boards of psychology and counseling require licensees to complete continuing education requirements for annual renewal of their license. The *Code of Ethics* presents an additional requirement that seems essential to maintaining competence: Counselors must monitor and assess the effectiveness of their professional activity as a stimulus for self-improvement (ACA, 1997, C.2.d). All therapists could certainly benefit from evaluating the effectiveness of their interventions with clients through peer supervision and by collecting outcome data or evaluations from their clients.

## THERAPIST IMPAIRMENT AND BURNOUT

Everyone goes through difficult periods in life. Therapists are no different. However, therapists have a professional and ethical obligation to monitor their effectiveness and not offer services when their effectiveness is impaired (ACA, 1997, C.2.d, g; APA, 1992, 1.13). Therapists, like others, can develop substance abuse problems, experience difficult and painful divorces, or become extremely upset and distracted by the illness or death of a loved one. Therapist impairment occurs when a therapist's personal problems spill over into his professional activity and reduce his therapeutic effectiveness. The potential for interpersonal difficulties in a therapist's life to result in inappropriate multiple relationships with clients, discussed earlier in this chapter, is an outstanding example of the potential for harm arising from therapist impairment.

Therapists have an obligation to recognize when they are experiencing emotional or physical problems that are affecting their professional effectiveness and to get help with their problems. Although it can be difficult for a therapist, who is accustomed to helping others, to seek help for his own problems, his concern for the welfare of his clients must take precedence over his personal reluctance to seek help. For instance, a therapist with a substance abuse problem cannot ethically continue to treat clients until his own problem has been resolved. Certainly, a therapist with unresolved feelings pertaining to his divorce should not conduct marital therapy (or perhaps even treat female clients). When appropriate, impaired therapists explain their personal situation to clients and arrange appropriate referrals. Impaired therapists have the same obligation as every other clinician not to abandon clients (ACA, 1995, A.11.a-b; APA, 1992, 4.09).

---

**Case Example 7.17**

*A clinical psychologist who is a heavy smoker asks clients if they mind if she smokes during sessions. If they express any discomfort with the idea, she does not smoke. She finds it very difficult to go for 50 minutes without a cigarette in such cases, but she manages. She has tried to quit smoking in the past, but with no success. She is no longer interested in quitting.*

*Is the psychologist's behavior ethically appropriate?*

---

Therapist burnout is a form of personal impairment that has received considerable attention in recent years. A therapist experiencing burnout generally perceives the demands of his work as being too much for him to handle, resulting in symptoms of emotional exhaustion, depersonalization, and feelings of reduced personal accomplishment (Skorupa & Agresti, 1993). For therapists, "burnout may manifest itself in a loss of empathy, respect, and positive feelings for their clients" (Skorupa & Agresti, 1993, p. 281). This loss of concern for clients may be evidenced by the development of a cynical attitude toward them and his work. As a result, he may become uncommunicative or irritable and uncooperative toward his clients and colleagues (Mills & Huebner, 1998). A therapist might feel that his clients do not appreciate his efforts on their behalf, or he might be disappointed and frustrated by his clients' lack of progress and feel that he has failed them.

Burnout can result from overwork, such as carrying too large a caseload. Therapists often feel that they are spread too thin: they have so many clients that they cannot devote sufficient attention to any of them. Correlational findings suggest that practitioners with smaller caseloads are less vulnerable to burnout (Skorupa & Agresti, 1993). More hours of contact with clients, as opposed to spending time on record keeping or administrative chores, are positively related to a sense of accomplishment (Vredenburgh, Carlozzi, & Stein, 1999). Also, therapists working in hospital settings are at greater risk for burnout than those in private practice; this finding could be a function of the perceived meaningfulness of conducting therapy in the two types of settings (Vredenburgh et al., 1999). On the other hand, working with inpatient clients who are often very severely disturbed might be a significant source of stress (Acker, 1999). In fact, several studies have suggested that burnout may relate to the degree of stress associated with a clinician's area of specialization (e.g., the stress of working with terminally ill children or trauma victims), although this correlational finding could also indicate that burnout causes therapists to report higher levels of stress (Miller, 1998; Mills & Huebner, 1998). Finally, age is related inversely to burnout among therapists (Vredenburgh et al., 1999), which is consistent with the idea that younger therapists may experience greater stress as they struggle to develop competency, manage boundary issues, and achieve some degree of professional security.

Therapists believe that burnout impairs one's professional competence (Skorupa & Agresti, 1993). The experience of burnout can cause a therapist to ignore his responsibilities and avoid his clients. Indeed, therapists suffering from burnout may be perceived more negatively by clients (Renjilian, Baum, & Landry, 1998). Also, clients rate the outcome of their therapy more negatively when their therapist displays symptoms of burnout (McCarthy & Frieze, 1999). As with other forms of impairment, it is extremely unprofessional and dangerous to the welfare of clients and the public trust in the mental health professions for a therapist experiencing burnout to fail to address the situation and continue to treat clients.

Burnout risks can be addressed by training and continuing education, providing adequate supervision and social support for therapists dealing with difficult populations, instilling a strong sense of purpose or mission in therapists, and encouraging treatment providers to recognize that they, too, need to access help when professional and/or personal stressors begin to build (Acker, 1999; Miller, 1998). Informal interaction with professional peers can provide an excellent outlet for discharging accumulating tension and accessing both emotional and professional support.

---

**Case Example 7.18**

*A counselor working in a state psychiatric hospital finds that the ever-increasing volume of paperwork keeps her from devoting as much time to her clients as she would like. On the other hand, she doesn't feel that most of her clients are really interested in treatment; they just come into the hospital for "three hots and a cot" when they run out of money. She complains to her colleagues about revolving-door admissions and needless paperwork. Some mornings she just can't face going to work. She calls in sick and takes what she and her colleagues refer to as a "mental health day." She dreams of the day when she will be able to establish a private practice and work with motivated clients who can really accomplish something with their lives, rather than a bunch of burned out, substance-abusing inpatient clients.*

---

## CONFLICT OF INTEREST

When conducting therapy, a mental health professional's primary concern is the best interest of her clients. She tries to improve the welfare of her clients while respecting their autonomy as persons. A conflict of interest exists when additional motivations affect the objectivity of a therapist's professional judgment. Multiple relationships, which were discussed earlier, are problematic and potentially harmful because they are likely to create conflicts of interest. In fact, they are the most common source of conflicts of interest. For example, if a counselor who is a college faculty member accepts a referral from the president of the college to treat a member of his family, the therapist might be concerned with how the outcome of the therapy will affect her chances for promotion to full professor, in addition to her concern about the welfare of her client. Her judgments in conducting the therapy might be less objective than usual because of her concern about impressing the president with the quality and brevity of the therapy.

Also, therapists in private practice frequently find themselves confronted with potential economic conflicts of interest. For example, a clinical psychologist in full-time private practice has been treating a woman for nine months for depression. Her condition has stabilized, but she shows no inclination to terminate therapy. The psychologist is concerned about the possibility that his client may be developing a dependency on him, yet he is hesitant to bring up the issue of termination, partly because he has not received any new referrals recently and cannot afford to lose the income from that weekly client hour. Economic pressures can easily affect a therapist's judgment regarding the value of a client continuing in therapy or the need to refer a client whose problems exceed the boundaries of the therapist's competence.

Clients frequently choose to bestow gifts on their therapist around the holidays. Permitting a client to express his appreciation by giving his therapist a small gift (e.g., a book) is certainly appropriate. To refuse the gift on the grounds that theirs is a "fee for service" relationship would embarrass and demean the client and misrepresent the nature and depth of the therapeutic relationship. However, if the gift becomes something more substantial (e.g., a set of golf clubs), the therapist might feel indebted to her client in a way that could affect her decision making regarding issues that arise in therapy. Large gifts should be refused politely to avoid a potential conflict of interest.

---

**Case Example 7.19**

*A clinical psychologist discovers that an outpatient client he is treating appears to be suffering from Dissociative Identity Disorder. He finds working with her different personalities a fascinating experience. With her consent, he audio- and videotapes sessions because he expects to write extensively about her case in the future. However, she says that her life problems are getting worse. Her marriage is falling apart. She says that she heard about an inpatient facility in another city that specializes in the treatment of dissociative disorders. She wonders if she would benefit from pursuing treatment there.*

*The psychologist tells her that inpatient programs are a last resort and encourages her to continue outpatient therapy with him. He offers to speak to her husband so that he will understand better what she is going through.*

*Is the psychologist's behavior ethically appropriate?*

---

## RESPECT FOR CLIENTS' AUTONOMY

Respect for the autonomy, values, and right to self-determination of clients is one of the most important principles guiding the behavior of mental health professionals. Although autonomy could be argued to be an American cultural value, mental health professionals mean simply that they respect a client's own self-directed decisions and view of life. Conducting therapy in a manner that is completely consistent with these principles can prove quite difficult, though. First of all, many clients who need treatment do not enter therapy voluntarily. They are manipulated (e.g., by threats of hospitalization) or persuaded to pursue therapy by family members, institutions, and therapists (Carroll, 1991). Second, clients struggling with life problems generally enter therapy needing assistance and direction. However, if the therapist provides direction out of concern for the client's welfare (e.g., suggests how the client might modify his behavior), she runs the risk of showing a lack of respect for the client's autonomy by, in essence, telling him how he ought to live. The principles of respect for autonomy and concern for the client's welfare can certainly conflict, most notably in cases of coercive suicide prevention and involuntary hospitalization.[23]

There is no question that therapists influence their clients, but this fact does not mean that therapy necessarily interferes with the autonomous functioning of clients. There are many ways in which therapists affect the belief systems and behavior of their clients. In all forms of therapy, therapists *influence* their clients. Influencing another person occurs in any intimate relationship and means that some aspect of the therapist's beliefs, values, or behavior "rubs off" on the client. This process may be deliberate or it might occur unintentionally. Many therapists give *advice* to their clients, suggesting more adaptive ways of dealing with situations. For example, a therapist might suggest methods a client can use to express his feelings assertively, rather than becoming aggressive. Another term used for this process of actively providing advice to clients is giving *direction* to clients. Therapists' use of their influence in imparting their clinical expertise to clients is related positively to clients' perception of the effectiveness of the therapy (McCarthy & Frieze, 1999). Keep in mind, however, that clients generally perceive therapists as authority figures and might tend to obey them without making an autonomous decision regarding the appropriateness of the advice. In other words, whenever therapists provide direction, they need to be aware that they may be fostering passivity and dependency in their clients, which is certainly not consistent with respecting clients' autonomy (ACA, 1997, A.1.b).

---

### Case Example 7.20

*A single mother is participating in individual therapy with a clinical psychologist. The therapy concerns primarily her conflict with her 15-year-old daughter. The mother asks if she and the daughter can see the psychologist for family therapy. When the three of them meet to discuss the possibility of family therapy, the daughter says that it is difficult for her to speak plainly in front of her mother. The daughter requests individual sessions, like her mother has.*

*The mother appears to be very controlling and strict about her daughter's behavior, based on her religious beliefs and the traditional Italian values instilled when the mother was a teenager. The psychologist tells the mother that the only chance she has of not losing her daughter completely is to allow her to pursue individual therapy that will enable her to better understand her mother's perspective. Privately, he wonders whether the individual therapy will promote the daughter's discontent and subvert the mother's authority, but he decides that this course of action is necessary to promote the autonomy of the daughter.*

*Is the psychologist taking the correct action?*

The most extreme form of potential therapist influence is *coercion*. Coercion involves forcing someone to do something against his will by exerting pressure, either psychologically or physically. A person is coerced to perform a behavior when he is put in a situation in which he has no meaningful alternative. Even though coercive interventions subvert a client's autonomy, they are sometimes employed in therapy, with the justification that it is the only means of protecting a client from serious harm. For example, when a therapist, acting out of concern for a suicidal client's welfare, tells him that he must agree to admit himself to a hospital for observation or the therapist will call the police to take him to the hospital, the client is being coerced. A more subtle form of coercion might involve a therapist showing obvious displeasure with a client's behavior or verbalizations. The use of personal coercive strategies has been shown to be negatively related to clients' perception of therapy outcome (McCarthy & Frieze, 1999).

An additional reason why it is not advisable to subvert a client's autonomy by coercing her to make life changes or adopt new behavioral strategies is that the client may be hurt as a result. Pushing a shy client to pursue relationships before she really feels ready could result in rejection and greater suffering. Also, therapists dealing with women who are in domestic abuse situations frequently urge them to muster the courage to leave. Unfortunately, many women have been murdered by their male partner because they were trying to leave.

Carl Rogers developed his person-centered approach to therapy because he believed that any sort of therapist influence demonstrated a lack of regard for the autonomy of clients (e.g., Raskin & Rogers, 1995). Rogers respected the autonomy of his clients by attempting to be as nondirective as possible. He believed that therapists should create an atmosphere of trust and support clients in choosing their own solutions to their life problems. Rogers' person-centered approach has been extremely influential in emphasizing the importance of respecting a client's autonomy and developing a therapeutic alliance based on mutual respect and trust. Although many models of therapy still incorporate varying degrees of directiveness in dealing with client problems, the Rogerian legacy has highlighted the ethically problematic nature of therapy techniques that involve deception or coercion (Cohen & Cohen, 1999). For example, some therapists employ a technique called "paradoxical intention" or "antisuggestion." For example, a marital therapist treating a couple who argue constantly and seem unwilling to work on improving their relationship realizes that he is reinforcing their combativeness by constantly urging them to deal with conflicts calmly. He decides to offer a paradoxical intention by saying that they have convinced him that their marriage has become one long battle and that the only solution to their situation is divorce. He does not really mean this, but is hoping that his statement will cause them to rally against him for dismissing their relationship so lightly. This type of strategy, often used by parents in old situation comedies on television, is referred to popularly as "reverse psychology." Dishonesty with clients is certainly disrespectful of them as persons. Also, therapists ask clients to be completely open and honest with them. In doing so, therapists certainly incur an obligation to be genuine and honest in return.[24] Clearly, there are ethical considerations involved even in selecting an approach to conducting therapy.

---

**Case Example 7.21**

*A counselor encourages a client suffering from depression and social anxiety to participate in a weekly therapy group he conducts. He does not tell the client that it is an Incest Survivors Group because he does not want to bias her approach to the group. The therapist believes it is possible that his client was a victim of sexual abuse at some point in her life. After attending the group for two months, the client reports that she has been remembering how, when she was a little girl, her father would "play" with her on her bed. The group explores these memories with her, and she becomes increasingly convinced that her father had actually abused her. Only then does the therapist mention that he had suspected all along that she had been a victim of sexual abuse.*

*Did the therapist behave appropriately?*

---

## RESPECT FOR CLIENT VALUES

Another facet of a mental health professional's respect for client autonomy and diversity is her regard for the personal values clients bring into therapy. The relationship between a therapist and a client is inherently value-laden, in that it necessarily reflects the values of each party involved. For example, the importance that therapists place on preserving their clients' autonomy represents a value position. Similarly, clients' willingness to endure the often uncomfortable process of therapy is evidence of the value they place on self-understanding and personal development. The fact that the values of all parties involved permeate the therapy relationship is not necessarily a problem; it is simply a fact.

However, this mixing of value systems does raise some important ethical issues. Allen Bergin (1980, 1991) pointed out that at least three sets of values are present in a therapy context: those of the therapist, those of the client, and those of the community or society in which they live. The role of values in the therapy process becomes an ethical issue when these different value orientations are discrepant. There is substantial empirical evidence that therapists' ratings of client improvement were correlated positively with clients' assimilation of the therapists' values. In other words, therapists seem to perceive clients as having changed for the better when the client's values become more like those of the therapist (e.g., Arizmendi, Beutler, Shanfield, Crago, & Hagaman, 1985; Beutler, Pollack, & Jobe, 1978; Kelly & Strupp, 1992; Richards & Davison, 1989). Although the empirical evidence regarding the tendency of clients to conform with their therapist by assimilating the therapist's values is somewhat contradictory, clients' values frequently do undergo significant change during the process of therapy (Kelly & Strupp, 1992; Schwehn & Schau, 1990). Thus, it is not unreasonable to suppose that some clients will be influenced by the values of their therapist as they work on clarifying their personal value system. Therapists might influence the values of their clients, although value imposition is not an explicit goal of therapy (Beutler et al., 1978; Schwehn & Schau, 1990).

Bergin focused on the issue of religious beliefs to illustrate this point. He asserted that psychotherapists are less religious than the general population (Bergin, 1980).

As the therapeutic relationship develops, the approach to understanding emotional conflicts and resolving behavioral problems taken by a nonreligious therapist and a religious client may very well differ because their perspectives would be a reflection of their personal value systems. For example, suppose a client who is a very devout religious believer is being treated for marital dissatisfaction by a psychologist who is an atheist. Bergin (1980) argued that the differences in the two individuals' values will necessarily affect the course of the therapy, even if the therapist never explicitly states her atheistic orientation. The psychologist might conceptualize her client's marital dissatisfaction and depression as an indication that he should consider obtaining a divorce. If the client responds that, as a Roman Catholic, divorce is out of the question, the psychologist might be inclined to view his difficulties as a function of personal rigidity or a punishing superego. The fundamental difference in value orientations could not help but come into play in a variety of ways. Some might be obvious, but others could be quite subtle. If the therapist is not a Roman Catholic, she now has an ethical obligation to become more familiar with her client's value system in order to understand his perspective better and work with him more effectively (ACA, 1997, A.2.b; APA, 1992, 1.08).

Bergin's (1980, 1991) concern was that clients tend to be influenced very strongly by their therapists, who are not only authority figures, but models of effective living. Therefore, when clients perceive a discrepancy between their thinking and that of their therapist, they might tend to modify their value position to bring it more in line with the "correct" perspective expressed by their therapist. In the example, the client might begin to question his religious values because the psychologist obviously thinks that divorce *is* an option for unhappily married people today.

Bergin is not asserting that the client's issues will be resolved more effectively within one value perspective or the other. He argues that therapists run the risk of subverting clients' value systems and imposing their own values on clients in their conduct of therapy. Such activity is profoundly disrespectful of clients' autonomy as individuals, which mental health professionals profess to believe in so strongly.

Bergin makes an excellent point. It certainly is ethically inappropriate for therapists to impose their values on clients, no matter how unintentionally (ACA, 1997, A.4.b; APA, 1992, 1.09). The issue then becomes, if value perspectives are indeed ubiquitous in therapy, how therapists can prevent or minimize the potential for their clients' value systems to be subtly influenced during the course of therapy. Unfortunately, there is no simple answer to such a complex issue.

Bergin suggested that therapists disclose their value orientation to potential clients as part of the informed consent process prior to beginning therapy, so that clients can make an informed choice of a therapist they will feel comfortable with (Bergin, 1980; Bergin, Payne, & Richards, 1996). However, this solution requires, first, that therapists increase their awareness of what their values are. Second, therapists need to determine what they should disclose to clients concerning their personal values. Both of these tasks will be quite difficult unless future therapists receive specific instruction in such matters in psychology and counseling training programs (Grimm, 1994).

Clearly, clients should not be subjected to long discourses regarding the therapist's beliefs, particularly those that are not directly relevant to the client's concerns (Tillman, 1998). In addition, if clients are indeed vulnerable to being unduly influenced by the therapist's values, it might be unwise to encourage such modeling by revealing too many of the therapist's beliefs. Nevertheless, a limited discussion of the therapist's values may be appropriate when the therapist can identify areas of potential value conflict based on information provided by the client during the intake process. In fact, as discussed earlier in this chapter, a therapist should talk with clients about her conceptualization of therapy and of the client's presenting problem prior to beginning therapy. This information should provide clients with a reasonable understanding of what they are likely to experience if they proceed with the therapy.

It would be extremely important for the therapist to make certain that her client understands that she is presenting her beliefs about certain issues to the client because they are relevant to concerns the client raised and that she is in no way suggesting that her beliefs are correct, or "scientific," or better in any way than the viewpoint of the client (Tillman, 1998). On the contrary, she should explain that mental health professionals have great respect for individual differences and people's right to choose their own values and beliefs. The therapist would need to emphasize repeatedly that she simply wants to make sure that they both understand the differences in their viewpoints so that the client can make an informed choice about whether to proceed with therapy with her. In taking such action, the therapist is modeling genuineness and respect for the autonomy of the client (Cohen & Cohen, 1999).

The discussion of values during the informed consent process, if deemed appropriate by the therapist, certainly should not be the end of the therapist's concern for the issue of value imposition. Therapists must continue to be sensitive to the potential for value conflict in each issue that arises in the therapeutic process. Value-related discussions could be initiated by therapists, as needed, to make certain that they do not impose their personal values on clients. Therapists cannot possibly know in advance which personal values might turn out to be relevant to the issues that come up during the course of therapy. As in all ethical matters, sensitivity to, and respect for, the client's welfare are key components of professional, competent practice. Vachon and Agresti (1992) have proposed a training model to assist therapists in clarifying their personal and professional values and better managing the role of values in the course of therapy. Their model is presented in the discussion of clinical supervision and training in Chapter 10.

The counterargument that therapists might decrease the likelihood of therapeutic success by revealing their religious values to clients has been raised by Zeiger and Lewis (1998). They assert that even religious clients do not generally approach psychotherapy with the expectation that it will involve substantial discussion of religious issues. Of course, there are exceptions, such as when clients seek out Christian counselors to address life problems. If a therapist initiates discussion of her religious values, clients' reactions would be extremely unpredictable. Quite possibly, the discussion of religious values on the part of the therapist could introduce powerful transferential and countertransferential complications into the therapeutic relationship (Tillman, 1998). Obviously, transferential and countertransferential issues will arise in the absence of any discussion of religious values, but Zeiger and Lewis (1998) question the wisdom of deliberately introducing such a powerful variable into the already complicated therapist-client relationship when, in their view, it is not necessary to do so.

---

**Case Example 7.22**

*A humanistically oriented, but not traditionally religious, therapist is assigned an inpatient client who asks the therapist to pray with her during a session for relief from her depression and despair.*
*What should the therapist do?*

---

Although Bergin (1980, 1991) argues that a therapist's religious values need to be disclosed so that the client can make an informed decision regarding whether to pursue therapy with someone whose religious beliefs are similar or dissimilar to his own, Zeiger and Lewis (1998) point out that the initial similarity of therapist and client values has not been demonstrated to be a valuable predictor of therapeutic outcome. Rather, it is the moderate convergence of their values over the course of therapy that is related to therapeutic success (Kelly & Strupp, 1992). Thus, a high level of value similarity at the outset of therapy may actually impede the development of a successful therapeutic process. An important benefit of therapy is learning new ways of thinking about and responding to situations, which is more likely to occur when the perspectives of client and therapist differ. There is generally little risk that a therapist-client dyad will lack value differences at the outset of therapy, unless the process is manipulated through the disclosure of the therapist's religious values.

On the other hand, if initial value dissimilarity is useful in therapy, therapists could be encouraged to disclose their religious values to make certain that a desirable degree of dissimilarity exists between the values of the therapist and client (Zeiger & Lewis, 1998). However, this approach of matching therapists and clients would make the manipulation of the client's values an explicit therapeutic goal, which would reflect an ethically unacceptable lack of respect for the client's values and autonomy. Zeiger and Lewis (1998) conclude that a therapist should not disclose his religious beliefs and values to clients in order to avoid imposing his values on clients and subverting their autonomy.

A final difficult issue concerning the role of a therapist's personal values in therapy is whether a client might present values or goals that so directly contradict the values of the therapist that he would feel he cannot treat the client effectively. For example, suppose a therapist is very strongly opposed to abortion on religious grounds. What should he do if a client comes in for an intake interview and reveals that she is trying to decide whether or not to terminate an unwanted pregnancy? Therapists are never obliged as professionals to behave in a manner that violates their personal moral principles. If a therapist were to deny his moral beliefs in an attempt to maintain a nonjudgmental stance in therapy, he would be behaving like an ethical relativist, which, as discussed in Chapter 4, is not an acceptable ethical position for a mental health professional (Bergin et al., 1996). However, the therapist cannot agree to work with the client, while hoping to convince her not to terminate the pregnancy, because intentionally attempting to alter the value perspective of a client would demonstrate an unethical lack of respect for the autonomy of the client. If the therapist realizes he cannot view the client's situation objectively and assist her effectively due to the depth of his personal moral convictions concerning abortion, he should show appropriate respect for her autonomy by arranging a referral to another therapist. However, what if the therapist worked in a rural area and referral were not a realistic option? Would this situation affect his duty to help the woman? It would certainly intensify the conflict between his concern for the welfare of the woman and her child and his desire not to subvert her autonomy and personal values. In such a circumstance, he might benefit from using the model of ethical decision making to devise a course of action that can serve both duties.

---

**Case Example 7.23**

*A couple participating in marital therapy tell the therapist that they have an "open" marriage, with each of them free to develop sexual relationships with other people. They perceive this to be a very positive aspect of their marriage. The therapist believes that their lack of a complete commitment to the marriage, which would involve sexual fidelity to each other, is a major problem. However, she wonders whether her perspective is clouded by her personal values concerning marriage.*

---

## TERMINATION

There are three reasons to end a therapy relationship through termination or referral (ACA, 1997, A.11; APA, 1992, 4.09). First, if the client no longer requires therapy because the issues that were troubling her have been resolved, the therapy has reached a successful conclusion. Second, if the client is no longer deriving any benefit from therapy, but is perhaps willing to continue due to dependency on the therapist, termination is indicated. If the therapist believes that his client might make better progress with another therapist, the possibility of a referral should be discussed. Third, clients are sometimes harmed by therapy (Lambert & Bergin, 1994). For example, an avoidant client might find the communication and intimacy demands of therapy unbearable. When the therapist believes that continuing the therapy relationship could be harmful to the client, the issue of termination or referral should definitely be addressed.

A termination or referral should not be done precipitously. When the issue of termination is raised by the therapist or client, the matter should be discussed thoroughly and the reasons for the proposed termination should be clear to both parties. Ethical therapists do not abandon clients (ACA, 1997, A.11.a; APA, 1992, 4.09[a]). In dealing with termination and referral, therapists must be careful not to let factors other than the best interest of the client influence their decision making. Earlier in this chapter, the possibility that a financial conflict of interest could affect a therapist's thinking about termination was discussed. On the other hand, a conflict of interest of a different sort could also be said to exist when a therapist is tempted to terminate prematurely with a client that he does not like personally. Therapists should carefully evaluate their motivations for considering termination in order to avoid potentially harming a client.

---

**Case Example 7.24**

*A client's insurance runs out, and he is no longer able to pay the full fee for sessions. The client is stable, but wants to continue the sessions to more fully address historical issues from his childhood. The therapist cannot afford to have him pay the greatly reduced fee for a regular weekly time slot due to overhead costs associated with her practice. The therapist and client agree that he can continue to attend sessions on a "standby" basis; that is, he can take the time slots of vacationing clients or clients who cancel appointments. He agrees to this arrangement in spite of the fact that, on some occasions, he might have as little as 24 hours notice of the availability of an appointment time. Of course, he can decline the opportunity for an appointment if it does not fit his schedule.*

*Is this an ethically appropriate therapy arrangement?*

---

Following the termination of a therapeutic relationship, therapists are ethically obligated to avoid pursuing any other sort of relationship with a former client because of the potential for the client to be harmed or exploited in a multiple relationship. Avoiding any sort of posttherapy relationship also serves the interests of clients because it preserves the possibility that they can resume therapy at some point in the future, should the need arise. Finally, therapists naturally wonder how their former clients' lives have progressed after therapy, but it is inappropriate for a therapist to contact a former client to find out.

## PRACTICE CASE INVOLVING THE MODEL OF ETHICAL DECISION MAKING

APA is currently involved in lobbying for licensed clinical psychologists to have the legal privilege to write prescriptions for certain medications used in the treatment of mental disorders (e.g., antidepressants). The American Medical Association opposes this initiative, arguing that psychologists are not trained as physicians and, therefore, cannot possibly be construed as being competent to dispense medications. APA has responded that doctoral-level training programs in clinical psychology could be redesigned to provide training that would make psychologists competent to provide such services. Those already licensed who desire to provide such services would be involved in a comprehensive continuing education program leading up to certification to prescribe. Psychologists favoring the initiative also argue that it would provide better continuity of care for clients.

Is this APA initiative ethically appropriate?

## SUMMARY

The ethical issues that arise inevitably in therapy are so numerous and complex that mental health professionals must possess the ability to reason ethically if they are to manage their responsibilities competently. During the informed consent process at the outset of therapy, therapists must address all relevant issues so that clients do not encounter any surprises during therapy. In language understandable to the client, the therapist must explain issues such as the length and duration of treatment, limits of confidentiality, fee arrangements, and the treatment plan to be implemented. If a client is legally incompetent to consent to treatment, a legally authorized person must provide consent. The assent of such a client must also be obtained. Additional informed consent issues in group, marital, and family therapy were discussed.

Therapists' respect for the autonomy and personhood of clients is demonstrated in the importance placed on confidentiality as an essential part of the therapeutic relationship. Providing clients with access to their treatment records is also done out of respect for clients' autonomy. Findings indicate that clients actually may benefit from viewing their records. Also, clients must know what is in their record before they can consent to the therapist sharing it with another professional. Therapists should be very careful to maintain and dispose of treatment records in a manner that will not endanger clients' confidentiality.

Multiple relationships occur when a therapist engages in another professional or social relationship with a client before, during, or after their therapy relationship. These relationships are problematic because they can cause a professional's judgment to be clouded by considerations other than the best interests of the client. Multiple relationships involving bartering and improper sexual relationships with current and former clients are a major source of ethics complaints.

Although therapists inevitably influence the thinking and behavior of their clients, the use of coercion is generally inappropriate. Therapists should be sensitive to the potential for their personal values to unduly influence clients during the course of therapy. Bergin (1980, 1991) pointed out the danger of a therapist subverting her clients' autonomy by subtly imposing her religious values in therapy. This controversial problem is discussed, along with proposed solutions.

Therapy should be terminated when it is apparent that a client has resolved her problem, is no longer benefiting significantly from therapy, or is actually being harmed by the therapy. Referral is the appropriate course of action if a client requires treatment but may derive greater benefit from working with a different therapist.

# 8 Professional Practice Within Organizational and Specialized Settings

Most mental health professionals become employees of organizations, rather than practicing completely independently. Psychologists and counselors work in hospitals, universities, clinics, penal institutions, corporations, schools, Health Maintenance Organizations (HMOs), and many other settings. In all of these professional contexts, mental health professionals are part of a larger organization (e.g., a company, hospital, state government, federal government). Working for an organization adds still another set of ethical considerations for mental health professionals because they now have professional obligations to the organization that employs them *and* to the clients or consumers they serve. This chapter will examine some of the organizations employing therapists and ways of dealing with the ethical issues and conflicts that can arise in these professional contexts. Special ethical issues involved in the treatment of children will also be addressed.

## WORKING WITHIN AN ORGANIZATION

When most people take a job with a company, institution, or government agency, they take on a straightforward set of responsibilities as an employee of the organization. However, the situation is somewhat more complex for a psychologist, counselor, or other mental health professional. These individuals already accepted a set of professional duties (e.g., ACA *Code of Ethics*) when they chose to work in their profession. In accepting a position within an organization, they assume a second set of obligations, prescribed by the employment policies and values of the organization. Generally, this dual role (e.g., psychologist and HMO employee) does not create an ethical problem for the professional. However, as discussed earlier, any situation involving multiple duties or obligations creates the potential for conflict.

In any organizational setting, the most fundamental ethical point for mental health professionals to remember is that the ethical principles and standards of their profession take precedence over their employer's regulations and policies when the two conflict. In a situation involving an apparent conflict, the professional should use the model of ethical decision making in an attempt to devise a solution that is consistent with the employer's guidelines and her ethical duties as a professional. If the outcome of her analysis indicates that the employer's policy genuinely conflicts with her ethical obligations, she would inform the relevant parties of her primary obligation to the ethical principles of her profession. She should not take on a holier-than-thou stance toward a supervisor or organization; rather, she should work with the organization, educating policy makers about potentially unethical institutional policies and attempting to modify and improve them. In some instances, the organization's values or policies may be so inconsistent with a professional's ethical duties that she cannot continue working there.

---

**Case Example 8.1**

*A therapist working in the counseling center of a Roman Catholic college is treating an adult female student who reveals that she is pregnant as the result of a date rape. She is extremely distraught and wants his help in obtaining information about abortion services. He is not personally uncomfortable about providing the information, but he knows that abortion is radically inconsistent with the values of the institution.*

*Should he discuss abortion with her as one of her alternatives?*

---

## CONFLICT OF INTEREST

Conflicts of interest occur when the objectivity of a professional's judgment is affected by personal interest in a situation, usually as the result of a multiple relationship. For example, a clinician who is an employee of a psychiatric inpatient facility has an outpatient practice as well. An outpatient client being seen by the clinician for depression becomes much worse and is threatening suicide. The clinician knows of a psychiatric hospital that specializes in the cognitive-behavioral treatment of depression, but she advises the client to enter the facility that she works for because it will enable them to continue their therapeutic relationship. Is this recommendation in the client's best interest, or is it motivated, at least in part, by the clinician's desire to generate business for the facility that employs her and/or to retain the client for outpatient treatment following his hospitalization?

A different type of conflict of interest can develop when a professional is asked to evaluate the effectiveness of a program offered by the agency that employs him (Hammond, 1998). For example, a clinician is currently serving as a consultant to a local Head Start facility when he is asked to conduct an evaluation of their Head Start program. This evaluation must be completed in order for the facility to qualify for continued federal funding. Even if the clinician has the competence in design, analysis, and report writing required for the evaluation, his vested interest in the outcome of the evaluation makes the arrangement ethically questionable (Hammond, 1998). First, he undoubtedly helped to structure at least some of the facility's programs. Second, the continuation of his contract as a consultant might be affected by the outcome of the evaluation; if the facility were to lose funding or if he were judged to have conducted a poor evaluation, he would likely not be retained. This situation involves an apparent conflict of interest because the consulting clinician is not in the best position to conduct an objective, unbiased evaluation of the Head Start program. How the evaluation turns out could impact his life directly. A competent evaluator who has no financial or personal stake in the outcome would be a much better choice to conduct the evaluation. In this situation, the clinician is obligated to point out this conflict of interest to the Head Start director and inform her that it is unethical for him to conduct the evaluation himself.

Professionals must be sensitive to the possibility of a conflict of interest, particularly when they are involved in multiple professional roles. When a situation does involve a conflict of interest, or has the potential to give rise to such a conflict, mental health professionals should clarify their roles with all parties concerned (APA, 1992, 1.17[b]). Specifically, they should inform the client, supervisor, student, or anyone else affected directly by the situation about the conflict and explain the limits they must place on their activity within the organization to avoid engaging in an unprofessional conflict of interest.

As in other instances discussed in this book, professionals should also avoid the appearance of conflicts of interest. If a situation arises that could be perceived by other professionals or the public as involving a conflict of interest, the professional should avoid becoming enmeshed in the situation, even if it technically does not involve a conflict.

---

**Case Example 8.2**

*A counselor frequently refers clients to a psychiatrist, who happens to be her husband, for medication consultations. She does not have the same last name as her husband, and she generally does not mention that he is her spouse because she does not want clients to feel pressured to accept the referral. She refers clients to him because she thinks he is the most competent psychiatrist in the local area.*

*Is the counselor behaving appropriately?*

---

## WORKING IN A PSYCHIATRIC HOSPITAL

Many therapists work with inpatients in hospitals. Inpatient therapy involves a number of special ethical issues, in addition to the ones discussed in the previous chapter. The dominant philosophy in psychiatric hospitals tends to be the *medical model,* which is the assumption that diagnosable conditions are a function of underlying, internal pathology or illnesses (Carson, Butcher, & Mineka, 2000). The dominance of biological explanations in psychiatric hospitals is not surprising, given that hospitals are medical facilities managed by psychiatrists. One implication of this medical philosophy is that psychiatric practitioners tend to behave in a paternalistic manner toward clients, feeling that clients cannot understand (nor do they need to understand) the complex explanations associated with their conditions. Clients just need to follow appropriate medical advice. A therapist must avoid letting this organizational culture of psychiatric institutions alter her perspective regarding her professional duties to clients. Respect for clients' autonomy and right to self-determination is particularly important in such settings. A mental health professional has a duty to argue for her clients if she believes that their rights are being infringed upon unreasonably.

## INFORMED CONSENT AND CONFIDENTIALITY

Informed consent for treatment is just as important in inpatient settings as it is in outpatient settings. Informed consent procedures for treatment are the same as those discussed in the previous chapter, with a few additions. First, inpatient clients might not be receiving treatment voluntarily. Their family might have pressured them to enter the hospital, or they might have been involuntarily committed to receive inpatient treatment.[25] Therapists must make certain that their clients, including those admitted involuntarily to the hospital, understand the voluntary nature of therapy and their right to refuse to participate.

---

### CASE EXAMPLE 8.3

*A voluntary inpatient client on a dual diagnosis unit (for clients diagnosed with both a mental disorder and substance abuse disorder) requests discharge. The clinical psychologist treating him does not feel that he is ready for discharge. She talks with the client for nearly two hours, trying to convince him that he needs further treatment before he will be ready to face the world again without resuming his substance abuse behavior. Finally, the client relents and agrees to stay.*

*Did the psychologist behave appropriately?*

---

Confidentiality issues are also more complex in inpatient settings. In a psychiatric hospital, the therapist will not be the only professional involved in a client's treatment. Psychiatrists, social workers, and nursing staff will also provide treatment and monitor the client's progress. As a result, information must be shared with others involved in the client's treatment; failure to provide the treatment team with relevant information obtained in therapy sessions will restrict the effectiveness of the client's treatment. The other team members are also professionals, so therapists should trust that they will behave in a competent, professional manner by protecting the client's confidentiality (ACA, 1997, B.1.i; APA, 1992, 1.20[b], 5.05[a]). During the informed consent process, therapists must, of course, inform clients that the treatment team exists and that information regarding the client will be shared with other team members. The client should be assured that the other members of the treatment team are also professionally obligated to protect his confidentiality.

If a therapist becomes aware of a member of the treatment team disclosing confidential information to anyone not directly involved in the client's treatment, he has an ethical duty to address the breach of confidentiality with the staff member and, if necessary, with the staff member's supervisor. In addition, members of the treatment team do not need to be informed of everything about a client's childhood history, family, sex life, marital history, etc., in order to provide effective treatment. Therapists should only share information in team meetings or in the client's record that is directly relevant to the client's treatment. For example, the fact that the client had been arrested for shoplifting as an adolescent might not be relevant to his treatment for depression as an adult, whereas his report of suicidal ideation definitely needs to be brought to the treatment team's attention.

There are additional federal guidelines governing the confidentiality of information in alcohol and drug abuse treatment programs. Therapists working in a facility of that type should become familiar with these rules, which generally place tighter restrictions on the release of treatment information. Even the names of clients pursuing treatment in such a facility cannot be revealed because, unlike admission to a medical or psychiatric hospital, entering a substance abuse treatment facility specifies the nature of clients' diagnoses (Arthur & Swanson, 1993).

## UTILIZATION REVIEW

Psychiatric hospitals frequently receive reimbursement from insurance companies, managed care organizations, and state and federal government agencies based on a client's diagnosis. For example, a health insurance provider might reimburse a hospital for 28 days of treatment if a client is diagnosed with Alcohol Dependence. According to this formula, if the client is discharged prior to the 28-day limit, the hospital comes out ahead financially. If a longer hospitalization is required to provide effective treatment, the hospital receives little or no additional reimbursement. Utilization review, then, is the process by which treatment facilities and health insurers monitor whether the length of a client's stay in a hospital is consistent with his diagnosis. This type of system puts considerable pressure on hospitals, and, in turn, mental health professionals, to complete treatment and discharge the client within a specified time limit. However, as always, the primary consideration for a mental health professional is the best interest of her client. A therapist must argue assertively for her clients if further treatment is clinically indicated when their diagnosis-related length of stay has been exhausted. She must be able to present documented clinical evidence to support her assertion. The administrative authorities of the hospital might be particularly receptive to her argument if she points out the litigation risk associated with discharging a client in need of continued treatment (e.g., a potential suicide risk).

---

**Case Example 8.4**

*A client suffering from chronic Alcohol Dependence and Borderline Personality Disorder is receiving treatment on an inpatient alcoholism treatment unit. Her psychologist lists her primary diagnosis as Borderline Personality Disorder, even though personality disorders are not the focus of treatment on the unit, because this diagnosis will permit her to stay longer on the unit for treatment. Her psychologist believes that it is a professional's duty to "work the system" whenever doing so serves the best interests of a client.*

---

## COERCION AND TREATMENT

Some hospitals use token economies and other operant conditioning programs to improve clients' self-care skills (e.g., on wards with long-term clients suffering from the schizophrenias) and to give clients a degree of responsibility for maintenance of their environment. Clients, particularly those who were admitted involuntarily, must be informed that participation in these programs is voluntary.[26] In addition, mental health professionals must ensure that only privileges (e.g., special snacks, additional trips off the ward) are used as reinforcers. Basic rights of hospital clients, such as regular meals, the ability to receive mail, and the right to the least restrictive treatment setting, cannot be withheld. If hospitalized clients are asked to do work normally performed by paid employees (e.g., cleaning or painting the ward) as part of a rehabilitation program, they should be paid for the work just like regular employees. Hospitals cannot exploit clients.

## MANAGED CARE PRACTICE

Most private insurance and some state-funded programs (e.g., Oregon Health Plan for Medicaid recipients) involve some form of managed care today. The goal of managed care organizations (MCOs) is to provide medical and mental health benefits for their customers in the most cost-effective manner possible (Ambrose, 1997). There are a variety of MCO formats; among the most common are Health Maintenance Organizations (HMOs), Preferred Provider Organizations (PPOs), and Employee Assistance Programs (EAPs). Each MCO is organized somewhat differently, with different allowable services and reimbursement schemes. Some programs only allow clients to use health care providers who are part of the managed care network, while some allow clients to use non-network providers, but at a lower rate of reimbursement. Also, many MCOs require a referral from a client's primary care physician or pre-approval through a separate review system before a client can receive behavioral or mental health treatment. What these different types of MCOs all have in common is that financial considerations play a greater role in decisions about treatment. Case management is no longer the exclusive province of treatment providers; rather, financial managers, focusing on cost containment, are involved actively in decisions about the provision and continuation of treatment services (Butcher, 1997a).

The increased focus on accountability, making sure that the nation's limited health care resources are expended effectively for needed and effective treatment, is a very positive aspect of managed care systems (Butcher, 1997a). However, many mental health professionals are extremely concerned about the ethicality of MCOs. These professionals believe that decisions regarding a client's treatment needs should be made by people who understand the client's problems and circumstances and put the client's best interest before economic considerations. This ethical concern has frequently put mental health professionals at odds with MCOs. Therapist-providers often feel like their professional work is being scrutinized by MCO case managers, who are constantly looking over their shoulders (Butcher, 1997a). However, professionals need to recognize that managed care is likely to exist for a long time and that viewing MCOs as enemies does not serve anyone's needs, including those of clients (Ambrose, 1997).

Therapist-providers can learn how to work within managed care systems to obtain needed services for clients in a cost-effective manner. This strategy will serve the needs of clients, providers, and MCOs. First, therapist-providers need to become competent in brief forms of therapy. Second, prior to initiating service, they should carefully research what a client's program will allow. Finally, therapist-providers should become proficient advocates for their clients by making a concise, reasonable case to demonstrate how providing needed services can benefit both clients and the organization (Ambrose, 1997). Therapist-providers may need to educate MCO case managers regarding the benefits to the organization and its clients of providing additional mental health services. For example, after spending ten sessions working to modify a client's inappropriate, explosive interpersonal behaviors, a follow-up session or two over the next few months is vitally important to make certain that the new skills are being employed effectively. An MCO that fails to recognize this need for follow-up is operating in a penny-wise, pound-foolish manner. The value of the ten sessions of treatment is seriously threatened by the MCO's lack of understanding of the behavior modification process. The MCO would be wasting its money because of its poor conceptualization of behavior therapy. Therapy certainly should not drag on interminably, but clients should not be denied a chance to complete their treatment.

Providing mental health services for an MCO requires that therapist-providers sharpen their assessment skills, so they can distinguish between clients who can benefit substantially from short-term treatment and those in need of longer-term care. Because diagnosis generally determines access to treatment in MCOs, therapist-providers must be competent diagnosticians and avoid the temptation to manipulate a client's diagnosis in order to provide him with the treatment he needs. For example, a therapist-provider might be tempted to misdiagnose a client suffering from a complex Adjustment Disorder with Depressed Mood as a case of Major Depression because the latter diagnosis will provide a larger allotment of treatment sessions. However, the ethical end of providing adequate treatment for the client does not justify the use of unethical means (i.e., deliberate falsification of treatment records). Therapist-providers have a professional obligation to their MCO to conduct themselves with integrity (ACA, 1997, C.5.c; APA, 1992, 1.06, 2.01[b]). (Issues pertaining to diagnosis are discussed more thoroughly in the next chapter.)

Mental health professionals working in HMOs must make certain that information they provide is not misunderstood or misapplied by other providers within the organization. For example, HMOs may use screening assessment techniques (e.g., psychological testing) for early detection of problems so that a primary care physician can make a timely referral for the client. Providing physicians with reports summarizing a client's emotional issues could contribute to the misdiagnosis of the client's physical symptoms as emotionally based (e.g., somatization). In fact, the more psychological information a physician receives, the greater his tendency might be to attribute symptoms to psychological issues (Belar, 1997). Obviously, psychological screening could harm such a client. The use of screening procedures and the information provided to primary care physicians must be weighed very carefully by mental health professionals. Mental health providers should consult directly with primary care physicians or provide continuing education workshops for them to reduce the likelihood that psychological assessment information will be misinterpreted.

When a therapist-provider is treating both network and non-network clients, who receive different levels of reimbursement, she is obligated not to vary the care and attention provided to the two groups of clients. A therapist's agreement to accept smaller fees from network clients is no justification for treating them differently than any other clients. For example, a therapist is ethically obligated to provide additional sessions for a network client if the sessions are needed to address the client's problems adequately, regardless of how much the therapist is being compensated for the treatment and regardless of whether a higher fee client is interested in initiating therapy during the time slot currently occupied by the network client.

## INFORMED CONSENT AND CONFIDENTIALITY

Therapist-providers in an MCO have informed consent obligations to both the organization employing them and to their clients. They need to clarify what their professional duties to the MCO are (e.g., to provide treatment summaries for each group of three sessions) and make certain that their clients are aware of these duties. Therapist-providers must also make sure that the MCO is, in turn, informed of their ethical duties to clients (Arthur & Swanson, 1993).

Prior to the initiation of therapy, providers should also inform clients about the permitted duration of treatment, the availability of alternative treatments, and the limits of client confidentiality. In addition to the limitations on confidentiality discussed in the previous chapter, issues that might arise in providing treatment for an MCO include the use of diagnostic and other information from a client's records in determining his need for treatment, the client's right to appeal decisions affecting access to treatment, and the types of information shared within the MCO system and with employers (and the potential impact of disclosures to employers). When providing services for an MCO, therapists are best served never to guarantee that any treatment information will be kept absolutely confidential.

Utilization reviews to monitor the need for continued treatment are part of any managed care setting. Therapist-providers should make certain that clients understand that the release of information for this purpose will be necessary in order for them to be treated in this setting. However, therapists should obtain a client's informed consent before releasing any information to utilization reviewers.

---

### Case Example 8.5

*A male high school teacher is referred through an EAP because, recently, he has frequently been unprepared for his classes. His principal is concerned because he has been a very effective teacher in the past. The client asks his therapist not to reveal the fact that he had a homosexual experience with another teacher at work that has caused him to become very anxious and confused about his sexual orientation. The therapist knows that revealing this information could cause the teacher to be fired, but it is very likely the reason he has been having so many difficulties with preparation for class.*

*What should the therapist do?*

*Would it affect the therapist's decision if the client had also mentioned having fantasies about some of the boys in his classes? Though he said he would never act on such ideas, the client has wondered about which boys might be receptive to sexual advances.*

---

## Multiple Relationships

Clients are very likely to view therapists working for an MCO as part of the system; therefore, therapist-providers must strive to establish that their primary concern is the client's welfare. To succeed in this task, the statement must be true. Providers must be very careful not to get caught up in any reward or reinforcement program provided by the MCO for containing client costs. The limited resources available within an MCO system encourage everyone involved (e.g., case managers, providers) to focus on utilitarian considerations in determining how benefits are to be rationed out to clients. Nevertheless, mental health professionals cannot lose sight of the Kantian basis for respecting the autonomy and needs of each individual client.

When health care providers work for an MCO, the potential for conflict between organizational profit and the best interest of clients always exists. Therapist-providers must bear in mind that they have an ethical duty to work within the organizations to make certain that clients' needs are met. Suppose a psychologist working for an MCO conducts an assessment that indicates the strong possibility of neurological impairment in a 35-year-old woman diagnosed with Major Depression. The psychologist recommends that the woman be referred for a neurological assessment. Her primary care physician makes the referral, but treatment review administrators refuse to approve the referral and request further information from the clinician. The psychologist speaks with an administrator and reiterates the justification for the referral stated in the assessment report, emphasizing that failure to obtain the assessment could be detrimental to the client's health. The psychologist is notified a week later that the referral has been disapproved again. The psychologist, genuinely believing that the referral is in the best interest of the client, has an ethical obligation to continue to advocate on the client's behalf in writing and to remind the managed care organization of its duty to provide services necessary to meet the needs of its clients. Even if the organization ultimately decides to drop the clinician as a service provider, the clinician's main responsibility is to her client. Mental health professionals must advocate for organizational change when they recognize that clients are being treated unjustly.

A final issue concerning a therapist's duties when working for an MCO is termination of treatment. When a client who is genuinely in need of continued treatment is denied additional coverage, her therapist cannot abandon her simply because an MCO case manager says that the maximum number of sessions has been reached. If advocating with the MCO on the client's behalf produces no results, the therapist is obligated to either provide services on a reduced fee or pro bono basis (ACA, 1997, A.10.d; APA, 1992, Principle F) or make an appropriate referral to another treatment provider (ACA, 1997, A.11; APA, 1992, 4.09).

## WORKING IN FORENSIC (CORRECTIONAL) SETTINGS

The number of convicts in the state and federal prison systems increased by 234% between 1985 and 1996. As a result, a growing number of mental health professionals provide assessment and treatment services as employees or consultants with the federal or state prison systems. They provide a range of assessment, diagnostic, and treatment services to convicts, many of whom suffer from mental disorders and/or mental retardation (Mobley, 1999). Crisis intervention services are also an important component of mental health services in prisons because the suicide rate among convicts is much higher than in the general population (Mobley, 1999).

Clients who are prison convicts are, quite literally, a captive population for mental health services. As a result, their participation in mental health treatment is never truly voluntary or completely free of coercion (Bell, 1999). This fact introduces a number of special ethical concerns for mental health professionals and obligations to protect the welfare of their clients. Correctional clinicians are also in a privileged position to contribute to the organizations in which they work by using their psychological expertise to foster the development of more humane and effective prison environments (Milan, Chin, & Nguyen, 1999).

## INFORMED CONSENT AND CONFIDENTIALITY

Although convicts are required to abide by the rules of the facility, mental health professionals are ethically bound to show the same respect for the rights of individual prisoners as for any other type of client. By demonstrating respect for the dignity of each convict as a person, mental health professionals may also be enhancing their therapeutic effectiveness: A convict is more likely to trust that these professionals are truly concerned with their welfare (Bell, 1999). For example, convicts entering a penal facility may be required to complete psychological testing, including intelligence and personality assessments. Although this testing is required, the clinician conducting the testing should nevertheless inform clients of the nature and purpose of the testing, the limits placed on the confidentiality of their interaction, the client's right to refuse testing (along with the consequences of such refusal), what, if any, feedback will be provided concerning the testing, and what use will be made of the results. The clinician should also attempt to answer any questions posed by the client.

Similarly, when conducting therapy with convicts, a therapist should make it clear that he is an employee of the institution and inform clients of the nature of the therapist-client relationship under those circumstances. Specifically, he should explain clients' rights to decline to participate, prison policies regarding the length and frequency of therapy sessions, the type of information included in their treatment record, and who will have access to their treatment record. Therapists working in prisons need to be aware of the combination of state and federal statutes affecting the privacy of client information so that they can inform clients about the extent of confidentiality in the relationship. The confidentiality of prison records is becoming more and more limited in many jurisdictions (Arthur & Swanson, 1993). In some settings, parole boards, mental health services, and others have relatively open access to the treatment records of convicts.

In group therapy settings, clinicians need to make clients aware of the possibility that other group members might reveal information to inmates outside the group. A discussion of group members' feelings about the importance of "respect" and their view of "snitching" can be helpful in clarifying confidentiality issues (Mobley, 1999). Another issue that should be addressed in both group and individual therapy is the implications of therapy participation in good conduct and parole reviews, to correct any misunderstandings clients might have developed.

---

**Case Example 8.6**

*A clinical psychologist working in a prison is told by an inmate client that another inmate has a knife and intends to stab the client's cell mate in retaliation for a previous altercation. The psychologist suggests that the client tell a correctional officer, but the client fears that word would get out that he had squealed on another inmate.*

*What, if anything, should the psychologist do?*

---

## GOAL SETTING

In working with convicts, therapists have the same concerns as with any other clients: promoting the self-determination and autonomy of clients and assisting them in resolving behavioral and emotional problems. An additional stated goal for incarcerated prisoners is rehabilitation, or developing the abilities needed to become productive members of society and avoid returning to prison (Mobley, 1999). Most clients receiving psychotherapy in prison are management problems (e.g., violent prisoners); prisoners with diagnosable mental disorders, identified upon admission and now receiving maintenance therapy; and participants in sex offender and substance abuse treatment programs. Within the limits imposed by the availability of mental health staff, convicts can also self-refer for therapy services (Mobley, 1999).

Therapists should communicate their professional purpose of helping clients deal with emotional problems, the prison environment, and reintroduction to society when their sentence is completed. Although therapy participation is not truly voluntary, as clinicians would like it to be, clients' autonomy in the situation can be maximized by involving them actively in establishing treatment goals. Although the goals should not be inconsistent with the rehabilitative goals of the penal system, they need not focus on making the client more manageable, or an easier "fit" in the system. Clients are much more likely to benefit from treatment if they are motivated to achieve the stated goals (Garfield, 1994).

---

**Case Example 8.7**

*An inmate requesting therapy is assigned to a male psychologist. In the initial interview, he tells the psychologist that he wants to address his long history of violence against women. He feels strongly that he can best accomplish this goal by working with the female colleague of the psychologist. The psychologist understands, and, to some extent, agrees with the client's reasoning, yet he wonders whether the request is a manipulation that could place his colleague at risk.*

*What should the psychologist do?*

---

## MULTIPLE RELATIONSHIPS

Mental health professionals working in prisons are employees of the correctional system; their function is to provide treatment services for prisoners. As such, therapists occupy an amorphous middle ground between corrections officers and inmates and are generally viewed with suspicion by both (Mobley, 1999). Avoiding drifting too far to one side or the other and becoming identified exclusively with one of these groups requires a very careful articulation of one's roles and responsibilities to all concerned parties (Mobley, 1999).

A mental health professional concerned with improving the prison system should be careful not to address this issue with her clients. Prison administrators will view such an employee as attempting to subvert the organization's structure and may retaliate against the clients with which the clinician is seen as having aligned herself (Mobley, 1999). Well-formulated ideas regarding positive changes in a prison's operations should be presented through the appropriate chain of command. Mental health professionals should utilize their training in devising effective, nonthreatening ways of proposing positive change.

Therapists working with prison populations are often interested in conducting research to increase society's understanding of both the causes of criminal behavior and the effects of incarceration. Prisoners are in great demand as research participants; in fact, this demand became so great that prison systems became inundated with requests from researchers. As a result, prison systems have greatly reduced researchers' access to prison populations. Therapists working in prisons should not take advantage of their position to encourage a client to participate in their research projects.

## COMPETENCE

With the majority of prisoners in the state and federal prison systems being African American or Hispanic, a therapist's understanding of cultural diversity is essential for competent provision of mental health services in a prison setting (Milan et al., 1999). Therapists cannot make assumptions about a client's cultural background based on his appearance. They must interview the client to learn about his cultural background and the extent to which he identifies with that culture (Milan et al., 1999). This process can help to prevent misdiagnosis and contribute to more effective treatment by forging a better understanding of the client's phenomenological experience.

Prison settings also require competence in other areas. Crisis intervention is an important area of competence therapists must develop to deal effectively with acts of violence and suicidal behavior (Mobley, 1999). In addition, a very large segment of prison populations is in need of substance abuse treatment (Milan et al., 1999). Providing competent substance abuse treatment requires expertise in substance abuse theory and the translation of this theory to the development of comprehensive treatment programs. Traditional rehabilitation strategies based on the disease model of addiction have proven relatively ineffective (Ford, 1996; Milan et al., 1999). In addition, competence in research is also needed to evaluate the effectiveness of substance abuse programs used in prison settings.

Therapists working in prison settings must learn to cope with the institutional environment and develop the skills needed to work effectively with a prison population. They must deal with the coercive reality of prison life without either withdrawing from offering needed services out of the desire to be noncoercive or becoming insensitive to the personhood of prisoners (Bell, 1999). Directive interventions have generally proven to be the most effective with prisoners. However, as discussed in the previous chapter, a therapist must learn how to be directive without diminishing the autonomy of the client (Mobley, 1999). Confrontation can be a very effective technique with convicts, but it is a skill that must be developed through supervised experience. Otherwise, confrontation can easily become little more than an unprofessional outlet for the therapist's own hostility.

Finally, therapist burnout is a significant threat to competence in prisons, as in other therapy contexts. Many therapists find it difficult to retain appropriate boundaries, becoming too close to their clients emotionally or maintaining too great a distance. Consequently, many therapists abandon prison work within a few years, leaving the prison system to cope with an ongoing shortage of trained forensic therapists (Mobley, 1999).

---

**Case Example 8.8**

*A counselor who has worked in prisons for 15 years feels that his younger, less experienced colleagues are constantly being manipulated by the inmates. He tells them that they need to always remain aware of the type of people they are dealing with: prison inmates, who would slit their own mother's throat to get something they want. His colleagues question how effective he can be as a therapist if he has so little regard for his clients. He says that he is very effective because he confronts them every time they attempt to manipulate him. Most of his clients want another therapist because all they want to do is manipulate.*

*Is there an ethical issue that needs to be addressed by the counselor and/or his colleagues? If so, how should it be addressed?*

---

## MENTAL HEALTH PROFESSIONALS IN THE MILITARY

Psychologists and other mental health professionals have been involved with the military throughout the past century. Many personnel testing methods were developed by psychologists working in the military during World War I. To this day, the armed forces remain the largest consumers of employment tests in the United States, both to screen applicants for military service and to assess job-related skills (Murphy & Davidshofer, 1994). Also, beginning in World War II, mental health professionals working in the military have become involved increasingly in the treatment of psychiatric disorders in military personnel in both peacetime and war.

An ethical tension has always existed for health care professionals working in support of the military. On the one hand, therapists working in the military are committed to supporting the goals of the armed forces and those of their individual clients. However, as mental health professionals, they also seek to support and protect the welfare of all humankind; they respect "the fundamental rights, dignity, and worth of all people" (APA, 1992, Principle D). In other words, they work to reduce human suffering.

Some ethicists have questioned whether the ethical concerns of mental health professionals are congruent with the goals of the military. They point out that there is nothing in the ethical codes of the mental health professions indicating that professionals are concerned with reducing the sufferings of Americans only or that national interests may take precedence over professionals' concern for the welfare of all people (Summers, 1992).

---

**Case Example 8.9**

*A clinical psychologist in the U.S. Army treated soldiers during the Vietnam conflict for combat-related stress disorders. At field hospitals near combat areas, he would assess a soldier's condition initially to determine whether the soldier might potentially regain his fitness for duty with treatment. The psychologist treated those who had the potential to function again as soldiers. The goal of this treatment was to enable soldiers to return to combat.*

*Throughout that period, and ever since, he has questioned whether his role as a facilitator of war and possibly the death of his clients was ethically appropriate for a psychologist.*

---

## MULTIPLE RELATIONSHIPS

The set of dual obligations faced by mental health professionals working in the military can be particularly difficult to clarify and resolve (Hines, Ader, Chang, & Rundell, 1998). Many clinicians working for the military are actually active duty military personnel. These mental health professionals are clearly part of the military organization, usually as officers. As military officers, they have a duty to abide by their oath of military service and to obey the orders of superior officers. However, as mental health professionals, they also have obligations to their clients. Therefore, therapists in the military must constantly balance and weigh the relative importance of these two sets of duties. Suppose a psychologist working in the military was ordered by a superior officer to document that a soldier-client of hers was unfit for duty because of his depressive symptoms, though she did not consider him incapacitated. She would need to inform the officer that she has a professional duty as a psychologist to consider what is in the best interest of her client, even if it means not carrying out an order from a superior officer.

## INFORMED CONSENT AND CONFIDENTIALITY

Therapists working in the military, like therapists working in forensic settings, must emphasize the voluntary nature of psychotherapy participation. Even when military personnel are ordered to seek psychological services, the therapist should inform the client that he can refuse to participate in therapy if he chooses. The client should also be informed of the likely consequences of such a refusal. Furthermore, the client should be told that the therapist will be functioning in the relationship as a mental health professional, not as a superior officer. For example, the client would never be ordered to self-disclose; what he reveals in therapy is his autonomous choice. The voluntary aspect of treatment can be further augmented by having the client play an active role in determining the goals of the therapy.

The APA Ethics Committee published a statement on the complex issues regarding confidentiality for psychologists working in the military ("Ethics Committee Statement on Military," 1993). According to this statement, therapists must strive to preserve the confidentiality of their clients, as they would in any other setting. However, they must also abide by Department of Defense rules regarding access to information. The limited nature of confidentiality in a military setting must be explained to the client at the beginning of the therapy (ACA, 1997, B.1.c; APA, 1992, 5.01). Therapists should not guarantee the confidentiality of mental health records. (For this reason, therapists should think very carefully about what they write in a client's record.) When the disclosure of confidential material is required, therapists should present the information in a manner designed to minimize the intrusion into the client's privacy (ACA, 1997, B.1.f; APA, 1992, 5.03).

Confidentiality should not be maintained regarding any information that could significantly affect a client's performance of his military duties. This limitation on the confidentiality of therapy relationships in the military, resulting from a military therapist's dual role as an officer and a mental health professional, can be confusing. For example, when a senior officer requests information about a soldier-client's substance abuse history, the clinician needs to weigh the importance of that information to the client's functioning as a soldier and to the welfare of his unit versus her duty to protect the privacy of her client. Again, the clinician must endeavor to minimize the intrusion of such disclosures into a client's privacy because revealing information about a client, even regarding diagnosis, can result in negative consequences for the client's military career (Arthur & Swanson, 1993).

---

**Case Example 8.10**

*A military psychologist is treating the adolescent son of an Air Force pilot. The client had gotten in trouble with the military police for drinking at a party. He tells the psychologist that his father is the one with a serious alcohol problem. He says that most nights his father passes out from drinking and then has a drink to get going in the morning.*

*The psychologist tells her client that, if this is true, she has a duty as a military officer to report his father's problem to a superior officer. The client refuses to provide his consent for the psychologist to violate his confidentiality, saying that his father would "kill" him if he found out about it. Then, he says that he exaggerated his father's drinking so the psychologist would not make too big a deal out of his own party incident.*

*What should the psychologist do?*

---

## PSYCHOTHERAPY WITH CHILDREN

There are a number of special ethical considerations that arise when children are treated by mental health professionals. First, as minors, children generally cannot legally consent to participate in therapy. Therefore, although the child is usually recognized to be the therapist's client, the child's parent(s) or legal guardian is involved directly in the consent process. The parents may also be involved in the treatment as clients if the decision is made to conduct family therapy or if the therapist provides parenting skills training to the parents separately from the child's sessions. Second, the legal limits of confidentiality are dramatically different for children. Third, children are more susceptible than adult clients to being influenced by a therapist's values (Cottone & Tarvydas, 1998).

## INFORMED CONSENT WITH CHILDREN

Informed consent for therapy with a minor must be obtained from the child's parent or legal guardian. The parents should be provided with a complete explanation of all issues pertaining to informed consent (as discussed in the previous chapter), including a thorough consideration of the potential risks (e.g., interacting with an adult they do not know well can be frightening to young children) and benefits of treatment. Alternative methods of resolving the presenting problems should also be described.

One problem with parents providing consent for their child's treatment is that parents might tend to focus more on the potential benefits of treatment than on any risks to the child. When parents bring a child to a therapist to address a behavioral problem, they frequently just want their child "fixed" (i.e., cured). Analogue informed consent research indicates that the severity of the child's symptoms is much more salient to mothers than the balance of risks and benefits associated with treatment (Gustafson, McNamara, & Jensen, 1994).

Therapists should always discuss the purpose of the therapy (e.g., to reduce the level of conflict between the child and her parents) and the methods that will be used in the sessions with the child (e.g., talking awhile, followed by playing a game together that the child will bring). Because a child cannot legally consent to treatment, the voluntariness of the therapy should be maximized by involving her as much as her age and understanding will permit in treatment planning and goal setting. Involving the child actively in treatment planning may also increase her motivation to participate in therapy, thereby reducing the likelihood of premature termination and increasing the effectiveness of treatment (Kazdin, 1994). Children who do not want to participate in therapy should not be coerced to do so by therapists (Yanagida, 1998). Unless there is a compelling need for treatment and the child's reasons for refusing to be treated are clearly irrational, therapists should point out to parents the futility of conducting therapy with an unwilling client. The limits of confidentiality, which will be discussed below, must also be described very carefully to the child, in a manner appropriate to her age and understanding.

In many states, there are special circumstances in which children do have a legal right to consent to treatment (e.g., if counseling is sought for physical and/or sexual abuse, substance abuse, pregnancy, sexually transmitted diseases, or contraception). These laws vary from state to state, so therapists need to become familiar with the relevant statutes in the state in which they practice. The issue of when adolescents become sufficiently mature to provide self-consent has been a matter of considerable controversy. No clear, empirically validated operationalization of "competence" in children's capacity to provide informed consent has yet been established (Hart, 1991;

Shields & Johnson, 1992). In some states, adolescents can legally self-consent for psychological treatment. Also, emancipated minors are generally regarded as adults in terms of their ability to provide informed consent.

## CONFIDENTIALITY CONSIDERATIONS WITH CHILDREN

Confidentiality should be protected for child clients in the same manner as for adults. The major difference concerning the confidentiality of child clients is that children do not generally have the right to have information kept private from their parents. Statutes concerning the confidentiality of minors vary from state to state, so a therapist working with children must be aware of the laws governing his practice, as well as the policies of his employing organization. In Texas, for example, therapists are not required to inform parents that their child has initiated therapy for suicide prevention, substance abuse, or physical, sexual, or emotional abuse (Texas Family Code, 2000). However, the statute does not prevent the therapist from notifying and involving the parents without the child's consent; the matter is simply left to the therapist's judgment of what best serves the interests of the child.

---

**Case Example 8.11**

*A 16-year-old female client being treated for depression with her parents' consent tells her psychologist that she underwent an abortion without the per-mission of her parents shortly before beginning treatment. (She resides in a state that does not require parental notification or consent prior to an abortion for a 16 year old.) The psychologist is acquainted with the parents and agrees with his client that the parents would punish her severely and kick her out of their home if they knew what she had done. On the other hand, the psychologist is concerned about his ethical and legal obligations to her parents. He is also concerned that his client's therapy would be terminated prematurely if her parents discovered that he knew of the abortion.*
*What should the psychologist do?*

---

Children, like any other clients, should be informed before confidential infor-mation is shared with anyone else, including parents, and their concerns about the sharing of information should be weighed carefully in a clinician's judgments of what to reveal to parents. Clearly, if a therapist were to reveal to the parents information their child had shared about the parents' behavior, the child-parent relationship might be negatively impacted. In general, parents should certainly be informed of anything the child communicates that suggests that she could be in danger (e.g., abuse, violence, drug use, suicidal ideation).

Prior to initiating treatment, therapists who work with children should always discuss the legal limitations on the confidentiality of children with the parents. Some therapists point out that children may be reluctant to discuss private issues that are affecting them after they have been informed that the information will be accessible to their parents. Parents are generally most concerned about the effectiveness of the treatment and do not want confidentiality issues to interfere with their child's full, voluntary participation. In some cases, the parents and therapist enter into a professional services agreement in which the parents allow the therapist to maintain confidentiality regarding the content of the child's therapy sessions, with agreed-upon limitations, such as dangerous behavior on the part of the child (Gustafson & McNamara, 1987). The terms of the agreement are presented to the child, with the parents present, to make certain that all parties understand the confidentiality ground rules for the therapy. The agreement is then signed by the parents, child, and therapist. Parents are left with the option of changing the terms of the agreement at a later date if they become uncomfortable with the arrangement, though parents seldom, if ever, exercise this option. If they did, the child would then be informed of the changes in the conditions of the therapy from that point forward in order to avoid "setting her up" by having promised her confidentiality. Of course, the child might then ask to terminate the therapy.

An interesting question about such an agreement is what would happen if the parents, in amending the agreement, exercise their legal parental right and demand to know what has occurred since the beginning of their child's therapy. The therapist is certainly obligated to resist the demand, but it is unclear whether the professional services agreement would be upheld in court. No legal challenge has ever been raised.

---

**Case Example 8.12**

*A 14-year-old, white client reveals to her counselor that she is secretly dating an African American classmate. She feels very positively about the relationship, but she says that her parents would never allow it if they knew. The counselor is uncertain about what he should do.*

*What are the relevant ethical and legal considerations in this case? What should the counselor do?*

---

## TERMINATION WITH A CHILD CLIENT

Parents often decide that their child's therapy ought to be terminated, regardless of the advice of the therapist and the feelings of the child. A therapist working with a child is obligated to urge the parents to allow an orderly ending to occur, so the child will not experience the termination of the relationship as an abandonment (Yanagida, 1998). In other situations, parents simply do not implement the treatment plan (e.g., a behavior modification program) at home, even though the critical importance of consistency in the child's environment was stressed in developing the treatment plan with the parents. If the parents are subverting the effectiveness of the treatment by not following the therapist's advice, the therapist should point out to the parents the limited value of continuing therapy with the child (Yanagida, 1998). On the other hand, terminating the relationship might eliminate the child's only opportunity to interact with a concerned, caring adult figure. A therapist must attempt to determine what is in the child's best interest in deciding how she will address this type of situation.

## Mandatory Reporting of Child Abuse and Neglect

In all 50 states, mental health professionals, like other professionals, are obligated to report suspicions that a child has been or may have been abused or neglected to state or local law enforcement personnel or a legally designated child protective agency (Kalichman, 1999).[27] Any person making a good faith report is generally protected against civil or criminal liability, should the report turn out to be false. Different forms of abuse (i.e., sexual, physical, and emotional) and neglect are covered by mandatory reporting laws.

Sexual abuse involves an adult's use of a child to achieve sexual gratification. Sexual abuse of a child can range from watching a child undress or bathe, to masturbating in the presence of a child, to acts of oral, vaginal, or anal penetration. The prevalence of child sexual abuse is difficult to determine, although prevalence studies are generally thought to underestimate rates of abuse. Recent national survey data indicate that 15.3% of girls and 5.9% of boys have been victims of sexual abuse (Swenson & Hanson, 1998). Only about 10% of all cases involve a stranger as the perpetrator of the abuse.

Physical abuse involves physically injuring a child, resulting in harm to the child (in some states, producing visible marks is the criterion), or the genuine threat of such injury. Mental or emotional abuse is emotional injury to the child that impairs the child's development or psychological functioning. Failure to prevent the abuse of a child can also be grounds for charges of abuse. Neglect can involve several different scenarios: leaving a child alone, leaving a child in a situation where the child is exposed to a significant risk of physical or emotional harm, not protecting the child's interests (e.g., leaving a child with caretakers who are known to be abusive, ignoring a serious medical problem), or abandonment (i.e., leaving a child with the demonstration of intent not to return). Overall, child abuse and neglect affect an estimated 2.7 million children in the United States (Greene & Kilili, 1998). In 1997, more than 3 million reports of child abuse and neglect were made (Kalichman, 1999).

It is extremely important that child abuse and neglect be identified and stopped and that both abuser and victim receive treatment. Child deaths resulting from abuse have increased dramatically during the past 15 years (Kalichman, 1999). Moreover, children, adolescents, and adults who were once victims of child abuse and neglect experience an increased incidence of depression, anxiety, posttraumatic stress disorder, alcohol abuse, interpersonal problems, and indiscriminate sexual behavior, as well as higher levels of anger, aggression, and suicidality (Briere & Elliott, 1994; Brown, Cohen, Johnson, & Smailes, 1999; Luster & Small, 1997; Muller & Diamond, 1999).

Reporting child abuse to legal authorities is frequently a very difficult and sensitive issue for mental health professionals. In many instances, therapists might question whether they have sufficient evidence to make a report, whether any positive results for the protection of the child will result from the report (e.g., report of excessive hair-pulling by a parent), and whether the report could interfere with the therapeutic relationship established between a therapist and a client suspected of abuse. A therapist might be concerned that an abuser-client will terminate therapy prematurely following a report, thereby actually increasing the likelihood that the abuse will recur. Might the report result in additional abuse, before the investigation by child protective services gets underway, as a means of pressuring the child to deny any history of abuse? As a result of considerations like these, many clinicians fail to comply consistently with mandatory reporting laws (Hess & Brinson, 1999; Kalichman, 1999).

Therapists need to carefully consider the motivations behind their reluctance to comply with the legal mandate to report abuse. It is certainly uncomfortable to confront, and possibly anger, violent people. It is awkward to place oneself in the middle of a potentially explosive family situation without having any control over the events that follow. The discomfort and sense of limited power experienced by therapists should help them to identify with the child, who has no protection within the family. Protection for the child must come from outside the family. Although the situation is not pleasant for anyone, the child's welfare is clearly best protected (though not necessarily perfectly so) by the legal authorities. Legislators and governmental policy makers in every state have come to that conclusion. If a therapist has reason to believe that the report of abuse will lead to greater harm to the child, she is obligated to inform legal authorities of this concern as well. Abusers should be put on notice that any further incidents will make the situation considerably worse. Also, it is difficult to understand how not reporting abuse in such an explosive context could possibly ensure protection for the child. Mental health professionals have both a legal and ethical obligation to report suspected child abuse or neglect. If a therapist ever doubts the appropriateness of making a report in a particular case, she should consult immediately with more experienced colleagues on the matter. In several cases, professionals have been held legally responsible for failing to report suspected child abuse (Kalichman, 1999). All the "what ifs" about the potential negative consequences of reporting simply place the therapist in an untenable position of predicting an abuser's response to treatment. The best means of protecting the interests of the child is to report.[28]

Mandatory reporting of child abuse and neglect again underscores the importance of providing comprehensive information to clients during the informed consent process prior to initiating therapy. Clients should be informed of the limits of confidentiality, including the therapist's legal obligation to report any suspicion of abuse (Kalichman, 1999). Addressing this issue proactively with clients can prevent them from experiencing mandatory reporting as an unexpected breach of confidentiality and from feeling betrayed by their therapist, should evidence of abuse arise. When a therapist suspects that abuse has occurred, she should inform her client of her concern and remind him of her legal duty to report suspected abuse. The critical importance of protecting the welfare of children can be presented as the rationale for the law. The client should be given the option of making the report himself, which, along with his participation in therapy, should suggest to child welfare authorities that he is attempting to address his behavioral problems. The client will need to make the report in the therapist's presence in order to absolve the therapist of her duty to report the abuse. The therapist can offer to speak to the child welfare authorities to corroborate her client's report that he is receiving treatment. Of course, the abuse of a child should also be addressed immediately as an important treatment issue. Anger management techniques, or whatever intervention is appropriate to the client's situation, should be discussed, and the client and therapist should begin to devise a treatment plan to address the abusive behavior and the emotional issues underlying it.

---

**Case Example 8.13**

*A school counselor is working with an 8-year-old girl who was sexually abused three years earlier by an older cousin. The case was investigated, and the cousin and his family no longer have any contact with the client's family. Her mother met with the school counselor several times about the girl's progress. The mother mentioned that she and her husband were under a great deal of financial stress and that her husband sometimes had trouble controlling his temper when the girl misbehaved. He "spanked her pretty hard" on those occasions.*

*The counselor had perceived symptoms of abuse in the child's behavior, but assumed they were the result of the sexual abuse incident. She now wonders whether the girl might be experiencing physical abuse, but she has not seen any physical evidence of abuse or injuries. The girl did not respond to the counselor's questions about physical abuse or being hurt by her father other than saying, "No." The counselor decided not to make a report.*

*Did the counselor behave appropriately?*

---

## SCHOOL PSYCHOLOGY AND COUNSELING

Another unusual aspect of providing mental health services to children is that they are seen in a wide variety of settings, including school (Kazdin, 1994). Mental health professionals working in school settings are generally either school psychologists or school counselors. School psychologists and counselors are typically master's-level practitioners with a specialized degree that requires coursework in education, in addition to counseling or psychology training. School psychologists provide assessment and treatment services to school children. School counselors provide students with academic and career guidance, in addition to mental health counseling.

### COMPETENCE IN SCHOOL PSYCHOLOGY AND COUNSELING

School psychologists are competent to administer a wide range of tests to school-age children to assess their personality and cognitive functioning. Frequently, school psychologists are called upon to conduct intellectual assessments to evaluate whether a child qualifies for a diagnosis of mental retardation or a learning disorder. School psychologists must be very familiar with federal and state statutes (e.g., ADA, 1990) and policies concerning the diagnosis of disabilities and the provision of educational services and accommodations for intellectually and physically challenged children.

Both school psychologists and counselors treat emotional and behavioral disorders affecting school behavior. An important aspect of competent practice as a school psychologist or counselor is recognizing when the issues affecting a child exceed the limits of school-based treatment. School professionals should have an established network of competent child psychiatrists and child-clinical psychologists to whom they can refer these students.

Suicide is an extremely serious and difficult issue to assess and treat effectively in children and adolescents. School psychologists and counselors must recognize the instability of adolescents' moods and the impulsivity that can characterize their behavior. Any mention of suicidal intent must be taken very seriously. Subsequent denial of suicidal thoughts does not necessarily mean that an adolescent is not at risk. Children and adolescents who are contemplating suicide need more intensive treatment than a school psychologist or counselor can provide, so, once again, competent practice requires identification and referral. Case precedents and legal guidelines for the state in which a school psychologist is practicing should be consulted carefully in determining whether it is appropriate to inform a student's parents if she seeks mental health services for suicidal thoughts and impulses (Fischer & Sorenson, 1996).

Currently, student violence in schools is a major concern of school districts. School psychologists and counselors need to pursue continuing education opportunities to work on developing competence in recognizing risk factors for violence and providing educational programs for students concerning the prevention of school violence.

---

**Case Example 8.14**

*A school psychologist working in a suburban high school is asked to develop an assessment plan for identifying students at elevated risk to commit violent acts against others. He points out to the principal that no valid method exists for accurately predicting such behavior in an adolescent population. He also questions what will be done with students considered to be at elevated risk. The principal says the assessment program will serve an important political purpose, showing parents that school officials are doing something about the school violence problem. Also, the parents of high-risk students will be notified, and these students will participate in a mandatory counseling program.*

*What should the school psychologist do?*

---

## INFORMED CONSENT AND CONFIDENTIALITY ISSUES

As discussed in the previous section, parental consent is generally required to provide mental health assessment or treatment services to children and adolescents. The child's assent to participate in an evaluation or treatment program is also essential, for two reasons. First, obtaining a child's assent shows a proper ethical regard for his autonomy as a person. Second, a child is likely to be more positively motivated to participate in and complete a procedure if it has been explained to him and he has agreed to it.

During the informed consent process, parents and children should both receive a thorough explanation of the purpose and nature of any testing or treatment procedure. When a child is going to be tested or evaluated by a school psychologist, his parents will be particularly interested in knowing what use will be made of the results of the procedure and what kind of feedback will be provided to them regarding their child's performance. The child who is assessed should also be provided with testing feedback, in language he will be able to understand.

Confidentiality is an extremely important duty for school-based mental health professionals. They are frequently faced with questions from teachers, other students, and concerned neighbors about the students who are being evaluated or treated. Information about a student should never be disclosed to any nonprofessional other than the student's parents or legally designated guardian. School staff members should only be given information about a student on a need-to-know basis. For example, a student's teacher will be provided with limited information regarding a student's functioning if he is being asked to implement a behavior modification program in his classroom. However, even when school personnel do become involved in delivering psychological services to a student, school psychologists and counselors should respect the student's confidentiality by limiting the disclosure of confidential information to what is absolutely necessary for the personnel to assist the student effectively (ACA, 1997, B.1.f; APA, 1992, 5.03). Teachers and administrators are not obligated to keep their interactions with students confidential, so they might not recognize that the professional duties of a school psychologist are different (Cottone & Tarvydas, 1998). School psychologists and counselors might need to educate their school colleagues about the obligation of mental health professionals to preserve students' confidentiality.

Students should be informed very carefully about the limits of confidentiality. Therefore, school psychologists and counselors must be familiar with federal and state statutes, as well as school board, state, and federal education policies regarding their duties to protect students' privacy and to inform parents about matters pertaining to their child (Arthur & Swanson, 1993). For example, school psychologists and counselors are required to report child abuse and neglect, but requirements regarding their obligation to inform parents about matters such as students' sexual activity or treatment for a sexually transmitted disease will vary from state to state (Fischer & Sorenson, 1996). School psychology and guidance counselor journals, along with state board newsletters, are excellent ways to stay abreast of legal developments that might impact school psychology practice. School psychologists and counselors should always inform students of what will be reported to their parents or anyone else.

Parents have a right to examine their child's school records under the Family Educational Rights and Privacy Act of 1974 (FERPA; Pub. L. No. 93-380), but parents are not entitled to inspect the mental health records created by school counselors and psychologists. However, parents can designate an appropriate professional to review the records on their behalf (Arthur & Swanson, 1993). FERPA does not require school psychologists and counselors to disclose information from confidential counseling sessions that is not provided in the child's records

(Anderson, 1996). Again, professionals should regard therapy and assessment records as legal documents and consider carefully the potential future implications for the student of the information they include.

## MULTIPLE RELATIONSHIPS

The issue of multiple relationships is one that most school-based mental health professionals confront. As residents of the community they serve, school psychologists or counselors may have preexisting relationships (e.g., as neighbors or friends) with the parents of the students they counsel. The professional's children might, particularly in smaller communities, attend the school where she works and know students being evaluated or treated by her. These relationships generally cannot be avoided, but they place a heavy responsibility on the school psychologist or counselor to remain as objective as possible in her judgments and recommendations. School administrators should be informed when a student requiring services has a preexisting relationship with the school psychologist or counselor that would be likely to interfere with her ability to assist the student in an objective, professional manner.

A school psychologist or counselor also faces a multiple role issue at her school. She is a professional colleague of the teachers and administrators at the school, but as a mental health professional, she is also obligated to advocate for the best interests of students by promoting the development of a more positive school environment and enhancing the effectiveness of educational programs. For example, she might need to voice her opposition to the use of corporal punishment in the school and offer alternative disciplinary strategies.

---

**Case Example 8.15**

*A principal refers a very troublesome student to a school counselor. The student is disruptive in class and, during a two-week suspension, allegedly flattened the tires on the principal's car. The principal tells the counselor that she believes the student suffers from Attention-Deficit/Hyperactivity Disorder. She asks the counselor to provide the diagnosis, so the student can be sent to an alternative school. She clearly wants the student out of her school.*

*What should the counselor do?*

---

## ENHANCING THE LEARNING ENVIRONMENT

For school-based mental health professionals, one of the most uncomfortable aspects of the learning and discipline strategies in schools is the frequent use of coercion with students (e.g., punishment, negative reinforcement). School psychologists and counselors have the expertise to recognize that even though coercion might reduce undesirable behaviors in the short run, it is not the most effective long-term behavior modification strategy (Sidman, 1999). School psychologists and counselors have a professional duty to educate school personnel about the effectiveness of positive reinforcement strategies (e.g., token economies) in modifying students' behavior and enhancing academic performance.

School-based mental health professionals are not teachers, nor do they have the authority of administrators. This ambiguous status complicates their role in that they are often involved in staff training and in consulting with teachers and administrators about methods of dealing with problem students. Input from school psychologists and counselors will be received much more positively if these professionals are perceived by teachers and administrators as a useful resource for solving practical problems with students. They will be less effective in promoting the best interests of students if they present themselves as mental health experts whose purpose is to tell teachers what they are doing wrong.

## COMPUTER-ASSISTED THERAPY

The information technology revolution is producing advances with exciting implications for the mental health professions. Technologically assisted therapy via teleconferencing, e-mail, and the Internet can, among other things, enhance the availability of mental health services to rural populations, ease the problem of scheduling therapy contacts, reduce the cost of therapy and assessment services for clients, allow clients to receive mental health services in the privacy of their homes, and simplify clients' completion of assessments and between-session homework assignments (Sampson, Kolodinsky, & Greeno, 1997). On the other hand, underserved populations of lower socioeconomic status are less likely to have access to the Internet, so this method of offering mental health services might do little to change the cultural inequality of access to treatment (Bloom, 1998).

At the same time, the development of computer-assisted therapy raises a number of serious ethical concerns, in addition to those affecting therapy in any context. To address these issues, the ACA Governing Council (1999) published a set of *Ethical Standards for Internet On-Line Counseling,* and the APA Ethics Committee published a statement concerning services offered by Internet ("Ethics Committee Issues Statement," 1998). The ACA standards emphasize confidentiality issues unique to Internet counseling. Confidentiality is difficult to guarantee on the Internet because few users understand the complexities of Internet security. At present, most providers of psychological services on the Internet use unsecured Web sites (Barak, 1999). Mental health professionals must utilize only secured sites (i.e., sites providing state-of-the-art data encryption security) for the transmission of confidential information. In addition, as with any computerized records on networked computers, therapists are responsible for taking all possible precautions, including the use of passwords to gain access to hidden files, to prevent unauthorized access to client information.

An additional confidentiality issue concerns the degree of privacy afforded clients in their homes as they interact with a therapist via a telephone or computer connection. Clients should be advised to address these concerns and to terminate a contact if they experience an intrusion into the privacy of a session. Counselors are required to execute a waiver agreement with clients stating that clients recognize that confidentiality cannot be guaranteed for information transmitted online, in spite of the best efforts of the counselor (ACA, 1999).

---

**Case Example 8.16**

*A counselor offering online services receives an inquiry from a man about providing counseling for his 10-year-old son, who is having increasing problems with abiding by the rules set for his behavior at home and at school. Although the counselor had expected his online practice to attract only adult clients, he says that he has no problem with the arrangement, as long as the parents fax him their consent for him to treat their son and the boy is agreeable. He says that he has treated children with behavioral problems in his practice before.*

*Are there ethical considerations that the counselor is overlooking?*

---

Therapists must be extremely careful to present their credentials and licensure status accurately on their own Web page and other Internet sites and to provide documentation of their credentials to potential clients who request it (Barak, 1999; Bloom, 1998). As in any other clinical context, competence is an extremely important issue. In addition to the "normal" competence issues relevant to conducting therapy and assessment, distance counseling should be regarded as a wholly new area of competence that a therapist must develop through study and supervised experience (Barak, 1999; Bloom, 1998). The APA Ethics Committee (1998) statement and the ACA ethical standards emphasize this point. Consulting with clients through the Internet is considerably different than meeting face to face. The burden is squarely on the therapist to determine, through a screening process, that online services are appropriate for a given client and to develop a clearly articulated treatment plan for clients treated online. The development of a therapeutic relationship is obviously very different if a client cannot see the therapist or hear his voice. The therapist, in turn, cannot perceive the client's vocal tone or observe her nonverbal behavior. Clearly, a great deal of research is needed regarding the additional variables affecting the efficacy of computer-assisted therapy (Sampson et al., 1997).

---

**Case Example 8.17**

*A Web site advertises individual and group therapy services via the Internet, provided by "a master's-level counseling student" with both individual and group counseling experience.*

*What are the potentially misleading and unethical elements of this announcement?*

---

An additional reason for caution in offering computer-assisted therapy services is the considerable potential for malpractice based on the limited supervision that therapists can provide via computer. For example, suppose a client being treated over the Internet commits suicide. A therapist's responsibility for protecting his client from harm is not diminished, though his ability to recognize and accurately assess suicidal potential through typed exchanges may be limited (Bloom, 1998; Sampson et al., 1997). Certainly, therapists should be extremely cautious in preparing themselves for, and in delivering, therapeutic services online.

## PRACTICE CASE INVOLVING THE MODEL OF ETHICAL DECISION MAKING

During the mid-1980's, New York City had several incidents of homeless citizens freezing to death overnight while living on the streets during the winter months. In response to this problem, Mayor Edward I. Koch initiated a policy of having police escort homeless individuals to shelters on dangerously cold nights (temperature below 20 degrees Fahrenheit). However, many homeless individuals refused to go to shelters, arguing that they were dangerous places where one's property was often stolen while one slept. Repeated attempts to reassure homeless individuals that shelters were being made safer (e.g., by the hiring of security personnel) had little effect.

Mayor Koch responded by initiating another policy that a homeless individual refusing to be transported to a shelter on such occasions would be taken into protective custody by the police and transported to a city psychiatric facility, with the rationale that exposing oneself to such imminent danger indicated that one's reasoning ability was seriously impaired and that one needed to be protected. These individuals would be evaluated by a psychiatrist the following day and then released, voluntarily admitted, or involuntarily committed, as deemed medically appropriate.

Is there a conflict for mental health professionals who are being asked to assess these homeless individuals between their duty as employees of the New York City health care system and their ethical obligations as professionals, delineated in their profession's ethical code?

## SUMMARY

This chapter dealt with the special ethical challenges faced by therapists practicing within organizations or with special populations. Mental health professionals in organizations must harmonize their duties as employees with their ethical obligations to their profession. Conflicts of interest can easily arise as professionals try to serve both their employing organization and the needs of their clients. Therapists working in psychiatric hospitals must deal with sharing confidential information within a treatment team and the pressure to discharge clients as quickly as possible. MCOs pose similar issues for professionals, who must be prepared to work on behalf of clients when they are denied needed services due to financial considerations.

Correctional therapists strive to minimize the coercive aspect of treatment in a prison setting by emphasizing clients' right to refuse treatment and having clients play an active role in setting therapy goals. Clients should be informed of the limits placed on the confidentiality of their treatment and records. Correctional therapists must avoid having their role as prison employees interfere with their professional duties to clients. Similarly, mental health professionals working in the military must strive to uphold professional standards of informed consent and confidentiality within the regimented military environment.

Psychotherapy with children is complicated by the inability of children to consent to treatment. Parents not only must consent for their child to be treated, but with only a few exceptions, they also have the right to know what is discussed during their child's therapy sessions. Professionals are legally required to report any suspicion that a child is a victim of neglect or physical, sexual, or emotional abuse. Nevertheless, many therapists are reluctant to comply with mandatory reporting laws. School psychologists and counselors must also report suspected abuse or neglect. They must look out for the best interests of their clients while promoting the safety and welfare of all students in their school and supporting its educational mission.

Computer-assisted therapy is a relatively recent development. Therapists offering services via the Internet face a number of special challenges in the areas of competence, informed consent, and confidentiality. Also, they must be careful to ensure that a client's needs can be addressed adequately in a computer-mediated therapy context or arrange an appropriate referral.

# 9 Ethical Issues in Assessment and Testing

Mental health professionals working in clinical and educational settings are involved continuously in assessment. In addition to formal intake assessment and psychological testing geared toward determining a client's needs and diagnosis, clinicians assess their client's condition and progress each time they meet. Similarly, school psychologists assess the personality, intellectual functioning, and academic achievement of students. This chapter will first examine the major ethical issues pertaining to clinical and educational assessment, beginning with diagnosis, which is a primary goal of clinical assessment. The remainder of the chapter will focus on ethical issues related specifically to psychological and educational testing.

## THE VALUE AND ETHICAL IMPLICATIONS OF PSYCHIATRIC DIAGNOSES

This is not a psychopathology textbook, so it might seem odd to address the issue of psychiatric diagnosis. However, the diagnostic process involves important ethical considerations because a diagnosis represents, among other things, a value judgment concerning the behavior and/or beliefs of a client (ACA, 1997, E.5; APA, 1992, 2.01[b]). In making a *DSM-IV* (American Psychiatric Association, 1994) diagnosis, the clinician is asserting that the client's behavior is not just unusual or different from most people's, but is disordered or "sick" (i.e., psychopathological).

### THE VALUES UNDERLYING THE DSM DIAGNOSTIC SCHEME

The *DSM-IV* (American Psychiatric Association, 1994) psychiatric diagnostic system uses a medical model to conceptualize behavioral disorders. Syndromes, such as the schizophrenias, are regarded as illnesses or diseases, presumably caused by some biological malfunction in the individual's central nervous system (Sarbin, 1990). Disorders are viewed within the context of the individual's biological functioning, thereby minimizing the significance of personality, social, and cultural factors in producing individual differences in behavior (Peele, 1990). The medical model appears to be inconsistent, then, with the ethical importance that mental health professionals attach to recognizing and respecting individual differences and sources of diversity in people (e.g., ACA, 1997, A.2, C.5.a, E.5.b, E.8; APA, 1992, 1.10, 2.04).

The *DSM-IV* has been designed to maximize the *reliability* of psychiatric diagnosis. Reliability is the extent to which independent evaluators would classify the same set of behaviors as fitting a particular diagnosis. This consistency of diagnostic classification is a prerequisite for a *valid* diagnostic system. Validity refers to the meaningfulness of a diagnosis; that is, whether the diagnosis provides important clinical information concerning a person's functioning and the prognosis for the individual's future adjustment.

Although the *DSM-IV* and its predecessors have long been accepted as the best system available for classifying behavioral syndromes, many aspects of the classification system, and of the diagnostic enterprise in general, have received criticism. Critics of the *DSM-IV* have focused primarily on the questionable validity of the classification system (Sarbin, 1997). The biological basis of mental illness, assumed by the medical model, has been supported by the identification of specific biological mechanisms in very few of the disorders listed in the *DSM-IV* (Lilienfeld and Marino, 1995). Even when biological factors have been identified as contributing to a syndrome (e.g., inadequate serotonin activity in Major Depression), there are many instances in which cognitive and social factors (e.g., the death of a spouse) appear to play a far more significant role in the development and persistence of the disorder. The validity of both the medical model and the practice of psychiatric diagnosis has been questioned increasingly as the number of mental disorders in the *DSM-IV* has burgeoned to over 300, with political support in the psychiatric community appearing to be a key factor in a syndrome gaining official "mental illness" status (Sharkey, 1997). American society appears to be moving closer and closer to the point where virtually everyone will qualify for some type of psychiatric diagnosis (Gergen, 1990). If everyone is "sick," the concept of mental illness ceases to make an important distinction between people. Critics have questioned whether the proliferation of diagnostic syndromes (e.g., "Road Rage") has been motivated, in part, by the desire of mental health professionals to increase their share of the health care funding pie (Sharkey, 1997). However, respect for the autonomy and capacity for self-determination of people should lead mental health professionals to emphasize the individual's responsibility for his behavior, rather than attributing all forms of socially inappropriate behavior to an illness or syndrome (Szasz, 1974).

## THE PROS AND CONS OF LABELING CLIENTS

Psychiatric diagnosis is intended to enhance clinicians' understanding of their clients' problems, thereby increasing the effectiveness of treatment. Diagnostic terminology has also provided mental health professionals with a universally recognized method of communicating about clients and disorders. However, the diagnostic process has been criticized on ethical grounds by clinicians and researchers who have argued that the use of diagnoses does more harm than good to clients. Many of these arguments have focused on the impact of diagnostic "labels" on clients. First, critics have asserted that once an individual receives a diagnosis of a mental disorder, it is difficult for others to ever view the person as normal again (e.g., Link, Cullen, Frank, & Wozniak, 1987). A famous case of this phenomenon involved Senator Thomas Eagleton, who was the Democratic Vice Presidential nominee in 1972. During the campaign, it was revealed that, years before, Senator Eagleton had been hospitalized in a psychiatric facility and treated successfully for depression with electroconvulsive therapy (Lydon, 1972). In spite of the fact that Senator Eagleton had not suffered any additional episodes and had served effectively for several years in the United States Senate, the outcry was so great against having a "nut" just a heartbeat away from becoming President that Senator Eagleton had to withdraw from the campaign (Naughton, 1972). Apparently, popular opinion still held that once an individual had developed a psychiatric condition, he would never be completely cured.

A second criticism is that being diagnosed with a mental disorder can result in an individual adopting a "sick role"; that is, the individual may devalue herself by perceiving herself as seriously incapacitated and cease to believe that she is capable of coping effectively or of improving her situation (Link, 1987). She might view herself as a disabled person and begin to focus more on obtaining relief from her responsibilities (e.g., by qualifying for disability compensation) than on resolving her problems and getting on with her life (Link, 1987; Link et al., 1987; Szasz, 1974).

Although proponents of psychiatric diagnosis assert that diagnostic information provides clinicians with a better understanding of their clients, critics argue that diagnosis actually *decreases* many clinicians' understanding of their clients as individual human beings. Diagnosis has become an end in itself, rather than representing one important piece of information in the process of understanding a client's experience and assisting her in making life changes (Tucker, 1998). Mental health professionals profess to have great respect for the autonomy of the individual and her capacity for self-determination, yet when individuals receive a psychiatric diagnosis, their individuality is too often subsumed by that label. Even clinicians will assume that they know the major facts about a person once they read the diagnosis of Schizophrenia, Paranoid Type in the individual's medical record. According to critics, diagnostic categorizations encourage a clinician to pigeonhole people rather than focus on their unique life history, current situation, and life goals. Effective treatment is based on a comprehensive understanding of an individual as an agent responsible for her behavioral choices, not on a diagnostic label (Sarbin, 1997).

On the basis of arguments like these, some mental health professionals believe that diagnosis is an unethical practice because of the enormous significance attached to such labels in current mental health practice. Clearly, ethical, competent diagnosis should be based on a comprehensive assessment of the individual's functioning by a highly competent clinician with a keen sensitivity to the potential impact that receiving a psychiatric label can have on a client's life (ACA, 1997, E.5; APA, 1992, 2.01).

## PREDICTION OF LOW BASE RATE BEHAVIORS

In many instances, the most important information in determining a psychiatric diagnosis is a person's score on a diagnostic test. The diagnosis is applied if the person's score exceeds a cutoff level that has been established as a valid indicator of the presence of the disorder. In fact, actuarial (i.e., statistical) prediction based on a client's assessment profile or test cutoff score yields greater diagnostic accuracy than the clinical judgment of even experienced clinicians (Walters, White, & Greene, 1988). However, Meehl and Rosen (1955) pointed out long ago that effective behavioral prediction cannot occur without an understanding of the *base rate,* or antecedent probability, of a behavior in the population being tested (i.e., how often the behavior or condition occurs in the population). Accurate classification is dependent on both the probability of detecting a condition by using a specific criterion and the proportion of the population that is actually affected by the condition (Gottesman & Prescott, 1989). Evaluating the efficiency of a diagnostic test involves comparing its rate of success in classifying people correctly, also known as the "hit rate," with the base rate of the condition in the population being studied.

For example, the MacAndrew Alcoholism Scale (MAC) was developed during the 1960s to differentiate clients who were in need of treatment for alcoholism from other psychiatric outpatient clients (MacAndrew, 1965). The MAC was included as a supplementary scale on the MMPI. In the original validation sample for the MAC, the base rate of alcoholism was 50%. Half of the sample consisted of alcoholics in treatment and half of nonalcoholic psychiatric clients. Using a cutoff score of 24, the MAC correctly classified 81.8% of the standardization sample as alcoholic or nonalcoholic, which is much better than the 50% hit rate that would have been obtained by randomly classifying individuals as alcoholic or nonalcoholic in that sample (Gottesman & Prescott, 1989).

However, the base rate, or lifetime prevalence, of alcoholism in the United States population is 13.4% (Grant, 1997). The MAC, with a hit rate of 81.8% (which sounds very impressive), would not provide an effective classification tool for such a low base rate behavior in the general population. Suppose, instead of administering the MAC, a psychologist decided to simply classify 100% of the general population as nonalcoholics. The hit rate (i.e., percentage of nonalcoholics correctly classified as nonalcoholics) would be 86.6% (100% − 13.4% = 86.6%), which is even better than the 81.8% hit rate of the MAC! Again, the evaluation of the hit rate of a diagnostic test must take the base rate of the behavior in the population into account. When a test is used with a population that has a significantly different base rate for a condition than the population used to validate the test, a high frequency of misdiagnoses will occur. In the case of the MAC, incorrect classifications would have tended to be false-positives (i.e., people classified as alcoholics who really were not). Using the MAC in a personnel screening context, then, would have led to the misclassification (and, presumably, the inappropriate rejection) of many job applicants as alcoholics. Clearly, this would have been an unethical use of the test.

Test developers have an ethical obligation to validate the use of cutoff scores and classification schemes for the population (e.g., male prison inmates) with which the test will be used (ACA, 1997, E.12; APA, 1992, 2.03). Likewise, professionals using tests should be aware of the population base rates of the behaviors being classified and should not use tests that have not compiled clear evidence of predictive efficacy for the population in question (ACA, 1997, E.6.a; APA, 1992, 2.02). Test users must also be sensitive to potential differences in base rates and appropriate cutoff scores based on ethnicity, age, and gender (Sandoval, 1998). Unfortunately, many clinicians have little understanding of the correct use of information regarding base rates (e.g., Walters et al., 1988; Whitecotton, Sanders, & Norris, 1998). When test scores and other relevant variables are used competently, specific predictors of low base rate behaviors can, in some instances, be identified (Janus & Meehl, 1997).

---

**Case Example 9.1**

*An African American job applicant is rejected by a construction firm because his score on the MAC is above the cutoff of 24, indicating that he is likely to abuse alcohol. Researchers subsequently discover that the mean score for African Americans is higher than it was for the norm group, making this test an even worse predictor of alcohol abuse for African Americans than for the population in general. When the norms for African Americans are published, the psychologist responsible for personnel testing at the firm stops using the test.*
*Are there any additional actions the psychologist should take?*

---

## PSYCHOLOGICAL AND EDUCATIONAL ASSESSMENT AND TESTING

Psychological assessment is the process of gathering information about an individual that will be useful in determining his need for treatment and which treatment methods will be most effective with him. It is essentially a problem-solving task, based on the questions regarding the individual that are being addressed in the assessment (Tallent, 1987). Testing is often a component of the assessment process. Whenever psychological testing is undertaken, it should have a clear purpose that serves the interests of the client. That is, the testing should yield important information that needs to be known in order to help the client more effectively. Unnecessary testing constitutes an unwarranted intrusion into the client's privacy and exploits the client financially. There should always be a legitimate referral question when testing is ordered.

There are two sets of specialty guidelines pertaining to the use of psychological and educational tests with which mental health professionals should be familiar. The American Educational Research Association, American Psychological Association, and National Council on Measurement in Education published a revised set of *Standards for Educational and Psychological Testing* in 1999. In addition, ACA and the Association for Assessment in Counseling published a set of specialty guidelines for users of standardized tests in 1989.

### INFORMED CONSENT ISSUES IN PSYCHOLOGICAL TESTING

Assessment procedures, like any other aspect of professional activity, require the informed consent of the individual(s) involved (ACA, 1997, E.3.a; APA, 1992, 1.07[a]). Many assessment referrals are made to clinicians by other practitioners or agencies that are providing treatment services to clients. It is extremely important that clinicians conducting assessments obtain informed consent themselves and never assume that the referring practitioner or agency provided an adequate explanation of the purpose of the assessment and the testing procedure.

The informed consent procedure for psychological testing is similar in many ways to the process described for therapy and counseling in Chapter 7. However, some significant differences do exist. For example, information provided during the interview and testing process is frequently not confidential between the client and the clinician in that all information provided by the client can be included in the test report to be generated for the referring agency. Because many assessment clients are either participating in therapy currently or have been in therapy in the past, it is extremely important to highlight this special limitation on the confidentiality of assessment information during the discussion of confidentiality issues. The client should also be told the types of tests that will be used, their purpose, and the types of responses she will be asked to provide (e.g., her impressions of inkblots, answers to true-false questions, drawings). The clinician should also tell the client who will be responsible for providing feedback to her regarding the results of the assessment, if a report will be generated, and the process that will be used to obtain her consent for the report to be sent to the referring agency, or any other professional or agency she designates.[29] Finally, the client must be informed of her right to refuse to participate in the assessment and any known consequences resulting from such a refusal.

---

**Case Example 9.2**

*A counseling psychologist is testing a client referred by a community mental health center. They want to know whether she is suffering from a mood disorder, a personality disorder, or both. The psychologist finds her to be very anxious and hostile when he interviews her. He explains the purpose of the testing as an attempt to find "how best to help [her]." The client continues to be hostile and evasive throughout the testing. When the testing is complete, the psychologist tells the referring agency that he has not obtained sufficient data from the client to make the differential diagnosis they requested. When the client's therapist asks her about the testing and explains the purpose of the procedure in greater detail, she looks greatly relieved and says that she thought the testing was being done to gather evidence to "put [her] away in a nuthouse."*

---

## INFORMED CONSENT ISSUES WHEN TESTING CHILDREN

When children are the focus of assessment, informed consent must be obtained from a parent or guardian prior to the initiation of the assessment process (ACA, 1997, E.3.a; APA, 1992, 4.02[b]). Clinicians must make certain that parents understand the purpose of the testing, which tests will be administered, and what use will be made of the test results. Children are often tested in situations where a particular diagnostic label is necessary for the child to receive services (e.g., to qualify for a special education program). The consent form signed by parents should specify the use to be made of any diagnosis resulting from the assessment and whether the parents' consent will be required after the procedure is completed for any further steps to be implemented (e.g., whether the parents will control the placement of their child in a special education program after receiving the assessment results or whether the child's diagnostic status will automatically trigger a placement decision). The nature and purpose of the testing should also be described to children, at a level commensurate with their understanding. The assent of the child to be tested should also be obtained (APA, 1992, 4.02[c]).

## CLIENT FEEDBACK

The informed consent process continues after the assessment has been completed. The clinician conducting the assessment is responsible for providing feedback to the client regarding the results (APA, 1992, 2.09), unless some other arrangement has been agreed upon with the referring agency (e.g., that feedback will be provided by the client's individual therapist). When testing a child, feedback is provided to the child's parents and to the child. Depending on the age of the child, the parents might receive feedback first, then sit in while the clinician explains the results to the child. Assessment feedback is considered an aspect of informed consent because clients must give their consent for copies of an assessment report to be sent to the referring agency or to any other professional. How can a client provide informed consent if she does not first obtain an understanding of the information in the assessment report?

It is desirable in most cases to provide the client (or, in the case of a young child, the child's parents) with some type of written summary of the assessment, based on the assessment report, but excluding scores and any other information that is liable to be misinterpreted by a nonprofessional. The written summary and supplementary information provided during the feedback session should be communicated in language consistent with the client's level of verbal achievement. Psychological jargon should be avoided.

When providing feedback to clients and/or the parents of a child, a clinician should make certain that clients and parents clearly understand any diagnosis that is being made and its implications. A very important component of assessment feedback is to eliminate or avoid clients' misunderstanding of the assessment results. Diagnostic information communicated to children should be based on the clinician's judgment of what the child can understand and benefit from knowing.

---

**Case Example 9.3**

*A psychologist receives a testing referral for an adult male client to determine the appropriate diagnosis for his apparently delusional beliefs about his neighbor. He is also suspicious about the testing process and agrees to be tested only after the psychologist agrees that she will provide him with feedback regarding the test results and any diagnostic conclusions. Throughout the testing, the client insists that there is nothing wrong with him and is clearly very upset about the possibility that he is "crazy." The results of the assessment clearly indicate that the client qualifies for a diagnosis of Schizophreniform Disorder. The psychologist feels that her client has the right to know this diagnosis and he clearly wants to know. On the other hand, she wants to protect him from being upset by the news because she fears he might decompensate further.*

*What should the psychologist do?*

---

## CONFIDENTIALITY ISSUES IN PSYCHOLOGICAL ASSESSMENT

The limitations of confidentiality in assessment situations may be quite different from those discussed for psychotherapy and counseling in Chapter 7. When clients are referred to a clinician for the sole purpose of assessment, they should be informed at the outset that all the information they provide will be used for the assessment report and may be communicated to the referring agency. This will prevent the client from assuming that, since he is speaking to a clinician, the assessment situation can be treated like an opportunity to receive therapy from a different therapist. Of course, clients should be assured that the clinician will not provide information regarding the assessment to anyone without their permission.

The same limitations of confidentiality discussed in Chapter 7 concerning risk of harm to self or others and abuse or neglect of children apply to the assessment situation (ACA, 1997, B.1.c; APA, 1992, 5.01). For example, suppose a client had not indicated any suicidal plan in her sessions with her therapist, but while completing the Thematic Apperception Test, she tells a story on Card 3BM about a suicidal individual. She then follows up the story by talking about her own plan to kill herself. The clinician administering the test would need to make a judgment regarding whether he should attempt to have the woman hospitalized to prevent her from carrying out her plan. The ethical responsibility to protect the client from harm while preserving the client's confidentiality to the greatest possible degree is no different than in therapy.[30]

Clinicians conducting assessments are also responsible for protecting the confidentiality of clients when sending test reports. After obtaining the informed consent of the client, a test report should always be sent to a specific person, designated by the client or the referral source, who is professionally qualified to understand the information provided in the report. The envelope should be marked "Confidential" to make certain that it will not be opened by anyone in a hospital mailroom or by clerical staff (ACA, 1997, B.4.e; APA, 1992, 5.03). An assessment report should be faxed only if immediate receipt of the report is in the best interest of the client and the clinician has been assured by the person receiving the report that the facility's fax machine is in a secure environment.

---

### Case Example 9.4

*A clinical psychologist conducts several days of testing with a client referred to her by his therapist. Her arrangement with the client is that he will pay the testing fee in full before the testing is finished. Although he makes partial payments, he still owes nearly half of the fee when the assessment is completed. The psychologist informs the client that she will not send the report to his therapist until he pays the remainder of the fee.*

*The testing indicated that the client is suffering from Major Depression and is a significant suicide risk. The psychologist is concerned about the delay in informing the referring therapist of the client's condition, but she feels that if she releases the report, the client will lose any motivation to pay her what she is owed. Is the psychologist behaving in an ethical manner?*

---

## COMPETENCE IN PSYCHOLOGICAL ASSESSMENT

A substantial proportion of successful malpractice claims arise within the context of psychological assessment. One reason for this phenomenon is that testing involves a permanent record that can easily be evaluated by independent experts to detect incompetent practice. A second major reason is that competent test administration, scoring, interpretation, and report writing require the development of a highly sophisticated set of clinical skills.

Many clinicians prefer doing therapy or counseling to conducting assessments, yet assessments can be a lucrative component of professional practice. As a result, many clinicians and agencies will hire practitioners beginning their professional careers to conduct assessments under the supervision of more experienced clinicians. Positive aspects of this situation are that assessment skills are a very marketable commodity for beginning clinicians and that these clinicians have the opportunity to obtain additional supervised clinical experience to enhance their assessment ability. However, people hired to conduct assessments need to be certain that they are competent to administer, score, and interpret each of the tests they are using (ACA, 1997, E.2.a; APA, 1992, 2.02). Before using a new test, clinicians should have knowledge of the test's development, the makeup of the normative sample, and its reliability and validity (ACA, 1997, E.2.a; APA, 1992, 2.04[a]). In addition, they must obtain experience by administering the test to a nonclinical population and then a clinical one, while under the supervision of a clinician knowledgeable about the test. Clinicians conducting assessments under supervision are responsible for demanding adequate supervision to be able to conduct the assessment correctly (APA, 1992, 2.06). The supervising clinician bears primary responsibility in such a situation, but the supervisee is equally responsible ethically for making certain that he does not exceed the limits of his competence in his clinical activities (ACA, 1997, F.1.g; APA, 1992, 1.22[b]).

A survey of departments training doctoral students in psychology found that a substantial majority of the departments did not believe that their graduates had developed competence in methods of assessing the reliability and validity of tests (Aiken et al., 1990). Geisinger and Carlson (1998) point out that although competent assessment does not require the ability to construct tests, an understanding of psychometric concepts is needed to recognize the potential for bias and invalidity when tests are used with different populations. They have suggested specific improvements in the training model for assessment and measurement. For instance, they recommend that instructors place greater emphasis on the applied contexts in which psychometric concepts play an important role to increase students' appreciation of the relevance of statistical issues to their competent use of tests in applied settings. Students must also develop competence in using the information provided in test manuals (Geisinger & Carlson, 1998).

## DIVERSITY ISSUES IN PSYCHOLOGICAL ASSESSMENT

When testing members of diverse groups, it is extremely important to make certain that the tests used and the conditions under which they are administered do not place members of any group at a relative disadvantage (ACA, 1997, E.8; APA, 1992, 2.04[c]). Tests must be selected carefully, with due attention to the makeup of normative groups

---

**Case Example 9.5**

*A counselor receives an assessment referral for an intellectual assessment of a child. The referral source asks specifically for the child to be assessed using the Stanford-Binet, rather than the WISC-III. The counselor has not used the Stanford-Binet, but he does not want to disappoint the referral source and decides that this would be an excellent opportunity to develop competence with a new test. He agrees to conduct the assessment.*

*Is the counselor's decision ethically appropriate?*

---

used in the construction of the test, to ensure that the test can provide useful, valid information for the groups in question (Geisinger, 1998). The professional's ability to understand the information provided in a test manual regarding normative samples and differences in test scores obtained by members of diverse groups is of critical importance to competent testing (ACA, 1997, E.6; APA, 1992, 2.04[a]).

Are some groups of test takers being placed at a disadvantage when a test is administered in English? If so, the professional should investigate whether translations of the test exist. If a translation does exist, evidence of the validity of the translation (i.e., that the translation measures the same constructs as the original language version) must be confirmed before using the translation (Geisinger, 1994). If a valid translation of the test is not available, perhaps a different test can be used to measure the same characteristics more effectively in linguistically diverse groups.

People with disabilities comprise a group whose special testing needs must also be considered. For example, large print, Braille, or audiotaped versions of a test might make it possible for visually impaired individuals to perform up to their true potential on a test. It is important to recognize, however, that whenever accommodations or variations are introduced, the nature of the test is altered. The professional using the test is responsible for considering whether the change from a standardized administration might affect the reliability and/or validity of the client's scores and the interpretation of those scores (Geisinger, 1998).

In training professionals to use psychological and educational tests, Geisinger and Carlson (1998) emphasize the importance of helping them to develop an understanding and appreciation of "individuality" (i.e., human differences resulting from each individual's unique experiential background). A knowledge and appreciation of individual and cultural differences is necessary in order to competently interpret the results of assessment procedures conducted with diverse groups of clients (Velasquez & Callahan, 1992). Like therapists, assessment professionals need to be capable of interpreting the meaning of clients' responses within a valid cultural context in order to draw valid conclusions. Obtaining supervised experience in testing diverse groups of clients is also extremely important to the development of competence in this area. Finally, consultation with professionals possessing greater expertise in issues of test administration and interpretation with diverse populations should not be presented in training as a rare or exceptional event, but as a commonplace practice of competent assessors concerned with delivering the highest quality assessment services possible to diverse groups of clients (Geisinger & Carlson, 1998).

---

**Case Example 9.6**

*A psychologist provides testing services for a number of nursing homes. She frequently finds it necessary to deviate from standardized administration procedures to accommodate the special needs of her elderly clients. She encourages them, reinforces their responses, takes breaks within a lengthy subtest, and repeats information to make sure they have heard it correctly. She believes that her methods ensure that the results reflect the client's optimal level of functioning. She is careful to mention the deviations from standardization in her assessment reports.*

*Is the psychologist's approach to testing with this group appropriate?*

---

## ETHICS AND TEST VALIDITY

For an assessment procedure to yield useful information, the tests used must be reliable and valid; that is, a client's performance on the test must convey important and meaningful information about him, corresponding to what the test was designed to measure. Test developers are responsible for establishing strong evidence of the reliability and validity of a test before publishing it (ACA, 1997, E.12; APA, 1992, 2.03). However, there are published tests whose reliability and validity have been criticized. For example, critics of the Rorschach have persistently questioned the ethicality of its widespread use in personality assessment, given the paucity of evidence regarding its reliability and validity as a predictor of personality functioning (Hunsley & Bailey, 1999).

Clinicians using a test need to be familiar with the test's construction and purpose, as well as its limitations, and must be careful to use it only with the populations for which it has been validated and only under the conditions specified for its use (ACA, 1997, E.8; APA, 1992, 2.02, 2.04). In other words, clinicians must be careful not to use a test for some purpose other than the one for which it was designed because conclusions drawn from such use could very well be invalid. For example, although the Beck Depression Inventory-II can be a valid measure of depression in college students, it would be invalid to infer that a student receiving a score of 10 is twice as depressed as a student producing a score of five (Beck, Steer, & Brown, 1996). First, the test is not designed to use a ratio scale of measurement; a score of zero does not indicate the complete absence of depression. Second, both scores fall within the range of "minimal" depression and the test is not designed to make discriminations within that range.

Clinicians should also be aware of variables that might affect a client's functioning in an assessment context (ACA, 1997, E.7.a; APA, 1992, 2.04[c]). A good rule to follow is that a clinician always wants to give clients the opportunity to perform as well as they can in assessment situations, consistent with the ethical dictum of nonmaleficence. To that end, clinicians should always provide test takers with the best test-taking conditions possible; tests should be administered under private, quiet, and physically comfortable conditions. Clients should be tested when they are physically alert and able to perform up to their potential. For example, if a client has an automobile accident on the way to the testing appointment, the testing should be postponed. If the client was tested on the day of the accident and produced a high score on an anxiety measure, it would not be reasonable to conclude that the results were indicative of the client's functioning in general. The result could very well have been affected by the anxiety induced by the day's disturbing events. Similarly, if a client arrives for a testing appointment and reports that he is quite upset because he broke up with his girlfriend earlier in the day, it is reasonable to assume that he would not be able to devote as much concentration to the assessment tasks as he would normally. The clinician would not know whether a lower than expected score on a memory task reflected a memory problem affecting the client or concentration difficulties related to his situational upset.

Whenever testing conditions are adapted to accommodate the special needs of test takers (e.g., presenting items orally to a visually impaired client), standardization is being violated. The clinician must evaluate the potential impact of nonstandardized administration on test takers' performance and on the validity of interpretations of scores (Geisinger, 1998).

Preserving test security is another important duty of mental health professionals (ACA, 1997, E.10; APA, 1992, 2.10). The validity of many psychological tests can be compromised if potential test takers have prior access to the test materials (American Educational Research Association et al., 1999). A clinician should be careful not to reveal too much about test stimuli and typical responses in her teaching or public presentations.[31] Also, she should not allow clients to look over test materials or discuss clients' responses with them in any detail, even after clients have completed the assessment process. She should always bear in mind that clients might need to take the same tests again in the future to evaluate changes in their condition.

A special case affecting the issue of test security for the Rorschach is the "testing the limits" procedure used by some clinicians with clients who produce a very limited Rorschach record (Exner, 1993). For example, if a client rejected (i.e., could not generate any response for) six of the ten cards during the Rorschach administration, the clinician might test the limits by showing the client Card V again and saying, "You did not see anything on this card. Some people see a _____ on this card. Can you see that?" Testing the limits on the Rorschach can be problematic because the procedure contaminates future testing of the client. The client will no longer be naive; she will know one or more of the "right" answers. Another reason to avoid testing the limits is that the clinician is communicating to the client that she did not perform well on the test. This information could significantly increase the client's anxiety level and affect her performance on the remaining tests in the assessment battery. For both reasons, testing the limits should generally be avoided. It is recommended only for use with severely disturbed schizophrenic clients who display little contact with reality, making them unlikely to remember the testing procedure clearly if they are tested again in the future (Exner, 1993).

## USE OF COMPUTERIZED TEST ADMINISTRATION, SCORING, AND INTERPRETATION

Computer-based test administration, scoring, and interpretation have become extremely popular in clinical practice, particularly during the past 30 years. The majority of psychologists involved in assessment have used these technological aids

(Pope, Butcher, & Seelen, 2000). Computer-based test scoring is a recommended procedure because it eliminates scoring errors, thereby increasing the reliability of scoring and making valid interpretation of the test data possible (Allard, Butler, Faust, & Shea, 1995; McMinn et al., 1999). Of course, clinicians and their staff must be competent in using the relevant software in order to realize these benefits (ACA, 1997, E.7.b; APA, 1992, 2.08[c]).

As discussed earlier, a clinician is obligated to provide clients with a testing environment that enables them to perform up to their full potential on the tests being administered. Computerized test administration affords clients greater privacy for test-taking and simplifies the process of responding to test items. However, for clients who have little or no experience with computers, computerized test administration can be extremely uncomfortable and anxiety provoking. Clients' discomfort with the test administration procedure could affect their test performance. For instance, clients with higher levels of computer anxiety have been shown to produce more negative mood ratings when questionnaires were administered on a computer rather than in a paper-and-pencil format (Tseng, Macleod, & Wright, 1997; Tseng, Tiplady, Macleod, & Wright, 1998). Clinicians are particularly likely to encounter this situation with rural, older, and low socioeconomic status populations in today's society. Clients should be asked about their experience and level of comfort with computer tasks prior to testing. Clients expressing reservations about using the computer should be permitted to practice making responses on the computer until they are comfortable doing so. If they remain uncomfortable or practice cannot be provided, an alternate testing format (e.g., responding on an answer sheet) should be used (APA, 1992, 2.04[c]). (The client's responses can be entered on the computer later, if desired.) Remember, the professional's ethical duty to clients is to create the most comfortable testing situation possible for *them* so that the assessment data will provide an accurate depiction of their current capabilities (ACA, 1997, E.7.d; APA, 1992, 2.02). Test publishers should provide data regarding any differences in performance that are likely to occur in computerized versus paper-and-pencil test administration so that interpretive assumptions made by clinicians are reasonable (Geisinger, 1998).[32]

Computer-based test interpretation can be a useful tool in the assessment process. Controlled studies have supported the superiority of actuarial interpretation over clinicians' judgment when the two had the same information available to them concerning the client (e.g., Tsemberis, Miller, & Gartner, 1996). The large empirical database underlying quality computer-based interpretive systems enables these systems to provide extremely valuable hypotheses concerning personality functioning and diagnosis, reflecting not only test scores, but also base rate information regarding various conditions in the relevant population. The closer the client comes to fitting a prototype score pattern, the more accurately the actuarial model is likely to describe the client's functioning (Butcher, 1997b). Computer-based reports also often provide treatment recommendations that might not otherwise be considered by a clinician (Butcher, 1997b; Tsemberis et al., 1996).

However, a computer-based interpretation should be viewed as one of several useful sources of information for a clinician interpreting assessment results, like a consultation with an experienced colleague, rather than as the final product of the assessment process (McMinn et al., 1999; Tallent, 1987). Clinicians should be able to obtain additional relevant information regarding a client's past and present functioning by interviewing the client, consulting his records, and administering a complete battery of tests, supplemented by behavioral observations obtained throughout the process (Carson, 1990; Tallent, 1987; Whitecotton et al., 1998). Nevertheless, computer-based test interpretations can provide an objective, unbiased perspective on the client's test performance (Pope et al., 2000). They can be an enormous time saver for the clinician, enabling her to provide other services to clients and substantially reduce the cost of assessment for clients and managed care organizations (Butcher, 1997b). Unquestionably, computer-based test interpretation using well-validated software programs can play an important and useful role in psychological assessment when combined with the skills and judgment of a competent clinician (Carson, 1990; Downey, Sinnett, & Seeberger, 1998; Whitecotton et al., 1998). Clinicians must achieve competence in the use of computerized tests and in general clinical assessment skills to make appropriate, ethical use of actuarial data and the other sources of information available to them (ACA, 1997, E.2; APA, 1992, 2.02, 2.08[c]). Professionals should carefully evaluate the quality of any computer-based test interpretation software they are considering using (ACA, 1997, E.2.b; APA, 1992, 2.08[b]). Research studies and reviews of the interpretive system are good sources of information. Also, the author of the program should have an excellent record of scholarship related to the validity of the test as well as the area of computer-based test interpretation (Moreland, 1987).

---

**Case Example 9.7**

*A counselor administers an MMPI-2 to a client in a substance abuse rehabilitation center. The computer-based test interpretation indicates that the client's profile could be consistent with a diagnosis of Schizophrenia, Paranoid Type. The counselor puts the computer-generated report in the client's record, along with the diagnosis. As a result, the client is transferred to a psychiatric facility. A clinical psychologist on the psychiatric unit reads the report and interviews the client. She believes the client is clearly not schizophrenic. She asks the client about a number of his MMPI-2 responses and finds that he answered that someone was trying to poison him because he was poisoning himself with alcohol. He reported strange and bizarre thought processes because they occurred when he was intoxicated. He said that people were trying to influence his mind because he was receiving therapy.*

*The psychologist changed the client's diagnosis back to Alcohol Dependence and transferred him back to the substance abuse rehabilitation unit.*

*Was the behavior of these clinicians ethically appropriate?*

---

## REPORT WRITING

In an assessment, the assessment report is generally the only information released to another professional (with the client's consent, of course). Test data and protocols are retained by the clinician who conducted the assessment (ACA, 1997, E.4.b; APA,

1992, 2.02[b]). Not releasing test data reduces the chance that the scores will be misinterpreted or misused and minimizes the invasion of the client's privacy. Test reports are released only to other professionals competent to understand the information provided (ACA, 1997, E.4; APA, 1992, 2.01[b]). With the client's consent, a clinician may release test data to another qualified professional who asks to review it in order to gain a better understanding of the client.

In preparing an assessment report, a clinician should, as always, be sensitive to the ethical importance of clear, understandable communication. The clinician should assume that professionals reading his assessment reports are not as familiar as he is with the tests used or with clinical terminology. After all, they did refer the client for testing, presumably to a clinician with more expertise in the area. The clinician should avoid using clinical terminology (e.g., paranoia) in a report because those terms have very weighty connotations for nonprofessionals and professionals alike (ACA, 1997, E.2.d). Rather, the goal of report writing is to describe the client's behavioral, cognitive, and emotional characteristics (i.e., how the client could be expected to behave, think, and feel in various situations, based on the assessment findings). The report should avoid value judgments concerning the client's behavior and focus on describing the person, in terms of both her strengths and weaknesses. The clinician should be certain to note any factors in the testing context that may have had a negative effect on the client's performance and might affect the accuracy of the interpretations provided in the report (ACA, 1997, E.9.a; APA, 1992, 2.05).

Providing an accurate sense of the individual's functioning is an important contribution to the client's future treatment, independent of a diagnosis. Any diagnosis that is provided in a report should be a clear implication of the description of the client contained in the report. Occasionally, a clinician perceives some pressure to provide a diagnosis in an assessment case because the client will not be eligible for services (e.g., accommodations for learning difficulties) without a qualifying diagnosis (i.e., learning disability). As a professional, it is certainly unethical to provide an invalid diagnosis, regardless of the potential benefit to the client (ACA, 1997, E.5.a; APA, 1992, 1.15, 2.01[b]). Always remember the potential costs to the client associated with diagnosis that were discussed earlier in this chapter.

A clinician should focus on answering the referral question in an assessment report. He should not include information in the report that is not directly relevant to the client's treatment (e.g., suggestions in projective data regarding possible sexual orientation issues in an assessment of the client's competency to stand trial). Such information could be harmful to the client (ACA, 1997, B.1.f; APA, 1992, 1.14, 5.03[a]).[33]

In making recommendations in an assessment report, a clinician should be clear and concise, and must bear in mind that, in making recommendations, he is an advocate for the client. Clinicians often confront issues regarding whether their recommendations should be based on what the client needs or what can realistically be provided for the client. For example, if a client has no health insurance coverage and is being treated at a small clinic, is it worthwhile to recommend that the client obtain a neurological evaluation if testing indicated the possibility of neurological impairment? The clinician might be concerned that the referring agency will be unable to act on such a recommendation, but that it might feel pressured to do so if the recommendation is included in the report and becomes part of the client's record.

This situation, in turn, could reduce the likelihood that the clinician will receive assessment referrals from the agency in the future.

In such a situation, the clinician's duty is clear: the best interest of the client must take precedence over the other considerations involved. A clinician's respect for other professionals entails that he should assume that a referring agency also has the best interests of the client in mind.[34] At the same time, a clinician should take reality factors into account by trying to think of recommendations that utilize available services in a creative manner. For example, a child with self-esteem and social skills deficits might benefit considerably from participation in a Big Brothers/Big Sisters program rather than more costly psychotherapy.

---

**Case Example 9.8**

*A counselor refers a client to a clinical psychologist for intellectual and personality assessment to evaluate the severity of the client's depressive symptoms and their impact on her cognitive functioning. The client calls the counselor after a feedback session with the psychologist. She is very upset and says that she needs to make an appointment with a neurologist because she is brain damaged. The counselor is very surprised by the finding. When he receives the test report from the psychologist the next day, he reads it carefully. He finds that her intellectual functioning is normal, though there is considerable variability between subtests. Personality testing indicated moderate depression. Nevertheless, there is a recommendation that she obtain a neurological evaluation for possible organicity.*

*After reassuring the client that there is no apparent evidence that she has suffered any brain damage, the counselor calls the psychologist and asks about the reason for the recommendation. The psychologist says that he always includes that recommendation in test reports to rule out the possibility that a client's psychiatric symptoms are the result of central nervous system pathology.*

*Is the psychologist's recommendation appropriate?*

---

## SPECIAL CONSIDERATIONS IN INDUSTRIAL/ORGANIZATIONAL ASSESSMENT

APA (1981b) has published a set of specialty guidelines for Industrial/Organizational (I/O) psychologists, who work in business settings. I/O professionals involved in assessment can also refer to the *Principles for the Validation and Use of Personnel Selection Procedures,* published by the Society for Industrial and Organizational Psychology (1987). I/O professionals are often involved in personnel assessment, which includes testing, interviewing, and reviewing applications and work samples (Murphy & Davidshofer, 1994). Testing is used in employment contexts both for screening job applicants and making promotion decisions. Tests used by personnel professionals provide information about a person's skills and abilities, personality functioning, and life experiences that can be useful in selecting the best qualified applicant for a job and in matching the right person with the right job.

When administering employment tests, personnel professionals should obtain the informed consent of test takers, as discussed earlier in the chapter. The major issues that should be addressed in the informed consent process are as follows: the nature and purpose of the test(s) to be taken; what the test scores will or might be used for, at present and in the future (e.g., employment selection, performance evaluations, promotion reviews); who will have access to the test scores (e.g., personnel professionals, potential supervisors, performance evaluators); what feedback will be provided after testing; and where the test data will be kept on file and for how long. Protection of the confidentiality of test data is as important in personnel settings as in any other assessment context.

Personnel professionals responsible for employment testing must be competent in the administration, scoring, and interpretation of the tests they use, like any other testing professional. Consultants who develop or recommend employment tests for organizations that do not have a staff psychologist or counselor competent in employment testing are obligated to ensure that the organization's personnel staff are sufficiently trained in the use of any tests being adopted (APA, 1992, 1.15, 2.06). Alternatively, the consultant should advise the organization to hire a competent testing service to conduct the employment testing.

A wide range of tests are used in employment settings, which can raise ethical issues. For example, the use of clinical tests (e.g., MMPI-2) in employment screening is certainly an invasion of the applicant's privacy and should be justified by the critical importance of the person's emotional state to his performance of the job (e.g., police officer) for which he is applying (ACA, 1997, E.2.b; APA, 1992, 2.02, 5.03). Clinical tests used in employment settings must also be well-validated for use with a nonclinical population. The Rorschach, for example, has questionable validity with normal populations, so it should not be used in personnel settings (Hunsley & Bailey, 1999). Also, the questionable validity of integrity (i.e., honesty) tests, which are sometimes used in personnel selection (Camara & Schneider, 1994), highlights the importance of personnel professionals possessing adequate knowledge of the validation of cutoff scores used in employment decisions for the groups being tested (ACA, 1997, E.6.a, E.8; APA, 1992, 2.04[c]).

Personnel professionals may also be called upon to develop employment tests. Competence to perform this task requires extensive knowledge and expertise in test development theory, psychometrics, and diversity issues (ACA, 1997, E.12; APA, 1992, 2.03). In most instances, a personnel professional does not possess the skills needed to produce a reliable, valid, and fair test. Her ethical duty, then, is to inform her supervisors that the task requires hiring a consultant competent to develop the test. As in other areas of professional practice, knowing the limits of one's abilities is a critical component of competence (ACA, 1997, E.2.a).

Decisions based on employment test results have significant economic implications for the applicants and employees affected, so it is not surprising that the use of tests in personnel settings has given rise to many legal challenges and to legislation concerning the appropriate use of tests in personnel decision making (Sireci & Geisinger, 1998). The two key issues in the appropriate use of tests in making personnel decisions are relevance and fairness. The relevance of a test for selecting the most qualified applicants for a particular job is a validity issue (Sireci &

Geisinger, 1998). A test is relevant if its content effectively addresses the skills, abilities, or characteristics relevant to the job (i.e., content validity) and if the possession of those skills, abilities, or characteristics can be demonstrated to be essential to the successful performance of the job (i.e., predictive or criterion validity). A comprehensive evaluation of what the job entails, referred to as a job analysis, is an important prerequisite for the development of a test with adequate content and criterion validity (Sireci & Geisinger, 1998). A valid test should predict job performance not just for workers in general, but for each group being tested (e.g., males, females, African Americans, Hispanics).

The issue of fairness concerns whether the test favors one group of applicants over another due to factors that are not essential to the performance of the job (Sireci & Geisinger, 1998). Personnel professionals have an ethical duty to identify situations in which an assessment device "may require adjustment in administration or interpretation" because of diversity issues such as gender, ethnicity, disability, or socioeconomic status (APA, 1992, 2.04[c]). For example, if the instructions on an accounting test are in English, it could place Hispanic applicants at a disadvantage, even though they might possess the skills needed to perform the job (ACA, 1997, E.8). If all applicants are required to take the test in English, then knowledge of English must be essential for performing the job. It still might be fairer to applicants from diverse groups to provide instructions in other languages, even if the test items are in English (Sireci & Geisinger, 1998).

Similarly, the Americans with Disabilities Act (ADA; Pub. L. No. 101-336) requires that an employer provide testing accommodations for disabled individuals if a disability prevents them from completing a standard test administration, but not from performing the job for which they are applying (ADA, 1990). Depending on the nature of the disability, accommodations might involve altering the time limit for a test, how the applicant's responses will be recorded, the format of the test (e.g., altering or eliminating items that present information graphically, providing large print or Braille version of the test), or how it will be administered (e.g., oral administration). For accommodations based on diversity or disability issues to be acceptable, they must not impact the validity of the test for its purpose of selecting the most qualified applicants or employees. Personnel professionals are responsible for empirically confirming the validity of the accommodated version of the test (Geisinger, 1994).

---

**Case Example 9.9**

*A visually impaired applicant for a police dispatcher position requests a large print version of the MMPI-2 for her employment testing. The personnel psychologist supervising the testing refuses her request because he cannot find any information concerning the effect of this altered format on the validity of MMPI-2 results.*

*Is the psychologist's action appropriate?*

---

## Adverse Impact in Employment Testing

When diverse groups of applicants produce substantially different scores on an employment test, the test is said to produce an *adverse impact* (Sireci & Geisinger, 1998). For example, if 80% of white applicants achieve passing grades on an employment screening test compared to only 60% of African American applicants, the test produces an adverse impact on African American applicants. In 1978, the Equal Employment Opportunities Commission, U.S. Civil Service Commission, U.S. Department of Labor, and U.S. Department of Justice adopted a set of Uniform Guidelines on Employee Selection Procedures. Adverse impact was defined in these rules as any situation in which the passing rate for a protected group is less than four-fifths (80%) of the passing rate for the highest scoring group.

The legality of a test used for employment purposes is questionable whenever the test is demonstrated to produce an adverse impact (Sireci & Geisinger, 1998). The company using the test is legally required to demonstrate the content and/or criterion validity of the test. Professionals using employment tests should be familiar with the procedures for establishing validity that are outlined in the *Standards for Educational and Psychological Testing* (American Educational Research Association et al., 1999). The adverse impact of a valid employment test can often be reduced by *banding* scores falling within a range determined by the standard error of difference (an index of statistical significance for the difference between test scores) of the test (Sireci & Geisinger, 1998). All scores within a band are treated as equal, which permits members of diverse groups with lower scores falling within the band interval to be selected when they would not have been selected based on raw test score alone. Although banding methods have been criticized, they do reduce adverse impact without ignoring the importance of selecting individuals with the best test scores (Sireci & Geisinger, 1998).

Personnel professionals involved in employment testing have an ethical obligation to make certain that the tests they use do not discriminate against any group of applicants (ACA, 1997, C.5.a; APA, 1992, 1.10). This ethical duty serves to protect both the firm employing the testing professional and the population being tested. When a test is demonstrated to be valid for predicting performance in a particular job, but produces adverse impact, the assessment professional has not completely fulfilled her duty to prevent discrimination and promote diversity within her organization. Also, the professional has an ethical duty to promote nondiscriminatory practices by investigating her organization's recruiting practices to determine why adequate numbers of qualified applicants from diverse groups are not applying for positions with the organization. She would then be expected to use this knowledge to improve the organization by developing better methods of recruiting and/or training applicants. The recruitment of effective minority, female, and disabled applicants is the best solution to increasing diversity (Sireci & Geisinger, 1998). If the ethics of a company do not involve an organizational concern about promoting diversity and eliminating discriminatory practices, the I/O professional should inform the organization of her commitment to the ethical standards of her profession (ACA, 1997, H.2.c; APA, 1992, 8.03).

The popularity of employment testing demonstrates that employers are very impressed with these tests as an objective, empirical method of making personnel decisions. Personnel professionals might, therefore, need to educate their organization about the limitations of the selection tests in predicting job performance by pointing out other variables (e.g., work history, performance appraisals, motivation) that may also be important predictors of performance.

Another common duty of personnel professionals is the development of methods to assess employees' job performance. Professionals can use performance appraisal as an additional means to promote the development of nondiscriminatory organizational practices and policies (ACA, 1997, C.5.a; APA, 1992, 1.10). Although the judgments and ratings of supervisors or other evaluators are never completely objective, professionals have an obligation to develop appraisal methods that are as objective and behaviorally based as possible (Murphy & Davidshofer, 1994). For instance, the use of multiple raters reduces the likelihood that the personal preferences of a supervisor will bias the appraisal. Also, I/O professionals can advocate for the development of a performance appraisal based on a careful job analysis, with input from the employee(s) doing the job, so the appraisal will comprehensively assess the tasks involved in an employee's job.

The performance appraisal system should incorporate adequate feedback to employees. Personnel professionals should encourage organizations to view performance appraisal as a learning experience and an opportunity for employees to improve their skills. Raters (e.g., supervisors) should be informed in advance whether their individual ratings or the average of several ratings will be provided to employees. Finally, the confidentiality of performance ratings, like any other assessment results, should be protected within the organization, but raters should be informed that their ratings will, in all likelihood, not remain confidential if an employee pursues a complaint concerning the fairness of her performance evaluation.

---

**Case Example 9.10**

*An accounting supervisor provides performance appraisal ratings for the six accountants under his supervision. When the employees receive feedback on the ratings, one accountant asks the supervisor why she received such a low rating on "collegiality." The supervisor replies that the accountant is very shy. The accountant informs the supervisor that he misunderstood the meaning of the term collegiality. The supervisor said that the term had not really been explained by the I/O psychologist who conducted the training session for supervisors, and he had thought it meant friendly and outgoing.*

---

## SPECIAL CONSIDERATIONS IN COLLEGE ORIENTATION TESTING

Many counselors and psychologists are involved in the testing of first-year college or university students during the student orientation process. Students may be asked to complete career interest tests, psychological adjustment screening measures, and even measures being used in faculty members' research. Group testing of this sort does not affect the testing professional's ethical duty to obtain the informed consent of each student. The tests should be described and the purpose of students' taking them should be explained. Any limitations on the confidentiality of students' test scores and responses must also be enumerated. Students must be informed that they have the right to refuse to complete the tests, without penalty. They should also have the opportunity to receive feedback on their test performance. It would be unprofessional and unethical to simply use students as a vehicle to amass assessment data. Finally, if the testing process is in any way related to a research study, students' informed consent as research participants must be obtained. Ethical issues pertaining to research participation are addressed in Chapter 11.

## PRACTICE CASE INVOLVING THE MODEL OF ETHICAL DECISION MAKING

A woman is hospitalized voluntarily for depression, although the admission was clearly influenced by her husband's insistence that she was "having a nervous breakdown." She was not very communicative when she was admitted. Most of the information obtained about her during the admission process was provided by her husband. At her husband's urging, she signed a consent form allowing hospital staff to continue to consult with him about all aspects of her treatment.

A counseling psychologist on the hospital staff conducts an intellectual and personality assessment to evaluate her condition. As the assessment progresses, the woman gradually becomes more comfortable and willing to discuss her situation with him. The psychologist learns that the client's depression had developed during the previous two months, largely as a result of the conflict she had been experiencing with her husband. She had found out that he had engaged in a series of extramarital affairs. The "breakdown" occurred when he filed for divorce. She reports feeling "totally overwhelmed" by the situation. Her biggest fear is that her husband will try to gain custody of their sons in the divorce proceedings.

The psychologist learns in a consultation with the woman's inpatient therapist that the husband denied having an affair. Her husband said that his wife had developed this strange belief as she became increasingly depressed and that the breakup was a result of her psychiatric deterioration, rather than a cause of it.

The testing reveals that she is indeed suffering from Major Depression and also qualifies for a diagnosis of Avoidant Personality Disorder. She is painfully shy, extremely sensitive, and very easily intimidated by other people. Her husband has managed her entire life, which is why the breakup has been so devastating for her. The psychologist does not believe that the woman's report of her husband's affairs is delusional in nature, so he decides not to include the information about the affairs in his assessment report.

The husband requests a copy of a summary of the assessment report, supposedly because he wants to make sure his wife receives appropriate outpatient care after she leaves the hospital. When the psychologist consults his client about releasing the information to her husband, she simply says, "Okay, whatever he wants." When the psychologist asks, "But what do you want?" she simply answers, "My children."

The psychologist is concerned that some of the information in the assessment summary could reflect negatively on his client in a custody determination and is hesitant to release it to the husband. The psychologist wishes he had included more of the client's statements about her husband's possible misbehavior during the marriage in the report.

What should the psychologist do?

## SUMMARY

This chapter addressed issues pertaining to diagnostic assessment and psychological and educational testing. Although psychiatric diagnosis is intended to enhance clinicians' understanding of their clients' problems, critics argue that clients are simply pigeonholed by diagnostic classifications, with little attention paid to their individual life circumstances. The fascination with diagnostic testing can also lead to the misclassification of clients if clinicians fail to take into account the population base rates of the conditions they are attempting to diagnose.

Informed consent issues for testing include discussing with clients the tests to be used and the purpose of testing, as well as providing feedback when testing is completed. Testing feedback enables clients to make an informed decision about sharing evaluation reports with other agencies or professionals. Clinicians should use only well-validated tests and only for the purpose for which they were developed and with the populations with which they were validated. Clinicians should be sensitive to diversity issues in assessment and avoid evaluating members of diverse groups by reference to norms developed with more homogeneous samples.

Computer-based test administration and scoring are very useful technological aids that reduce response and scoring errors. However, taking a test on a computer may have an adverse effect on the performance of clients who are not used to computers. Actuarial computer-based test interpretations are a useful component in the interpretation process, but assessment reports should not simply be printouts of actuarial interpretations. Reports should integrate information from all the sources available to a competent assessment professional.

Personnel professionals should use selection tests that are valid predictors of job performance. These professionals are concerned with fairness in testing and work to ensure that the tests they use do not discriminate unfairly against members of diverse groups. They design objective, behaviorally based methods of evaluating employee performance.

# 10 Ethical Issues in Teaching and Supervision

A substantial proportion of counselors and psychologists take on the role of faculty and/or supervisor, on a full- or part-time basis, to train the next generation of professionals. Instead of working with clients, faculty provide professional services to students. However, many of the ethical issues of concern to faculty members addressed in this chapter are related to those affecting the therapist-client relationship. Additional issues that are unique to instructional contexts will also be presented.

## COMPETENCE

College and university faculty are expected to make professional contributions in the areas of teaching, scholarship (e.g., research), and service to their institution, profession, and community. Effective faculty must develop competence in each of these areas (ACA, 1997, C.2.a-b; APA, 1992, 1.04).

### DEVELOPING COMPETENCE IN TEACHING

Historically, mental health professionals received relatively little graduate training in providing instruction to students. This situation was not unique to the mental health disciplines; graduate programs in all fields focused primarily on familiarizing students with major academic content areas and providing training in research methods that would enable students to complete their theses or dissertations. Professionals beginning their teaching career were generally well-versed in their specialty area and in their academic field in general, but had little or no specific training in methods of conveying these ideas effectively to students. Of course, they had been exposed to numerous teaching styles as undergraduate and graduate students and many had also been employed as graduate teaching assistants, which gave them an opportunity to learn more about the mechanics of organizing a course, grading students' work, and preparing and delivering an occasional class lecture. However, for the most part, beginning faculty members learned teaching skills on the job. Initially, they generally attempted to blend the styles of a few of their favorite teachers and, over time, developed their own teaching style based on feedback on their teaching performance obtained from colleagues, supervisors, and students.

In recent years, the importance of assisting graduate students and faculty members in developing teaching competence has received much more attention. Many graduate programs in the mental health professions provide courses devoted specifically to instructional theories and methods. These courses address both theoretical issues and the development of specific skills that are important to effective teaching, such as syllabus and exam preparation, textbook selection, classroom management and methods of preventing academic dishonesty (i.e., plagiarism and cheating), ethical and diversity issues, and lecture preparation. Graduate students are also frequently afforded the opportunity to teach one or more courses as teaching apprentices.

APA has long recognized the teaching of psychology as a distinct area of specialization and research. APA Division 2 (Society for the Teaching of Psychology) is devoted specifically to teaching issues and publishes its own journal, *Teaching of Psychology*. A number of other journals have also been developed that provide information about innovative teaching theories and methods.[35] National and regional teaching institutes and conferences provide additional resources for graduate students and faculty to augment their repertoire of instructional skills.

---

**Case Example 10.1**

*A first-year member of the counseling faculty thinks that he might have a tendency to identify too strongly with the struggles of his students. He does not want to be perceived as an "easy" instructor, so he sets out to create difficult, challenging assignments for his students and has more rigorous requirements in his sections of courses than anyone else in the department. He makes a point of telling his colleagues about the high percentage of students failing his exams.*

---

## Maintaining Competence as a Teacher

Although faculty members are generally well-trained today prior to beginning their instructional careers, it is extremely important that they remain up-to-date concerning developments in teaching theory, applications, and technology, as well as in the content areas they teach (ACA, 1997, C.2.f; APA, 1992, 1.05). Like all other fields of human endeavor, the mental health professions are producing new research discoveries and information at a continually increasing rate. As discussed in Chapter 2, Dubin estimated in 1972 that half of the knowledge gained in graduate study in psychology was outdated within 10 to 12 years. The revolution in information technology that has occurred during the past 25 years has undoubtedly caused professionals' knowledge to become outdated even more quickly today. New editions of textbooks are certainly helpful in maintaining competence, but faculty must also stay current by reading journals in their areas of specialization as well as those devoted to instructional issues and methods, attending teaching conferences and other professional meetings, and pursuing continuing education opportunities.

Competent faculty should incorporate updated information into their class presentations, rather than relying on old lecture notes. Students become extremely frustrated when outdated information presented in class is inconsistent with what they read in their textbook. Also, faculty members should always be aware of diversity issues relevant to the subject matter they are presenting (ACA, 1997, F.1.a; APA, 1992, 1.08). For example, in discussing the issue of diagnosis, the potential significance of cultural, ethnicity, gender, age, and socioeconomic factors for the validity of diagnostic assumptions should be discussed. The task of maintaining competence as a faculty member, like most ethical duties, is a very challenging, though not impossible one.

---

**Case Example 10.2**

*A very senior faculty member uses the same lecture notes for her classes as she did 10 years ago. She becomes annoyed with students who point out the discrepancies between information she presents in class and more current information presented in the textbook. She finally tells students that on exams, they should stick with the information she presents in class when it is inconsistent with the erroneous information provided by the textbook.*

---

## "Jack" of All Subject Areas, Master of None?

The challenges encountered by faculty members in developing and maintaining competence vary considerably depending on the context in which they teach. At a large, doctoral degree-granting institution, a faculty member might teach one or two courses each semester within his specific area of expertise. On the other hand, a faculty member at a small undergraduate college might be expected to teach a wide variety of courses as part of a small department. In a single semester, a clinical psychologist might be asked to teach Introductory Psychology, Abnormal Psychology, Developmental Psychology, and Statistics. Consequently, faculty members at "teaching institutions" must devote considerably greater energy to becoming and remaining competent in these varied teaching areas (ACA, 1997, C.2.b; APA, 1992, 1.04[b]). (This demand is one of the reasons why, historically, faculty members at such institutions have not been expected to engage in as much research activity as those with less diverse or lighter teaching loads.) Regardless of their situations, faculty members should remember that it is ethically inappropriate for them to teach a course outside the boundaries of their competence (ACA, 1997, C.2.a; APA, 1992, 1.04[a]).

## Burnout

Like clinicians, faculty members can become discouraged and cynical about their work. Personal problems, professional setbacks, and negative feedback from students (particularly if it is felt to be undeserved) can all cause a faculty member to feel like a failure who is not achieving her goals in life. Her perceived lack of personal accomplishment will likely cause her to become less committed to maintaining a high level of professional performance (Vredenburgh et al., 1999). Like clinicians, faculty members suffering burnout may become withdrawn and irritable. A faculty member may evidence signs of burnout in adopting an adversarial relationship with students. She might react to student criticism of her performance by complaining that students are lazy, unmotivated, and always seeking to blame someone else for their own failures. The faculty member might then set unreasonably difficult standards in her classes, ostensibly to motivate students, but perhaps with the added motivation to punish them for their criticism of her. In other cases, genuine disappointment in students' lack of interest in her chosen field can reduce a faculty member's investment in and enjoyment of teaching.

The "publish or perish" expectations for scholarly productivity at many academic institutions can also contribute significantly to faculty burnout. The externally imposed pressure on faculty to produce meaningful research in order to earn tenure and/or promotion can make research activity extremely stressful and interfere with a faculty member's experiencing any intrinsic enjoyment from conducting research (Singh, Mishra, & Kim, 1998). Clearly, when people no longer enjoy their work, they are at elevated risk for burnout.

Obviously, any decline in the motivation or professionalism of a faculty member impairs her competence as a teacher (ACA, 1997, C.2.g; APA, 1992, 1.13, 1.14). It is the faculty member's ethical obligation to identify and seek help for any emotional problems she is experiencing that could impinge on her professional performance. Remediation might involve a break from teaching, the pursuit of faculty development opportunities to enhance her skills, or, in extreme cases, a recognition that teaching is not an appropriate career path for her.

---

**Case Example 10.3**

*A psychology faculty member has developed a very unfavorable opinion of students over the years. He feels that all they care about is their grade for a course, not about how much they learn. He tells students that they are the only group of consumers who demand less for their money. He sees his task as being to challenge students to think. He asks extremely difficult exam questions that require students to go well beyond the information presented in the lectures and textbooks in order to synthesize a comprehensive answer. A substantial majority of students fail his courses, even his graduate courses.*

*When students complain about the exams, the chair of the department finds that even she cannot answer several of the questions. She discusses the matter with the faculty member, suggesting that perhaps he expects too much of his students. He replies that everyone else in the department expects too little.*

---

## INFORMED CONSENT

### PROVIDING A SYLLABUS

When students enroll in a course, the ethical duty of informed consent obligates the faculty member to provide students with information regarding the scheduled meeting times for the course, goals of the course and material to be covered, the course requirements and assessment methods to be used, and the grading procedures for the course (ACA, 1997, F.2.c; APA, 1992, 6.02[b]). The course syllabus serves as the primary informed consent document in academic courses. It should be distributed at the first meeting, or at least early enough that students can still elect to change their schedule if the course is not one they want to take. The instructor should make certain that students adding the class after the first meeting also receive a syllabus and the opportunity to pose any questions they might have about the course. Once the syllabus has been distributed, instructors should make every effort to conform to the schedule and terms set forth in it. The syllabus should be viewed as an informal contract between the instructor and students. If changes in the schedule or requirements for the course do become necessary, they should not impact students negatively (ACA, 1997, F.2.c; APA, 1992, 1.14, 6.05[b]).

---

**Case Example 10.4**

*After the semester has begun, a psychology instructor takes on a research project that will require a great deal of his time near the end of the term. He realizes that he will not have sufficient time to grade the term papers he had assigned in one of his classes. He notifies students at mid-semester that he is canceling the research paper that had been listed in the syllabus and that the final exam will now account for 40% of the course grade, instead of the 20% stated in the syllabus.*

*Is there an ethical problem with the instructor's solution?*

---

### PROVIDING LETTERS OF REFERENCE TO STUDENTS AND SUPERVISEES

Faculty members and supervisors are frequently asked to provide references for students seeking admission to further academic training, or applying for academic awards, financial aid, certification and licensure, or employment. A letter of reference is a public statement made by the professional; she is ethically obligated to be truthful and forthright in all such statements (APA, 1992, 3.03[a]). Therefore, a faculty member or supervisor should not agree to provide a letter of reference unless she is very comfortable with the student's qualifications (ACA, 1997, F.1.h).

Providing letters of reference involves informed consent issues because students are often asked to waive their right to review the letters, thereby protecting the confidentiality of the writer. As with other informed consent situations discussed previously, it would be difficult for a student to meaningfully consent to waive his legal right to review the letter unless he had at least a general notion of its contents. If a faculty member feels that she cannot write a very positive, helpful letter, she should model professional integrity for the student by simply being honest with him regarding any reservations she has (and would need to include in a letter) about his qualifications. A faculty member who agrees to write a letter for a student she feels is not well-qualified is really not doing him a favor. From a student's point of view, it is much better to have a professor or supervisor decline to provide a letter of reference than to have her write a lukewarm or negative letter.

## MULTIPLE RELATIONSHIPS

There are several types of dual relationships that can and do occur in the context of teaching. Mental health professionals endeavor to avoid multiple relationships in teaching, as they do in other areas of their professional activity (ACA, 1997, F.1.b; APA, 1992, 1.17). When a multiple relationship cannot be avoided, the faculty member should be sensitive to the potential for students to be harmed by such relationships and take appropriate steps to protect students' interests (ACA, 1997, D.1.k; APA, 1992, 1.19). A common multiple relationship in teaching involves students taking courses from a faculty member and being involved simultaneously in an employee-employer/supervisor relationship with the faculty member. For example, graduate students often take a class from the professor they are assigned to as a teaching assistant for the semester. While there is nothing inherently improper about such an arrangement, it does fit the definition of a *dual* relationship and, thus, requires that the faculty member be vigilant in ensuring that the relationship does not in any way exploit or harm the student or his classmates. For example, in the context of interacting with the student as an assistant, the faculty member should not provide any information regarding the class in which the assistant is a student that would not be equally available to the other graduate students in the class. Also, the faculty member should be particularly careful not to assign duties to the assistant that exceed his job description. A student with a 20-hour per week assistantship might be less likely to object to being assigned 25 hours of work each week by a professor from whom he is also taking a class, fearing that the protest might adversely affect the professor's perception of him and, in turn, his grade in the professor's course.

A similar issue could arise if a faculty member were to ask a student enrolled in her class if he would like to earn some extra money by babysitting her children or by doing yard work for her. This type of multiple relationship is potentially problematic because the student might feel, rightly or wrongly, that if he declined the faculty member's offer, it would negatively impact his grade in her course. If the student did decline the offer and performed poorly in the class, the student might attribute his low grade to the multiple relationship issue. It would be difficult for the faculty member to alter the student's perception of the matter, particularly if the grading for the course included an element of subjectivity (e.g., essay exams). An ethical professional is sensitive not only to avoiding treating students unequally, but also to the potential for students to believe that they have been treated unequally.

Alternatively, a multiple relationship with a student might be perceived by *others* as affecting the faculty member's evaluation of that student's performance (Blevins-Knabe, 1992). For example, a graduate assistant might interact with the faculty member in a more informal manner than other students, resulting in other students perceiving the assistant as the "teacher's pet" and believing that he receives preferential treatment from the professor. The same situation could develop with an undergraduate student who works as a babysitter for the faculty member or assists him with his research. Again, the important element to be aware of here is students' *perceptions* of the situation. Faculty must be careful not to create an impression of possible bias or impropriety in their professional roles.

The issue of multiple relationships outside the college or university is much more likely to arise in a smaller town, as was mentioned in Chapter 7 (ACA, 1997, A.6.a; APA, 1992, 1.17[a]). A faculty member in a small college town encounters her students everywhere — working in the grocery store, the bank, her child's preschool, etc. Her neighbors' children might well become students in her classes. While such multiple relationships are a fact of life in such contexts, it is the professional's obligation to ensure that there is no potential for students to be harmed or exploited in any way. If such potential exists, the professional must refrain from entering into the multiple relationship. If the relationship already exists and is found to be problematic, the professional "attempts to resolve it with due regard for the best interests of the affected person and maximal compliance with the Ethics Code" (APA, 1992, 1.17[c]).

No matter how tempting it may be for a faculty member with a part-time private practice to treat current or former students, it is not a good idea because the preexisting relationship results in a mixing of professional roles (ACA, 1997, A.6; APA, 1992, 1.17[b]). Students will ask a clinical faculty member to provide therapy for them because they trust and admire her, but she should recognize that it is better for them to begin therapy with someone they can approach on a more equal footing, as opposed to someone who is already an authority figure for them in another context (Pearson & Piazza, 1997).

---

**Case Example 10.5**

*A neighbor and close friend of a counseling faculty member tells him that she will be taking a counseling course as part of her Interdisciplinary Studies degree. She indicates that she will be enrolling in the section of the course he teaches because the time at which his section meets is more convenient for her schedule than the other time at which the course is offered. The faculty member is aware of the multiple relationship issue involved in the situation, but he questions whether he has the right to prevent her from taking the course at a time that is convenient for her. The course involves objective (true-false) exams, so he does not envision a problem with the objectivity of his judgment regarding her academic performance. He decides to say nothing and allow her to enroll.*
*Should the counselor have taken some other action?*

---

## SEXUAL RELATIONSHIPS WITH STUDENTS AND SUPERVISEES

The appropriate limits on multiple relationships in academic settings have proven much more controversial than those in therapy contexts. While sexual relationships with clients have long been recognized as unethical, psychology's ethical principles had never stated that such relationships with consenting adult students were strictly unethical until the 1992 revision (ACA, 1997, F.1.c; APA, 1992, 1.19[b]). Prior to that, a faculty member was prohibited only from being involved with a student taking his class (APA, 1990, Principle 7[d]). One reason for the slow development of these guidelines, as well as the controversy surrounding them, is that historically, it was not uncommon for faculty to become involved with, and even marry, currently enrolled graduate students.

Eventually, the ethical codes of the mental health professions were expanded to address more comprehensively the significant inequality of power present in teacher-student relationships. The "Ethical Principles" now states that a sexual relationship is inappropriate if a faculty member has any "evaluative or direct authority" over the student or supervisee "because such relationships are so likely to impair judgment or be exploitative" (APA, 1992, 1.19). However, this standard still leaves considerable ambiguity regarding whether a faculty member can have a relationship with a graduate student if the student never takes a class from him. Although professional ethical codes have not eliminated this "loophole" in the prohibition of teacher-student sexual relationships, most colleges and universities have institutional policies prohibiting such relationships between a faculty member and any enrolled student. Also, some state boards have developed guidelines more restrictive than those of the APA and ACA ethical codes. For example, the Texas State Board of Examiners of Psychologists prohibits any sexual relationship with a student matriculating in the faculty member's department (Hays & Costello, 1994).

APA and ACA do not prohibit a faculty member from having a relationship with a former student following graduation because this situation is recognized as being quite different from a sexual involvement with a currently enrolled student. Also, faculty members are not generally as authoritative and emotionally significant to their students as therapists are to their clients. Consequently, unlike sexual relationships between therapists and former clients, sexual involvements between faculty members and former students are not viewed as interfering with the current or future needs of the former student or as involving a greater potential for emotional harm than any other intimate relationship. However, the potential for inequality in such relationships remains an important consideration for ethical professionals.

### Using Students as Research Participants

Faculty members are often tempted to use the students in their own classes as research participants. If the instructor offers her students the opportunity to participate in her research project, she is initiating a multiple relationship with them. In such a situation, it would be improper for the instructor to coerce her students in any manner to participate in her particular research study by, for example, making participation in the study a course requirement (ACA, 1997, G.2.c; APA, 1992, 6.11). Even if participation is voluntary, the instructor should also be sensitive to the fact that students in her class might be more reluctant to refuse to participate in her research than in a study conducted by another researcher (Galassi, 1991). Therefore, if the instructor has a research participation requirement, it must apply to a wider range of studies, perhaps to all projects using the student subject pool. Also, if the instructor offers her students any incentive (e.g., extra credit in her course) to participate in her study, the same benefit must be available if students choose to participate instead in a different study being conducted in the department. Finally, the instructor should have alternative means available for students to earn the extra credit if they choose not to participate in a research study (APA, 1992, 6.11[d]).

## CONFIDENTIALITY

Student records, including information regarding a student's performance in a faculty member's course (e.g., test grades), are confidential (APA, 1992, 5.03[b]). The release of student information is protected by the Family Educational Rights and Privacy Act of 1974 (FERPA, Pub. L. No. 93-380), often referred to as the "Buckley Amendment." Faculty members cannot post a student's grades by name or Social Security number because she could be identified by other students. Faculty members wishing to post grades should obtain the student's consent to do so; the student should be identified by a code number or name known only to the faculty member and student.

However, other communications between a student and a faculty member are not typically regarded as confidential, unless both parties agree in advance to make it so. This fact can pose a problem for faculty members in the mental health professions because students often equate a discussion with their psychology or counseling professor (even one who is not a clinician) with a psychotherapy context, assuming that anything they communicate will be treated as confidential. Mental health professionals should be sensitive to this perception and avoid potentially harming a student by being very careful about sharing any personal information revealed by a student (APA, 1992, 1.14).

---

**Case Example 10.6**

*A faculty member posts his students' grades using only the last four numbers of their social security numbers after obtaining their consent to do so. One of his classes has only six students. They quickly figure out that, although students' names do not appear on the grade sheet, the grades are posted in alphabetical order. One of the students complains that the faculty member's procedure for posting grades violates her right to privacy.*

*Does she have a legitimate complaint?*

---

## PROFESSIONAL AND SCIENTIFIC RESPONSIBILITY

### ADMINISTERING AN UNDERGRADUATE OR GRADUATE CURRICULUM

Mental health professionals who have a role in the administration of academic programs are responsible for making certain that those programs operate in a manner consistent with the ethical code of their profession and federal and state statutes. Selection criteria for admitting students into an academic program must be unbiased, objective, and valid predictors of academic performance. Policies for admission to a program, retention, academic probation, and dismissal must be explained thoroughly to students during their orientation to the program and administered fairly (ACA, 1997, F.2.a). Furthermore, students must be provided with timely evaluative feedback regarding their performance in a program (ACA, 1997, F.2.c; APA, 1992, 6.05).

### PRESENTING A BALANCED VIEWPOINT ON CONTROVERSIAL ISSUES

All mental health professionals have personal preferences for particular theoretical perspectives in psychology or counseling based, to a significant extent, on their personal values. When presenting information in class, it is important to remember that models in psychology, including those a faculty member has adopted, are theories, not facts. Thus, if an instructor presents only his perspective, a Rogerian one, for example, regarding psychopathology, he is arbitrarily imposing his values on the students (ACA, 1997, A.5.b; APA, 1992, 1.09, 6.03[b]). Instead, a responsible faculty member is careful to present a variety of models in an unbiased fashion, so that students get as much information as possible on the topic (ACA, 1997, F.2.f; APA,

1992, 6.03[a]). An instructor should consider it a credit to the objectivity of his class presentations if, at the end of the semester, his students are unsure which model he prefers. An instructor should always be respectful of the viewpoints expressed by students, particularly those that disagree with his perspective (APA, 1992, 6.03[b]).

A related point is that it is highly unprofessional to derogate or belittle other professions or areas of specialization when presenting information to students (ACA, 1997, C.6.a; APA, 1992, Principle B). Such behavior demonstrates a lack of respect for other professionals and serves only to betray the limited competence and lack of integrity of the instructor. Irresponsible public statements of this sort can harm students by causing them to question their commitment to a future profession or to reconsider taking courses from a particular instructor. Instructors should, instead, serve as role models of professional, ethical behavior (ACA, 1997, F.1.a).

## MAKING STUDENTS SKEPTICAL CONSUMERS OF RESEARCH FINDINGS

The task of a faculty member is to educate, not to try to convince students that her research or profession is infallible. Faculty members must exercise great care to avoid overstating the evidence in support of a particular theory or research finding. (This point is similar to the one regarding professionals' public statements in general in Chapters 2 and 3.) For example, in presenting research results, instructors should be careful to distinguish *statistical* and *practical* significance to prevent students from overinterpreting the meaningfulness of research findings. Instructors should explain that statistical significance refers to the probability that observed group differences reflect genuine differences in the underlying populations (Keppel, Saufley, & Tokunaga, 1992). Furthermore, instructors should point out that statistically significant differences between groups are affected by sample size, such that with large samples, very small differences of little practical importance can sometimes achieve statistical significance. For example, in studies of gender differences in children's cognitive abilities, small differences in the average scores achieved by boys and girls constituted a statistically significant difference due to the very large samples of boys and girls used for the studies. Instructors presenting these research findings should also point out that the variation in performance within each gender group (e.g., among girls) was much greater than the difference between the two groups (Maccoby, 1990).

---

### Case Example 10.7

*A psychology faculty member takes every opportunity to criticize projective assessment as "voodoo psychology" in his classes. When clinical faculty members hear about these criticisms, they ask him to discuss his criticisms with them. He is not a clinician and has no expertise in projective assessment. He responds that voluminous empirical literature exists that attests to the invalidity of projective techniques. He says that he talks about this issue in his classes not to present his clinical colleagues in a negative light, but to make his students skeptical consumers of their psychology training.*

*Is the faculty member's behavior ethically appropriate?*

## DISTANCE LEARNING

Increasingly, academic programs are making courses available through distance learning arrangements with other institutions or over the Internet. The instructional technologies used in these initiatives hold tremendous promise for making academic and professional training resources more accessible to potential students. Although distance learning arrangements may involve learning environments that are very different from a traditional classroom, they do not in any way alter the obligations of program administrators and faculty members to their students. All students accepted for enrollment in a distance learning course must be given the same opportunity to succeed. For example, all students must have access to study materials, which can be a problem if students at a distant location cannot get to the university library to read materials placed on reserve. The ethical concerns about distance learning become much greater if all or most of a training curriculum is delivered in this format, as opposed to just a course or two. It is considerably easier to teach courses addressing a content area (e.g., statistics) via distance learning than a skills development course (e.g., personality assessment). Training programs must determine that competent instruction and student mastery of a course's subject matter can be achieved through distance learning before offering the course in such a format.

# TEACHING STUDENTS ABOUT VALUES AND PROFESSIONAL ETHICS

## TEACHING STUDENTS ABOUT ETHICS IN COURSES OTHER THAN ETHICS

Faculty members teaching undergraduate and graduate courses in psychology, counseling, and social work deal generally with one or more of the content areas addressed in this book: therapy, assessment, and research. Each of these areas involves a substantial number of serious ethical issues. It is very important that instructors communicate ethical standards and values to their students whenever the opportunity arises in the context of their courses (ACA, 1997, F.2.d). For example, when teaching a research methods course, an instructor should discuss issues of informed consent, confidentiality, and debriefing, as well as explaining to students how IRBs function to protect the interests of research participants. An early introduction to ethical considerations in their field of study will serve to increase students' sensitivity to these issues as they prepare to enter their chosen profession. Ethics training should not be reserved for ethics courses.

## ADDRESSING THE ISSUE OF THERAPIST VALUES IN TRAINING MENTAL HEALTH PROFESSIONALS

In Chapter 7, the important role of therapist values in the conduct of psychotherapy was discussed. Vachon and Agresti (1992) have developed a three-phase model that graduate training programs can use to increase novice therapists' awareness of their personal and professional values and to help them more effectively manage the role of therapist and client values in the psychotherapy process.

Phase 1 involves increasing a therapist's awareness of her personal values. This phase of values training encourages the therapist to identify and explore the personal values underlying her views about psychotherapy, different types of clients, diagnosis, and other issues (e.g., religious belief) that play a role in her approach to working with clients. This process will enable the therapist to reflect consciously on the personal, subjective values that guided her choices of an orientation to therapy and a style of relating to clients, as well as her positions on other professional issues. This book addresses some of these issues (e.g., psychotherapy orientation and values in Chapter 7, and the values operative in the diagnostic process in Chapter 9). In fact, each topic addressed in this book is intended to encourage readers to reflect consciously on their personal values concerning fundamental issues in professional practice.

Phase 2 of the training model helps a therapist develop an ethical framework that integrates her increased conscious awareness of her personal values from Phase 1 and her knowledge of her ethical obligations as a professional. In other words, in Phase 2 the therapist can apply her increased sensitivity to the personal values and issues of self-interest that might influence her professional judgments to her ethical decision-making process. Her awareness of her personal values represents important information for her to consider in Step 2 of the model of ethical decision making presented in Chapter 6.

Phase 3 develops methods to deal with religious values and issues involving "a client's general philosophy of life" in therapy (Vachon & Agresti, 1992). Clearly, respect for the values of clients is fundamental to the therapy process. However, a therapist's personal values will influence her perception of a client's perspective on life. For example, a behavior therapist who views life in a baldly empirical manner and firmly believes that a scientific model is the best perspective for understanding each and every aspect of human existence can respect a client's religious beliefs, but cannot relate fully to the phenomenological experience of the client. Much as she might try, she will not be able to avoid viewing the client's beliefs as an ultimately incorrect attempt to comprehend the nature of existence. Vachon and Agresti (1992) suggest that such a therapist employ a "levels of analysis" approach to better understand the perspective of her client. Instead of viewing a phenomenon from only one perspective (e.g., a client's religious belief as a failure to comprehend the true contingencies influencing events in his life), therapists can be encouraged to consider other levels of meaning associated with religious beliefs (e.g., as philosophies of life or mythic systems). The behavior analyst might be better able to relate to the logical rigor of the philosophical and theological tenets of religious systems. The important thing is the therapist's ability to find points of connection with her clients' philosophy of life, so she can relate to them more fully and genuinely. This effort will enable the therapist to understand her clients and be respectful of their religious values or philosophy of life (Kelly & Strupp, 1992). Similarly, an important aspect of multicultural sensitivity is to develop a better understanding of various religious philosophies (Grimm, 1994).

---

**Case Example 10.8**

*A counseling graduate student objects to the values training component of her Counseling Methods course. She argues that self-disclosure of her personal values to a faculty member or to other students is an unwarranted invasion of her privacy. She also asserts that the exercise is pointless because students do not present their true personal values. They simply talk about values that they know the instructor will approve of. "They just tell her what they think she wants to hear."*

*Does the student present a legitimate argument for removing values training from the content of the course?*

---

## ETHICAL AND LEGAL ISSUES IN SUPERVISION

When providing supervision for students completing practica or internships in such areas as counseling, clinical psychology, school psychology, and I/O psychology, faculty members incur obligations to the clients being served by the students, in addition to their obligations to the students themselves. For example, supervisors can be held legally responsible for the actions of their supervisees. In addition to the guidance provided for supervisors in professional ethical codes (ACA, 1997, F.1-3; APA, 1992, 1.22), counseling supervisors can consult the "Standards for Counseling Supervisors," published by the Association for Counselor Education (1990).

### COMPETENCE ISSUES IN SUPERVISION

Supervision involves a combination of theoretical and applied knowledge and skills that is not possessed by all faculty members in the mental health professions. Faculty should have received additional preparation in models and methods of supervision prior to entering into supervisory relationships (ACA, 1997, F.1.f). Some graduate training programs assist counseling and psychology students in developing supervision skills by providing students with the opportunity to function as peer supervisors to other trainees. Peer supervisors are themselves supervised by a fully qualified, licensed supervisor (ACA, 1997, F.1.f, F.2.e). In the absence of this type of training opportunity, novice supervisors should have the opportunity to observe and work with more experienced supervisors before taking on full supervisory responsibilities themselves. This process will help the novice supervisor to develop a clearer conception of the skill level of practicum students or interns, rather than basing his expectations for their performance on his own abilities. An accurate assessment of the capabilities of supervisees is essential in protecting them and the clients they serve from harm (ACA, 1997, F.1.g; APA, 1992, 1.22[a]).

Supervisors should have a clear sense of the model of supervision they will employ with their students and of the theoretical orientations to which they want students exposed (ACA, 1997, F.2.f). In addition, supervisors must have a thorough knowledge of the ethical, professional, and legal issues that supervisees should learn during their initial opportunities to function as mental health professionals (ACA, 1997, F.2.d; APA, 1992, 1.22[b]). Many of the issues that students are exposed to in their academic training (e.g., confidentiality, cultural diversity) need to be reinforced strongly as students enter an applied setting so that they will develop an appropriate sensitivity to the issues affecting their work with clients.

## INFORMED CONSENT AND CONFIDENTIALITY ISSUES IN SUPERVISION

There are two sets of informed consent issues in supervisory relationships, one set concerning supervisees, the other concerning the clients they serve. A clear, detailed syllabus is every bit as important in a practicum course as in the more traditional classroom setting. Supervisors tend to underestimate the importance of a practicum syllabus because of the relatively informal organization of a practicum "class." Actually, there is an enormous amount of information that needs to be provided to practicum students regarding the supervisor's expectations of them (e.g., if they must self-disclose personal issues that may give rise to countertransferential experiences), the evaluation methods that will be used in the course, the procedures to be used in contacting and dealing with clients, the mechanics of keeping track of practicum hours, and the nature and frequency of supervision meetings (ACA, 1997, F.2.a; APA, 1992, 6.02[b]). Practicum students, particularly those working at off-campus agencies, should be told whether they are permitted to communicate with their supervisor about client issues by e-mail. If they are permitted to use e-mail, correct procedures to protect the client's confidentiality should be explained.[36]

---

**Case Example 10.9**

*A psychology practicum supervisor conducts individual initial meetings with each of his supervisees on the first day of the semester to discuss their practicum duties and to assign clients to each of them. The supervisor is struck by one student who seems very depressed. She becomes tearful during the session while discussing the recent breakup of her marriage. The supervisor suggests that she postpone her practicum, but she assures him that she will fulfill all of her obligations, though she thinks it would be wise not to assign any marital therapy cases to her.*

*The supervisor decides that, at present, the student lacks the emotional stability needed to work with clients effectively and to complete the practicum successfully. He informs her that he is canceling her registration for the course and suggests that she pursue psychotherapy to resolve her personal issues. The student complains to the department chair that the supervisor's actions were inappropriate.*

*What are the ethical considerations relevant to this situation? Did the supervisor act appropriately?*

---

The supervisor-supervisee relationship is more informal and involves more one-on-one interaction than is typical between faculty and students. As a result, there is an even greater tendency for inappropriate multiple relationships to develop (Thoreson et al., 1993; Thoreson et al., 1995). Supervisors are obligated to clearly define appropriate relationship boundaries for their supervisees and to discuss the ethical importance of these boundaries with them (ACA, 1997, F.1.b; APA, 1992, 1.17[a]). This discussion provides an excellent opportunity for supervisors to begin the process of educating supervisees about the importance of maintaining professional boundaries in their relationships with clients and anyone else they serve in a professional capacity.

In addition to the usual informed consent information provided to clients in a given professional context, clients served by supervisees must be informed that professional services are being provided by a trainee under the supervision of a licensed professional. The qualifications of the supervisee providing services and the supervisor must be specified (ACA, 1997, F.3.d; APA, 1992, 4.01[c]). Also, clients served by trainees receiving supervision must be informed of the nature of the supervisory relationship and its effect on the confidentiality of information disclosed by the client. Clients need to be told that all aspects of their interactions with the trainee will be shared with her supervisor. The supervisor's professional obligation to maintain the client's confidentiality should also be explained. In many training settings, sessions are observed by other practicum students and aspects of the client's treatment are discussed in group practicum meetings. Of course, the client's informed consent must be obtained for these procedures, as well as for any electronic recording of sessions (ACA, 1997, B.4.c, F.3.d; APA, 1992, 5.01[c]). If a client is uncomfortable with confidential information being shared with the supervisor or other practicum students, she should be referred to a licensed professional who does not require supervision.

## CONFLICTS OF INTEREST IN SUPERVISION

The potential for conflicts of interest, discussed in Chapter 8, can also arise in supervising students. For example, suppose an I/O faculty member is responsible for placing students in practicum settings. Suppose further that the faculty member serves as a paid consultant to one of the agencies serving as a practicum site. Clearly, the faculty member has a dual relationship with this agency (i.e., as a practicum supervisor and as a paid consultant). The potential for conflict of interest arises because he might want to place the best student with this agency, both because she would be the best student to supervise and because the agency might be more likely to retain him as a consultant if he proves to be a reliable source of excellent practicum students (ACA, 1997, F.2.h). The supervisor can minimize the potential for conflicts of interest by avoiding placing students with agencies where he has a consulting relationship and by declining opportunities to work as a consultant with agencies where he places students. Of course, as discussed in Chapter 8, what makes such issues complex is that the agency for which he serves as a consultant might provide the best quality practicum experience. Again, this is particularly possible in a smaller city. In such a case, a professional must weigh the relevant concerns and attempt to rationally devise a solution that will minimize the likelihood that a conflict of interest will arise.

## LEGAL RESPONSIBILITIES OF SUPERVISORS

Supervisors are ethically and legally responsible for the actions of supervisees (ACA, 1997, F.1.a, F.1.g; APA, 1992, 1.22). Supervision is a formal, structured relationship, developed to ensure an adequate standard of care for clients (Anderson, 1996). Therefore, supervisors can be held liable for actions of a supervisee that are harmful to a client, though the courts generally consider the question of whether the supervisor could have reasonably been expected to have known of the danger and prevented it. For example, suppose a supervisee meets his client in a campus bar, and they wind up spending the night together. The next week, she files a complaint against both the supervisee and his supervisor. If the supervisor had taken the proper pains at the beginning of the practicum to make certain that his supervisees were aware of the ethical rules prohibiting sexual relationships with clients, it would be unlikely that the supervisor would be held legally accountable for the inappropriate behavior of the supervisee, unless the supervisee had discussed his attraction to the client in supervision and the supervisor had failed to take appropriate action.

A supervisor must be careful to document his supervision in writing, including the decision-making process conducted for all complex treatment matters, such as termination, referral, suicidal ideation, and child abuse (Anderson, 1996). He should discuss with supervisees at the outset of the relationship the shared nature of their ethical and legal responsibility for the treatment of clients. Supervisees should perceive the supervisor as a resource who will enable them to avoid making potentially serious errors in the treatment of clients through timely consultation.

## PRACTICE CASE INVOLVING THE MODEL OF ETHICAL DECISION MAKING

As a result of a sudden serious illness to a colleague, a clinical psychologist is asked to teach a course in Physiological Psychology, which is definitely outside his area of expertise. The course is to begin in one week. The department chair recognizes that the psychologist is not competent in this area, but is as qualified as anyone else in the department and is the only person whose schedule could be altered to accommodate the course. The course is required for graduation, and several seniors will be unable to graduate at the end of the semester if they do not take the course now.

What should the faculty member do?

## SUMMARY

This chapter addressed issues pertaining to the teaching and supervision activities of mental health professionals. Establishing and maintaining competence as an instructor requires specialized training and scholarly diligence. Faculty members should regard their course syllabus as an informed consent document and employ grading procedures that are fair and equitable to all students. Multiple relationships with students should be avoided because they can impair the objectivity of faculty members and supervisors, or be perceived by students as doing so.

Faculty members should remember that the privacy of students' academic performance is protected by federal law. Also, faculty in the mental health professions should be circumspect about discussing a student's personal disclosures with colleagues because the student might assume that psychology and counseling faculty maintain confidentiality in nontherapy settings as well.

Providing ethics training should not be limited to ethics courses. Vachon and Agresti's (1992) model for instructing future therapists about the role of values in therapy was presented to highlight the importance of addressing this issue in training programs. Practicum and internship supervisors must recognize that supervision is a specialized area of competence. The development of this competence is essential in order for supervisors to fulfill their legal and ethical responsibilities to both supervisees and practicum clients.

# 11 Ethical Issues in Research

Most mental health professionals conduct research during their academic training and many continue to pursue research as an important part of their professional activity. Behavioral research is generally conducted to test specific hypotheses arising from psychological theories. That is, researchers have ideas about the variables influencing some psychological phenomenon, and they test their expectations about those variables under specified conditions. Thus, the first topic to be addressed in this chapter is the ethical significance of psychological theory construction.

Unfortunately, some researchers fail to recognize the tremendous importance of the ethical issues that arise in planning and conducting research, perhaps because they assume that they are simply conducting objective "science" when they take on the role of researcher. However, ethical considerations are as important in research settings as they are in clinical practice. In both cases, there is great potential for harm, as well as benefit, to those affected by the professionals' decision making. Concern about the potential for harm to human research participants initially focused on biomedical research. However, notable instances of participants being harmed emotionally by behavioral studies, like Milgram's (1963) research on obedience to authority, increased awareness of the ethical complexity of behavioral research.

Milgram (1963) deceived the participants in his study by making them believe they were administering shocks each time the participant they were paired with (actually, a confederate of the experimenter) made an error on a paired associates learning task. Actually, no one was being shocked. Participants became increasingly upset as they were instructed to administer stronger and stronger shocks, but most of them continued to obey the experimenter's instructions. Although they were debriefed and told they had not harmed anyone, many of the participants were extremely upset and embarrassed about how they had behaved in the study.

Milgram's participants were deceived about the true purpose of the study, about the confederates, and about the fact that no shocks were really administered. The study raised questions about the appropriateness of the common practice of deceiving research participants. Also, Milgram had not warned the participants in advance about the risk of emotional harm. This chapter will present the ethical standards concerning informed consent and protecting participants from harm that were developed in response to behavioral studies like Milgram's. Because researchers still deceive participants in some studies, the complex ethical considerations involved in the decision to use deception and the consequences of deceiving participants will also be discussed. In addition, the confidentiality of research data, as well as ethical concerns related to data collection, analysis, and the publication of research findings, will be presented. Finally, ethical issues unique to research conducted on the Internet and research using animals will be addressed.

## ETHICS, VALUES, AND THEORY CONSTRUCTION IN THE MENTAL HEALTH PROFESSIONS

A research program is a reflection of the researcher's theoretical perspective. A researcher decides which questions about human and/or animal behavior will be the most interesting ones to address based upon her views of how motivation, behavior, and human nature are best explained. It is important to realize that a researcher's choice of a theoretical viewpoint develops primarily from her subjectively held values regarding these phenomena, rather than from an objective scientific appraisal of the issues. As discussed in Chapter 7, mental health professionals adopt theoretical viewpoints that have proven useful to them for understanding themselves and the people they know. Similarly, a researcher's choice of a model of human personality, for example, is based upon her own values and beliefs regarding such issues as human freedom of choice, personal responsibility, and the relative contributions of emotion and cognition to behavior.

This point is important because it illustrates again the ubiquitous role of subjective, personal values in every aspect of mental health professionals' activities. If values are involved in a researcher's choice of which phenomena to study, it follows that the choice has a potential ethical significance. For example, a researcher who views human nature in a very positive, hopeful light might choose to study altruism (i.e., helping behavior), whereas a researcher who believes that women are cognitively inferior to men might be interested in finding evidence to support that viewpoint. This issue raises the ethical question of whether there are research questions that should or should not be studied. Obviously, a study that involves deliberately harming human participants would be unethical, but what about studies that are potentially socially divisive, like those looking for racial differences in intelligence? This is an extremely complex ethical question because defenders of these studies point out that scientific research should never avoid issues for social or political reasons and that uncovering social problems is a necessary first step toward remediating them. Nevertheless, each researcher must address her motivations for pursuing a particular research program and consider the potential social implications of the results she might obtain.

A researcher's personal values might not only affect what issues she studies, but how she evaluates the evidence (i.e., data) she obtains. Research is a scientific enterprise in which data are to be evaluated in an objective, dispassionate manner. However, in reality, researchers might be more open to accepting data that support their assumptions, even when these data are flawed. Researchers must always strive to be as objective as possible in their activities, which requires that they consciously acknowledge their theoretical biases and approach research as a quest to *disconfirm* their theories.

## CONDUCTING RESEARCH WITH HUMAN PARTICIPANTS

In 1977, the National Commission for the Protection of Human Subjects of Biomedical and Behavioral Research (NCPHS) was created under the National Research

Act of 1974 (Pub. L. No. 93-348). The primary purpose of the commission was to identify the ethical principles involved in research with human participants and to make recommendations to the Department of Health and Human Services (DHHS) for improving government regulations for protecting human research participants. The work of the commission resulted in *The Belmont Report* (1979). The three ethical principles identified in *The Belmont Report* are respect for persons, beneficence, and justice. Respect for persons is "recognition of the personal dignity and autonomy of individuals and special protection of those persons with diminished autonomy." Beneficence is "the obligation to protect persons from harm by maximizing anticipated benefits and minimizing possible risks of harm." Justice is "fairness in the distribution of research benefits and burdens" (*The Belmont Report,* 1979, p. 4). In addition, in 1982, APA's Committee for the Protection of Human Participants in Research published its own guidelines for research with human participants.

## INSTITUTIONAL REVIEW BOARDS (IRBs)

Based on the principles articulated in *The Belmont Report,* DHHS published federal regulations in 1981 that formalized the role of the Institutional Review Board for the Protection of Human Subjects in Research (IRB) in protecting the interests of human research participants. In an institution where research is conducted (e.g., hospital, university, medical school), the IRB is the official entity that reviews research proposals involving human participants to determine whether the proposed studies are ethically acceptable. The IRB is composed of at least five members of varying backgrounds who will provide expertise to the board in the areas of research commonly conducted at the institution. At least one member of the board must have no affiliation with the institution, one member must have a scientific background, and one member must have a primary interest in a nonscientific area. These members have a responsibility to ensure the following: that the risks and benefits to participants are reasonable, that consent is informed and voluntary, that research conditions are safe, that the privacy of data is protected, that the selection of participants is equitable, and that vulnerable groups such as children are protected (Porter, 1996). Also, DHHS regulations draw a distinction between biomedical and behavioral research by exempting most survey and interview research and most observation studies in public settings from the regulations, unless the research concerns "sensitive matters" and the participants can be identified and linked to their responses (Areen, 1992).

---

**Case Example 11.1**

*The Director of the Research Development Office at a university is appointed coordinator of the university's IRB. The person was chosen because it was felt that her duties in encouraging faculty to develop proposals for extramural research funding dovetailed very well with overseeing the protection of human research participants.*

*Is there a potential ethical problem with this arrangement?*

## INFORMED CONSENT

A researcher must obtain the informed consent of research participants prior to their participation in a study (ACA, 1997, G.2; APA, 1992, 6.11). Obtaining consent simply means that participants agree to participate. It is the "informed" aspect of informed consent that involves most of the tricky ethical issues. Ideally, participants should be fully informed regarding the purpose of the research and every aspect of their participation. The following information should be explained in the informed consent process:

1. the voluntary nature of participation
2. the amount of time required for participation
3. the procedure(s) participants will complete
4. any risks that participants might encounter as a result of their participation in the study
5. what use will be made of the results of the study
6. any inducement (e.g., money) that will be provided to participants
7. the right to withdraw from participation
8. addresses and telephone numbers of the primary researcher and the chair of the IRB so that participants can contact someone regarding any questions or concerns about their participation
9. the right to ask the researcher(s) any questions at any point during the study or afterwards
10. the protections used to insure the confidentiality of non-anonymous data and any potential limitations on confidentiality
11. how to obtain information regarding the results of the study
12. any debriefing procedure that will occur following their participation
13. participants' legal rights, including their right to sue the researcher, even though they have consented to participate.

### VOLUNTARY RESEARCH PARTICIPATION

Participation in research should be voluntary. IRBs require that participants be free to decide whether or not they want to participate and to choose to withdraw from participation at any time (ACA, 1997, G.2.c; APA, 1992, 6.11[b]). Research in institutional settings, or in any other context involving perceived differences in power between participants and researchers (e.g., research with involuntarily committed clients or prisoners), is scrutinized very carefully by IRBs because it can fail to meet the standard of voluntary consent for research participation (Draine, 1997; Grisso, 1996). The use of incentives (e.g., extra credit for students, toys for children, free treatment following participation for depressed participants) can also potentially affect the voluntariness of research participation.

### CONSENT FORMS

Researchers generally obtain the informed consent of research participants by having them read and sign a consent form. Participants' signatures attest to the fact that they

---

**Case Example 11.2**

*Researchers at an inpatient facility are preparing to conduct a study concerning the schizophrenias. They do not feel comfortable recruiting participants themselves because they treat many schizophrenic clients and do not want to create multiple relationships. They hire a research assistant to handle participant recruitment. The assistant is a young, friendly woman to whom they think the schizophrenic clients will respond positively. They plan to have her spend time on each of the wards talking to the clients, so the clients can "get used to her." The researchers expect that the positive attention the clients receive from the research assistant will facilitate the process of recruiting them as research participants.*

*Could this recruitment strategy potentially affect the voluntariness of clients' decision to participate in the study?*

---

have read and understood the consent form and are agreeable to participating in the study. The use of consent forms to provide information concerning a study to potential participants is only an effective means of obtaining informed consent if the potential participants actually do read and understand the information provided. A number of studies have indicated that consent forms tend to be written at a reading level higher than would be appropriate for the participant population (e.g., Hochhauser, 1999; Ogloff & Otto, 1991; Young, Hooker, & Freeberg, 1990). However, researchers are obligated to make certain that their informed consent forms can be understood by potential participants. Helpful strategies for increasing participants' comprehension of informed consent information include having a member of the participant population review the form and provide suggestions for making the form more readable, checking the vocabulary level of the form using a word processing program, focusing on finding the simplest way to express an idea, providing visual illustrations to accompany the verbal information presented in the form, and presenting information orally as well as in writing (Hochhauser, 1999; Murphy et al., 1999; Tymchuk & Ouslander, 1990).

Informed consent research has also raised questions about whether participants really bother to read consent forms carefully and ask questions about matters they do not understand. There is evidence that shorter consent forms are understood better than longer ones, so it is probably desirable not to include every minute detail of the research procedure (Mann, 1994). Researchers should instead cover the key issues listed earlier that might affect participants' willingness to take part in the study, using terminology familiar to the participants (Young et al., 1990). As previously mentioned, consent forms should state that participants do not relinquish any of their legal rights, including the right to sue the researcher, by signing the consent form. Participants often misunderstand this point, so it is recommended that the point be reinforced orally by the researcher (Mann, 1994).

Participants must be informed of any potential risks to their well-being (ACA, 1997, G.2.a; APA, 1992, 6.11[b]). If a study involves greater risk for particular groups of participants, the researcher must make certain that these additional risks are communicated. For example, a retrospective study about childhood memories may involve special risks for individuals who experienced traumatic events (e.g., abuse, death of a parent or sibling) as children. Participants should be informed of this potential risk because it may not occur to them that participation could be upsetting due to their personal history (APA, 1992, 6.07[d]). The issue of risk will be discussed in greater detail later in this chapter.

In research involving deception, researchers cannot lie to participants on the consent form because such a practice is radically incompatible with the purpose of informed consent. Withholding information is more acceptable. Of course, information regarding potential risks to participants in the study can never be withheld (Bersoff & Bersoff, 1999).

In studies involving data that are not anonymous, informed consent documents should state the extent of confidentiality afforded to participants and the protections in place to insure the confidentiality of participants' data (e.g., using numerical codes for data files so that an individual participant's data cannot be identified). The limits of confidentiality, which will be discussed later in the chapter, should also be presented (ACA, 1997, G.2.d; APA, 1992, 6.11[b]).

Some research projects involve agencies as well as individual participants. In such cases, researchers must also develop an informed consent agreement with the agency to delineate the responsibilities of each party (ACA, 1997, G.2.i; APA, 1992, 6.19). For example, a community mental health clinic might agree to provide access to their clients as potential participants in a study of rural mental health care. Researchers should create a contract with the agency stipulating the records or information the agency will provide, the role agency personnel will play in the data collection process, and the types of information the researchers will provide to the agency (e.g., group or individual results). Researchers are ethically bound to fulfill these commitments.

---

**Case Example 11.3**

*A psychology instructor teaching a Research Methods course at a university requires each student to conduct his or her own research project for the class. One of her students is especially interested in the topic of therapist bias, with particular emphasis on sexism. The student suggests that, for her research project, she will pose as a client at various clinics in town and gather data regarding sexist behavior of male and female therapists toward female clients.*

*Are there ethical issues the instructor should point out to the students?*

---

## INFORMED CONSENT WITH PARTICIPANTS OF REDUCED CAPACITY

The decision-making capacity of potential research participants must be assessed if their competence to provide consent is questionable. Visual and auditory functioning, mental status, and reading comprehension are all relevant to the consent process. Each of these factors can be assessed through interview and testing procedures. Elderly populations, poorly educated individuals, or participants for whom English is a second language might require modifications of the forms and procedures used in the informed consent process (Tymchuk & Ouslander, 1990). The assessment of participants' ability to consent should be made by competent professionals who are not otherwise involved in the research study. Disinterested experts can provide a more objective assessment than researchers, who have a vested interest in recruiting participants.

Individuals who lack a capacity that is important to the consent process, as well as anyone who is not legally competent to consent to participate in research, require proxy consent from a legally authorized guardian (ACA, 1997, G.2.e; APA, 1992, 6.11[e]). Potential participants with an impaired ability to consent are often encountered by researchers evaluating the effectiveness of new treatments for severe mental disorders. In addition to proxy consent, the *assent* of these participants (i.e., their agreement to participate after being given an explanation of the nature and purpose of the research that they can comprehend) is ethically required. Because these individuals cannot legally consent to participate in research, a stronger justification is needed for invading their privacy by including them in a study, even though proxy consent has been obtained and the participants have assented. The justification for using participants of diminished capacity in research should involve some direct benefits to them or others suffering from similar problems (Delano & Zucker, 1994). For example, it is inappropriate to involve these participants in a study that demonstrates only that the scores obtained by institutionalized populations on a personality test differ from those of a normal population.

Another important issue in working with research participants of reduced capacity is how to make certain that their right to withdraw from participation at any time is respected. These participants may be less likely to exercise this right because of their willingness to comply with the directions of authority figures (Fisher & Rosendahl, 1990). They can be told during the informed consent procedure how to communicate their desire to end their participation or to request a break. Fisher and Rosendahl (1990) suggest that participants "can simply be instructed to say 'I'd like to stop now,' or to signal their reluctance to continue by picking up an arrow provided by the experimenter and pointing it toward the door" (p. 50). Behavioral indications of discomfort in the research situation, such as crying, yawning, wringing of hands, looking away from the task, or requesting to use the bathroom, are also obvious indications of a participant's desire to stop.

## INDUCEMENTS TO RESEARCH PARTICIPANTS

In studies evaluating the effectiveness of new treatments for physical illnesses or emotional problems, participants are frequently offered free treatment in exchange for their participation. The offer of free treatment would be a strong inducement to an individual who is suffering. Thus, the promise of relief could be viewed as coercive because the person might feel compelled to participate by her desire to obtain effective treatment. Researchers conducting treatment studies must explain the nature of the treatment services, the length of treatment provided in the study, any risks and limitations associated with the treatment, and the possibility that the participant could be assigned to a control group condition and not receive the experimental treatment (APA, 1992, 6.14[a]). Participants in treatment studies should be offered the opportunity to receive the new treatment at no cost if it proves effective.

Researchers conducting nontreatment studies also frequently offer to compensate research participants in some way for their time and effort, consistent with the respect mental health professionals have for their participants' value as persons. However, inducements can interfere with the voluntariness of a participant's decision regarding whether or not to participate (APA, 1992, 6.14[b]). For example, offering poor families money as an inducement to participate in family research could be construed as coercive (Bersoff & Bersoff, 1999). There is no straightforward formula that researchers can use to determine what constitutes reasonable, noncoercive compensation for participants' time and effort. First, the degree of effort associated with participation varies tremendously across studies. Second, the coercive potential of a financial inducement depends largely on a participant's economic situation and/or the value he places on money. Offering a financial inducement equivalent to the federal minimum wage might not be a coercive influence for most university students, but it certainly could be for homeless individuals.

Any inducement offered to children is potentially coercive, even though the parents are actually providing consent. If a child is aware of a desirable inducement to participate (e.g., a toy that most children want), he might insist that his parents sign the consent form so that he can obtain it. Researchers should just give children the inducement after they participate, if the parents are agreeable, without advertising the inducement to the child beforehand (Powell & Vacha-Haase, 1994). Otherwise, knowing about the inducement might also interfere with the child's concentration while he is participating. He might rush to complete the research task in order to obtain the inducement more quickly. Paying money to preadolescent children for participating in research is also an ethically ill-advised procedure (Powell & Vacha-Haase, 1994). First, the money might be a coercive influence on the process of obtaining parental consent. Second, because the money is generally given to the child's parents, researchers do not know whether the child will ever receive the inducement intended for him.

---

**Case Example 11.4**

*College students recruited for a study comparing scores on a short form of the MMPI-2 with scores on the complete test are offered an inducement of receiving a free copy of a computer-based interpretive report based on their MMPI-2 performance. Participants will be able to pick up their report the day after they complete the tests.*

*Are there ethical issues that need to be considered prior to offering this inducement?*

---

## DEBRIEFING PARTICIPANTS

Researchers are obligated to provide participants with comprehensive information regarding the study after they have participated (ACA, 1997, G.2.g; APA, 1992, 6.18[a]). Debriefing procedures are intended to correct any misconceptions and answer any questions participants might have about the study. In addition, if participants were not fully informed regarding the purpose and procedures for the study, or if they were actively deceived about the nature of the study, they must be fully informed as soon as possible following their participation in order to reduce any anxieties about their participation and ameliorate any negative experiences that may have resulted from the study (Blanck, Bellack, Rosnow, Rotheram-Borus, & Schooler, 1992). Debriefing is the responsibility of the principal researcher and must be done carefully and effectively because debriefing, particularly following a study involving deception, can actually evoke anger, suspicion, and emotional upset (Oliansky, 1991).

Although debriefing should occur immediately following the conclusion of the individual's participation in the study, debriefing is delayed in many cases until all of the data for the study have been collected because researchers fear that participants will reveal the true details of the study to future participants (ACA, 1997, G.2.g; APA, 1992, 6.18[b]). Evidence supports this concern about participant contamination, particularly when participants are recruited from a student subject pool (Klein & Cheuvront, 1990). Having students sign a pledge to maintain confidentiality regarding the study reduced, but did not eliminate, the problem. Although the practice of delaying debriefing (i.e., debriefing all participants at the end of a study) is not prohibited, it is ethically problematic because it once again gives priority to the concerns of researchers over their duties to participants. For their part, researchers question whether delayed debriefing is of any value because most participants do not bother to attend the sessions. The option of contacting participants later by mail is costly and complicated by address changes, especially with student participants. Notwithstanding the arguments of some researchers to skip debriefing entirely when it must be delayed, the failure to make certain that participants are debriefed and have the opportunity to ask questions about the study and their participation is a serious ethical violation. When it comes to debriefing, later is better than never.

Debriefing participants is also intended to serve an educational function. In some studies, participants are able to obtain feedback regarding their personal performance in the study (Blanck et al., 1992). For example, in clinical research concerning depression, clients can be provided feedback about their depression score and any change that occurred from pretest to posttest. When college students are the population studied, debriefing affords an excellent opportunity to enhance participants' understanding of the research process. If debriefing is delayed until all the data have been collected, the results and conclusions of the study can also be presented. In any case, participants should always be given the opportunity to obtain a copy of the results and conclusions of the study (APA, 1992, 6.18[a]).

Delayed debriefing and providing participants with study results is now much easier, thanks to Internet technology. At the time of their participation, participants can be given the researcher's Web address and the date that the results of the study will be posted there. Participants can then view a summary of the study, its results, and conclusions on the researcher's Web site. If they have questions, they can contact the researcher by telephone, mail, or e-mail. This online method of debriefing participants does not require finding a way to contact participants again at the end of the study. Of course, participants who do not have Internet access would be given the option of receiving debriefing materials by mail.

Gurman (1994) raises an additional issue about a researcher's ethical duty to debrief participants who complete a pretesting or prescreening procedure for a study, but are not selected to participate in the main study. These individuals are frequently ignored because they are not regarded as study participants, leaving them to develop their own hypotheses regarding why they were not included in the final sample. For example, in conducting depression research with college students, a major concern of researchers is that the population of depression scores for any sample will be positively skewed (i.e., most students will have low depression scores and relatively few will score toward the high end of the distribution). As a result, researchers will sometimes pretest a very large sample of students, then select a stratified random sample for the actual study to insure equal numbers of participants for each level of depression score (e.g., low, moderate, high). In such studies, students who are chosen to participate in the study frequently assume that they had high depression scores. Their misconceptions can be corrected during debriefing following their participation. However, students who were not selected might also believe that they scored too high on the depression measure to be useful to the study, but their misconceptions are never corrected. Therefore, it is extremely important to debrief the entire sample that participated in pretesting after the study is completed to make certain that everyone understands the criteria for participant selection and the nature and purpose of the study. Also, the pretesting participants invested time and energy in making the study possible, so they deserve an explanation of the results of the study and their role in it.

Researchers should also regard debriefing as a personal educational opportunity (Blanck et al., 1992). In general, researchers do not take great advantage of the opportunity to find out from participants how well the methodology of the study worked, what expectations and beliefs participants had, and whether participants' behavior was affected by any extraneous variables. For example, in studies using deception, researchers should learn whether participants were at all suspicious of the manipulation. Previous experiences in research involving deception can increase participants' suspiciousness about manipulations in studies they participate in subsequently (Epley & Huff, 1998; Oliansky, 1991).

## INFORMED CONSENT ISSUES WITH CHILDREN

In 1983, DHHS adopted additional guidelines for research with children based on commission recommendations issued in a report entitled *Research Involving Children* (NCPHS, 1977). These guidelines are found in 45 CFR 46, Subpart D: "Additional Protections for Children Involved as Subjects in Research." (The most recent version of 45 CFR 46 was issued on June 18, 1991.) The general exemption from DHHS policy for research involving survey and interview procedures does not apply to research conducted with child participants. Subpart D of the regulations requires that research with children involve no greater than minimal risk to the children and adequate provision for obtaining the assent of the child and the informed consent of the parent as specified in the regulations. "Minimal risk" means that the "probability and magnitude of harm or discomfort anticipated in the research are not greater in and of themselves than those ordinarily encountered in daily life or during the performance of routine physical or psychological examinations or tests" (Protection of Human Subjects, 1991, 45 CFR 46.102[i]). Research that poses more than minimal risk will generally be approved by an IRB only if it holds out the prospect of direct benefit to the child participant. Understandably, the standards for approval of research with children are more stringent because children are not able to provide consent (Mordock, 1995).

Obtaining parental informed consent protects both child participants and researchers against a number of potential ethical problems. First, this process reduces the pressure on researchers to make certain that children understand every implication of the consent agreement and that children's interests are protected adequately (Grisso, 1992). Second, the parental consent form can involve a more complete explanation of the details of the study than might be given to participants because of the potential for participants' behavior to be affected by knowledge of the true purpose of the study. For example, an incidental learning procedure (e.g., instructing children to attend to the different colors of cards with printed words, then testing their ability to recall the words) can be explained completely in the parental consent form, whereas it will spoil the study if participants are told about this aspect of the research in advance. Finally, obtaining parental informed consent provides researchers with the opportunity to inform parents that, as mental health professionals, researchers have an ethical and legal duty to report any suspicions of child abuse or neglect that might arise in the course of the research (Kalichman, 1999).

Researchers are, in most cases, also required to obtain the assent of children to participate in research (ACA, 1997, G.2.e; APA, 1992, 6.11[e]). Assent is "a child's affirmative agreement to participate in research" (Protection of Human Subjects, 1991, 45 CFR 46.402[b]). The IRB will consider the age, maturity, and psychological state of the children involved in determining whether assent is needed (Protection of Human Subjects, 1991, 45 CFR 46.408[a]). For example, the assent of infants is obviously not required. Children cannot meaningfully assent to participate until they are able to understand that they could refuse.

Furthermore, when appropriate, the IRB may waive or alter the parental consent requirement if four conditions apply: (a) the research poses no more than minimal risk, (b) the waiver or alteration will not jeopardize the rights and welfare of the participants, (c) the research cannot be conducted without the waiver or alteration of the consent process, and (d) if appropriate, the participant may be informed of pertinent information after the research is completed (Porter, 1996). A waiver is also permitted in situations in which parental consent is not a reasonable requirement for the protection of the child participant, such as in research with neglected or abused children (Protection of Human Subjects, 1991, 45 CFR 46.408[c]). In spite of IRBs' ability to waive parental consent in some research (if such a waiver does not conflict with state or local law), IRBs are usually very reluctant to grant a waiver. In some cases, the IRB's own uncertainty about how to interpret legal requirements for adolescent populations leads to seemingly unnecessarily restrictive interpretations of rules, thereby limiting research that would more likely benefit than harm participants (English, 1995).[37] Finally, children of any age should be informed that they can stop if they no longer want to participate. Parental consent should never involve coercing a child to participate against his or her will.

## ACTIVE VERSUS PASSIVE PARENTAL INFORMED CONSENT

The ethical requirement to obtain parental informed consent has proven to be a significant issue in some types of survey research conducted with children in a school setting. Researchers proposing minimal risk survey and interview research with children and adolescents have, in some instances, sought and gained approval from IRBs to obtain the passive, rather than active, informed consent of parents (Mumford, 1996). "Active parental consent" is a consent procedure wherein parents are provided information regarding a research study, usually by mail, and asked to return a form or contact the researcher if they want their child to participate in the study. Conversely, in "passive parental consent," parents are contacted and asked to return a form or contact the researcher if they do *not* want their child to participate in the study. In other words, the child will participate in the study, after she assents, unless explicitly prohibited from doing so by a parent. The federal regulations (45 CFR 46, Subpart D[b]) require "that adequate provisions are made for soliciting the permission of each child's parents or guardian" for the child's participation. Although this regulation requires that researchers obtain the informed consent of parents, it does not stipulate that the parent must respond actively to the information provided by the researcher in order to consent; providing parents with the opportunity to respond only if they do not want their child to participate still constitutes "soliciting the permission" of parents.

This practice was undertaken because active consent procedures were thought by researchers to diminish participation rates significantly in survey research, often to unacceptable levels of 50% or lower, and to impact the representativeness of research samples in areas such as ethnicity (Dent et al., 1993) and the inclusion of "at-risk" participants (e.g., Ellickson & Hawes, 1989; Shope, Copeland, & Dielman, 1994). Furthermore, it was argued that the differences in participation rates were largely a function not of parental objections to the proposed research, but of parents' losing or forgetting to return the consent form (Ellickson & Hawes, 1989).

The use of active versus passive parental consent procedures in research with children and adolescents has created considerable controversy among those involved in the consent process, with critics of passive consent asserting that parents' right to consent to their child's participation in research was being abridged (Fisher, Hoagwood, & Jensen, 1996). Furthermore, they argue, it is not reasonable to assume that parents have consented to their child's participation in a research study solely on the basis that the parents have not contacted the researcher to indicate their refusal to consent. The passive consent letter might not have reached the parents, they might not have opened it, they might have misread the instructions, or they might have intended to refuse, but forgot to return the appropriate form. Although the federal regulations may not specify how parental consent should be obtained, the ethical duty of researchers to obtain parental consent requires that they be absolutely certain they have the parents' consent. This certainty can only be achieved by means of an active parental consent procedure. Ethically, researchers' concern about the adequacy of their research samples is simply not a compelling consideration when weighed against the right of parents to provide informed consent for their child to be asked to participate in a research study. In recent years, IRBs have become increasingly reluctant to accept passive consent for any study in which parental consent is required.

## DEBRIEFING CHILD PARTICIPANTS

Ethical issues concerning debriefing are even more complex in research involving child participants. When children are deceived or manipulated to engage in negative behaviors, debriefing is necessary to reduce the possibility that the children will make negative self-attributions regarding their behavior in the study (Fisher & Rosendahl, 1990). However, debriefing children is not the same as debriefing adults. The terminology used must be understandable to the children, and they should be asked to demonstrate their understanding of the points communicated in the debriefing. Pilot testing of the debriefing procedure prior to conducting a study is certainly indicated; if an effective debriefing procedure that eliminates all risk of lingering emotional or behavioral harm to the participants cannot be developed, the researchers cannot ethically conduct the study (Fisher & Rosendahl, 1990).

---

**Case Example 11.5**

*A researcher conducts a study with 7 year olds concerning honesty. Specifically, children are left in a room with loose change on a table. The researcher tells one group of children that they will be watched through a one-way mirror when she leaves the room; the researcher does not tell the other group of children anything. The researcher anticipates that a child who does not expect to be monitored will pick up some of the money. The researcher decides not to debrief the children or their parents following children's participation because she thinks that both the children who took money and their parents will be embarrassed and will think that she is calling the children thieves.*

*What ethical considerations are relevant to this decision? Is this an ethically appropriate course of action?*

---

## THE IMPORTANCE OF CONDUCTING RESEARCH WITH CHILD PARTICIPANTS

The additional safeguards required for research involving children, such as obtaining parental informed consent, has at times affected researchers' willingness to conduct research with children. However, in most research studies, excluding children from health-related research samples does an injustice to them as a group and involves greater risk than their participation because the exclusion of children will result in a lack of valid information regarding the effects of proposed behavioral and biomedical treatments on them (Levine, 1995b). In addition, accurate data on the prevalence of health-threatening behaviors in children (e.g., substance abuse, suicidal behavior, depression) will be lacking. Furthermore, the generalizability, or population validity, of research results can only be insured by including children representing the gender, age, cultural, and ethnic groups that the researchers intend for the treatment to benefit (Laosa, 1990). Therefore, the National Institutes of Health (NIH) instituted a policy requiring the inclusion of children in federally funded research samples unless there are compelling scientific or ethical reasons for excluding them (NIH, 1998).

## PROTECTING RESEARCH PARTICIPANTS FROM HARM

The ethical duty to protect research participants from physical and psychological harm was stated in the Nuremberg Code, which was developed after the Nuremberg trial of Nazi medical researchers following World War II (Beecher, 1970). Compared to medical research, most psychological research involves relatively little risk to participants' health (and correspondingly, little potential benefit). For the most part, the potential risks associated with psychological research concern harm to participants' emotional well-being. Nevertheless, the potential for negative impact on mood, lowered self-esteem, embarrassment at being manipulated to perform negative behaviors, emotional upset from recalling painful life events, negative reactions to being deceived, and harm from potential breaches of confidentiality can be very real risks in mental health research (Bersoff & Bersoff, 1999). For example, psychologists studying the effects of childhood trauma on adult adjustment can potentially worsen PTSD symptoms in some participants (Newman, Kaloupek, Keane, & Folstein, 1997). Although it is extremely difficult to assess and predict the level of psychological risk in a study of this type, particularly given the individual differences in participants' reactions to stimuli, researchers are obligated to inform research participants of any potential risks associated with participating in the study (Thompson, 1992).

Generally, however, behavioral research involves a short-term manipulation of variables like anxiety, and generally not a very powerful manipulation (i.e., the manipulation often does not even generate a significant effect on the dependent variable in the study). It is very difficult to produce chronic, intense anxiety by means of an ethically acceptable experimental manipulation. Nevertheless, researchers have no right to place participants at even short-term risk without informing them of the potential for emotional upset.

The assessment of research risk always involves weighing the potential risks to participants against the potential benefits to participants and others who could be affected by the research. The potential benefits associated with a study should always outweigh the potential risks. For example, in a behavioral study of honesty in children, there is little potential for direct benefit to the participants. Consequently, an IRB will approve such a study only if it involves no more than minimal risk. On the other hand, an ethically acceptable treatment study of an aversive conditioning method to reduce head banging behavior in autistic children might involve a higher level of risk, but is balanced by the potential for the direct benefit to the child participants of reducing the frequency of such a dangerous behavior (Thompson, 1992). In addition to the risks to participants, researchers must consider a study's potential risks to their academic discipline. For example, studies involving deception may diminish public trust in psychology and related professions. As discussed earlier in the chapter, there can also be potential risks to society associated with conducting a research study. For example, in a study of the relation between IQ and race, there is a strong possibility that the results of the study will be misinterpreted by individuals and misrepresented in the media (Bersoff & Bersoff, 1999).

As Thompson (1992) points out, risk-benefit assessment appears initially to be a purely utilitarian calculation of what will produce the greatest positive balance of pleasure over pain to the greatest number of people, but researchers have an ethical duty to always minimize risks to participants, reflecting the principle of nonmalef-icence, and to only conduct research that benefits participants, consistent with the principle of beneficence (ACA, 1997, G.1.c; APA, 1992, 1.14). Respect for the autonomy of participants is also evident in the requirement that participants must be informed of any potential risks associated with their participation in a study.

Everyone agrees that researchers have an ethical duty to inform participants of any potential risks associated with a study; what they sometimes disagree about is what constitutes a risk that needs to be mentioned. For example, a researcher wants to elicit anxiety by providing participants with false feedback concerning the results of a "personality" test. The items will not really be scored, but half the participants will be shown a set of negative trait terms and told that the testing software generated these descriptors of their personality. They will be debriefed immediately following their participation. Does this procedure involve a significant risk of harm to participants?

Most of the potential risk factors in behavioral research are not expected to affect all participants equally. For example, participants affected by anxiety or mood disorders are at considerably greater risk than other participants in a study designed to induce anxiety. When conducting such a study, the researcher might be required by an IRB to use a screening procedure to identify high-risk individuals who should not be subjected to the manipulation. Prebriefing procedures, in which potential participants are informed of risk factors in solicitations for the study, can also be helpful in reducing the potential for participants to be upset by stimuli, such as traumatic childhood experiences, snakes, vignettes depicting violent crimes, or sex-ually explicit material (Allen, D'Alessio, Emmers, & Gebhardt, 1996).

---

### Case Example 11.6

*A student in an Experimental Psychology class has a large python snake as a pet. For his experiment, he proposes to have college students attempt to complete a set of 10 anagrams in five minutes under one of two conditions. He will walk around the room with his pet snake around his shoulders while Group 1 completes the anagrams. He will walk around the room without his snake while Group 2 completes the anagrams. He is interested in knowing whether most people's concentration is affected by anxiety about snakes.*

*After receiving assurances that the snake will not attempt to molest any of the students, the instructor gives him permission to conduct the study.*

*What ethical considerations are involved in this situation? Was this an ethically appropriate decision?*

Risk is a particularly potent concern in research with children. However, adult researchers and IRB members often experience difficulty in effectively evaluating a research study's potential risks to children. In general, the younger the child, the greater her vulnerability to the risks associated with research participation (Thompson, 1992). However, older children may actually be more vulnerable to self-esteem damage than younger children because self-concept becomes more sophisticated over time. Therefore, adolescents might be more troubled by procedures that reflect negatively on their personal characteristics, such as their ethnicity (Thompson, 1992). Risks to child participants must be minimal or nonexistent in most cases for a study to receive IRB approval because children must depend on someone else (i.e., their parent or guardian) to make consent decisions for them. The only exception might be therapeutic research concerning life-threatening problems, where the promise of direct benefit to the child participants reasonably outweighs the risk involved. The informed consent agreement in such a study should stipulate that all participants, including the children in control groups, will be provided access to any therapeutic benefit resulting from the study.

IRBs look very carefully at the potential risks to research participants. However, critics point out that most IRB members are researchers themselves, which makes them more likely to view the situation from a researcher's perspective. Although all IRB members take their duty to protect participants from risk seriously, the assessment of risk is a major reason why IRBs include a community member who has no investment in research. This individual is best able to represent the perspective of potential participants in evaluating risks associated with participation in a proposed study.

Of course, research risk to participants could be eliminated completely if IRBs refused to approve any study involving greater than minimal risk, but at what cost to the scientific, educational, and applied goals of research? For example, social psychology researchers conduct studies investigating anger and antisocial behavior, such as the phenomenon of road rage. When researchers elicit negative emotions or behavior in these studies, the risk for harm to participants is very real. Participants might be embarrassed about their behavior in the study after they are debriefed, or they may carry the anger elicited by the study with them to the next interpersonal context in their lives. However, these are important phenomena for researchers to investigate because the results could assist in generating solutions to a serious social problem. In this way, researchers and IRB members weigh the risks to participants against the potential benefits of conducting the research. Whenever there is any risk to participants in a proposed study, researchers' responsibility for demonstrating the potential value of the study becomes much greater. For example, it is inappropriate to place participants at significant risk merely to replicate a well-documented behavioral phenomenon; a study involving risk should have the potential to make an important unique scientific and/or social contribution.

## RISKS TO CONTROL GROUP PARTICIPANTS

A final issue pertaining to research risks concerns control group participants. In studies testing the effectiveness of new treatments for physical illnesses or emotional problems (e.g., depression), researchers must use a control group. Otherwise, the effectiveness of the new treatment cannot be compared with that of existing interventions and/or the likelihood of spontaneous remission. However, it is not ethically appropriate to place people suffering from the disorder at increased risk by denying them treatment (ACA, 1997, G.1.c; APA, 1992, Principle E). Researchers should provide these control group participants with a baseline level of treatment; ideally, this treatment will be the most popular intervention currently used for the participants' problem. Comparing an experimental treatment with the current preferred treatment will provide a robust test of the effectiveness of the new intervention, in addition to minimizing the risk of harm to control group participants. At a minimum, concern for the welfare of control group participants requires the use of an attention-placebo control condition so that the condition of control group participants can be monitored carefully (Bersoff & Bersoff, 1999).

## THE USE OF DECEPTION IN RESEARCH

Informed consent procedures are supposed to provide a research participant with all the information that is relevant to his decision regarding whether or not to participate in a study. The most common limitation placed on the duty to obtain informed consent in psychological research involves the use of deception. Deceptive methodologies are used quite frequently, particularly in social psychology and personality research.

In 1985, for example, 47% of published studies in social psychology utilized deception (Adair, Dushenko, & Lindsay, 1985). In such studies, the ethical duty to obtain informed consent is not being compromised by behavioral researchers due to a lack of ethical sensitivity; rather, it is done in the interest of using the best methodology possible in their research. Deception is used when (a) the researcher believes that informing participants fully regarding a study's purpose and/or procedures will affect participants' responses, thereby threatening the validity of the study, and (b) there is no workable nondeceptive method of addressing the research question. For example, if participants are told in advance that the purpose of a study is to evaluate people's honesty in different situations, their behavior will likely reflect a social desirability response set (i.e., they will behave honestly to create a positive impression on the researcher). The use of deception reduces the response cues available to participants, thereby improving the methodology of the study and making the results more straightforwardly interpretable and valid.

The ethical justification for using deception is conceptualized in terms of a cost/benefit analysis. The potential cost to participants of being deceived is weighed against the potential benefit to science, or in some instances, to the participants themselves, of conducting the study (ACA, 1997, G.2.b; APA, 1992, 6.15[a]). One problem with this analysis is that all the costs affect participants, while the benefits generally accrue to the researcher or to "society." Moreover, the costs of deception are quite apparent, but the potential future benefits of the research are extremely difficult to predict. Michaels and Oetting (1979) found that participants' views of the ethicality of hypothetical research projects varied as a function of the costs, whereas researchers focused on the potential benefits. The major problem with a cost/benefit analysis to justify deception is that informed consent is based on a Kantian ethical regard for persons, and deception depends primarily on utilitarian ethical justifications. Thus, deception involves more than just a conflict between ethical principles; it involves a mixing of incompatible metaethical models. Therefore, the relative importance of informed consent considerations and potential research benefits cannot usually be directly and meaningfully compared. Nevertheless, researchers are instructed to weigh these competing considerations in deciding whether it is necessary and appropriate to use deception.

Some researchers have argued that intentional deception is never appropriate in psychological research because it denies participants the right to self-determination and causes professionals to violate their duty to be trustworthy (Baumrind, 1990; Ortmann & Hertwig, 1997). These researchers point to the fact that many participants now approach research studies assuming that they will be deceived. Even if no deception is involved, participants wonder what is really going on in the study. This phenomenon suggests that the use of deception might reduce the respect participants have for psychological research and researchers and impact the quality of data obtained by researchers (Ortmann & Hertwig, 1997). Also, even after debriefing, participants may still be upset about having been deceived.

Even if researchers do use deception in their studies, there are some issues about which researchers are never permitted to deceive participants. First, participants must be informed of any potential risks or other factors that might affect their willingness to participate in the study (APA, 1992, 6.15[b]). Second, researchers cannot promise participants an incentive for participating without fulfilling the promise. Third, researchers cannot create audio or video recordings of participants without first obtaining their informed consent (ACA, 1997, B.4.c; APA, 1992, 6.13).

As discussed in Chapter 3, two types of deception are employed in behavioral research. The first, which counseling's *Code of Ethics* refers to as "concealment," occurs when researchers fail to tell participants the "whole truth" about a study (ACA, 1997, G.2.b). For example, a researcher studying the relation between depression and interpersonal behavior tells participants that they will be asked to complete a questionnaire about some of their *behaviors and attitudes,* then discuss their experiences in research studies with the other participants. Participants are not actively deceived in the description of the study procedure; however, they are not told that the questionnaire concerns depressive symptoms, even though this information could be important to some participants' decisions regarding whether to take part in the study. This limited type of deception is present in a large proportion of psychological studies.

The second type of deception involves actively deceiving participants regarding the true purpose and procedures of the study. Milgram's (1963) study concerning obedience to authority is a classic example of researchers actively lying to participants. Nevertheless, deception is condoned when the potential value of the research is believed to justify its use and the researchers have considered alternative methodologies and concluded that the research question cannot be addressed effectively without deception (ACA, 1997, G.2.b; APA, 1992, 6.15[a]).

> **Case Example 11.7**
>
> *Participants in a study are told that they will complete a mood questionnaire, followed by a cognitive task. Two participants are assigned to each small room being used for the study. However, the actual participants are not told that the person they are paired with is a confederate of the experimenter. The confederate in each pair will either talk and act like a very bright, confident person or like a very dumb person. The study is designed to investigate whether interpersonal influences on cognitive performance vary as a function of depression.*

The statement in the "Ethical Principles" that "psychologists never deceive research participants about significant aspects that would affect their willingness to participate" is of questionable validity (APA, 1992, 6.15[b]). It is difficult to imagine that knowing a study involves deception would not, in and of itself, potentially affect a participant's willingness to take part in the study. One suggested method of operationalizing this ethical requirement more effectively is to have members of the proposed participant population evaluate the acceptability of research designs involving deception (Fisher & Fyrberg, 1994). Prospective participants can offer a unique perspective on the cost/benefit balance of a study, which is so critical to evaluating the ethical status of the research. Interestingly, potential participants are not uniformly opposed to deceptive research. They recognize its potential value to society and feel that the potential benefits of such research can outweigh the costs to participants (Fisher & Fyrberg, 1994). At the same time, they believe participants would be less likely to agree to participate in the research using deception if they were fully informed prior to their participation.

Researchers are obligated to fully disclose to participants the true nature and purpose of the study and the reason deception was used as soon as possible following the completion of their participation.[38] Effective and timely debriefing is extremely important in eliminating any negative effects the deception may have had on participants, in addition to providing the educational benefits associated with debriefing. For example, false self-perceptions created by an experimental condition tend to persist; explicit discussion during debriefing might be needed to draw participants' attention to this issue (Stanley & Guido, 1996).

The use of deception in research with children is particularly problematic (Thompson, 1992). Children are more easily deceived because of their trust of adults; therefore, they are more susceptible to being harmed. Debriefing procedures used to resolve issues of deception following a study are also potentially harmful to children. First, children may not benefit from debriefing; in fact, the procedure might increase their confusion about their experiences in the study (Thompson, 1992). Second, if they do understand the nature of the deception, their trust in adult authority may be shaken, which could also be an upsetting and harmful experience for them (Macklin, 1992).

---

**Case Example 11.8**

*A researcher conducts a correlational study of the relation between locus of control and sociability. Participants complete paper-and-pencil measures of the two variables. Unfortunately for the researcher, the only room available for conducting the study is a research room with an entire wall of one-way mirrors and microphones hanging from the ceiling. Several participants ask whether they are being observed and recorded. The researcher assures them that they are not and tells them that he would have had to obtain their written consent to monitor their behavior in that manner. One participant responds that the researcher is probably lying to them because psychology research always involves "some kind of trick." The participants remain very suspicious, looking at the mirrored wall repeatedly. When the papers have been collected, another participant asks, "Now will you tell us what was really going on?" The researcher wonders about the validity of his data.*

---

## CONFIDENTIALITY

Researchers, like therapists, have an ethical duty to protect the privacy of participants by not revealing the information participants disclose to them to any other party (ACA, 1997, G.2.d; APA, 1992, 5.02). In the ideal situation, participants provide data anonymously. Research participation is only truly anonymous when there is no practical way to determine which participant provided a particular set of data. Just because a participant's name does not appear on the data sheets does not mean that the data are necessarily anonymous. If participants provided demographic data that could be used to identify any of them individually, the data are not anonymous. For example, if there are very few participants that are not of traditional college age in a university sample, a 44-year-old, divorced woman's data might easily be connected with her. If the researcher gives each participant a number to avoid having them put their names on questionnaires, but keeps a list of the name-number combinations in case any data sets are incomplete, the data are not anonymous (at least until the list is destroyed).

When research data are not anonymous, researchers have an ethical obligation to keep the identity of the participants and any identifying data confidential. When sharing data with other researchers or reporting the results of a study in books, articles, or presentations, the individual participants should not be identifiable (ACA, 1997, G.3.d; APA, 1992, 5.07[b], 6.16). In general, only group results are presented. If the shared or presented data do reveal the identities of individual participants, the researcher must obtain the participants' consent to use the data (APA, 1992, 5.07[c]).

Research participants are sometimes asked to report illegal behaviors (e.g., drug use). Studies of this type can involve additional confidentiality issues because research data are not necessarily protected from subpoena. However, DHHS will provide a "Certificate of Confidentiality" to the researcher that will protect the privacy of research data (Hoagwood, 1994). Many Department of Justice research programs require researchers to obtain this certificate in order to apply for funding.

Any researcher planning a study in areas such as drug use and antisocial behavior should request a Certificate of Confidentiality from DHHS prior to actually conducting the study.

---

**Case Example 11.9**

*A researcher is conducting a study on the relation between anxiety and locus of control. To encourage participants to be honest in reporting their depressive symptoms, she guarantees the confidentiality of their responses in the consent form they sign. One of the participants receives a clinically significant anxiety score. The researcher is concerned that the participant might be suffering a great deal of tension and unhappiness as a result of his anxiety. As a mental health professional, the researcher wonders whether she has an ethical duty to contact the participant and recommend therapy.*

*What should the researcher do?*

---

## LIMITS OF CONFIDENTIALITY IN RESEARCH

There are limitations on the confidentiality of information provided by research participants, just as there are for therapy clients. Researchers are obligated to explain these limitations to participants during the informed consent process. Such limitations arise primarily from researchers' ethical obligation to protect the welfare of research participants (Bersoff & Bersoff, 1999). For example, clinical research regarding psychiatric symptomatology can evoke information about severe depressive symptoms that indicates an acute need for intervention. The researcher is obligated to provide an appropriate referral to a participant, or perhaps even to take the participant, with his consent, to be assessed by a clinician. If a study involves the possibility of clinical referrals based on participants' responses to the research protocol, participants should be told in the consent form. An alternative procedure is to express to participants in the consent form the importance of pursuing treatment if they experience symptoms like those described in the protocol and to provide all participants with information sheets regarding treatment referrals. In research with children, the children and their parents should be told during the consent process whether the parents will be informed of data indicating their child's involvement in suicidal activity, substance abuse, or other (specified) risky behaviors. Parents and children should also be made aware of the researcher's legal obligation to report suspected child abuse and neglect to the appropriate legal authorities.

Research involving the observation or interviewing of families presents a number of ethical complexities concerning confidentiality. The researchers cannot necessarily know in advance what sorts of issues might arise in the interactions among family members. Statements or behavior indicating child abuse or suicidal potential can place researchers in a situation in which they are legally and ethically obligated to violate a participant's confidentiality and report their concerns to parents or legal authorities (Bussell, 1994). This limitation on the confidentiality of the interview or observational data must be explained to participants beforehand.

---

**Case Example 11.10**

*A social psychologist is conducting research with families. In her interview with an adolescent male family member, he discusses his use of alcohol and marijuana, both of which are illegal activities. Although his drug use has not created any dangerous consequences in his life yet, the researcher wonders if she has an ethical and/or legal duty to inform his parents. After all, he could be injured while intoxicated or go on to experiment with other drugs.*
*What should the researcher do?*

---

## CAN THERE BE A "DUTY TO WARN" IN A RESEARCH CONTEXT?

Researchers do have an ethical and legal obligation to report suspicions of child abuse and neglect arising in research contexts (Kalichman, 1999). Mental health professionals also frequently collect interview or questionnaire data regarding participants' mood, anger, psychiatric symptoms, family functioning, and traumatic experiences. Suppose a research participant reports severe depressive symptoms and a very strong intention to commit suicide. The mental health professional conducting the research study could incur an ethical obligation to prevent suicide, just as a therapist would. In clinical settings, the obligation to prevent clients from harming themselves or others is also a legal duty, referred to as a duty to warn (*Tarasoff v. Board of Regents of the University of California*, 1974/1976). Although the existence of a clinical researcher's legal duty to warn has never been tested in court, it is certainly possible that mental health researchers could be viewed by the courts as having a similar legal duty to prevent research participants from harming themselves or someone else (Appelbaum & Rosenbaum, 1989). When conducting behavioral studies, researchers need to consider what their ethical responsibilities would be if a participant reported very severe depressive symptoms, significant suicidal potential, or a familial situation involving child abuse, as either a victim or an abuser (Stanton, Burker, & Kershaw, 1991).

A major consideration in the possible existence of a legal duty to warn in behavioral research is that a clinical researcher may not obtain sufficiently detailed information in a research protocol to make the research context analogous to a clinical intervention. For example, if a participant reports a very high level of anger on a questionnaire, a clinical researcher is not in a position to judge whether the individual represents a serious risk for violence. Research designs that employ participant interviews, in which researchers can probe further to evaluate the seriousness of a participant's potential for violence toward himself or particular individuals in his life, are likely to be considered much more similar to a therapist-client context (Appelbaum & Rosenbaum, 1989).

Of course, many behavioral researchers are not clinicians, which further complicates the issue of a potential duty to warn in research. For example, suppose a participant is being debriefed after participating in a cognitive psychologist's analogue study concerning the effect of stress on cognitive functioning. The participant reveals that he was already extremely stressed out when he arrived to participate because he had just learned that his 18-year-old son had been arrested for armed robbery. The participant then says that he is so ashamed of his son's behavior that he wants "to go home and kill [him]self." Although the study was not intended to involve such matters, the researcher now has to decide whether her ethical duty to protect the welfare of the participant requires her to report her concerns to the authorities (APA, 1992, Principle E). On the other hand, if she informs the authorities, she is violating her ethical duty to keep his participation confidential, a commitment she had, unfortunately, made unconditionally in the consent form. Many questions can be raised about the existence of a duty to warn in the study just described. For example, the cognitive researcher, as a nonclinician, can be viewed as lacking the training to form the type of "special relationship" that exists between a clinician and a client; therefore, the cognitive researcher is not competent to make a meaningful and valid professional judgment regarding her participant's dangerousness (Appelbaum & Rosenbaum, 1989).

Whether or not a legal duty to warn can be established for researchers, the preceding discussion indicates clearly that the research process can elicit information that would create serious ethical concerns for a researcher about her professional obligation to protect a participant, or someone else, from harm by intervening in the participant's life. Both clinical and nonclinical researchers should address the potential clinical implications of their data collection procedures proactively, while the study is being designed. Researchers should be certain not to guarantee unconditional confidentiality during the informed consent process if there is any foreseeable circumstance in which they might find it necessary to violate a participant's confidentiality. If a study does involve the potential for intervention by the researchers or others, the consent forms for the study must state this possibility in the section on the limits of confidentiality (ACA, 1997, G.2.a; APA, 1992, 6.11[b]).

Nonclinicians should seriously consider consulting with a clinical colleague to obtain input about the sorts of clinically significant responses that their research protocol might evoke and how researchers might want to react to participants' clinically provocative statements. It would also be prudent for nonclinicians conducting family interview research or research about suicidal behavior, anger, or other clinical topics to have a clinician on their research team. The clinician can competently evaluate videotape or audio recordings of interviews, as well as questionnaire responses, to assess the presence of clinical risk factors (Fisher & Rosendahl, 1990). Then, the clinician can follow up with at-risk participants and provide appropriate referrals (Bussell, 1994). A clinician might also be useful during the debriefing process in helping participants resolve emotional reactions evoked by the study, especially in family interview research studies. Family members might need to work through the disclosures they have made regarding each other during the data collection sessions.

## ETHICAL ISSUES CONCERNING THE USE OF STUDENT SUBJECT POOLS

Many universities require students taking freshman-level psychology courses to participate in one or more research studies during the semester. Some programs give students extra credit points for fulfilling this course requirement; others do not. Sieber and Saks (1989) reported that 74% of psychology departments with graduate programs had subject pools; Landrum and Chastain (1999) found that 32.7% of undergraduate psychology departments had them. A major ethical issue regarding student subject pools is whether research participation for these students is truly voluntary. To provide students with a voluntary choice regarding whether to participate in research, the "Ethical Principles" requires that subject pool students be given "equitable alternative activities" they can complete to fulfill their research requirement or earn extra credit (APA, 1992, 6.11[d]). Alternatives might include reading and summarizing a research article, designing a study to investigate a phenomenon of interest to the student, or attending a public lecture on campus. The major question about such alternatives is whether they are truly equitable; that is, are they really equivalent to participation in a research study, or do they require a greater investment of the student's time and effort? If the alternatives are not equitable, students are again being coerced to participate in research.

The justification mentioned most often for having a departmental subject pool is that research participation is educational for the students. Students are afforded firsthand experience of how behavioral research is conducted, providing a valuable experiential supplement to the information concerning research methods they learn in class and from their reading. Some empirical support does exist for the viewpoint that students develop a greater appreciation of behavioral research through their subject pool experience, although the quality of this educational component depends largely on researchers' efforts to make educational information, including handouts, available to participants and to provide thorough debriefing explanations that address all questions the student-participants raise (Nimmer & Handelsman, 1992; Sieber, 1999; Waite & Bowman, 1999).[39] Just as IRBs protect the best interests of research participants, academic departments incur an obligation when they create a subject pool to promote the interests of these participants. Departments using a subject pool should appoint a faculty member or graduate assistant as subject pool coordinator to oversee the ethical treatment of subject pool participants, deal with participant complaints, and ensure that the educational goals of the subject pool are being addressed effectively.

The other, arguably more salient justifications for the use of subject pools are the familiar utilitarian considerations that are so prominent in research contexts. Faculty and students conducting research need participants, but students do not volunteer in sufficient numbers to satisfy this need. Furthermore, students who do volunteer are arguably not representative of the general student population of the institution. Therefore, in the interest of science (and to provide students with firsthand experience with behavioral research), students are coerced, at least to some extent, to participate. In some cases, students might be provided with brief descriptions of studies and allowed to select the studies in which they prefer to participate. However, other institutions, wishing to minimize the potential for sampling bias based on students' preferences for particular types of studies, simply provide students with dates, times, and locations of data collection sessions. This practice can be problematic because it can be argued that after students appear for a research session and read the consent form, it is uncomfortable for many of them to refuse to participate, even if there is something about the description of the study that they do not like. This sort of situation introduces another element of potential coercion to the subject pool procedure.

Subject pool students must have the same freedom as any other research participant to withdraw from participation in a study without penalty. It must be made clear to these students that if they do not wish to participate in the study after reading the consent form, they can withdraw and still receive credit for attending the research session. Fortunately for researchers, students very rarely elect this option.

A problem for researchers using student participants is the high rate of "no-shows" (i.e., students who sign up to participate, but do not appear at the appointed time). No-show rates in the range of 20 to 25% are extremely common; reminding students by telephone or mail helps to reduce this number (Butler, 1999). An ethical issue pertaining to this phenomenon is faculty members' punishment of no-show behavior. Some faculty require additional (penalty) hours of research participation when students are reported as no-shows for experiments; other students might lose points toward their course grade if slots are no longer available to sign up for other studies. Faculty members should remember that failure to appear to participate in a study is not necessarily an indication of laziness. Research participation is not an element of a student's usual routine; therefore, it is easily forgotten. Faculty members certainly have their share of difficulty remembering appointments. Also, everyone experiences an unavoidable circumstance occasionally (e.g., car trouble) that prevents him from keeping an appointment. Penalizing no-shows again highlights the tension between the ethical expectation of voluntary research participation and participation as a course requirement.

## ETHICS AND THE SCIENTIFIC MERIT OF RESEARCH

A researcher faces a host of ethical obligations when he decides to conduct a research study using human participants. In addition to issues like informed consent, confidentiality, and debriefing, researchers incur obligations based simply on the fact that they are using participants' time. Wasting participants' time on a meaningless research study demonstrates a lack of respect for participants as persons. Therefore, one of a researcher's most basic ethical obligations in designing a study is to make certain, by reviewing the relevant literature and consulting with colleagues, that her project has the potential to produce findings that will make a significant contribution to her field and/or to the participants (APA, 1992, 6.06). Of course, a researcher can never know in advance what the outcome of her study will be.[40] Nevertheless, IRBs will typically ask researchers to provide information regarding the potential contributions of a proposed study. The IRB can reject a proposal on ethical grounds if they believe the study is not of sufficient potential value to justify the demands being placed on the participants.

The justifications typically given for the value of research in the mental health professions are largely utilitarian. If it is the potential value of the research results that justifies the economic and human costs of conducting the research, it would follow that inadequate research design can compromise the ethical acceptability of a research study. Even a study involving minimal risk uses the time and effort of participants and expends important resources (Rosenthal, 1994). Therefore, IRBs will also comment on issues concerning the internal validity of the research design (e.g., lack of random assignment of participants to conditions). Researchers also incur an ethical obligation to make certain that their research results are valid and generalizable to the population they are sampling (i.e., possess external validity). A related concept, *ecological validity,* concerns how closely the research procedure mirrors behavioral contexts people confront in real life. The greater the ecological validity, the greater the potential practical implications of the research findings.

## ETHICAL ISSUES IN SELECTING RESEARCH SAMPLES

A study's value also depends on the representativeness and diversity of its participants. For example, research on the effectiveness of cognitive-behavioral therapy in the treatment of depression is less valuable if the sample consists exclusively of adult white males. The importance of including children in research samples for studies evaluating treatments that may benefit children was discussed earlier (NIH, 1998). NIH has also issued regulations concerning the inclusion of women and minorities in federally funded research (NIH Guidelines, 1994). Researchers should not conduct studies without adequate representation of women and minorities in their samples if the results of the studies could potentially benefit, or have implications for, these diverse groups (ACA, 1997, G.1.f). In other words, diverse groups should be included in research samples unless there is a compelling justification for not doing so.

## ETHICAL ISSUES IN DATA COLLECTION AND ANALYSIS

The principal researcher on a project has an ethical responsibility to make certain that data collection procedures are conducted competently and professionally, whether he collects the data himself or has colleagues, students, or others under his supervision conduct the sessions (ACA, 1997, G.1.d; APA, 1992, 6.07). The researcher is also responsible for insuring that protocols are scored correctly and that computer entry of data is accurate (Rosenthal, 1994). Too often, these clerical tasks are assigned to students with inadequate training and investment in the project. Computer data files should be proofread by at least spot-checking the accuracy of data entry. If errors exist, the entire file should be proofread line by line. Failure to do so could compromise the validity of the research results.

Fabricating data that were never collected and altering data are clearly the two most serious types of unethical behavior associated with data collection and analysis (ACA, 1997, G.3.b; APA, 1992, 6.21[a]). In addition, when researchers publish or present the results of a study, they are obligated to report nonsignificant findings and any results that disconfirm their hypotheses, along with significant results consistent with their hypotheses (ACA, 1997, G.3.c).

The decision to drop participants from a data set for any reason or to handle statistical outliers in a special way also has ethical implications. Whenever the collected data are manipulated in these ways, the researcher incurs an ethical duty to report how the data were handled and to provide the results that would have been obtained if the original data set had been left intact (Rosenthal, 1994).

Analyzing and reanalyzing data, which has been called "cooking the data," is a practice that is considered inappropriate by many psychometricians. However, Rosenthal (1994) regards such activities as making full use of the data that researchers and participants invested so much energy in creating. Of course, statistical techniques to adjust probability values should be employed when the same data are analyzed in a number of different ways so that the likelihood of obtaining statistically significant results is not inflated.

If errors pertaining to the analysis or reporting of results are discovered after a study has been published, the professional should endeavor to correct the error (APA, 1992, 6.21[b]). In such a circumstance, contacting the publisher to make arrangements for a printed correction or retraction statement is an appropriate course of action.

---

**Case Example 11.11**

*A researcher is interested in studying the effect of different counseling styles on clients' perception of the therapist in an initial meeting. Each "client" (actually, college student) is interviewed by two therapists, in counterbalanced order. The researcher hypothesizes that a person-centered counseling style will be perceived more positively than a more directive, confrontational approach. He collects pilot data and finds that the directive style was rated more positively. The researcher wonders whether a difference in the attractiveness of the two therapists, rather than their counseling style, would account for the results of the pilot study.*

*He conducts another study in which only one therapist is used. She uses a person-centered approach with half of the participants and a directive approach with the other half. Participants are assigned randomly to the two conditions. The results of the second study are consistent with the researcher's hypothesis. The researcher concludes that the pilot data were invalid due to the confounding variable of therapist attractiveness. When he publishes the study, he reports only the methodology and results of the second study because he believes he should not publish invalid data.*

*Did the researcher behave ethically?*

---

## ETHICAL ISSUES IN PUBLISHING RESEARCH RESULTS

### Assigning Authorship Credit

Many researchers collaborate on projects with colleagues and/or students. When presenting or publishing research articles or books, it is necessary to determine which contributors to a project merit listing as authors (ACA, 1997, G.4.b; APA, 1992, 6.23[a]). Authorship entails more than just assisting with data collection or making useful editorial contributions in the preparation of a research paper (Fine & Kurdek, 1993). The authors of a project are "those who have made substantial scientific contributions to a study," as well as those who have written the report of the research (APA, 1994b, p. 4).

In addition, authors are not listed randomly or alphabetically. The order in which authors are listed on a project is intended to indicate "the relative scientific or professional contributions of the individuals involved, regardless of their relative status" (APA, 1992, 6.23[b]). In other words, the senior researcher will not be listed first if her contributions to conceptualizing the study, collecting and interpreting the data, and writing up the report are not as substantial as those of other members of the research team. Similarly, as discussed in Chapter 3, the faculty mentor of a student's dissertation study will generally not be the first author of an article based on the research because students should receive authorship credit commensurate with their contribution to a project (ACA, 1997, G.4.c; APA, 1992, 6.23[c]). However, if a student completes his master's thesis requirement by taking primary responsibility for one study that is part of a four-study project conceptualized and developed by a faculty member, the student is not ethically entitled to claim first authorship for the project merely because one part of it was his thesis (Shadish, 1994). It is extremely desirable for the members of a research team to discuss the issue of authorship early on, so there are no misunderstandings later regarding who the authors will be or in what order the authors will be listed. Senior members of the research team bear primary responsibility for attending to these matters because they should be more familiar with the issues involved than students or first-time researchers.

## PLAGIARISM

When information obtained from a published or unpublished source is used in a publication or presentation, mental health professionals are ethically obligated to cite the source of the information or idea (ACA, 1997, G.4.a; APA, 1992, 6.22). Failure to do so constitutes plagiarism, which is the act of stealing another person's idea and presenting it as one's own. When the exact words of a source are presented, quotation marks should be used and a citation, including the page number on which the quoted material appeared in the original source, should be provided (APA, 1994b). Also, each time an idea from another source is paraphrased, rather than quoted directly, a citation of the source should be included (APA, 1994b).

## MEDIA PRESENTATIONS OF RESEARCH FINDINGS

When a professional's research findings are presented on television or in a newspaper article, he cannot necessarily prevent the commentator or journalist from misrepresenting or misinterpreting the research results. Nevertheless, mental health professionals have an ethical obligation to try to minimize the probability of such mistakes and, if possible, to correct mistakes that are presented to the public (ACA, 1997, C.5.d; APA, 1992, 3.02[b, c]). There are several ways professionals can try to prevent their work from being misunderstood or misrepresented by the media. First, a professional should carefully consider the media outlets with which he agrees to discuss his research. For example, a request for information from a legitimate news organization like the *New York Times* is much safer to pursue than a request from the *National Enquirer.* Second, a professional should explain his findings very carefully and straightforwardly to media people, remembering that they are not mental health professionals and may not understand technical terms and statistical analyses. Third, he should ask to review the articles or video presentations prior to their release to the public to ensure that no misrepresentation has occurred. Finally, researchers should keep in mind that professional outlets (e.g., journals, books, organizational newsletters) are generally best for their work. Professionals who seek the glamour of mass media exposure always invite the risk of having their work misrepresented to the public, which could reduce public confidence in their profession.

## SUBMITTING MANUSCRIPTS FOR JOURNAL PUBLICATION

Before submitting articles to academic journals, researchers should always review the journals' "instructions to authors" section. These instructions usually specify the format and style to be used in the article, where to submit the manuscript, and how to contact the editor. There are some additional guidelines for submission that may or may not be explicitly stated, but professionals are still obligated to abide by them. For example, researchers should not submit data for publication to a journal if they have already published the data elsewhere because an author cannot give the copyright to more than one publisher (ACA, 1997, G.4.d; APA, 1992, 6.24). Neither should researchers submit a report of the same study to more than one journal at a time, hoping that at least one of the journals will accept the article (APA, 1994b). If an article is rejected by a journal, the author is then free to pursue another outlet.

## ETHICAL ISSUES IN CONDUCTING RESEARCH ON THE INTERNET

The development of the Internet has opened up exciting opportunities for research with human participants. Now researchers can reach larger and more specialized samples of participants. For example, a substantial sample of people with eating disorders might be recruited simply by contacting an Internet-based support and discussion group on the subject. Also, researchers are becoming increasingly interested in studying Internet behavior (e.g., patterns of Internet use).

However, Internet research does introduce several additional ethical concerns for researchers and IRBs. Obtaining informed consent is a tricky issue since, at present, it is not feasible to get a signed consent form over the Internet. For studies concerning nonsensitive topics (e.g., a survey of television viewing habits), informed consent can be obtained using a "portal." Participants read a consent document screen, then click with their mouse on a button to indicate their consent and gain access to the survey. For sensitive research topics (e.g., a survey of substance abuse behavior), researchers should present a consent form that participants can print out, sign, and return to the researcher. (Alternatively, participants could request a consent form and postage-paid return envelope via e-mail so that they will not incur any expense.) When the researcher receives a signed consent form, he can provide the participant with a password that will enable her to access the survey questions.

Confidentiality is a very tricky topic in Internet research. It is impossible to absolutely guarantee the confidentiality of information transmitted over the Internet. Breaches of confidentiality can occur inadvertently or through the deliberate acts of "hackers." An example of an inadvertent breach of confidentiality is if a participant responds to an e-mail recruiting message sent to a large pool of potential participants by using the "reply" function in her e-mail program. The reply is then received by everyone on the mailing list for the recruitment message. Participants in Internet research must be informed of the potential risks pertaining to confidentiality that are an inevitable part of transmitting data over the Internet.

Another ethical concern in conducting Internet research is that the researcher has no way of knowing for certain the identity of a participant. For example, a researcher might believe that he has received data for his sexual behavior study from a 30-year-old woman when the survey was actually completed by her 9-year-old son. Although there are monitoring services that can check the adult status of users of Web sites and prevent inappropriate participation by minors in a study, these services translate into additional effort on the part of participants and further intrusion into their privacy. Nevertheless, validity concerns require that a researcher be able to document precisely the characteristics of research participants. As use of the Internet for research purposes increases, Internet researchers and IRB members will both need to receive training in the nuances of Internet technology so that researchers can provide technical information regarding security procedures to IRBs, and IRB members, in turn, can ask pertinent questions and provide competent consultation and recommendations.

---

**Case Example 11.12**

*A researcher submits a proposal to the IRB at his university requesting permission to conduct a study monitoring the frequency with which counselors and psychologists visit sexually explicit Web sites. He plans to send an e-mail message describing an online survey of Internet behavior to the members of ACA and APA. Participants will complete the online survey about the types of Web sites they visit most frequently and submit their data without indicating their name. However, when they submit their data, the researcher's server will deposit a "cookie" on the participant's computer that will enable the researcher to track the participant's online behavior for the next year. The researcher asserts that he will not record the identity of the participants, so there is no risk of their being harmed by the deception. He argues that the deception is necessary because participants would alter the sites they visit if they were informed that their behavior was being monitored. Finally, he asserts that it is very important that we learn more about the nature of professional people's Internet behavior.*
*Should the IRB approve the research proposal?*

---

## ETHICAL ISSUES IN CONDUCTING ANIMAL RESEARCH

Throughout the 20th century, animal researchers and government agencies (e.g., NIH) have created and supported regulations concerning the humane treatment of animals in research. During the 1960s, the Pet Protection Act, subsequently known as the Animal Welfare Act (AWA) of 1966 (Pub. L. No. 89-544), was enacted by

Congress to address the use of animals in research. Of major concern at that time were press reports of pets being used in research. The AWA gave the United States Department of Agriculture (USDA) responsibility for enforcement of the new law.

Institutions conducting behavioral and biomedical research involving animals are required to establish an Institutional Animal Care and Use Committee (IACUC), in accordance with guidelines published by NIH, the Applied Research Ethics National Association (ARENA), and the Office for Protection from Research Risks (OPRR), to review and approve such research (NIH, ARENA, and OPRR, 1992). The IACUC also inspects all animal facilities at its institution twice each year to make certain USDA regulations are being observed.

The use of animals in biomedical and behavioral research has become extremely controversial in recent years (Gluck & Kubacki, 1991; Plous, 1996a). Critics of animal research argue that it is unethical to cause animals pain and suffering unnecessarily. Supporters of animal research offer utilitarian justifications: animal research furthers our understanding of human behavior, assists in developing solutions to medical problems affecting human beings, and, in some instances, actually promotes the survival of the animal species involved. Psychologists' support for animal research has declined over time, and the positions of opponents and proponents of animal research have become increasingly polarized (Gluck & Kubacki, 1991).

Psychology students are somewhat ambivalent about animal research. They oppose animal research involving pain or death and do not think that psychology majors should be required to take an animal laboratory course (Plous, 1996b). One reason for their opposition to animal learning courses is that the animals are typically killed at the conclusion of the course. On the other hand, students are not opposed in general to the use of animals in research or teaching. They believe that observational studies of animal learning and behavior are appropriate (Plous, 1996b).

However, both biomedical and behavioral research with animals has produced important findings that have benefited humankind. Proponents of the value of well-designed biomedical animal studies have countered the argument about the cost to animals of conducting such studies by pointing out the costs to people with serious illnesses of *not* conducting the studies (Kaplan, 1988).

Researchers conducting animal studies incur ethical and professional duties to treat animals humanely and to comply with relevant laws and government regulations (APA, 1992, 6.20). One or more researchers competent and experienced in the care of laboratory animals are responsible for providing training and supervision for all procedures in their laboratory. Clearly, ultimate responsibility for any problem or mistreatment that occurs in the lab rests with these researchers. Students and other personnel working in an animal lab must be adequately trained in research methods and in the care and handling of the species they will be dealing with (APA, 1992, 6.20[d]). Supervising researchers are obligated to monitor the behavior of their students and assistants to make certain that the animals are not harmed (APA, 1992, 6.20[c]).

Research procedures that involve pain or suffering for the animals are only permitted when no alternative methodology is available that will produce less suffering and when "the goal is justified by its prospective scientific, educational, or applied value" (APA, 1992, 6.20[g]). An institution's IACUC is responsible for evaluating the adequacy of researchers' justification for inflicting pain or suffering on animals.

For example, it would be difficult to justify subjecting animals to any pain or deprivation for the purpose of a teaching demonstration, when there are computer simulations of animal learning available now that make live demonstrations unnecessary.

Finally, the "Ethical Principles" stipulates that when the animals must be killed, the methods used should be quick and minimize pain (APA, 1992, 6.20[i]). Based on the growing ethical misgivings of psychologists, psychology students, and the general public regarding animal research, it is likely that the decline in the use of animals in psychological research will continue (Plous, 1996b).

## PRACTICE CASE INVOLVING THE MODEL OF ETHICAL DECISION MAKING

An experimental social psychologist undertakes a survey research project concerning anger. She has participants rate scenarios depicting different responses to anger-provoking stimuli in terms of the "appropriateness" of each response as a method of coping with anger. She then completes a structured interview with individual participants regarding their own methods of dealing with anger. The consent form signed by participants guarantees unconditionally the confidentiality of their data.

She interviews one participant who reports homicidal fantasies about his ex-wife, who was recently granted custody of their two young children following a hotly contested custody battle in court. She completes the structured interview protocol, but feels uncomfortable later about the seriousness of the threat this man might pose to his ex-wife and family. She knows the participant's name, but is unsure about what action, if any, she should take.

Does the researcher have an ethical obligation to take some sort of action in this situation?

## SUMMARY

Research is an important aspect of many mental health professionals' work. Because a professional's personal values influence her theoretical orientation and research interests, she must guard against conducting studies or presenting findings in such a way that they are biased toward her subjective viewpoint.

The role of Institutional Review Boards for the Protection of Human Subjects (IRBs) is to review their organization's proposed research studies to ensure that participants will not be harmed and that the studies are of sufficient quality to justify the use of participants' time and effort. Evaluating the relative importance of the risks and potential benefits associated with a study is one of the most difficult tasks that IRBs and researchers have. IRBs also review informed consent procedures. The consent form provided to participants must be easily understandable to them and explain the study in such a way that they can make an informed decision about their participation. For example, researchers are obligated to inform participants about any potential risks associated with the study and any limitations on the confidentiality of the data they provide (e.g., mandatory reporting of child abuse). Additional informed consent considerations arise with special participant populations, such as legally incompetent individuals and children. For example, in school-based research, the issue of active versus passive parental consent frequently arises.

After participating in a study, participants should be debriefed as soon as possible. If information has been withheld or deception has been used for the sake of the study's validity, then full disclosure must be made during debriefing. Debriefing is also supposed to serve an educational purpose for participants, particularly when the research sample is drawn from a student subject pool.

The Internet presents exciting new opportunities for researchers, but it also presents significant challenges to the ethical duties of informed consent and confidentiality. Researchers and IRBs will need to master this new technology to ensure that ethical standards for the protection of human participants are not compromised in Internet research studies.

The use of animals in research has become increasingly controversial in recent years. IACUCs oversee the ethical and legal standards governing animal research. In any animal research laboratory, one or more supervising researchers are designated as having ultimate responsibility for the care and treatment of animals by all lab personnel. Today, animal research plays a more important role in biomedical research than in traditional behavioral studies.

# 12 Mental Health Professions and the Law

As discussed in Chapter 1, many of the professional activities of psychologists and counselors are guided by legal statutes, as well as by ethical guidelines. Some legal duties are mandated under federal laws, but the majority of statutes governing the treatment of emotionally disturbed and mentally retarded clients are established by individual states. Although there is considerable overlap, the laws of individual states do vary. Thus, it is extremely important for mental health professionals to become familiar with the specific laws governing mental health practice in their state.

Mental health professionals encounter the legal system whenever they are involved in the involuntary commitment of a client to a psychiatric hospital. Suicide prevention, for example, frequently requires hospitalizing a client temporarily. The issues of voluntary and involuntary treatment, and the ethical arguments for and against the use of coercive methods in preventing suicide, are discussed in this chapter.

Mental health professionals also function in a variety of roles within the legal system. These areas of professional specialization are referred to collectively as *forensic psychology*. Forensic psychologists are involved in matters pertaining to both criminal law, which involves criminal acts prosecuted by the government, and civil law, which involves noncriminal legal issues, including lawsuits, commitment procedures, and family law (Anderson, 1996). In criminal matters, forensic experts might assist in determining a defendant's competence to stand trial or mental state at the time of the crime. In civil matters, forensic psychologists might offer testimony regarding a person's need for involuntary hospitalization, based on an assessment of the individual's mental status and potential for violence. Forensic experts also frequently conduct child custody and child protective evaluations. A number of issues facing forensic psychologists are addressed in this chapter. Finally, situations in which legal and ethical considerations appear to conflict are discussed as yet another context in which the ethical reasoning skills of professionals are tested.

## LEGAL ISSUES CONCERNING ADMISSION FOR INPATIENT PSYCHIATRIC TREATMENT

Each state provides psychiatric facilities to serve its citizens' need for outpatient and inpatient mental health treatment. Most inpatient clients are admitted voluntarily, a process that assumes the client is competent to choose to pursue treatment.

### COMPETENCE

A person can exercise a right or privilege only to the extent that she can make an autonomous choice to do so. In Chapter 4, the concept of personal autonomy was shown to arise from Kant's (1785/1964a) view of personhood. Kant believed that what distinguishes persons from everything else that exists is their ability to reason; people are rational beings. Legally, the concept of personal competence centers on the ability of the person to understand what is going on, both within her and around her, and to make rational, deliberative decisions based on her accurate understanding of her circumstances. Moreover, autonomous beings are self-directing; that is, they make rational choices consistent with their personal values. Thus, when the issue of an individual's competence to make decisions for herself is raised, the question to be decided is whether she understands what is going on and has the rational capacity to make deliberative choices based on the values she has adhered to during the course of her life.

## VOLUNTARY TREATMENT

The U.S. Supreme Court ruled that an incompetent individual cannot provide the informed consent necessary for voluntary hospitalization (*Zinermon v. Burch,* 1990). For treatment to be truly voluntary, the client must be competent to make an autonomous choice to pursue treatment. Autonomous choice entails, first, the absence of coercion (Carroll, 1991). In other words, the client is not being pressured to enter treatment with the threat of negative consequences (e.g., going to jail) for not pursuing treatment. Second, acting autonomously requires that the client be capable of understanding her situation and options and of making a rational, deliberative decision consistent with her values and beliefs. For example, if a client chooses to seek admission to the hospital because it is the only safe haven that will permit her to escape the visitors from Mars who wish to extract her cerebrospinal fluid, it is unlikely that her decision would be deemed autonomous.

Clearly, there are degrees of autonomous functioning, falling along a continuum. Some clients request admission to a psychiatric facility based on their deliberative judgment that they need assistance with their emotional and/or substance abuse problems. These individuals demonstrate a high degree of autonomy. In many cases, a client's family or outpatient therapist will urge him to enter the hospital, with the assurance that he will be free to leave if he no longer wishes to continue treatment. In deciding to take this advice, the individual still may be acting autonomously (i.e., consistent with his personal values and perceptions of the situation), though it could be argued that he demonstrates less autonomy than a person making an independent decision to pursue treatment (Wrightsman, Nietzel, & Fortune, 1998). In other cases, a client's family will threaten him with involuntary hospitalization if he refuses to accept voluntary admission to the hospital (Solomon, 1996). Mental health professionals making admissions evaluations at psychiatric hospitals sometimes present a client with the same limited menu of options. This client has very little choice in accepting "voluntary" admission (Carroll, 1991).

Once admitted, even voluntary inpatient clients can face legal obstacles in attempting to leave the hospital if the mental health professionals responsible for their treatment do not believe they are ready for discharge. Essentially, any client deemed mentally ill and either potentially dangerous or incapable of attending to his basic physical needs can be held while civil commitment procedures are initiated, even though he has made a written request to be discharged. In most states, a client can be held up to three days after requesting discharge, even if commitment is not being sought, while the professionals responsible for his treatment determine whether his psychiatric condition requires additional hospitalization. Voluntary clients generally cannot be committed unless they demand to be discharged, leave the facility without medical permission, or refuse to consent to needed treatment.

---

**Case Example 12.1**

*A clinical psychologist working in a psychiatric hospital has a client who requests discharge from an alcoholism treatment unit. The client has a history of depression and has made suicide attempts in the past. The psychologist is concerned that the client will start drinking again if he is discharged. She urges the client to stay in the program, but to no avail. Finally, she tells him she believes that if he leaves the hospital, he will drink, become depressed, and attempt suicide. Therefore, if he demands to be discharged, commitment proceedings will be initiated on the basis that he poses a danger to himself. He agrees to stay voluntarily and complete the alcohol rehabilitation program.*

*What ethical considerations are involved in this situation? Did the psychologist behave ethically?*

---

## INVOLUNTARY HOSPITALIZATION: THE PSYCHIATRIC COMMITMENT PROCESS

Being deemed mentally ill is not sufficient grounds for hospitalizing a person against his will. The vague and problematic nature of the concept of mental illness, discussed in Chapter 9, certainly raises questions about the appropriateness of using it as the sole criterion for depriving individuals of their civil liberties (Szasz, 1974). Although the legal requirements for commitment vary from state to state, usually a person who is committed must (a) suffer from mental illness, (b) be dangerous to himself or others or incapable of tending adequately to his basic physical needs, and (c) need inpatient hospitalization for treatment or care (Wrightsman et al., 1998).

The key element justifying most instances of involuntary commitment is the individual's inability to take care of his own basic needs (Turkheimer & Parry, 1992). Most courts do not require that the person pose an "imminent" danger to himself or others in order to commit him (Litwack & Schlesinger, 1999). In all cases, the ethical basis of involuntary hospitalization is concern for the welfare of the client and others potentially affected by his behavior. In other words, to be committed, a client must be judged to be incompetent as a function of mental illness in a way that threatens serious harm to himself or others (Cohen & Cohen, 1999). Involuntary hospitalization is the most extreme expression of paternalism in mental health practice; mental health professionals actually decide to suspend a client's civil liberties "for his own good."

There are three types of legal psychiatric commitment. The most common type is emergency commitment, which occurs when a client is admitted involuntarily to a psychiatric hospital on an emergency basis, usually on the assertion that he is dangerous to himself or others (Wrightsman et al., 1998). Emergency commitment does not require a court order and can be initiated by a law enforcement officer or mental health professional. The client is examined by a physician or mental health professional prior to emergency admission and committed on the basis of the professional's judgment. In most states, a commitment of this type has a maximum duration of 48 to 72 hours (Wrightsman et al., 1998). A preliminary hearing before a judge is needed to detain a person any longer.

The other two types of involuntary commitment require a court order committing the individual to receive treatment. Involuntary hospitalization in an inpatient facility, which is the second type of commitment, involves an examination of the individual by a psychiatrist or other qualified mental health professional, followed by a court hearing concerning the results of the examination. If the supposedly mentally ill person does not have an attorney, one is appointed to represent her interests at the hearing. The hearing is generally before a judge, though, in some states, the person for whom commitment is sought can elect to have a jury hear the case. Witnesses present evidence at the hearing and are cross-examined (Wrightsman et al., 1998). If the outcome of the hearing is that the person should be committed to a state facility, the commitment is generally not open-ended, particularly if the individual has not been committed before. If the person still meets the legal criteria for involuntary confinement after the initial period has elapsed, the commitment will need to be extended at another court hearing.

The third type of involuntary commitment, called "outpatient commitment," mandates that the person must attend treatment sessions at an outpatient facility (Wrightsman et al., 1998). It was developed to address the right of psychiatric clients, even involuntary ones, to be treated in the least restrictive setting appropriate to their treatment needs. Clients committed to outpatient treatment require treatment, but can tend to their basic physical needs and do not require the protection of an inpatient setting to avoid being dangerous to themselves or others (Hiday, 1996).

Consumer advocacy groups have questioned the ethical appropriateness of outpatient commitment on the grounds that these clients are not dangerous to themselves or others (or they would require inpatient hospitalization), and therefore should not be compelled to participate in treatment (Draine, 1997). Nevertheless, various forms of outpatient commitment have become increasingly popular as a means to prevent decompensation in outpatient clients, thereby avoiding inpatient admission, and to increase the probability that conditionally discharged inpatient clients will pursue treatment in the community (Draine, 1997). Outpatient commitment has also been used to ensure that treatment will be pursued by an individual who is ordered to receive psychiatric and/or substance abuse treatment by a court as a condition of probation or some other resolution of criminal charges. The limited research that has been conducted on the effectiveness of outpatient commitment, summarized by Hiday (1996), indicates that the procedure is generally effective in improving clients' adjustment and reducing the likelihood of hospitalization, although more research is urgently needed (Draine, 1997).

Outpatient commitment does have its problems. A major issue is client non-compliance. For example, when a client misses several sessions or does not take her medication consistently, but is not imminently dangerous to herself, the clinician must decide whether to report her to the court (Arthur & Swanson, 1993). Also, a great deal more paperwork is associated with outpatient commitment than with voluntary outpatient treatment, so some clinicians might use the threat of outpatient commitment to "persuade" a client to voluntarily continue outpatient treatment. This informal use of coercion is an ethically questionable practice, as discussed earlier in the case of voluntary inpatient treatment (Hiday, 1996).

---

**Case Example 12.2**

*An adult heroin addict is arrested for drug dealing. The court grants him probation provided he goes directly into an inpatient drug treatment facility and completes a three-month drug rehabilitation program successfully. Otherwise, he will be sent to prison. The individual enters a drug treatment program, but he makes little effort to benefit from the program. He follows all the rules, but he is not really invested in understanding his problems and changing his life. A drug counselor accuses him of "jailing" (i.e., just passing time in the program without participating actively) and threatens to discharge him unless he shows greater urgency about changing his life. A week later, in spite of not having broken any program rules, the client is discharged, resulting in his being sentenced to prison.*

*What are the relevant ethical considerations in this situation? Was the client treated fairly?*

---

## THE RIGHTS OF PSYCHIATRIC INPATIENT CLIENTS

A right is defined as a legitimate claim to something. When people have legal rights, everyone else has a *duty* not to interfere with their exercise of those rights. Inpatient clients, whether voluntary or committed, have a number of civil and political rights enumerated in court decisions and state statutes that psychiatric facilities must provide (Slovenko, 1999). This "patient's bill of rights" includes the right to live in a safe environment, receive adequate food and shelter, have visitors, and participate in developing an individualized treatment plan. Several additional rights of clients are discussed below.

### RIGHT TO TREATMENT

Once a person is committed because she is in need of psychiatric treatment, the right to treatment follows naturally as part of the state's obligation for having deprived her of her liberty. A person cannot be committed to a psychiatric facility simply to get her "off the streets"; she must receive treatment intended to improve her condition. It might be surprising to learn that an involuntarily confined client's right to treatment is a rather recent development. The right was established in a 1971 court decision (*Wyatt v. Stickney,* 1971/1972). In addition, involuntarily committed clients are entitled to treatment by the least intrusive or restrictive means possible.

## Right to Refuse Treatment

When clients are committed involuntarily, the mental health professionals working with them are ethically obligated to provide treatment, but committed clients do not relinquish the right to refuse treatment. In other words, a committed client, like a voluntary client, can waive her right to treatment. However, mental health professionals responsible for her treatment might question whether she is competent to make this decision. They can deny a client the right to refuse treatment if she is deemed incompetent to make such a judgment and if her refusal is likely to result in harm to herself or others (Wrightsman et al., 1998).

The crucial issue is *why* she is refusing to comply with the treatment plan, as well as the behavioral consequences of her refusal. For example, a client suffering from Schizophrenia, Paranoid Type is committed to a state hospital. She refuses to take the antipsychotic medication prescribed. When asked why she refuses, she tells her psychiatrist that the pills are poison and will kill her instantly. She has been assaultive toward the treatment staff on a number of occasions, believing that the food, toothpaste, and water on the ward are also being used to poison her. If a client's reason for refusing treatment is clearly irrational, her psychiatrist can argue that she is delusional and is not capable at present of understanding her situation rationally or perceiving her circumstances accurately. Furthermore, her assaultiveness in her unmedicated delusional state makes it dangerous *not* to medicate her. On that basis, the psychiatrist can deem her incompetent to make such a decision and coerce her to take her medication.

If, on the other hand, a client refuses to take her medication and her reasons are not clearly irrational or based upon a misperception of reality, coercion is inappropriate. For example, if the same client refused antipsychotic medication because she was concerned that she was being harmed by the medication, based on the serious side effects she had experienced from taking it, and she displayed no signs of being dangerous to herself or others, there would be no adequate justification for forcing her to accept treatment. The burden of proof in this matter is always on those wanting to use coercion. Medicating a person involuntarily is a very serious violation of her right to bodily privacy, which is protected by the First, Eighth, and Fourteenth Amendments of the United States Constitution.

## Right to Least Restrictive Treatment

All clients, including involuntary ones, are entitled to treatment by the least intrusive or restrictive means possible. The "least restrictive appropriate setting for treatment" refers to the available treatment setting that provides the client with the greatest likelihood of improvement or cure and restricts the client's physical and social liberties no more than is necessary for effective treatment and for adequate protection against any dangers the client might pose to himself or others (*Dixon v. Weinberger,* 1975). An implication of the least restrictive treatment right is that court-mandated outpatient care (i.e., outpatient commitment) is possible, if such a setting is deemed appropriate for carrying out the client's treatment plan.

---

**Case Example 12.3**

*A client suffering from Schizophrenia, Undifferentiated Type has been treated in an inpatient facility for the past three months. Her condition is now stable, and she does not need to be in the hospital. However, she does not have a place to live, and there are no placements available in halfway houses or other community care facilities. The hospital administration insists that she be discharged because it is illegal to keep her in the restrictive hospital environment when she does not require that level of supervision. The treatment team discharges her, with the plan that she will seek temporary housing at a nearby YWCA. Within days, she violates a YWCA rule and is told to leave. She becomes homeless.*
*Did the treatment team behave appropriately?*

---

## ETHICAL CONSIDERATIONS IN SUICIDE PREVENTION

One of the most common reasons for considering hospitalizing a client involuntarily is to prevent her from committing suicide. The ethical codes of the mental health professions state that it is appropriate for a professional to violate his client's confidentiality by informing the police or medical personnel if he believes that she represents a danger to her own life (ACA, 1997, B.1.c; APA, 1992, 5.05). However, suicide prevention is a matter of considerable ethical complexity because mental health professionals also profess a deep respect for the autonomy and personhood of each client. Clinicians believe that a client knows what is best for her and should be afforded the respect to make her own decisions about how she wants to direct her life (ACA, 1997, A.1.a; APA, 1992, Principle D). Professionals avoid imposing their values on a client out of this same respect for the client's personhood (ACA, 1997, A.5.b; APA, 1992, 1.09).

Nevertheless, clinicians engage in coercive, paternalistic suicide prevention procedures. Their ethical justification for doing so is their duty to protect the welfare of the client; interestingly, this duty is also based on their regard for her as a person (Fairbairn, 1995). The ethical duty of nonmaleficence is also an important consideration in deciding whether to intervene to prevent a client from committing suicide. Clinicians do not want to cause harm to a client, yet they are divided regarding which course of action produces the most harm: preventing suicide and abridging the client's autonomy and right to self-determination, or allowing her to make her own choice and possibly lose her life as a result. Legitimate ethical duties conflict in the case of a suicidal client, creating an ethical dilemma for the clinician.

### WHY DO PEOPLE COMMIT SUICIDE?

The traditional view of suicide among mental health professionals was that suicide is always an irrational act, resulting from depression, hopelessness, intense emotional pain, or psychosis (Shneidman, 1992). It is certainly true that individuals suffering from depressive disorders and the schizophrenias are at significantly elevated risk for suicide (Isometsa et al., 1994; Reid, 1998). However, one of the factors that makes the issue of suicide so complex ethically is that there are actually many different motivations for suicide. Suicidal acts are committed out of a sense of hopelessness or the perception that existence is meaningless, for cultural and religious reasons, out of altruistic concerns, to obtain revenge against others, for political reasons, as a sort of judicial self-punishment, and as a reaction to the behavior of others (Fairbairn, 1995).

Some suicidologists have argued that although suicide is frequently an irrational act, suicide can also be a rational, autonomous act. To act autonomously, however, it must be the case that a person "has the capacity to make considered choices and is aware of acting for reasons that are connected to her goals and purposes" (Fairbairn, 1995, p. 164). That is, a person cannot be said to make a truly free choice if she is not capable of reasoning clearly. Battin (1999) has added that a rational person must also be capable of making a realistic appraisal of the world and her situation (i.e., not be delusional or seriously misinformed), have adequate information about present and likely future circumstances in her life, and be acting to avoid harm to herself or others. For example, a person who is extremely depressed might not be considered rational because she is incapable of perceiving the possibility that her life circumstances could improve considerably.

Cases cited in support of the idea of rational suicide frequently involve the decisions of terminally ill people to end their lives in a painless manner or to be withdrawn from life-sustaining medical treatment (e.g., kidney dialysis). For example, in 1994, voters approved the Oregon Death with Dignity Act that makes it legal for a primary care physician to prescribe a medication for a competent, terminally ill person that will end the person's life (Ganzini, Fenn, Lee, Heintz, & Bloom, 1996). However, Thomas Szasz (1999) has argued that euthanasia is really suicide, so mental health professionals must decide where they stand on the fundamental issue of a person's right to commit suicide before they can determine the ethical acceptability of passive and active euthanasia. For instance, if the removal of life support (passive euthanasia) or the administration of a lethal drug (active euthanasia) is initiated by a patient, these acts are intended to cause the patient's own death. Thus, they are cases of suicide, though in cases of passive euthanasia the cause of death is often reported to be the disease from which the person was dying. Szasz (1999) points out that if a patient refused to continue life-sustaining dialysis, but was shot on the way home, it would be a case of murder, not death from kidney disease. In the same manner, voluntarily withdrawing life-sustaining treatment is suicide, not death from kidney disease. Just as people decide to keep themselves from dying by pursuing medical treatment, so they decide to die by withdrawing from life-sustaining treatment.[41]

Critics of the notion of "rational suicide" have asserted that a person can never choose death rationally because she cannot have adequate knowledge of what she is choosing. No one knows what death is like; there is something "uncanny" about it (Devine, 1990). A person can only make a rational choice about suicide if she possesses knowledge of the following alternatives: what she does not like about living and what awaits her in death. However, no one can claim knowledge of the latter.

---

**Case Example 12.4**

*A counselor is working with a 68-year-old, white female, whose husband died three years before. She has recently been diagnosed with Alzheimer's disease, for which there is no cure. The diagnosis has been confirmed by several independent evaluations. She has been informed that she will gradually become increasingly demented. At present, she is not significantly demented, though she has developed severe memory difficulties. She has no desire to experience a decline into dementia and wants to spare her family the experience of watching her sink into a vegetative state. She desires instead to be allowed to terminate her life now in a painless manner, so her family can remember her as a healthy, vibrant person. She asks the counselor to help her gain a physician's assistance to end her life painlessly. She is apparently rational and has maintained her position regarding the desirability of taking her own life for the past three months.*

*What should the position of mental health professionals be on the subject of assisted suicide?*

---

## PREDICTING SUICIDAL BEHAVIOR

Predicting future suicidality is about as difficult as predicting a person's potential for violence, which will be discussed later in this chapter. In both situations, clinicians tend to overpredict, rating individuals as being at higher risk for suicide than they really are (Joiner, Walker, Rudd, & Jobes, 1999; Murphy, 1988; Shergill & Szmukler, 1998). This tendency is quite understandable because a single instance of understated suicidal risk can result in a client's death.

Joiner and his colleagues (1999) have developed a method of rating the severity of risk for suicide that enables clinicians to evaluate individual clients' suicidality on a continuum from nonexistent to severe. The key variables they have identified for predicting suicidality are a history of multiple attempts, a resolved plan and preparations for an attempt, and suicidal desire and ideation. Additional risk factors can be incorporated into the process as "significant findings." This model of suicidality provides behavioral criteria that can help clinicians to identify the more severe indications of suicidal risk, rather than worry that every mention of suicidal ideation is an indication that the client is at serious risk for suicide.

## THE ETHICAL ARGUMENT FOR SUICIDE PREVENTION

The justification for coercive intervention to prevent suicide (e.g., involuntary hospitalization of the individual) is concern for the client's welfare, consistent with the ethical principle of nonmaleficence. According to active suicide prevention proponents, people who are depressed, intoxicated, psychotic, or in intense physical pain might perceive suicide as a rational solution to the problems in their life, but their belief is clearly irrational. They generally change their minds with the passage of time and/or after receiving mental health treatment (Goldblatt, 1999). Even terminally ill individuals are more likely to accept the continued use of life-prolonging medical treatment following successful treatment for depression (Farrenkopf & Bryan, 1999). Concern for the welfare of the survivors of the suicide (e.g., a client's family) is also an important consideration in preventing suicide.

Although the use of coercion, which involves controlling or exercising power over another person, does not appear to be consistent with respect for a client's autonomy, those favoring coercive suicide prevention argue that suicide is an irrational act, and irrational acts are never truly autonomous. For example, Kant, the major philosophical source of the ethical duty to respect personal autonomy, argued that "to use the power of a free will for its own destruction is self-contradictory" (Kant, 1924/1963, p. 148). The notion of suicide involves the deliberate elimination of the ultimate source of all of a person's duties toward herself, and, indirectly, the source of her duties to others (i.e., respect for the absolute value of personhood). According to Kant, it makes no logical sense to exercise freedom by killing it.[42] Thus, according to Kant, in preventing a person from committing suicide, the clinician is not abridging her autonomy. Rather, he is working toward restoring her ability to engage in free, truly autonomous decision making by providing treatment for her psychiatric and emotional problems.

Proponents of active suicide prevention argue that coercive interventions following a suicide attempt are also done out of respect for the person's autonomy. Providing medical treatment to save a person's life following a suicide attempt is no different than providing medical care when someone finds a person unconscious and assumes that the person did not intend to harm herself (Fairbairn, 1995). Also, suicidal behavior indicates that an individual is mentally ill and not capable of fully autonomous intention and action. Society does not question the appropriateness of using coercive methods in other contexts to prevent harm from occurring to people who are not regarded as fully autonomous, such as children or mentally retarded adults.

A final argument in support of active suicide prevention is that when clinicians fail to intervene and a client does commit suicide, the clinician can be viewed as ethically and legally negligent for having failed to prevent the client's death. If a clinician is expected to protect her clients from harming themselves, she needs to take positive action when she feels a client is at risk (Shergill & Szmukler, 1998).

## THE ETHICAL ARGUMENT AGAINST SUICIDE PREVENTION

One extreme position in this debate is that "coercive psychiatric suicide prevention" (i.e., hospitalizing a client involuntarily) is never appropriate (Szasz, 1999, p. 19). Active suicide prevention strips the client of his status as an autonomous moral agent in the name of protecting his life. It involves the use of coercion to deprive the suicidal individual of his civil liberties, which is radically inconsistent with the values of a mental health professional (Szasz, 1986). A person has a right to direct his own life in the manner he chooses, including making the autonomous decision to end it. The introduction of the concept of mental illness to explain suicidal behavior makes the suicidal individual less than a person. In reality, there are many motivations to commit suicide, just as there are many motivations to join the army in wartime or to smoke cigarettes, both of which can be viewed as suicidal acts. Suicide prevention also involves the imposition of the clinician's values on the suicidal individual, specifically, the arbitrary values that suicidal acts are always "wrong" or "crazy." A clinician cannot legitimately claim to respect a client's autonomy if she is only willing to do so when his free choices are consistent with her values. Clinicians are supposed to respect autonomy unconditionally. Psychiatrists supportive of the Oregon Death with Dignity Act placed greater emphasis on a patient's right to self-determination, whereas opponents weighted the duty to protect and preserve life more strongly (Ganzini et al., 1996).

Historically, prior to 1800, taking one's own life was regarded as a sin or crime, for which the actor bore responsibility (Szasz, 1986). Since that time, the supposed role of mental illness in suicide has become increasingly prominent, resulting in the view that suicide is an insane act and that a suicidal individual must be protected from his own irrational impulses by a mental health professional. As a result of this line of reasoning, an individual can be deprived of his civil rights and hospitalized involuntarily if he speaks of committing suicide in a manner that leads a clinician to believe that he poses a danger to himself (Szasz, 1986).

While most people experience suicidal thoughts and even discuss the possibility of committing suicide at one or more points in their lives, suicide is actually another example of a low base rate behavior (discussed in Chapter 9), which means that the vast majority of individuals judged to be at risk for suicide will not actually attempt it (Murphy, 1988; Shergill & Szmukler, 1998). Those opposed to coercive suicide prevention argue that clinicians' inability to accurately predict the future further diminishes the legitimacy of depriving an individual of his civil liberties based on the clinician's belief that he is a suicide risk. The seriousness of suicidal threats is very difficult to determine.

Although proponents of suicide prevention frequently cite the principle of non-maleficence in support of their position, critics argue that coercive psychiatric suicide prevention actually does enormous harm to a client. The result of suicide prevention procedures "is the utter infantilization and dehumanization of the suicidal person" (Szasz, 1999, p. 55). The suicidal client is not regarded as responsible for his behavior, but as a "crazy" person incapable of controlling himself or making autonomous choices. Clinicians "define suicide as an illness and thus deny that it is an act; or they acknowledge that it is an act but deny that it is 'rational' or 'truly voluntary,' annulling the moral significance of their acknowledgment" (Szasz, 1999, p. 128). Szasz's point is that coercive psychiatric suicide prevention subverts the sense of autonomy and personal responsibility that clinicians supposedly seek to foster in clients. The suicidal individual's responsibility for controlling his suicidal impulses is not acknowledged. Instead, mental health professionals assume responsibility for stopping the person. Does this pattern of "therapeutic" interaction not encourage dependency, which clinicians are ethically bound to avoid creating in clients (ACA, 1997, A.1.b; APA, 1992, Principle D)? The manipulative display of suicidal behavior by some clients to "test" the extent of the therapist's concern suggests that clients perceive their therapist as responsible for preventing them from killing themselves.

Furthermore, a client who is hospitalized involuntarily after discussing his suicidal intentions with his therapist is extremely unlikely to ever again trust a therapist sufficiently to disclose intimate information and may well suffer an additional loss of self-esteem as a result of his humiliating experience (and permanent record) of a psychiatric hospitalization. Szasz (1999) points out that the considerable ethical costs of engaging in this infantalizing and dehumanizing practice are not even justified by the effectiveness of suicide prevention. Coercive psychiatric suicide prevention does not prevent suicide; the suicide rate has not decreased as a result of using these procedures (Szasz, 1999). In fact, some clients might act on a suicide threat out of fear of being put away in a mental hospital. Suicide has occurred throughout human history, ever since people discovered that they could cause their own deaths. Unfortunately, it will continue to occur, no matter what steps mental health professionals take to prevent it. The possibility of unwise, self-destructive choices is the price a society pays for truly valuing the freedom and autonomy of its people (Szasz, 1999).

## METHODS OF SUICIDE PREVENTION

The primary focus of methods of treating suicidal clients tends to be the management and control of suicidal behavior (Hendin, 1988). The least coercive intervention is to discuss the matter with a client, which usually involves attempts to persuade him that suicide is not the answer. Discussing a client's suicidal ideation affords him the opportunity to explore the issue. Opponents of coercive suicide prevention are comfortable with this method of intervention. "Those who desire to prevent a particular person from committing suicide must be content with their power, such as it might be, to persuade him to change his mind" (Szasz, 1999, p. 110). Intervening noncoercively will, in many cases, effectively eliminate a client's serious intent to kill himself (Fairbairn, 1995). Interestingly, proponents of more active, coercive methods of suicide prevention point out that, if a client is dissuaded from suicide that easily, it is unlikely that the suicidal intent ever represented a reflective, autonomous plan. Any action that is highly consistent with a person's goals and values would not likely be abandoned so easily.

Coercive suicide prevention involves actively preventing an attempt or undoing the effects of the attempt after the fact, without the client's consent. Again, the justification for preventing suicide by removing the means to commit suicide (e.g., confiscating a client's gun) or by hospitalizing him involuntarily is that he was not acting autonomously, or at least not fully autonomously, when he decided to commit suicide (Fairbairn, 1995).

## LEGAL ASPECTS OF SUICIDE PREVENTION

Legal authorities' acceptance of the expert judgments of psychiatrists and other mental health professionals as sufficient grounds for committing a person involuntarily to a psychiatric hospital has opened up the possibility of malpractice litigation against a clinician for failing to accurately recognize and predict suicidal potential when an individual under his care does commit suicide (Szasz, 1986). Fairbairn (1995) suggests that many cases of involuntary hospitalization of potentially suicidal clients might represent the self-interested paternalism of mental health professionals. The professional in such cases is more concerned about the legal, financial, and professional consequences for himself of even the remote possibility of having a client commit suicide than he is about the consequences for the person who is being hospitalized against her will. Many clinicians might believe that, in theory, respect for personal autonomy does entail that people have a right to kill themselves, but, regardless, they will never risk allowing their clients to exercise an autonomous choice of that type (Ganzini et al., 1996). In other words, people are free to decide to commit suicide, but not on the clinician's watch.

Fairbairn (1995) argues that a clinician has the right to prevent a client from exercising his autonomy and committing suicide because this autonomous act threatens to harm the clinician, legally as well as personally. However, this justification is not valid for a mental health professional because of her ethical duty to always give the best interests of her client priority over her own. The clinician at least has to weigh the client's reasons for contemplating suicide (e.g., his physical and emotional pain following the death of his spouse after 40 years of marriage) against the potential cost to herself and others affected by the action. However, a clinician really needs other types of justification that are rationally defensible (e.g., the welfare of the client) in order to ethically engage in coercive suicide prevention.

---

**Case Example 12.5**

*A clinical psychologist receives a call from a neighbor who is concerned about her 16-year-old daughter. Her daughter has seemed depressed recently and, at dinner the previous night, asked whether there was any history of suicide in their family. The mother asks the psychologist if he will talk with her daughter to determine whether she is seriously contemplating suicide. The psychologist explains that he is headed out of town on vacation with his family, but says he will stop by to talk with the daughter before leaving town.*

*The psychologist, who knows the daughter well, talks with her for 15 minutes. She is somewhat embarrassed about her mother's call to the psychologist. She says that she recently broke up with her boyfriend and has been wondering whether life is worth living. She becomes very tearful during this discussion. She tells the psychologist that if she did attempt suicide, she would do it by taking an overdose of pills. She denies that she is going to try to kill herself, though. The psychologist asks her to promise not to harm herself and to go and talk to a colleague of his. She gives him her promise and thanks him for his concern.*

*The psychologist tells her parents they should make an appointment with his colleague, keep an eye on their daughter for any change in her condition, and remove any pills from their medicine cabinet. They thank him and offer to pay him for his time. He refuses politely, saying "What are friends for?" Two days later, the daughter kills herself by taking pills she had hidden in her room a week earlier.*

*Her parents sue the psychologist for malpractice, claiming that he failed to accurately assess their daughter's suicidal potential.*

*Do the parents have a case? What ethical and legal considerations are involved?*

A final consideration that again highlights the ethical dilemma involved in coercive suicide prevention is that, when a clinician violates a client's confidentiality by informing medical or legal authorities about her suicidal potential, the client can bring a civil malpractice suit against the clinician, claiming that the breach of confidentiality was unjustified. A jury would determine whether the clinician acted appropriately.

## FORENSIC PRACTICE IN THE MENTAL HEALTH PROFESSIONS

The role of mental health professionals in the legal system has expanded steadily since the mid-1800s. However, until fairly recently, expert testimony on such matters as competency, insanity, and civil commitment was nearly exclusively the province of psychiatrists. It was only during the 1960s that clinical psychologists began to be recognized as forensic "experts." During the 1970s, specialized graduate training in forensic psychology was introduced (Bartol & Bartol, 1999). Since that time, forensic psychology has become an important, popular, and lucrative area of practice for mental health professionals (Hagen, 1997). Mental health professionals acting as forensic experts can provide testimony concerning a wide range of civil and criminal matters. However, they are ethically obligated to present only truthful testimony, including the limitations of their knowledge and conclusions (APA, 1992, 7.02[c]).

The different aspects of forensic psychology are best conceptualized today as unique specialty areas of professional practice. As such, practicing in an area of forensic psychology (e.g., conducting child custody evaluations) should be preceded by the development of appropriate expertise through specialized training and supervised experience, along the lines promulgated by APA for psychologists wishing to change their specialty area (Conger, 1976). In addition, the American Academy of Forensic Psychology and Division 41 of APA have published "Specialty Guidelines for Forensic Psychologists" to address professional and ethical issues affecting forensic specialists, including competence (Committee on Ethical Guidelines for Forensic Psychologists, 1991). Ideally, forensic experts will introduce unbiased scientific information into a legal proceeding. They have a "special responsibility for fairness and accuracy in their public statements" (Committee on Ethical Guidelines for Forensic Psychologists, 1991, VII.B). However, forensic psychology has become a very controversial area of mental health practice because of "experts" who will offer under oath whatever testimony a lawyer requests in exchange for a substantial fee (Pope et al., 2000).

This section will first discuss special ethical considerations in forensic assessment contexts. Then, the legal procedures governing competency determinations and insanity pleas will be presented, followed by a consideration of ethical issues pertaining to expert testimony on dangerousness, defendants' past mental state (i.e., at the time a crime was committed), and parental fitness in custody disputes. Finally, ethical issues concerning the presentation of expert testimony in general will be addressed.

### Special Considerations in Forensic Assessment

In conducting assessments for legal proceedings (e.g., insanity evaluations, child custody evaluations), it is especially important for a clinician to clarify her role with all parties involved in the assessment (APA, 1992, 7.03). The client being assessed needs to understand that the clinician is not his therapist, but has been retained to conduct an evaluation in connection with his current legal involvement. Also, the clinician should explain to the client who hired her to conduct the assessment (e.g., the court, defense attorney, prosecutor's office) both the purpose of the assessment (e.g., a determination of his competence to stand trial) and what the results of the procedure will be used for (e.g., report provided to the court). It is extremely important that the client understand the limits placed on the confidentiality of information he reveals during the assessment. In general, all information obtained from the client can be included in the assessment report. A forensic clinician should never assume that the judge or lawyers in a case have fully informed the client, or have done so accurately; the clinician should always obtain the client's informed consent herself prior to conducting the assessment. In competency determinations, where there is likely reason to question the client's ability to provide autonomous informed consent, the client's legal counsel should also be a party to the informed consent discussion. Forensic assessment generally involves a significant amount of coercion in forcing the client to agree to be evaluated. Nonetheless, as in every other assessment context, the clinician must inform the client that he has the right to refuse to participate. However, he should understand clearly, in consultation with his attorney, the consequences of such a refusal (e.g., potentially stricter sentence).

Countertransferential issues that can affect the objectivity of clinicians' judgment might be more likely to arise in forensic contexts. Specifically, certain types of criminal charges (e.g., sexual assaults against children) or defendants (e.g., attractive females) might evoke positive or negative countertransferential biases in the clinician. The clinician needs to be aware that her subjective value biases are potentially as important in this context as in conducting therapy.

---

### Case Example 12.6

At the request of the district attorney's office, a forensic psychologist is conducting an evaluation of a defendant charged with killing two children. She explains to the client who she is and what her role in the case is. She informs him that anything he tells her during the evaluation will not remain confidential and can be used in her evaluation report and/or testimony at the trial. He indicates his understanding and signs an informed consent document.

She begins the evaluation with intelligence testing. During the testing, the client says, "You're a head doctor, right?" She replies that she is a psychologist. He then says, "Why did I kill them?" She reminds him that she is not his therapist and of the limits on the confidentiality of their discussion. She then completes the intelligence testing and finds that he is mildly mentally retarded.

She is no longer confident that he understood the informed consent procedure and is unsure how she should treat his admission of guilt.

Should the psychologist inform the district attorney of the defendant's admission to her? What ethical considerations are involved?

## EVALUATING A DEFENDANT'S COMPETENCY TO STAND TRIAL

Competency determinations permit a criminal trial to be postponed if a defendant is considered unable to consult rationally with his lawyer and participate in his own defense or lacks a rational understanding of the charges brought against him as a result of mental or physical illness or disability (Roesch, Zapf, Golding, & Skeem, 1999). People are presumed to be competent; therefore, incompetency must be proven by a preponderance of the evidence.

The issue of a defendant's competency can be raised before or during the criminal trial (Roesch et al., 1999). Competency determinations are conducted separately from the criminal proceedings. If the question of a defendant's competency is raised, the judge orders an evaluation of the defendant by a psychiatrist or psychologist with expertise in forensic assessment. The evaluation can be conducted in a psychiatric hospital, outpatient mental health center, or jail, as ordered by the judge (Roesch et al., 1999). Then, the evaluation report is submitted to the judge. The mental health professional conducting the forensic evaluation does not decide the issue of the defendant's competency to stand trial. Competency is a legal issue, decided by a judge or jury. A forensic evaluator simply presents data to the court and offers her opinion as to whether the defendant's current mental status meets the criteria for competency. However, a formal competency hearing is generally not held; most judges simply accept the evaluators' opinion (Roesch et al., 1999). If the evaluator concludes that the defendant is incompetent at present, she is generally required to address the issue of whether the defendant is likely to attain competence to stand trial in the foreseeable future. Also, if the defendant is believed to be incompetent, the professional who conducted the evaluation must submit a separate report regarding the mental illness or disability responsible for the defendant's incompetency. The report should contain recommendations regarding appropriate treatment and the advisability of commitment.

In most jurisdictions, there are three possible outcomes in a competency determination. First, the defendant can be found competent to stand trial, and the trial will proceed. Second, the defendant can be judged incompetent, but with the future prospect that he may become competent. In this case, the defendant will generally be committed to a psychiatric facility for a specified period to attain competency. The length of commitment varies by state statute (Roesch et al., 1999). Third, the defendant can be judged incompetent and unlikely to become competent in the future, resulting in dismissal of the charges against him. In the final scenario, civil commitment proceedings are undertaken if the defendant is believed to be mentally ill or mentally retarded and in need of hospitalization. If hospitalization is not warranted, the defendant will be discharged.

## INSANITY AS A LEGAL DEFENSE

In most states, a defendant pleads "Not Guilty by Reason of Insanity" (NGRI) to claim that she was insane at the time she committed the crime with which she is charged. An insanity plea entails that the defendant admit she committed the crime. In 36 states (and the District of Columbia), the defense must then establish, by a preponderance of the evidence, that the defendant was insane at the time she committed the act. In 14 states, the prosecution must prove beyond a reasonable doubt that the defendant was sane, a much more difficult task (Steadman et al., 1993).

The issue of insanity must be raised, before the trial begins, as the defendant's plea in response to the charge. After an insanity plea is entered, the defendant is required to undergo an evaluation by one or more forensic clinicians (psychiatrists or clinical psychologists). Both sides in the case (i.e., defense and prosecution) have the right to appoint experts to examine the defendant and to call these clinicians as expert witnesses in the trial (Wrightsman et al., 1998). The clinicians conducting the evaluation will report their findings on whether the defendant was mentally ill at the time the act was committed. If the court finds the defendant NGRI, the defendant is committed to a psychiatric facility for evaluation of her need for treatment based on her current level of dangerousness due to her mental illness. Jurors are not generally informed of the commitment process that follows an NGRI verdict (Golding, Skeem, Roesch, & Zapf, 1999).

In some states, those acquitted by reason of insanity spend less time in psychiatric hospitals on the average than people convicted of the same crimes spend in prison; in other states, they are confined for a longer period than people convicted of the same crimes (Wrightsman et al., 1998). The NGRI defense is used in less than 1% of felony indictments and results in acquittal in approximately 28% of those cases (Cirincione, Steadman, & McGreevy, 1995). Also, this defense is used in less than 2% of capital (i.e., murder) cases in the United States (Steadman et al., 1993). Contrary to popular belief, faking insanity has not generally been a successful method of avoiding punishment for clever defendants with slick lawyers (Lymburner & Roesch, 1999). However, defense claims of diminished capacity (resulting in diminished responsibility) as a consequence of mental retardation, temporary insanity, or intoxication at the time of the criminal act have increased in frequency over the years (Hagan, 1997).

There are five rules and standards that have been used by courts to establish whether a defendant is insane. The first is the M'Naughten Rule, which dates back to 1843. Daniel M'Naughten had attempted to assassinate the Prime Minister of England, but had instead killed the Prime Minister's secretary. His legal defense was that he was delusional and did not know right from wrong (Wrightsman et al., 1998). The M'Naughten criterion states that a defect of reason, resulting from a mental disease, prevented the defendant from knowing the nature and quality of the act he performed, or, if he knew he was performing the act, from understanding that the act was wrong (Steadman et al., 1993). Basically, psychotic disorders are the only potentially excusing conditions under the M'Naughten Rule. This rule was the criterion used by courts in most states until the 1960s (Steadman et al., 1993).

The Irresistible Impulse Rule was established in 1887. This precedent states that even if a defendant knew that what he was doing was wrong, he could not stop himself from performing the act because he was compelled beyond his will to commit the act. In other words, he had lost the power to choose between right and wrong (Wrightsman et al., 1998).

In 1954, the insanity defense was broadened further by a decision that established the Durham Rule (*Durham v. United States,* 1954). The rule, which is presently used only in New Hampshire, states that a defendant is not criminally responsible if the unlawful act was the product of mental disease or defect. Under this rule, insanity can also be interpreted as involving a dissociative disorder or personality disorder (Wrightsman et al., 1998).

The American Law Institute (ALI) standard, developed in 1962, states that the defendant is not responsible for her criminal act if, at the time of the act, owing to mental disease or defect, she lacked the capacity to appreciate the criminal character of the act or to conform her behavior to the law. The ALI standard combines aspects of the M'Naughten and Irresistible Impulse rules.

The Insanity Defense Reform Act (IDRA) was passed by the United States Congress in 1984 (Pub. L. No. 98-473) as the standard for insanity pleas in all federal courts. It is quite close to the standard set in the M'Naughten Rule. The defense must prove by clear and convincing evidence that the defendant was suffering from a severe mental disorder that made him unable to appreciate the nature and quality of the act he was performing or that the act was wrong. Congress enacted the law in response to complaints that insanity pleas were too frequently successful. Public discontent with the insanity defense had become particularly vocal when John Hinkley was found NGRI after he attempted to assassinate President Reagan (Steadman et al., 1993).

At present, the vast majority of state courts use versions of the M'Naughten Rule or the ALI standard (Golding et al., 1999). Three states (Idaho, Montana, and Utah) have no provision for an insanity defense.

Another reform in the insanity defense was the "Guilty, But Mentally Ill" (GBMI) verdict that was first enacted in Michigan in 1975 (Steadman et al., 1993). This verdict does not eliminate the insanity defense, but offers an additional alternative in arriving at a verdict for mentally ill defendants. When the GBMI verdict is applied, the defendant receives the same sentence as others convicted of the crime, with the addition of requirements for mental health treatment during incarceration.

The key ethical issue involved in the insanity defense is the ability of mental health professionals to determine a person's past mental state. Although this judgment can be extremely difficult to make, particularly in cases of temporary insanity, many forensic clinicians are very willing to offer opinions on cases that require this sort of "retrospective diagnostic clairvoyance" (Hagan, 1997, p. 123). Expert testimony is frequently presented on both sides of the issue, which is not surprising, but makes it quite clear that a final, objective, scientific determination on the matter is not possible at present (Weiner, 1999). For example, a central issue in NGRI determinations is delusionality because the insanity defense relieves a mentally disordered individual of legal responsibility if she "acts upon a pathological, uncontrollable belief system that distorts her sense of reality, thereby impairing her capacity for rational choice" (Golding et al., 1999, p. 390). In contested cases, experts frequently disagree regarding the presence of delusions, as opposed to zealously held beliefs.

It is important to remember that forensic expert witnesses do not actually decide the issue of insanity, though verdicts generally are consistent with the clinical evaluations of forensic experts (Lymburner & Roesch, 1999). These witnesses simply present assessment information that the court uses to decide the legal issue of insanity.

---

**Case Example 12.7**

*An extremely intoxicated woman drives her car up onto the sidewalk and kills a pedestrian. At her trial for manslaughter, she pleads NGRI. She claims that as a result of a mental illness, Alcohol Dependence, she was temporarily insane and unable to control her behavior when the incident occurred. She says that the accident happened during an alcohol-induced blackout and that she has no memory of anything that happened that night.*
*Does she have a case?*

---

## PREDICTION OF DANGEROUSNESS

Predicting violent or suicidal behavior requires a mental health professional to make a judgment about a person's future behavior based on current mental status and assessment data as well as information about his past behavior (Weiner, 1999). Predicting dangerousness is the reverse of the insanity defense evaluation process, which involves the clinician "predicting" the defendant's past mental status. Both are formidable undertakings. Nevertheless, researchers in the area of risk assessment argue that actuarial prediction of risk for violence has improved considerably in recent years due to progress in identifying and validating risk factors for violence (Litwack & Schlesinger, 1999).

Many forensic clinicians use actuarial data from personality tests and interview assessments in determining a person's potential for violence. As discussed in Chapter 9, actuarial prediction can be a powerful tool in making clinical predictions and judgments, particularly for low base rate behaviors like violence (Arango, Calcedo Barba, Gonzalez-Salvador, & Calcedo Ordonez, 1999; Rice & Harris, 1995), provided that the model is sound and the individual being assessed is a member of a class of people (e.g., persons experiencing delusional thinking) for whom actuarial data have been compiled (Garb, 1998; Janus & Meehl, 1997; Shergill & Szmukler, 1998). Sound actuarial models can provide an objective standard that can be applied fairly and consistently by the courts (Janus & Meehl, 1997; Pope et al., 2000). Indeed, actuarial methods have proven more effective than clinical judgments in predicting violence in psychiatric populations (Arango et al., 1999; Rice & Harris, 1995).

There is compelling evidence that an individual currently experiencing psychotic symptoms involving a sense of being threatened and having his life controlled by external forces is at increased risk to commit violent acts against himself or others, particularly when statements of violent intentions have been associated with the psychosis (Link & Steuve, 1994; Litwack & Schlesinger, 1999; Monahan, 1992). A history of repeated violence, particularly a recent history, and the likelihood that the individual will confront circumstances similar to ones that resulted in violent behavior in the past are also potent risk factors for violence (Arango et al., 1995; Litwack & Schlesinger, 1999; Megargee, 1993).

Critics have argued that most people in our society associate these predictors with an individual's potential for violence, so their use does not demonstrate any special capacity peculiar to mental health professionals (Hagen, 1997). As a result, the unique ability of clinicians to accurately predict violent behavior remains a matter of considerable controversy. An obvious limitation of such predictions is that violent behavior is not simply a function of personality variables; situational factors, such as the behavior of the victim, play an extremely important part in violent acts (Megargee, 1995). In general, clinicians tend to focus too much on the individual's psychiatric condition in predicting violence, while underemphasizing the importance of interpersonal contexts and social variables, such as employment (Mulvey & Lidz, 1998). In fact, the vast majority of people suffering from mental disorders are not violent; alcoholism and drug abuse are much more potent predictors of violent behavior (Monahan, 1992). In addition, it is impossible to develop and scientifically evaluate any set of predictors of violence without releasing people judged to be very dangerous to see whether the predictions are accurate (Litwack, 1997). An experiment of this type would place the welfare of citizen nonparticipants at considerable potential risk, making it ethically unacceptable. Such a scheme introduces the additional ethical problem of not providing appropriate treatment for psychotic individuals (Monahan, 1992).

---

**Case Example 12.8**

*A voluntary client suffering from Schizophrenia, Paranoid Type requests discharge from a psychiatric hospital. When evaluated by a clinical psychologist, the client's condition is stable, though he still shows evidence of delusional beliefs that others intend to harm him. The client has a history of violence against people, but those incidents occurred when he was not taking his medication. He says that he intends to stay on his medication now, so that he does not have to return to the hospital. The psychologist does not believe the client meets the legal standard for psychiatric commitment, so she recommends that he be discharged.*

*Five days later, having stopped taking his medication, he is questioned by a police officer who notices him running down a residential street, stopping to hide behind each tree. He gets into an altercation with the officer, manages to get the officer's gun, and kills him.*

*The police officer's family sues the hospital and the psychologist for malpractice for discharging an individual who represented a significant risk for violence. Do they have a case?*

---

Clinicians should not (and generally do not) make simplistic yes-or-no predictions regarding dangerousness. Rather, they assess the degree of risk an individual represents for violence against himself or others (Litwack & Schlesinger, 1999). In other words, the conclusion that an individual is a serious risk for violence is not necessarily false, even if the individual does not commit a violent act. The criticism that clinicians produce a high rate of "false positive" judgments in their predictions of dangerousness is based on a misunderstanding of the methods and goals associated with the assessment of risk for violence. Clinicians' ethical duty to protect the welfare of others leads quite naturally to the tendency to overpredict violent behavior. As in the case of suicidal risk, the potentially dire consequences of failing to recognize the dangerousness of someone who then goes on to harm another person causes clinicians to guard very carefully against underestimating an individual's potential for violent behavior (Grisso & Appelbaum, 1992).

The key question in evaluating clinicians' ability to predict violence effectively is whether clinicians can identify, with reasonable accuracy, the point at which an individual's risk for becoming violent constitutes an unacceptable threat to his own or others' welfare (Litwack & Schlesinger, 1999). Forensic experts make violence predictions in court that result in individuals being deprived of their civil liberties. Although the courts are generally very receptive to assessments of dangerousness by mental health professionals with scientifically based expertise in this area (Litwack & Schlesinger, 1999), the question remains: Is the expertise of forensic clinicians adequate to take on the huge responsibility of recommending that an individual be deprived of his civil liberties and committed involuntarily to a psychiatric facility (Hagen, 1997)?

The degree of difficulty in predicting future violence becomes apparent whenever a recently discharged psychiatric client does commit a violent act: The clinicians responsible for his release assert that they are not legally or morally responsible for the person's actions because they had no way of knowing that the person would get into that situation or respond in that manner. However, legal responsibility for the violent acts of clients is something that mental health professionals have brought on themselves by asserting to judges and juries that they are indeed capable of predicting violence.

None of this is to say that clinicians cannot develop the competence to predict violence better than the average person. To generate their predictions, clinicians can use the following types of information: a skilled clinical assessment of the individual; the most effective actuarial prediction models, including base rate information for violence in the population to which the individual belongs; knowledge of recidivism rates for violent behavior; the circumstances of the individual's previous violent behavior and their similarity to circumstances he is likely to face in the short-term future; his capacity for empathy; his mental status; his response to treatment; and the evidence supporting the validity of each of these variables (APA, 1992, 7.02[b]; Litwack & Schlesinger, 1999; Weiner, 1999). However, it is clearly inappropriate for a clinician to testify as a forensic "expert" in matters of violence without having developed a high degree of competence in this area (APA, 1992, 7.01). Mental health professionals are always ethically concerned with the welfare of others, they respect people's rights and dignity, and they recognize the limits of their professional competence. Clinicians should give careful consideration to these ethical duties before assuming the role of expert witness concerning a person's risk for violence. Also, clinicians should consider how willing they are to draw various conclusions, along with their degree of certainty regarding those conclusions, while under oath (APA, 1992, 7.04[b]).

## CHILD CUSTODY EVALUATIONS

Each year, more than one million families in the U.S. experience divorce (Bailey, 1998). Domestic courts generally become involved in determining child custody when the involved parties cannot informally resolve the amount and type of contact each parent (or other party seeking custody) will have with a child and the extent to which each will have decision-making authority for the child. In such cases, the court determines what arrangement is in the best interest of the child. The criteria taken into account in custody determinations are the following: the age and gender of the child; the child's preferences regarding a custodian; the quality of interaction of the child with each person seeking custody, as well as with any siblings or others (e.g., stepparents, stepsiblings) residing in the households; and the emotional and physical health of everyone relevant to the decision (Hess & Brinson, 1999). These cases are another setting in which mental health professionals conduct evaluations and offer expert testimony involving predictions about future behavior and events. APA has published guidelines for professionals involved in child custody evaluations (APA, 1994a). In spite of the guidance provided, the questions involved in child custody determinations are sometimes extremely difficult for experts to address effectively based on the data available to them (Weiner, 1999).

Child custody evaluators conduct assessments that are designed to determine the parenting capacities of one or both parents, based on interview, testing, and observational data. The evaluation also assesses the personality functioning, developmental needs, and preferences of each child involved. Others living in the custodial households, including stepparents, stepsiblings, half siblings, and grandparents, are generally included in the examination of the home environment (Weiner, 1999). Clearly, the expertise of mental health professionals who are trained to make these evaluations can make a very positive contribution to the custody determination process "by providing competent, impartial information" (APA, 1994a, p. 677).

As in other areas of forensic assessment, evaluators must be careful to obtain the informed consent of the individuals being evaluated, including the parent or guardian of any children being evaluated. The purpose of the evaluation and how the results will be used must be explained thoroughly. Parents should be informed at the outset of the significant limitations placed on their confidentiality in the evaluation; everything they discuss with the evaluator can be included in his report (APA, 1992, 7.03).

Child custody decisions involve extremely weighty issues and difficult predictions. It is interesting that the guidelines mention that complaints have arisen about "the misuse of psychologists' influence" in such cases (APA, 1994a, p. 677). Like assessments of dangerousness, differentiations of parenting capabilities are extremely difficult to make unless the parent is exceptionally and obviously unfit. For example, a clinician might pick up on particular personality attributes in an assessment, such as "unresolved anger," but it would be extraordinarily speculative to testify as to how those attributes will affect the client's ability to function as a father. It would be far better to avoid presenting an opinion to the court regarding the relative merits of parents in the absence of considerable behavioral evidence. Clinicians should never be hesitant to admit when they simply do not have any valid data that will enable them to make a definite prediction (APA, 1992, 7.04). After all, the best long-term adjustment of children of divorce is related to their frequent contact with both parents, provided the parents do not experience ongoing personal conflict (Hess & Brinson, 1999).

This area of professional practice requires competence concerning issues well beyond the range of normal clinical assessment (APA, 1994a). Always remember that an important component of the ethical principle of competence is to recognize and acknowledge the limits of one's professional abilities. Even a clinician experienced in personality assessment does not qualify as competent in forensic assessment. A professional competent to conduct custody evaluations using the MMPI-2, for example, should not only be familiar with the literature regarding the interpretation of MMPI-2 profiles, but of the differences they should expect between the profiles of individuals from the normative sample and those undergoing custody evaluations, two entirely different populations (Pope et al., 2000). Professionals are obligated to inform attorneys who contact them in connection with a case of the limits of their competence and make appropriate referrals to more qualified or experienced colleagues as needed (Pope et al., 2000). In addition, the ethical principle of professional and scientific responsibility requires that an expert never present empirical evidence to support a conclusion (e.g., that children raised by their mothers have better long-term adjustment), unless the conclusion has been validated with the population represented by the family in question and no other variables are known to affect this relation significantly, such as the relative parenting competence of the mother and father (Hess, 1999b). Bailey (1998) argues that unvalidated, biased viewpoints expressed by mental health professionals concerning paternal custody contributed to custody being awarded to fathers in only 10% of cases in 1990.

As in other legal applications of mental health expertise, many clinicians are drawn to perform child custody evaluations because of the lucrative reimbursement available for this service. Most evaluators are hired by one "side" in a case, and when clients and lawyers pay for an expensive evaluation, they expect the results to support their side. The failure to make a case for that parent (and, if possible, against the other parent) can have direct implications for the clinician's future business in conducting custody evaluations. Nevertheless, professional guidelines clearly require that "the psychologist should be impartial regardless of whether he or she is retained by the court or by a party to the proceedings" (APA, 1994a, p. 678). Psychologists experienced in custody evaluations prefer to be appointed by the court or to be retained jointly by both attorneys in the case (Hess & Brinson, 1999).

The professional guidelines state that the parents' values that are relevant to parenting are an important aspect of the evaluation, which introduces considerable potential for the value biases of evaluators to influence the process (APA, 1994a). An extremely difficult, yet important duty for evaluators is to avoid favoring parents whose approach to child rearing resembles their own (ACA, 1997, A.5.b; APA, 1992, 1.09). This potential for bias increases when there is little in the way of objective determinants to guide a clinician's judgment. The personal values of an evaluator may also affect the objectivity of an evaluation. For example, if an evaluator believes strongly in supporting the rights and autonomy of women within a male-dominated legal system, her value orientation could bias her perceptions and interpretations of the relative desirability of granting custody to the mother, as opposed to the father (Keller, 1999).

The issue of physical, emotional, and sexual abuse of children is often raised in child custody cases, with or without justification (Hagan, 1997). Clinicians must be extraordinarily careful not to go beyond well-validated sources of behavioral data or unambiguous self-report information in offering professional judgments regarding these issues. For example, the interpretation of children's play with toys as data relevant to the issue of child abuse requires extensive validation in controlled behavioral studies, rather than being dependent on clinical lore. Ethical mental health professionals should not make statements about "classic signs" of abuse, or of anything else, in the absence of objective, empirical evidence to support them (Hagen, 1997). The guidelines specifically mention that even evaluators competent to perform child custody evaluations may not be competent "to address these complex issues" of abuse (APA, 1994a, p. 678). For example, professionals who have experienced abuse may well lack the objectivity to make effective assessments in such matters (Pope et al., 2000).

A final issue pertaining to mental health professionals' role in child custody evaluations is that these evaluations tend to be quite expensive for parents. As a result, the process of obtaining expert testimony based on these evaluations to support parental fitness is inherently discriminatory against one parent (e.g., nonworking mother) if she has inadequate financial resources to obtain a competent evaluator. To avoid the unethical practice of discriminating against people based on their socioeconomic status (ACA, 1997, A.2.a; APA, 1992, 1.10), professionals can discuss their concern that both parents receive competent evaluations with the attorney that contacts them about conducting an evaluation.

---

**Case Example 12.9**

*A counselor is treating a male client for problems in his marital relationship. He has been working with her to learn better methods of controlling his anger. His wife decides to divorce him and requests that he not have access to their son, alleging that he has physically and verbally abused the child. The counselor is subpoenaed to appear at the child custody hearing. Her client does not want her to testify. He denies the abuse allegations and is concerned that testimony about the anger management work, taken out of context, could be very damaging to his case. His lawyer attempts, unsuccessfully, to have the subpoena quashed.*
*What should the counselor do?*

---

## CHILD PROTECTION EVALUATIONS

In cases of alleged abuse or neglect of a child, forensic experts in the area of child protection are frequently called upon to conduct evaluations of parents and children on behalf of the court, child welfare authorities, or some other interested party (e.g., parents) to determine whether a child should be removed from the parents' home for his own protection. APA has published a set of specialty guidelines for clinicians conducting these forensic evaluations (APA Committee on Professional Practice and Standards, 1998). The guidelines emphasize that the best interest and well-being of the child are the most important considerations in these situations. Above all else, children must be protected from harm (i.e., abuse and neglect).

Like child custody evaluators, clinicians conducting child protection evaluations need to develop a very specialized competence. Child protection evaluators are asked to provide complex judgments about the future behavior of parents (i.e., whether parents are likely to abuse their child) and make difficult predictions regarding the future impact of events on children (e.g., whether a child will suffer emotional harm as a consequence of being separated from his parents). These tasks require an exceptionally high level of expertise and should only be undertaken by people possessing an extremely high degree of competence in these matters. Their areas of professional expertise should include the following: forensic practice, child and family development and psychopathology, the different types of child abuse, and the effect on a child of being separated from his biological family (APA Committee on Professional Practice and Standards, 1998). Any expert opinion presented by an evaluator in an evaluation report or as an expert witness should be based on scientific knowledge that is valid for the population represented by the parents (e.g., African Americans) and children (e.g., adolescents) involved in the case. If a sound knowledge base is not available to support an evaluator's judgment, he should refrain from offering an opinion.

Evaluators must also be aware of their biases for and against different types of people (e.g., based on gender, age, race, ethnicity, sexual orientation, socioeconomic status, etc.) in order to avoid discriminating against parents from diverse groups. If an evaluator recognizes that he cannot maintain his objectivity in a case, he should not conduct the evaluation (APA Committee on Professional Practice and Standards, 1998). Again, the welfare of the child should never be compromised for any other consideration.

## GENERAL ETHICAL CONCERNS ABOUT FUNCTIONING AS AN EXPERT WITNESS

Sales and Simon (1993) stated that "a dramatic improvement in the quality of expert testimony could occur if experts reflected on their ethical obligations prior to becoming expert witnesses" (p. 244). They make an excellent point. Providing expert testimony, particularly in complex clinical matters (e.g., the assessment of an individual's potential for violence), is an extremely difficult task and one that has enormous potential implications for the lives of the people involved. A professional should recognize the considerable ethical obligations he incurs when he agrees to present himself as an expert witness in a legal proceeding.

The highest level of competence is absolutely crucial for professionals presenting themselves as forensic experts. They must qualify as genuine experts concerning the specific issues (e.g., the prediction of dangerousness) involved in their testimony based on their training, experience, and knowledge of the relevant literature (Sales & Simon, 1993). Professionals should not undertake the role of an expert witness until they have developed competence in a forensic specialty area. Continuing education opportunities that will assist professionals in becoming competent in these areas are plentiful today. Developing competence as an expert witness is extremely difficult and time consuming, however.

To ethically claim competence to provide expert testimony in a case, the professional should be familiar with the scientific knowledge base for the testimony he will offer and possess an excellent knowledge of the laws and procedures relevant to his role as a forensic expert (APA, 1992, 7.06). He should also understand the legal theories relevant to the testimony he will offer, so that his testimony will be pertinent. In addition, before agreeing to participate in a specific case, the professional has an ethical duty to make certain that he will have adequate time to prepare his testimony.

When conducting a forensic evaluation, the professional needs to obtain the informed consent of the individual being evaluated. The person needs to understand the purpose of the evaluation and the use that will be made of the findings in court. The individual must also understand the limits placed on the confidentiality of the information provided in the evaluation. The forensic professional must make certain that all involved parties (e.g., defendant, lawyer, family) understand his role in the process as an evaluator and witness (APA, 1992, 7.03). Each of these ethical obligations is important to the welfare of clients and others affected by the professional's testimony. Acting ethically by restricting their forensic activities to areas in which they are genuinely expert and demonstrating regard for their obligations in each of their cases will also enable forensic experts to avoid ethical and legal difficulties (e.g., malpractice complaints) themselves.

Many lawyers will try to influence the interpretation of a forensic evaluator's findings or how they will be presented in court to support the lawyer's case. Forensic professionals must be very careful to insist upon reporting their findings honestly and candidly in their testimony (APA, 1992, 4.04[a]). The honesty and objectivity of the forensic expert is what distinguishes him from a "hired gun," whose job it is to support the case of the lawyer who retained him (Hess, 1999a). The professional has a social responsibility not to assist a lawyer in constructing a case with no scientific basis (APA, 1992, Principle F; Hess, 1999b). The biased, unethical testimony of professionals selling their services as hired guns has compromised the integrity of the mental health professions (Sales & Simon, 1993).

A forensic expert should be retained by the court or by an attorney in the case. If the professional is hired by a party in the case, the client could claim legal privilege in an attempt to prevent the professional from disclosing information in his testimony. In addition, lawyers have a clearer understanding of professional fees. Due to conflict of interest, forensic professionals cannot work on a contingent fee basis, as many lawyers do. In other words, a professional's fee cannot depend on his "side" winning the case (Pope et al., 2000).

As in all of the professional activities of clinicians, a primary obligation of a clinical professional consulting with defense attorneys or providing expert testimony for the defense is to protect the welfare of the defendant. In a recent case in New York state, a man with a long history of violence and hospitalizations for schizophrenia pleaded NGRI after murdering a woman by throwing her in front of a subway train (Barnes, 2000). His first trial ended in a hung jury. The defense team then decided to take him off his antipsychotic medication prior to his testimony at his second trial, so the jury could get a clearer picture of his mental state at the time of the crime (when he had also stopped taking his medication). The legal strategy did not work because the defendant struck a social worker and the judge ordered that he had to be offered his medication on a daily basis (Barnes, 2000). The defendant resumed taking his medication when it was offered and did not testify at the trial. A mental health professional involved in the defense of this individual would have an ethical obligation to object to the defense team's attempt to deliberately withhold treatment from the defendant without his consent.

Juries and judges place great importance on the testimony of forensic experts, so these experts must be extremely careful to offer only well-validated conclusions in their evidence. In forensic testimony, professionals should not draw conclusions from tests that the tests are not validated to support. For example, a forensic expert should not offer Rorschach data as evidence that a defendant is delusional (Weiner, 1999). Using computer-based test interpretations from a well-validated source can minimize the extent to which the subjective impressions of a forensic expert could affect her evaluation of an individual (Pope et al., 2000). However, the expert must be familiar with the evidence supporting the validity of the particular interpretation software she uses (Pope et al., 2000). A forensic professional must guard against the tendency to put too much faith in her judgments and be careful not to overstate her degree of certainty regarding an interpretation of assessment data in her testimony (Faust & Ziskin, 1988). She should always use a graded system of levels of confidence in presenting assessment interpretations, ranging from certain, based on the well-developed literature supporting an interpretation, to no expert opinion on an issue (Hess, 1999b). This point is important because when a person thinks of herself as an expert, as she would when she is consulted as one, she may tend to overstate her legitimate statistical confidence in a judgment (Garb, 1998). Similarly, a forensic expert should not present a theory regarding behavior as fact. She is also obligated to point out whether any alternative theories have been developed in the profession that would lead to conclusions different from those she presented (Sales & Simon, 1993).

---

### Case Example 12.10

*A forensic psychologist has an excellent reputation among defense attorneys for presenting credible evidence in favor of a defendant that a jury will find compelling. He has been criticized by fellow forensic experts and prosecutors as a "hired gun" who will say anything under oath to assist the defense in exchange for a large fee. The psychologist feels that there are at least two sides to every case. He enjoys the intellectual challenge of examining different perspectives on a case until he finds the one that meets the two conditions of presenting the defendant in a positive light and being as consistent as possible with the evidence in the case, including the evidence obtained in his evaluation of the client. He believes that criminal proceedings involve an adversarial system and that his job is to present as strong a scientific case as possible for his side.*

*Is the psychologist's perspective on forensic work correct? Is his behavior ethically appropriate?*

---

Finally, the personal values of a forensic professional should not enter into her role as an expert witness. For example, a child custody evaluator should not support separating siblings of different genders because she did not get along with her own brother (Hess, 1999b). The objectivity required of a forensic professional also entails that she avoid subjective judgments regarding the merit of a client's legal case and simply present information consistent with her scientific knowledge.

Dr. Elizabeth Loftus, an experimental psychologist, has been a strong advocate of the need for a standard of unbiased professionalism in the forensic treatment of memory issues, grounded in objective experimental evidence (e.g., Loftus & Ketcham, 1994). Dr. Loftus was perceived by many as having violated her own standard when she refused to testify about her research findings in the trial of an accused Nazi, John Demjanjuk (Loftus & Ketcham, 1991). Scientists cannot ethically pick and choose the cases and causes entitled to the benefit of their objective data, based on their personal biases. This is a lesson that forensic psychology needs to learn from the American Civil Liberties Union. Everyone has an equal right to protection under the law, not just the people with whom you sympathize. Dr. Loftus expressed discomfort about possibly advocating on behalf of a guilty individual if she had taken the witness stand (Loftus, 1987). Of course, a forensic psychologist's job is not to determine guilt or innocence, but merely to present relevant research findings. On the other hand, if an expert witness's testimony is potentially influenced by personal bias, or is open to serious misinterpretation by a jury, questions arise as to whether the findings are appropriate in the courtroom.

## WHAT IF ETHICS AND THE LAW CONFLICT?

As discussed in Chapter 1, ethics and law are not the same thing, but both involve important duties for mental health professionals. Professionals have an ethical obligation to obey the federal, state, and local laws and policies relevant to their profession (APA, 1992, Principle F), just as they have a duty to behave in accordance with their professional ethical code (ACA, 1997, Preamble; APA, 1992, 1.01). This book has emphasized that, to function ethically, professionals must become familiar with the laws pertaining to the practice of the mental health professions. However, in some instances, legal and ethical duties can conflict. This type of scenario presents mental health professionals with a different sort of ethical dilemma.

When a legal requirement conflicts with a professional ethical duty, a mental health professional must make the relevant parties aware of her commitment to the ethical code of her profession and endeavor to resolve the conflict (APA, 1992, 1.02). For example, suppose a counselor has been treating a couple in marital therapy for six months when their child dies of injuries that the authorities suspect may have resulted from abuse. The counselor receives a subpoena to appear, along with his therapy records for the couple, to testify about the content of the sessions in the prosecution of his clients for aggravated child abuse and manslaughter. The couple explained the circumstances of their child's death to the counselor, and he believes that they are not guilty of any abuse. Also, the couple repeatedly told the counselor that they did *not* wish any material to be discussed in court regarding their sessions. The counselor has a legal duty to comply with the subpoena, but he has an ethical duty to preserve the confidentiality of his clients. This type of ethical dilemma is not uncommon in mental health practice.

A subpoena is a court document that requires the named individual to appear at a hearing, or at another location, to provide a deposition or courtroom testimony

(Anderson, 1996). Whenever a mental health professional is served with a subpoena, as in the example, he must still consider his ethical duty to protect the privileged communications of his clients. In determining how to respond to the subpoena, he should first review the statutes concerning legal privilege for the state in which he practices. Suppose he discovers that, in his state, there is no therapist-client privilege in criminal proceedings. (Actually, this would be true of most states.) Second, he should find out whether his clients want the information disclosed. If they do, he should obtain their consent to release the information and comply with the subpoena. If, as in the present case, the clients do not want the information released, or if the therapist believes that releasing the information is not in the clients' best interest, he should obtain their permission to contact their attorney. He would inform the attorney that providing the court with the information sought in the subpoena will place him in violation of the ethical code of his profession (ACA, 1997, B.1.e; APA, 1992, 1.02). He would also inform the attorney that his clients do not want him to testify and ask the attorney to file a motion to block the subpoena (ACA, 1997, B.1.a; Anderson, 1996; Arthur & Swanson, 1993). He should also seek legal advice himself about any unresolved concerns and keep very careful records of his entire decision-making process (Anderson, 1996; Arthur & Swanson, 1993). If the subpoena is not withdrawn, the counselor would have to decide whether to testify or risk being charged with contempt. Although a mental health professional is expected to support his clients' right to privacy with legal authorities, professional ethical codes do not require that he subject himself to arrest by resisting a legally mandated disclosure order (ACA, 1997, B.1.c; APA, 1992, 5.05). However, even if legally required to testify, the counselor should still endeavor to minimize the intrusion into his clients' privacy by providing only information directly required by the court (ACA, 1997, B.1.f; APA, 1992, 5.03[a]).

One final note is that mental health professionals have an ethical obligation to work, individually and through their professional organizations, to change laws that are harmful to the people they serve.

## PRACTICE CASE INVOLVING THE MODEL OF ETHICAL DECISION MAKING

In 1991, APA canceled its plans to hold its 1997 annual convention in New Orleans, Louisiana, after the state of Louisiana passed what the leadership of APA considered an unreasonably restrictive abortion law. APA acknowledged publicly that this law was the reason for canceling the convention plans, arguing that the decision was consistent with the ethical principle of social responsibility (APA, 1992, Principle F).

Was this an ethically appropriate decision?

## SUMMARY

This chapter addressed the areas in which the mental health professions interface with the legal system. Each state has statutes concerning the rights of hospitalized psychiatric clients, hospital discharge procedures, and the involuntary commitment process. Clients can be hospitalized involuntarily on a temporary, emergency basis. Longer-term commitment requires a judge's order, as does commitment to mandated outpatient treatment. The process of suicide prevention often involves hospitalizing clients involuntarily to prevent them from carrying out their plans. Suicide prevention has proven very controversial because it is inconsistent with the respect for the autonomy of clients that mental health professionals avow. The opposing schools of thought on this issue were presented in detail.

Forensic psychology is the specialty area of mental health professionals who conduct evaluations and provide expert testimony in connection with civil or criminal legal proceedings. Professionals evaluate the competency of criminal defendants to stand trial when the issue is raised, and they evaluate defendants who enter a plea of NGRI. Forensic experts also provide testimony in their area of expertise (e.g., long-term effects of abuse, accuracy of eyewitness testimony) when retained to do so in a criminal or civil case. Forensic clinicians also conduct child protection and child custody evaluations. Expert witnesses should only offer an opinion in a court proceeding when they have valid data to support their statements. In addition, they should be sensitive to their duty to explain their role in the evaluation process to those involved (e.g., clients and attorneys).

Mental health professionals occasionally become involved in legal proceedings unintentionally when their client records are subpoenaed in connection with a criminal or civil case. If the client does not want the information presented, the professional should claim privilege on the client's behalf and attempt to have the subpoena withdrawn.

# 13 State Boards, Ethics Committees, and Ethics Complaints

State governments regulate the practice of professions when such regulation is considered to be in the public interest. This chapter focuses specifically on the operation of state boards of psychology and counseling as well as the ethics committees of national professional organizations. The methods that such entities use to investigate and resolve ethical complaints are discussed, along with the most common types of ethical complaints brought against mental health professionals. In addition, professionals will learn how to respond to an ethics inquiry. Because ethics complaints are quite different from malpractice suits, the distinction between these two potential consequences of unethical behavior is clarified.

Another troublesome issue for mental health professionals is how to handle situations in which they become aware of apparently unethical behavior on the part of professional colleagues. The appropriate steps to take in responding to the unethical behavior of other professionals is described. The final section of the chapter summarizes the major themes of this book in a discussion of how to avoid ethical difficulties.

## STATE BOARDS OF PSYCHOLOGY AND COUNSELING

As discussed in Chapter 1, state boards for psychology and counseling set requirements for licensure, evaluate the credentials and test the qualifications of candidates for licensure, and investigate and adjudicate ethical complaints against licensed professionals. As gatekeepers for professions, state boards screen applicants for certification and licensure for past or current records of felony convictions, ethics complaints, ethics investigations, judgments affecting their license status, and malpractice lawsuits to make certain that individuals of questionable moral character are not permitted to be licensed as professionals in their state. Once a professional is licensed in a jurisdiction, the state board for the profession is the governmental agency that will receive, investigate, and adjudicate any ethics complaints brought against the professional. As a consequence of being licensed, professionals place themselves under the authority of their state board.

### STATE BOARD PROCEDURES FOR INVESTIGATING ETHICS COMPLAINTS

When a client, student, supervisee, fellow professional, or other recipient of professional services files a complaint against a psychologist or counselor, the state board of the profession will initiate an investigation. A complaint may also be referred to the board by the ethics committee of a state or national professional organization.

Furthermore, if a professional is convicted of a felony or violation of a law involving moral turpitude, the board will pursue action against him. Anonymous complaints are not accepted.

Although the procedures used by state boards to investigate ethics complaints vary from state to state, complaints are generally prioritized based on the risk of harm to the public represented by the alleged violation (e.g., a client's allegation of therapist sexual abuse would be addressed before a dispute over fees). The board's first step is contacting the complainant to obtain sufficient information to evaluate whether the complaint falls within the jurisdiction of the board. If it does, the professional is then asked to provide a written response to the complaint. This preliminary investigation will result in either a recommendation to dismiss the complaint or, if probable cause exists that a board rule has been violated, referral to a disciplinary panel of the board.

The board's disciplinary panel will conduct any further investigation needed before recommending dismissal of the complaint or sanctions against a professional. The investigation might include meeting with the professional. There might also be an option of an informal hearing to resolve the investigation. Of course, professionals always have the right to contest a complaint more formally and request an adjudicative hearing.

---

### Case Example 13.1

*A university student tells the instructor of her Abnormal Psychology course that she was sexually abused by her therapist during the previous year. The instructor encourages her to file a formal complaint with the state board of psychology, but she says she is too uncomfortable about signing a complaint and confronting him publicly.*

*What, if anything, should the psychologist do?*

---

## STATE BOARD SANCTIONS FOR UNETHICAL CONDUCT

When an ethical complaint against a mental health professional is supported adequately by the facts obtained by the state board, the board can impose sanctions against the professional, including the following: temporary suspension of his professional license, license revocation, probation, reprimand (sometimes referred to as a "letter of instruction"), and/or monetary fine. Any sanction other than revocation of a license can, and usually will, involve rehabilitation in the form of additional continuing education requirements, completion of a professional ethics course, reexamination for licensure, supervision of practice for a period of time, limitations on services the professional can provide or on classes of clients he can work with, and/or restrictions on his ability to supervise others.

A professional facing serious ethics charges will sometimes choose to resign his license to avoid formal adjudication of a complaint. However, a record of the circumstances of his resignation, like that of sanctions imposed against him, will follow him if he ever attempts to apply for licensure elsewhere.

## PROFESSIONAL ORGANIZATIONS' ETHICS COMMITTEES

Professional organizations (e.g., APA, ACA) have standing ethics committees that formulate the ethical code of the profession and receive, investigate, and adjudicate complaints of unethical conduct against their members (ACA Ethics Committee, 1997b; APA Ethics Committee, 1996). The ethics committee can also require a member to "show cause" why he should not be expelled from membership if a judgment (e.g., license revocation, expulsion from membership, felony conviction) involving a serious ethical infraction has been made against him by a state licensing board, state professional association, or criminal court (APA Ethics Committee, 1996). Finally, the ethics committee also addresses the ethical acceptability of applicants for membership in the organization if the applicants have reported prior or current ethics complaints, investigations, and lawsuits on their membership application (Flescher, 1991).

### ETHICS COMMITTEE PROCEDURES FOR
### INVESTIGATING ETHICAL VIOLATIONS[43]

In addition to complaints arising from the adjudication of ethics violations by state boards or state professional organizations, an ethics committee also responds to complaints of professional misconduct filed with them by members of the association or by the general public (ACA Ethics Committee, 1997b; APA Ethics Committee, 1996). Complaints cannot be filed anonymously. When the complaint falls within the jurisdiction of the committee (i.e., involves a complaint against a member of the organization), the committee will first determine whether there is sufficient cause for action on the complaint (ACA Ethics Committee, 1997b; APA Ethics Committee, 1996). This determination may require requesting additional information from the complainant. The matter will be closed if the information provided does not constitute sufficient grounds for the committee to investigate (ACA Ethics Committee, 1997b; APA Ethics Committee, 1996).

If, on the other hand, the alleged behavior of the professional constitutes a violation of the ethical code, the professional will be notified of the complaint (ACA Ethics Committee, 1997b; APA Ethics Committee, 1996). The professional then has 30 days to respond to the complaint. The professional is free to consult legal counsel, but he must respond to the complaint himself. If, at the conclusion of this process, cause for action is believed to exist, a formal investigation will be initiated. A formal letter delineating the charges arising from the complaint will be sent to the professional (APA Ethics Committee, 1996). The ethics committee may request the professional to appear before them to provide pertinent information. At the conclusion of the investigation, the ethics committee will make a decision and inform the professional and the complainant of the outcome (ACA Ethics Committee, 1997b; APA Ethics Committee, 1996).

### MOST COMMON TYPES OF ETHICS COMPLAINTS

In 1998, the APA Ethics Committee received a total of 85 ethics complaints, representing a rate of one complaint for every 1,000 APA members, the lowest rate in recent years (APA Ethics Committee, 1999). Sexual misconduct with adults was the most frequent category of complaint, and was involved in 44% of the complaints filed. Insurance and fee problems were a factor in 15% of complaints, followed by nonsexual dual relationship (13%), child custody evaluation (11%), confidentiality (7%), and competency (5%) complaints (APA Ethics Committee, 1999).[44]

### SANCTIONS FOR UNETHICAL CONDUCT

The ethics committees of professional organizations may dismiss the charges for a violation if it is trivial or has already been corrected. The ethics committee may still send the professional an educative letter, though, concerning the violation. In 1998 APA dismissed only 8% of cases arising from ethics complaints (APA Ethics Committee, 1999). For violations not likely to cause harm to another person or seriously damage the profession, the ethics committee can decide to reprimand the professional (APA Ethics Committee, 1996). When a violation is likely to cause harm to another person, but not significant harm, the ethics committee might recommend that the professional be censured or placed on probation by the organization (ACA Ethics Committee, 1997b; APA Ethics Committee, 1996). In 1998, APA recommended reprimand or censure in 19% of cases (APA Ethics Committee, 1999). The ACA Ethics Committee (1997b) has the additional option of suspending a counselor from membership in the organization for a period of time, generally with remedial requirements that must be completed during the suspension. The most severe action that a professional organization can take against a member who has committed a serious ethical violation is to recommend to its board of directors that he be expelled from membership in the organization or allowed to resign under stipulated conditions (ACA Ethics Committee, 1997b; APA Ethics Committee, 1996).[45] In taking this action, the ethics committee can also inform the offender's state board of the complaint and of the committee's action (APA Ethics Committee, 1996). The state board may then decide to investigate the complaint and potentially take action against the professional's license. In 1998, 66% of ethics cases investigated by the APA Ethics Committee resulted in recommendations for loss of APA membership; 53% of the recommendations for loss of membership concerned sexual misconduct complaints (APA Ethics Committee, 1999).

The professional can accept the decision of the ethics committee or request a formal hearing on the charges before a three-member hearing committee, which must include at least two members of the organization (APA Ethics Committee, 1996). The hearing committee will call witnesses if needed, and then decide whether to accept the recommendation of the ethics committee, alter the sanctions, or dismiss the charges (APA Ethics Committee, 1996).

## DEALING APPROPRIATELY WITH A STATE BOARD OR ETHICS COMMITTEE INQUIRY

Mental health professionals have an obligation to cooperate fully with an ethics investigation undertaken by their state board or any duly authorized ethics committee

(ACA, 1997, H.3; APA, 1992, 8.06). Although every professional hopes she will never be contacted regarding an ethics inquiry, it is important to know how to handle such an inquiry in an appropriate, professional manner. First, before launching into a defense of her behavior, the professional should make certain that she does not exacerbate the situation by violating the confidentiality of a complainant or anyone else. If a professional receives a phone call from a member of an ethics committee, it would be inappropriate for her to even acknowledge that she knows or has treated a client until she receives a written waiver, signed by the complainant, permitting her to disclose information to the committee. The professional should inform the caller that she would be glad to cooperate in any way she can as soon as she has received the permission form required in order to discuss the matter with the committee.

Second, when the nature of the complaint and the formal documentation have been provided to the professional, she should definitely consult an attorney who is competent and experienced in handling such matters. A professional should not assume that, because she knows she is totally blameless in the situation, she does not need expert guidance in preparing her response to the complaint. The investigation and adjudication of ethics complaints are legal matters; attorneys have a great deal more expertise in handling them than most mental health professionals.

Finally, the professional should provide relevant documentation to her attorney and, as instructed, to the state board or ethics committee. She certainly should not attempt to create, alter, or destroy records to support her case. If documentation concerning the matter does not exist, the professional should simply report that fact.

---

**Case Example 13.2**

*A counselor receives a phone call from a person who says she is from his state board. The caller names one of the counselor's clients and says that the client has filed a complaint against him for sexual harassment. The caller goes on to say that she has obtained the permission of the client to discuss the matter with him and that she wants to hear his version of the events in question. He responds by pointing out that the client has received a diagnosis of Borderline Personality Disorder and that she is frequently very manipulative.*

*The caller then says, "So, you think I'm manipulative? Well, just wait until I play the recording of this conversation for the state board. You've violated my confidentiality, as well as displaying your total contempt for me. You're finished as a therapist, Charlie!"*

*What should the counselor do? Is he in trouble?*

---

## LEGAL COMPLAINTS AGAINST MENTAL HEALTH PROFESSIONALS

Most legal proceedings brought against the professional conduct of mental health professionals are civil actions (e.g., malpractice suits). However, some circumstances can result in criminal charges against a professional, such as Medicaid or insurance fraud. Also, in some states, sexual relations with a client can result in a felony sexual misconduct charge. These legal proceedings are conducted independently of any ethics committee or state board investigation of professional ethics violations. However, it is possible that, in at least some states, the records of an ethics investigation could be subpoenaed as part of a civil or criminal case.

As stated earlier, conviction of a felony or a crime involving moral turpitude can also be grounds for sanctions against a professional by a state board and/or ethics committee. Even if the crime (e.g., bank robbery) has no apparent relation to the individual's professional conduct, the dishonesty and disregard for the law involved in such an act will likely constitute sufficient grounds for revoking the individual's license and/or expelling him from membership in a professional organization.

## WHEN PROFESSIONALS IDENTIFY UNETHICAL CONDUCT

Mental health professionals have an obligation to uphold the ethical standards of their profession in their own behavior. They also have the right to expect their colleagues to behave as ethical professionals (ACA, 1997, H.2.a). If a professional is unsure about the ethical appropriateness of a situation or proposed course of action, involving either herself or a fellow professional, she should gather information from consultations with more experienced colleagues or the ethics committee of her state or national professional organization (ACA, 1997, H.2.b; APA, 1992, 8.02). Again, ethical violations are best avoided by proactive reflection and consultation.

### INFORMAL RESOLUTION

Professionals are collegial, which means that they regard each other as equals and as colleagues. In the spirit of collegiality, if a mental health professional believes that another professional may be violating an ethical principle or standard, his first step should be to informally point out the violation to the professional involved (ACA, 1995, H.2.d; APA, 1992, 8.04). Suppose a psychologist had observed his colleague drinking from a flask in the restroom between therapy sessions and became concerned that his colleague's drinking was interfering with his competence as a therapist. It would be the psychologist's ethical duty to bring the issue to the colleague's attention. Many ethical violations can be avoided or resolved by an informal discussion in which one professional approaches the other as a concerned colleague interested in protecting the colleague from placing himself in professional jeopardy and from potentially harming the people he serves (APA, 1992, Principle C). These situations should be addressed in a nonjudgmental, supportive manner.

At the same time, the psychologist should make it clear that the interests of his colleague's clients and those of the profession will not allow him to ignore a continuation of the potentially unethical behavior. The members of a profession have a duty to uphold the ethical standards of the profession and to serve as the first line of defense against ethical violations that can harm others and erode public confidence in the profession. If the psychologist was convinced that he had addressed the issue effectively, he need not take any further action, other than to monitor the situation.

On the other hand, suppose one of the psychologist's clients told him she had observed the other professional's unethical behavior. If the psychologist believed that his colleague would know that the client was the source of the information, the psychologist would have a duty to preserve his client's confidentiality and would not be able to discuss that specific incident with his colleague (ACA, 1997, H.2.d; APA, 1992, 8.04). Suspected ethical violations by a fellow professional do not constitute sufficient grounds to violate anyone's right to confidentiality. The psychologist could look for other evidence of a drinking problem that he could discuss with his colleague. He could also ask the client's permission to discuss her report with his colleague; however, in general, it is not desirable to ask clients to waive their right to confidentiality unless the ethical violation is of an extremely serious nature, involving the strong potential for direct harm to clients. The reason a therapist should be hesitant to make such a request of a client is that the client might feel pressured to agree to the waiver, even though she feels very uncomfortable about the other professional finding out what she said.

If a professional's efforts to resolve a colleague's apparent ethical violation informally are not successful, or if the unethical behavior is so severe that it does not lend itself to an informal resolution (e.g., a faculty member was involved in an inappropriate sexual relationship with a student that contributed to the student's suicide attempt), the professional should report the matter to his colleague's state licensing board and/or to the ethics committee of the colleague's state or national professional organization (ACA, 1997, H.2.e; APA, 1992, 8.05).

In all of these matters, protecting the confidentiality of people reporting possible violations is a major concern of professionals. Recipients of professional services (e.g., clients, students, supervisees) reporting ethical complaints should be encouraged to proceed with a formal complaint themselves. The procedure for filing a complaint should be explained to them, as well as the protections provided to prevent retaliation against them for making a legitimate complaint. Ultimately, though, a state board or an ethics committee must be able to identify and interview a complainant in order to investigate and, if necessary, adjudicate a complaint.

---

**Case Example 13.3**

*A counseling psychologist observes a colleague shoplifting at the local K-Mart. She wonders whether it would be appropriate to say something to him about it, to encourage him to get professional help for his problem before he is caught in the act and humiliated publicly. She consults a colleague who agrees with her that it would be appropriate to discuss the matter with him out of concern for his well-being and professional standing in the community. She arranges to have lunch with the psychologist and mentions the incident. He tells her he has never stolen anything and that she should mind her own business. He accuses her of harassing him out of professional jealousy.*

*Her attempt to achieve an informal resolution of the matter was unsuccessful, and she wonders if she should pursue the matter any further.*

*What should the psychologist do?*

## Dealing with More Serious Unethical Behavior

Serious ethical violations that involve the potential for harm to clients (e.g., a sexual relationship with a client) should not be resolved informally between colleagues. Rather, such violations should be reported to the appropriate ethics committee and/or state board to make certain that the victim of the abuse receives adequate assistance in resolving the emotional harm produced by the situation and that the professional receives the supervision and rehabilitation needed before he is permitted to practice again (ACA, 1997, H.2.e; APA, 1992, 8.05). Professionals' failure to report such serious violations is unethical. This type of behavior threatens the trust that the public bestows on mental health professionals because it suggests that professionals are simply covering up for one another (Quadrio, 1994). If a client, student, supervisee, research participant, or other recipient of a mental health professional's services informs another professional of a serious ethical violation, the person should be encouraged to contact the state board and/or ethics committee of the professional's national organization to file a complaint.

In academic settings, a problem that sometimes develops is that the person with firsthand knowledge of the ethical violation (e.g., a student who was berated and demeaned repeatedly by a faculty member because he had effectively disagreed with the professor during a class discussion early in the semester) might be unwilling to file a complaint because he will need to take additional classes from the professor. He might believe he can avoid the problem in the future by never disagreeing with the faculty member, but he might tell another faculty member about the situation in confidence just to ventilate to someone. In such a circumstance, the professional who learns of a colleague's unethical behavior could be guilty of violating the student's confidentiality if *she* files a complaint on the student's behalf. A professional in this situation must try to resolve the confidentiality issue with the student (e.g., by encouraging him to report the unethical instructor's actions to prevent future harm to other students), but if it cannot be resolved, the professional still must not file the complaint herself (ACA, 1997, H.2.e; APA, 1992, 8.05). The student's wish for the matter to remain confidential must be given priority.

---

**Case Example 13.4**

*A counseling psychologist working in an outpatient clinic hears rumors about a male therapist at the clinic, who is not a psychologist. The rumors concern his inappropriate sexual behavior with female clients. No complaints have been made by the clients.*

*What, if anything, should the psychologist do?*

---

## AVOIDING ETHICAL DIFFICULTIES BY FUNCTIONING AS AN ETHICAL PROFESSIONAL

Throughout this book, the ethical mental health professional has been shown to combine virtue with knowledge. An ethical professional wants to serve humankind in a positive manner through her teaching, research, and/or applied work. She respects those she serves as persons and does not seek opportunities to exploit them. She feels a professional responsibility to each individual affected by her work, to her profession, and to society as a whole to provide only the highest quality professional services possible. These virtuous motivations are fundamental to ethical professional practice.

However, behaving ethically as a mental health professional also requires knowledge. An ethical professional must understand the metaethical origins of her professional ethical duties if she is to be capable of rationally resolving situations involving apparent conflicts between ethical duties. She must strive to develop competence in ethical reasoning, so she will recognize when a situation involves ethical complexity and can devise a rational, ethically appropriate course of action that gives each relevant ethical consideration the respect it merits. Functioning as an ethical professional is difficult; it requires "a personal commitment to a lifelong effort to act ethically" (APA, 1992, Preamble). Nevertheless, ethical competence is certainly achievable. The purpose of this book was to provide mental health professionals with the tools they need to develop this competence and to demonstrate how these tools apply in various professional contexts.

To prevent proactively the occurrence of unethical behavior, an ethical professional scrupulously avoids engaging in any professional activity outside the range of her competence. Also, she has a sound working knowledge of the ethical code of her profession. She knows that in many situations an ethical course of action is prescribed by state board rules; federal, state, and local statutes relevant to her professional activities; and the organizational or institutional policies of her employer.

An ethical professional must always be sensitive to her duty to obtain the informed consent of clients, research participants, and students. She reflects carefully on the informed consent procedure she intends to use to make certain it will be understood by the people she will be working with and that she identifies and explains any potential risks arising from people's agreement to interact with her professionally. She also considers the possibility that some or all of the people from whom she requests consent may not be competent to provide consent. She takes appropriate steps to avoid exploiting such individuals.

An ethical professional understands the importance of keeping careful, confidential records of her professional activities. Thorough documentation of professional activities can be extremely helpful in resolving complex ethical situations. Good records are also a tremendous asset if any aspect of her professional activity is reviewed by an ethics panel. Conscientiously kept records provide reviewers and investigators with information regarding a professional's behavior, attitudes, and professionalism at the time a situation occurred. There is no substitute for accurate, timely documentation.

In recording personal information about people she works with, she is always sensitive to the fact that her records could be reviewed in a legal setting at some point (APA Committee on Professional Practice and Standards, 1993). She works to minimize any potential harm to the people she serves that could result from such a review. An ethical professional is always aware of the confidential nature of many of her professional activities. She deeply respects the individual's right to privacy and develops positive habits regarding the protection of the privacy of those she serves. When it is unclear whether a communication (e.g., with a student or research participant) qualifies as confidential, she errs on the side of caution by not disclosing the information to anyone. An ethical professional is not a gossip.

Whenever an ethical professional is uncertain about the correct ethical response to a particular situation or about the ethicality of a proposed course of action, she realizes that the best way to avoid ethical mistakes is to consult with more experienced colleagues, members of the ethics committee of her professional organization (ACA Ethics Committee, 1997a), competent legal authorities, or other resources appropriate to the context. Consultation with colleagues was discussed earlier as an important aspect of gathering information in preparing to address a complex ethical situation. Consultation takes time and is often overlooked because of the time pressure a professional is under to make a decision and *do something*. An ethical professional always remembers that when it comes to sound ethical decision making, haste makes mistakes. She prevents ethical problems from developing by avoiding impulsive action; she takes the time needed to reflect on situations that are outside the range of her everyday professional experience. She does not allow herself to be pressured into acting without careful forethought.

---

**Case Example 13.5**

*A clinical psychologist in private practice finishes his last session of the day. He and the client engage in a bit of small talk, and she says she will walk out to the parking lot with him. The statement catches him off guard, but he wants to leave and sees no harm in leaving with her, so he agrees and gathers his belongings. When they get out to the parking lot, they stand by his car and the client asks him about his plans for the weekend. He is a bit uncomfortable with this inquiry about his personal life, but he decides he would appear defensive if he evaded the question, so he says that he'll probably stay at home and catch up on some reading. She touches his arm and suggests that since she has no plans either, maybe they could get together for lunch on Saturday. At this point, he is totally flustered. He does not feel it would be appropriate to get into a discussion of professional boundaries in the parking lot, so he just says that he thinks he will be busy on Saturday and quickly jumps into his car. She says, "Well, I'll give you a call."*

*He wonders how things got so out of hand so quickly after a very productive session. He also wonders what his client is thinking about the whole conversation and how he should respond if she does call.*

*Should the psychologist have handled things any differently?*

---

Finally, self-awareness is a key aspect of professionalism. An ethical professional must understand the subtleties of professional relationships in order to be sensitive to the ethical dimension present in every aspect of her work. For example, she needs to be aware of her personal values, so she can identify situations in which they might affect her perception of and/or behavior toward those she serves professionally. Self-awareness is also the key to preventing personal problems from impairing her professional performance. An ethical professional recognizes that unresolved personal issues can gradually subvert her professional competence and grease the slide into the abyss of burnout or an unethical dual relationship.

An ethical professional needs to be sensitive to the many warning signs of impairment. For example, she might recognize that she is not concentrating as well on her work, that she is looking forward more than she reasonably should to seeing a particular client each week, or that she is missing supervision sessions with her employees with increasing frequency. Each of these scenarios, along with countless others described throughout this book, should be clear indicators to an ethical professional that she is not operating at her normal level of professionalism. Simply paying attention to these signs and not assuming that she is invulnerable to professional impairment will enable her to recognize when she is overextended in her personal and professional life and needs to reduce her burden somehow. Resolving her personal problems may involve seeking professional help (a very difficult admission for many clinicians, although they think everyone else would benefit from talking to a professional), or perhaps just cutting back on her caseload or taking a vacation. The point is that an ethical professional recognizes that taking care of herself and her own problems are among her *professional* duties; she cannot function competently as a professional if she fails to attend to the important issues in her personal life. An ethical professional is aware of both her strengths and limitations.

## PRACTICE CASE INVOLVING THE MODEL OF ETHICAL DECISION MAKING

A 22-year-old, African American female client consults a counselor for complaints of depression and low self-esteem. During the intake interview, she reveals that she had been in treatment with another counselor in a nearby town for the previous three years. However, when the counselor asks for her permission to contact her previous counselor, she refuses. After some further probing by the counselor, she reveals that she had been involved in a sexual relationship with her former counselor for most of the time she saw him professionally. The counselor had ended the sexual relationship recently, and she had then stopped seeing him for counseling. She suspected that he had become sexually involved with another of his clients because she had seen him at a restaurant with a young woman she had seen and talked to once in his waiting room.

The counselor expressed her dismay about how the client had been exploited by her previous counselor and encouraged her to file a formal complaint with the state board so that disciplinary action could be taken against him. The client refused. She said that her husband did not know about the affair, and she did not want him to find out. She also said that she was in love with the counselor and still hoped for a reconciliation. She said that even if they did not get back together, she would never do anything to hurt her former counselor because she had wanted the relationship as much as he did. She again expressed an interest in working with the new counselor on her feelings of depression and her low self-esteem. However, she made it quite clear that she wanted the situation with her former counselor to be kept confidential.

What should the counselor do?

## SUMMARY

Both state boards for counseling and psychology and national professional organizations (e.g., ACA, APA) are responsible for handling ethics complaints against professionals. If the state board or ethics committee of an organization determines that sufficient cause exists to pursue an investigation, professionals are obligated to cooperate fully. The procedure for handling a complaint was described in this chapter. State board sanctions for misconduct include suspension or revocation of the professional's license to practice, mandatory training, or monetary fine, whereas ethics committees can force a professional to resign from the professional organization.

If a mental health professional is aware of a colleague's unethical behavior, the professional is obligated to try to resolve the issue informally with the colleague. If this attempt fails or the misconduct is too serious for informal resolution, the professional should report the behavior to the applicable state board or professional organization. If a student, supervisee, therapy client, or other person served by a mental health professional indicates knowledge of professional misconduct, this person should be encouraged to file a complaint.

Ethical professionals are motivated to uphold the standards of their profession by functioning in a competent manner. They value those they serve and show respect for persons' autonomy and right to privacy. Furthermore, ethical professionals strive to attain the knowledge that will allow them to reason ethically. They are familiar with their profession's code of ethics as well as pertinent federal, state, and local laws and regulations. Professionals who are sensitive to their personal values and to the warning signs of impairment will be able to prevent many ethical problems from developing. Finally, ethical professionals do not make decisions without deliberating about them sufficiently. They think through the relevant considerations carefully, gathering information as needed, and use their ethical reasoning skills to resolve ethical dilemmas effectively.

# References

AAAPP declares its own "war on drugs." (1995, March). The Scientist Practitioner, 4(3), 2-5.

Acker, G. M. (1999). The impact of clients' mental illness on social workers' job satisfaction and burnout. Health and Social Work, 24, 112-119.

Adair, J. G., Dushenko, T. W., & Lindsay, R. C. L. (1985). Ethical regulations and their impact on research practice. American Psychologist, 40, 59-72.

Aiken, L. S., West, S. G., Sechrest, L., Reno, R. R., Roediger, H. L., III, Scarr, S, Kazdin, A. E., & Sherman, S. J. (1990). Graduate training in statistics, methodology, and measurement in psychology: A survey of PhD programs in North America. American Psychologist, 45, 721-734.

Allard, G., Butler, J., Faust, D., & Shea, M. T. (1995). Errors in hand scoring objective personality tests: The case of the Personality Diagnostic Questionnaire--Revised (PDQ-R). Professional Psychology: Research and Practice, 26, 304-308.

Allen, M., D'Alessio, D., Emmers, T. M., & Gebhardt, L. (1996). The role of educational briefings in mitigating effects of experimental exposure to violent sexually explicit material: A meta-analysis. Journal of Sex Research, 33, 135-141.

Ambrose, P. A., Jr. (1997). Challenges for mental health service providers: The perspective of managed care organizations. In J. N. Butcher (Ed.), Personality assessment in managed health care: Using the MMPI-2 in treatment planning (pp. 61-72). New York: Oxford University Press.

American Association for Marriage and Family Therapy. (1991). AAMFT code of ethics. Washington, DC: Author.

American Counseling Association. (1997). Code of ethics and standards of practice. Alexandria, VA: Author.

American Counseling Association. (1999). Ethical standards for internet on-line counseling. Alexandria, VA: Author.

American Counseling Association (in cooperation with the Association for Assessment in Counseling). (1989). Responsibilities of users of standardized tests. Alexandria, VA: Author.

American Counseling Association Ethics Committee. (1997a). Policies and procedures for responding to members' requests for interpretations of the ethical standards. Alexandria, VA: American Counseling Association.

American Counseling Association Ethics Committee. (1997b). Policies and procedures for processing complaints of ethical violations. Alexandria, VA: American Counseling Association.

American Educational Research Association, American Psychological Association, & National Council on Measurement in Education. (1999). Standards for educational and psychological testing. Washington, DC: American Educational Research Association.

American Law Institute. (1962). Model Penal Code § 4.01.74, Proposed Official Draft. Philadelphia, PA: Author.

American Psychiatric Association. (1993). The principles of medical ethics, with annotations especially applicable to psychiatry. Washington, DC: Author.

American Psychiatric Association. (1994). Diagnostic and statistical manual of mental disorders (DSM-IV) (4th ed.). Washington, DC: Author.

American Psychological Association. (1952). Discussion on ethics. American Psychologist, 7, 425-455.

American Psychological Association. (1953). Ethical standards of psychologists. Washington, DC: Author.

American Psychological Association. (1958). Standards of ethical behavior for psychologists. American Psychologist, 13, 268-271.

American Psychological Association. (1963). Ethical standards of psychologists. American Psychologist, 18, 56-60.

American Psychological Association. (1968). Ethical standards of psychologists. American Psychologist, 23, 357-361.

American Psychological Association. (1979). Ethical standards of psychologists. Washington, DC: Author.

American Psychological Association. (1981a). Ethical principles of psychologists. American Psychologist, 36, 633-638.

American Psychological Association. (1981b). Specialty guidelines for the delivery of services by clinical (counseling, industrial/organizational, and school) psychologists. American Psychologist, 36, 639-681.

American Psychological Association. (1987). General guidelines for providers of psychological services. American Psychologist, 42, 712-723.

American Psychological Association. (1990). Ethical principles of psychologists (Amended June 2, 1989). American Psychologist, 45, 390-395.

American Psychological Association. (1992). Ethical principles of psychologists and code of conduct. American Psychologist, 47, 1597-1611.

American Psychological Association. (1993a). Guidelines for providers of psychological services to ethnic, linguistic, and culturally diverse populations. American Psychologist, 48, 45-48.

American Psychological Association. (1993b). Guidelines for ethical conduct in the care and use of animals. Washington, DC: Author.

American Psychological Association. (1994a). Guidelines for child custody evaluations in divorce proceedings. American Psychologist, 49, 677-680.

American Psychological Association. (1994b). Publication manual of the American Psychological Association (4th ed.). Washington, DC: Author.

American Psychological Association, Committee for the Protection of Human Participants in Research. (1982). Ethical principles in the conduct of research with human participants. Washington, DC: Author.

American Psychological Association, Committee on Ethical Standards of Psychologists. (1958). Standards of ethical behavior for psychologists: Report of the committee on ethical standards of psychologists. American Psychologist, 13, 266-267.

American Psychological Association, Committee on Professional Practice and Standards. (1993). Record keeping guidelines. American Psychologist, 48, 984-986.

American Psychological Association, Committee on Professional Practice and Standards. (1998). Guidelines for psychological evaluations in child protection matters. Washington, DC: American Psychological Association.

American Psychological Association, Committee on Subdoctoral Education, Education and Training Board. (1955). The training of technical workers in psychology at the subdoctoral level. American Psychologist, 10, 541-545.

American Psychological Association Ethics Committee. (1994). Report of the ethics committee, 1993. American Psychologist, 49, 659-666.

American Psychological Association Ethics Committee. (1996). Rules and procedures. American Psychologist, 51, 529-548.

American Psychological Association Ethics Committee. (1999). Report of the ethics committee, 1998. American Psychologist, 54, 701-710.

Americans With Disabilities Act of 1990, 42 U.S.C.A. § 1201 et seq. (West 1993).

Anderson, B. S. (1996). The counselor and the law (4th. ed.). Alexandria, VA: American Counseling Association.

Animal Welfare Act of 1966, 7 U.S.C. § 2131 et seq. (West 1994).

Appelbaum, P. S., & Rosenbaum, A. (1989). Tarasoff and the researcher: Does the duty to protect apply in the research setting? American Psychologist, 44, 885-894.

Arango, C., Calcedo Barba, A., Gonzalez-Salvador, T., & Calcedo Ordonez, A. (1999). Violence in inpatients with schizophrenia: A prospective study. Schizophrenia Bulletin, 25, 493-503.

Areen, J. (1992). Legal constraints on social research with children. In B. Stanley & J. E. Sieber (Eds.), Social research on children and adolescents: Ethical issues (pp. 7-28). Newbury Park, CA: Sage.

Aristotle. (1947). Nicomachean ethics (W. D. Ross, Trans.). In R. McKeon (Ed.), Introduction to Aristotle (pp. 300-543). New York: Modern Library.

Arizmendi, T. G., Beutler, L. E., Shanfield, S. B., Crago, M., & Hagaman, R. (1985). Client-therapist value similarity and psychotherapy outcome: A microscopic analysis. Psychotherapy: Theory, Research, and Practice, 22, 16-21.

Arnhoff, F. N., & Jenkins, J. W. (1969). Subdoctoral education in psychology: A study of issues and attitudes. American Psychologist, 24, 430-443.

Aronow, H. A. (1993, May). Sex between HIV+ partners: What are the options? Being Alive, 3, 13.

Arthur, G. L., Jr., & Swanson, C. D. (1993). The ACA legal series: Vol 4. Confidentiality and privileged communication (T. P. Remley, Jr., Series Ed.). Alexandria, VA: American Counseling Association.

Association for Counselor Education. (1990). Standards for counseling supervisors. Journal of Counseling and Development, 69, 30-32.

Bailey, G. R., Jr. (1998). Ethical and professional considerations in child custody evaluations. Journal of Psychological Practice, 4, 1-19.

Barak, A. (1999). Psychological applications on the internet: A discipline on the threshold of a new millennium. Applied and Preventive Psychology, 8, 231-245.

Barnes, J. E. (2000, March 23). Insanity defense fails for man who threw woman onto track. The New York Times, pp. A1, A29.

Bartol, C. R., & Bartol, A. M. (1999). History of forensic psychology. In A. K. Hess & I B. Weiner (Eds.), The handbook of forensic psychology (2nd ed., pp. 3-23). New York: Wiley.

Battin, M. P. (1999). Can suicide be rational? Yes, sometimes. In J. L. Werth, Jr. (Ed.), Contemporary perspectives on rational suicide (pp. 13-21). Philadelphia: Brunner/Mazel.

Baumrind, D. (1990). Doing good well. In I. E. Sigel (Series Ed.), C. B. Fisher & W. W. Tryon (Vol. Eds.), Annual advances in applied developmental psychology: Vol. 4. Ethics in applied developmental psychology: Emerging issues in an emerging field (pp. 17-28). Norwood, NJ: Ablex Publishing.

Beauchamp, T. L., & Childress, J. F. (1979). Principles of biomedical ethics. Oxford: Oxford University Press.

Beck, A. T., Steer, R. A., & Brown, G. K. (1996). BDI-II manual. San Antonio: The Psychological Corporation.

Beecher, H. K. (1970). Research and the individual: Human studies. Boston: Little, Brown.

Belar, C. D. (1997). Psychological assessment in capitated care: Challenges and opportunities. In J. N. Butcher (Ed.), Personality assessment in managed health care: Using the MMPI-2 in treatment planning (pp. 73-80). New York: Oxford University Press.

Bell, D. (1999). Ethical issues in the prevention of suicide in prison. Australian and New Zealand Journal of Psychiatry, 33, 723-728.

The Belmont Report: Ethical Principles and Guidelines for the Protection of Human Subjects of Research, 44 Fed. Reg. 23192 (1979).

Bentham, J. (1948). An introduction to the principles of morals and legislation. In W. Harrison (Ed.), A fragment on government and An introduction to the principles of morals and legislation (pp. 113-435). Oxford: Basil Blackwell. (Original work published 1789)

Bergin, A. E. (1980). Psychotherapy and religious values. Journal of Consulting and Clinical Psychology, 48, 95-105.

Bergin, A. E. (1991). Values and religious issues in psychotherapy and mental health. American Psychologist, 46, 394-403.

Bergin, A. E., Payne, I. R., & Richards, P. S. (1996). Values in psychotherapy. In E. P. Shafranske (Ed.), Religion and the clinical practice of psychology (pp. 297-325). Washington, DC: American Psychological Association.

Bersoff, D. M., & Bersoff, D. N. (1999). Ethical perspectives in clinical research. In P. C. Kendall, J. N. Butcher, & G. N. Holmbeck (Eds.), Handbook of research methods in clinical psychology (2nd. ed, pp. 31-53). New York: Wiley.

Beutler, L. E., Pollack, S., & Jobe, A. (1978). "Acceptance," values, and therapeutic change. Journal of Consulting and Clinical Psychology, 46, 198-199.

Blanck, P. D., Bellack, A. S., Rosnow, R. L., Rotheram-Borus, M. J., & Schooler, N. R. (1992). Scientific rewards and conflicts of ethical choices in human subjects research. American Psychologist, 47, 959-965.

Blevins-Knabe, B. (1992). The ethics of dual relationships in higher education. Ethics and Behavior, 2, 151-163.

Bloom, J. W. (1998). The ethical practice of WebCounseling. British Journal of Guidance and Counselling, 26, 53-59.

Bodenheimer, T. (1997). The Oregon health plan: Lessons for the nation. New England Journal of Medicine, 337, 720-723.

Brandt, R. B. (1959). Ethical theory: The problems of normative and critical ethics. Englewood Cliffs, NJ: Prentice-Hall.

Bridwell, A. M., & Ford, G. G. (1996). Interpersonal variables affecting attributions of defensiveness. Current Psychology, 15, 137-146.

Briere, J. N., & Elliott, D. M. (1994). Immediate and long-term impacts of child sexual abuse. The Future of Children, 4, 54-69.

Brown, F. (1982). The ethics of psychodiagnostic assessment. In M. Rosenbaum (Ed.), Ethics and values in psychotherapy (pp. 96-106). New York: Free Press.

Brown, J., Cohen, P., Johnson, J. G., & Smailes, E. M. (1999). Childhood abuse and neglect: Specificity and effects on adolescent and young adult depression and suicidality. Journal of the American Academy of Child and Adolescent Psychiatry, 38, 1490-1496.

Bussell, D. A. (1994). Ethical issues in observational family research. Family Process, 33, 361-376.

Butcher, J. N. (1997a). Assessment and treatment in the era of managed care. In J. N. Butcher (Ed.), Personality assessment in managed health care: Using the MMPI-2 in treatment planning (pp. 3-12). New York: Oxford University Press.

Butcher, J. N. (1997b). Use of computer-based personality test reports in treatment planning. In J. N. Butcher (Ed.), Personality assessment in managed health care: Using the MMPI-2 in treatment planning (pp. 153-172). New York: Oxford University Press.

Butler, D. L. (1999). Why do students miss psychology experiments and what can be done about it? In G. Chastain & R. E. Landrum (Eds.), Protecting human subjects: Departmental subject pools and institutional review boards (pp. 109-125). Washington, DC: American Psychological Association.

Butler, J. (1950). Five sermons preached at the Rolls Chapel and a dissertation upon the nature of virtue. Indianapolis: Bobbs-Merrill. (Original work published 1726)

Camara, W. J., & Schneider, D. L. (1994). Integrity tests: Facts and unresolved issues. American Psychologist, 49, 112-119.

Carroll, J. S. (1991). Consent to mental health treatment: A theoretical analysis of coercion, freedom, and control. Behavioral Sciences and the Law, 9, 129-142.

Carson, R. C. (1990). Assessment: What role the assessor? Journal of Personality Assessment, 54, 435-445.

Carson, R. C., Butcher, J. N., & Mineka, S. (2000). Abnormal psychology and modern life (11th ed.). Boston: Allyn and Bacon.

Catalano, S. (1997). The challenges of clinical practice in small or rural communities: Case studies in managing dual relationships in and outside of therapy. Journal of Contemporary Psychotherapy, 27, 23-35.

Chafetz, M. D., & Buelow, G. (1994). A training model for psychologists with prescription privileges: Clinical pharmacopsychologists. Professional Psychology: Research and Practice, 25, 149-153.

Cirincione, C., Steadman, H. J., & McGreevy, M. A. (1995). Rates of insanity acquittals and the factors associated with successful insanity pleas. Bulletin of the American Academy of Psychiatry and the Law, 23, 399-409.

Cohen, E. D., & Cohen, G. S. (1999). The virtuous therapist: Ethical practice of counseling & psychotherapy. Belmont, CA: Wadsworth.

Committee on Ethical Guidelines for Forensic Psychologists. (1991). Specialty guidelines for forensic psychologists. Law and Human Behavior, 15, 655-665.

Conger, J. J. (1976). Proceedings of the American Psychological Association, Incorporated, for the year 1975: Minutes of the annual meeting of the Council of Representatives, August 29 and September 2, 1975, Chicago, Illinois, and January 23-25, 1976, Washington, DC. American Psychologist, 31, 406-434.

Cottone, R. R., Mannis, J., & Lewis, T. (1996). Uncovering secret extramarital affairs in marriage counseling. The Family Journal, 4, 109-115.

Cottone, R. R., & Tarvydas, V. M. (1998). Ethical and professional issues in counseling. Upper Saddle River, NJ: Prentice Hall.

Croxton, T. A., Churchill, S. R., & Fellin, P. (1988). Counseling minors without parental consent. Child Welfare, 67, 3-14.

Cutler, D. L., McFarland, B. H., & Winthrop, K. (1998). Mental health in the Oregon health plan: Fragmentation or integration? Administration and Policy in Mental Health, 25, 361-386.

DeAngelis, T. (1991, August). Board approves budget, nixes Big Easy for 1997. APA Monitor, pp. 1, 5.

DeAngelis, T. (1993, March). Practitioner advertising affected by FTC order. APA Monitor, p. 7.

Delano, S. J., & Zucker, J. L. (1994). Protecting mental health research subjects without prohibiting progress. Hospital and Community Psychology, 45, 601-603.

Dent, C. W., Galaif, J., Sussman, S., Stacy, A., Burton, D., & Flay, B. R. (1993). Demographic, psychosocial, and behavioral differences in samples of actively and passively consented adolescents. Addictive Behaviors, 18, 51-56.

Devine, P. E. (1990). On choosing death. In J. Donnelly (Ed.), Suicide: Right or wrong? (pp. 201-205). Buffalo, NY: Prometheus Books.

Dewey, J. (1930). Human nature and conduct. New York: Modern Library.

Dixon v. Weinberger, 405 F. Supp. 974 (D.C. 1975).

Downey, R. G., Sinnett, E. R., & Seeberger, W. (1998). The changing face of MMPI practice. Psychological Reports, 83, 1267-1272.

Downs, A. M., & De Vincenzi, I. (1996). Probability of heterosexual transmission of HIV: Relationship to the number of unprotected sexual contacts. Journal of Acquired Immune Deficiency Syndromes and Human Retrovirology, 11, 388-395.

Draine, J. (1997). Conceptualizing services research on outpatient commitment. Journal of Mental Health Administration, 24, 306-315.

Dubin, S. S. (1972). Obsolescence or lifelong education: A choice for the professional. American Psychologist, 27, 486-496.

Durham v. United States, 214 F.2d 862 (1954).

Ellickson, P. L., & Hawes, J. A. (1989). An assessment of active versus passive methods for obtaining parental consent. Evaluation Review, 13, 45-55.

English, A. (1995). Guidelines for adolescent health research: Legal perspectives. Journal of Adolescent Health, 17, 277-286.

Epley, N., & Huff, C. (1998). Suspicion, affective response, and educational benefit as a result of deception in psychology research. Personality and Social Psychology Bulletin, 24, 759-768.

Ethics Committee issues statement on services by telephone, teleconferencing, and internet. (1998, January). APA Monitor, p. 38.

Ethics Committee statement on military and confidentiality. (1993, September). APA Monitor, p. 51.

Exner, J. E., Jr. (1993). The Rorschach: A comprehensive system. Vol. 1. Basic Foundations (3rd ed.). New York: Wiley.

Fairbairn, G. J. (1995). Contemplating suicide: The language and ethics of self harm. London, UK: Routledge.

Family Educational Rights and Privacy Act, 20 U.S.C. § 1232g (1974).

Farrenkopf, T., & Bryan, J. (1999). Psychological consultation under Oregon's 1994 Death With Dignity Act: Ethics and procedures. Professional Psychology: Research and Practice, 30, 245-249.

Faust, D., & Ziskin, J. (1988, July 1). The expert witness in psychology and psychiatry. Science, 241, 31-35.

Fellows, L. K. (1998). Competency and consent in dementia. Journal of the American Geriatrics Society, 46, 922-926.

Fine, M. A., & Kurdek, L. A. (1993). Reflections on determining authorship credit and authorship order on faculty-student collaborations. American Psychologist, 48, 1141-1147.

Fiscal year 1998 enforcement statistics. (1999, Spring). Texas State Board of Examiners of Psychologists (TSBEP) Newsletter, 12, 2-3.

Fischer, L. & Sorenson, G. P. (1996). School law for counselors, psychologists, and social workers (3rd ed.). White Plains, NY: Longman.

Fisher, C. B., & Fyrberg, D. (1994). Participant partners: College students weigh the costs and benefits of deceptive research. American Psychologist, 49, 417-427.

Fisher, C. B., Hoagwood, K., & Jensen, P. S. (1996). Casebook on ethical issues in research with children and adolescents with mental disorders. In K. Hoagwood, P. S. Jensen, & C. B. Fisher (Eds.), Ethical issues in mental health research with children and adolescents (pp. 135-266). Mahwah, NJ: Lawrence Erlbaum.

Fisher, C. B., & Rosendahl, S. A. (1990). Psychological risks and remedies of research participation. In I. E. Sigel (Series Ed.), C. B. Fisher & W. W. Tryon (Vol. Eds.), Annual advances in applied developmental psychology: Vol. 4. Ethics in applied developmental psychology: Emerging issues in an emerging field (pp. 43-59). Norwood, NJ: Ablex Publishing.

Flescher, I. (1991). Ethical implications in screening for ethics violations. Ethics and Behavior, 1, 259-271.

Fletcher, J. (1966). Situation ethics: The new morality. Philadelphia: Westminster Press.

Ford, G. G. (1996). An existential model for promoting life change: Confronting the disease concept. Journal of Substance Abuse Treatment, 13, 151-158.

Frankl, V. E. (1963). Man's search for meaning. New York: Washington Square Press.

Freud, S. (1961). The ego and the id. In J. Strachey (Ed. and Trans.), The standard edition of the complete psychological works of Sigmund Freud (Vol. 19, pp. 3-66). London: Hogarth Press. (Original work published 1923)

Gabbard, G. O. (1994). Reconsidering the American Psychological Association's policy on sex with former patients: Is it justifiable? Professional Psychology: Research and Practice, 25, 329-335.

Galassi, J. P. (1991). Issues in clinical-analogue research versus issues in research compliance. Psychological Reports, 69, 82.

Ganzini, L., Fenn, D. S., Lee, M. A., Heintz, R. T., & Bloom, J. D. (1996). Attitudes of Oregon psychiatrists toward physician-assisted suicide. American Journal of Psychiatry, 153, 1469-1475.

Garb, H. N. (1998). Studying the clinician: Judgment research and psychological assessment. Washington, DC: American Psychological Association.

Garfield, S. L. (1994). Research on client variables in psychotherapy. In A. E. Bergin & S. L. Garfield (Eds.), Handbook of psychotherapy and behavior change (4th ed., pp. 190-228). New York: Wiley.

Geisinger, K. F. (1994). Cross-cultural normative assessment: Translation and adaptation issues influencing the normative interpretation of assessment instruments. Psychological Assessment, 6, 304-312.

Geisinger, K. F. (1998). Psychometric issues in test interpretation. In J. Sandoval, C. L. Frisby, K. F. Geisinger, J. D. Scheuneman, & J. R. Grenier (Eds.), Test interpretation and diversity: Achieving equity in assessment (pp. 17-30). Washington, DC: American Psychological Association.

Geisinger, K. F., & Carlson, J. F. (1998). Training psychologists to assess members of a diverse society. In J. Sandoval, C. L. Frisby, K. F. Geisinger, J. D. Scheuneman, & J. R. Grenier (Eds.), Test interpretation and diversity: Achieving equity in assessment (pp. 375-386). Washington, DC: American Psychological Association.

Gergen, K. J. (1990). Therapeutic professions and the diffusion of deficit. Journal of Mind and Behavior, 11, 353-367.

Glancy, G. D., Regehr, C., & Bryant, A. G. (1998). Confidentiality in crisis: Part II--Confidentiality of treatment records. Canadian Journal of Psychiatry, 43, 1006-1011.

Glass, T. A. (1998). Ethical issues in group therapy. In R. M. Anderson, Jr., T. L. Needels, & H. V. Hall (Eds.), Avoiding ethical misconduct in psychology specialty areas (pp. 95-126). Springfield, IL: Charles C. Thomas.

Gluck, J. P., & Kubacki, S. R. (1991). Animals in biomedical research: The undermining effect of the rhetoric of the besieged. Ethics and Behavior, 1, 157-173.

Golann, S. E. (1970). Ethical standards for psychology: Development and revision, 1938-1968. Annals of the New York Academy of Sciences, 169, 398-405.

Goldblatt, M. J. (1999). Rational suicide: A psychiatrist against. In J. L. Werth, Jr. (Ed.), Contemporary perspectives on rational suicide (pp. 114-120). Philadelphia: Brunner/Mazel.

Golding, S. L., Skeem, J. L., Roesch, R., & Zapf, P. A. (1999). The assessment of criminal responsibility: Current controversies. In A. K. Hess & I. B. Weiner (Eds.), The handbook of forensic psychology (2nd. ed, pp. 379-408). New York: Wiley.

Gottesman, I. I., & Prescott, C. A. (1989). Abuses of the MacAndrew MMPI Alcoholism Scale: A critical review. Clinical Psychology Review, 9, 223-242.

Grant, B. F. (1997). Prevalence and correlates of alcohol use and DSM-IV alcohol dependence in the United States: Results of the National Longitudinal Alcohol Epidemiologic Survey. Journal of Studies on Alcohol, 58, 464-473.

Greene, B. F., & Kilili, S. (1998). How good does a parent have to be? Issues and examples associated with empirical assessments of parenting adequacy in cases of child abuse and neglect. In J. R. Lutzker (Ed.), Handbook of child abuse research and treatment (pp. 53-72). New York: Plenum.

Grimm, D. W. (1994). Therapist spiritual and religious values in psychotherapy. Counseling and Values, 38, 154-164.

Grisso, T. (1992). Minors' assent to behavioral research without parental consent. In B. Stanley & J. E. Sieber (Eds.), Social research on children and adolescents: Ethical issues (pp. 109-127). Newbury Park, CA: Sage.

Grisso, T. (1996). Voluntary consent to research participation in the institutional context. In B. H. Stanley, J. E. Sieber, & G. B. Melton (Eds.), Research ethics: A psychological approach (pp. 203-224). Lincoln, NE: University of Nebraska Press.

Grisso, T., & Appelbaum, P. S. (1992). Is it unethical to offer predictions of future violence? Law and Human Behavior, 16, 621-633.

Gurman, E. B. (1994). Debriefing for all concerned: Ethical treatment of human subjects. Psychological Science, 5, 139.

Gustafson, K. E., & McNamara, J. R. (1987). Confidentiality with minor clients: Issues and guidelines for therapists. Professional Psychology: Research and Practice, 18, 503-508.

Gustafson, K. E., McNamara, J. R., & Jensen, J. A. (1994). Parents' informed consent decisions regarding psychotherapy for their children: Consideration of therapeutic risks and benefits. Professional Psychology: Research and Practice, 25, 16-22.

Haas, L. J., Malouf, J. L., & Mayerson, N. H. (1986). Ethical dilemmas in psychological practice: Results of a national survey. Professional Psychology: Research and Practice, 17, 316-321.

Hagen, M. A. (1997). Whores of the court: The fraud of psychiatric testimony and the rape of American justice. New York: HarperCollins.

Hammond, O. W. (1998). Ethical considerations in program evaluation. In R. M. Anderson, Jr., T. L. Needels, & H. V. Hall (Eds.), Avoiding ethical misconduct in psychology specialty areas (pp. 142-153). Springfield, IL: Charles C. Thomas.

Hargrove, D. S. (1991). Training Ph.D. psychologists for rural service: A report from Nebraska. Community Mental Health Journal, 27, 293-298.

Hart, S. N. (1991). From property to person status: Historical perspective on children's rights. American Psychologist, 46, 53-59.

Hays, J. R., & Costello, R. M. (1994). Texas law and the practice of psychology. Austin, TX: Texas Psychological Association.

Hendin, H. (1988). Psychotherapy and suicide. In S. Lesse (Ed.), What we know about suicidal behavior and how to treat it (pp. 265-281). Northvale, NJ: Jason Aronson.

Hess, A. K. (1999a). Serving as an expert witness. In A. K. Hess & I. B. Weiner (Eds.), The handbook of forensic psychology (2nd ed., pp. 521-555). New York: Wiley.

Hess, A. K. (1999b). Practicing principled forensic psychology: Legal, ethical, and moral considerations. In A. K. Hess & I. B. Weiner (Eds.), The handbook of forensic psychology (2nd. ed, pp. 673-699). New York: Wiley.

Hess, K. D., & Brinson, P. (1999). Mediating domestic law issues. In A. K. Hess & I. B. Weiner (Eds.), The handbook of forensic psychology (2nd ed., pp. 63-103). New York: Wiley.

Hiday, V. A. (1996). Outpatient commitment: Official coercion in the community. In D. L. Dennis & J. Monahan (Eds.), <u>Coercion and aggressive community treatment: A new frontier in mental health law</u> (pp. 29-47). New York: Plenum.

Hines, A. H., Ader, D. N., Chang, A. S., & Rundell, J. R. (1998). Dual agency, dual relationships, boundary crossings, and associated boundary violations: A survey of military and civilian psychiatrists. <u>Military Medicine, 163,</u> 826-833.

Hoagwood, K. (1994). The certificate of confidentiality at the National Institute of Mental Health: Discretionary considerations in its applicability in research on child and adolescent mental disorders. <u>Ethics and Behavior, 4,</u> 123-131.

Hochhauser, M. (1999). Informed consent and patient's rights documents: A right, a rite, or a rewrite? <u>Ethics and Behavior, 9,</u> 1-20.

Hoffman, R. M. (1995). Sexual dual relationships in counseling: Confronting the issues. <u>Counseling and Values, 40,</u> 15-23.

Holmes, D. S. (1976). Debriefing after psychological experiments. <u>American Psychologist, 31,</u> 858-875.

Holroyd, J. C., & Brodsky, A. M. (1977). Psychologists' attitudes and practices regarding erotic and nonerotic physical contact with patients. <u>American Psychologist, 32,</u> 843-849.

Houghkirk, E. (1977). Everything you have always wanted your clients to know but have been afraid to tell them. <u>Journal of Marriage and Family Counseling, 3,</u> 27-33.

Howard, K. I., Kopta, S. M., Krause, M. S., & Orlinsky, D. E. (1986). The dose-effect relationship in psychotherapy. <u>American Psychologist, 41,</u> 159-164.

Hunsley, J., & Bailey, J. M. (1999). The clinical utility of the Rorschach: Unfulfilled promises and an uncertain future. <u>Psychological Assessment, 11,</u> 266-277.

Insanity Defense Reform Act of 1984, 18 U.S.C.S. § 17 (West 1998).

Isometsa, E. T., Henriksson, M. M., Aro, H. M., Heikkinen, M. E., Kuoppasalmi, K. I., & Lonnqvist, J. K. (1994). Suicide in major depression. <u>American Journal of Psychiatry, 151,</u> 530-536.

Jaffe v. Redmond, 518 U.S. 1 (1996).

Jamison, S. (1999). Psychology and rational suicide: The special case of assisted dying. In J. L. Werth, Jr. (Ed.), <u>Contemporary perspectives on rational suicide</u> (pp. 128-134). Philadelphia: Brunner/Mazel.

Janus, E. S., & Meehl, P. E. (1997). Assessing the legal standard for predictions of dangerousness in sex offender commitment proceedings. <u>Psychology, Public Policy, and Law, 3,</u> 33-64.

Jellinek, M., & Parmelee, D. (1977). Is there a role for medical ethics in postgraduate psychiatry courses? <u>American Journal of Psychiatry, 134,</u> 1438-1439.

Joiner, T. E., Jr., Walker, R. L., Rudd, M. D., & Jobes, D. A. (1999). Scientizing and routinizing the assessment of suicidality in outpatient practice. <u>Professional Psychology: Research and Practice, 5,</u> 447-453.

Kalichman, S. C. (1999). <u>Mandated reporting of suspected child abuse: Ethics, law, and policy</u> (2nd ed.). Washington, DC: American Psychological Association.

Kant, I. (1909). On a supposed right to tell lies from benevolent motives. In T. K. Abbott (Trans.), <u>Kant's critique of practical reason and other works on the theory of ethics</u> (pp. 361-365). London: Longmans, Green, & Co. (Original work published 1797)

Kant, I. (1956). <u>Critique of practical reason</u> (L. W. Beck, Trans.). New York: Bobbs-Merrill. (Original work published 1788)

Kant, I. (1963). <u>Lectures on ethics</u> (L. Infield, Trans.). New York: Harper & Row. (Original work published 1924)

Kant, I. (1964a). <u>Groundwork of the metaphysic of morals</u> (H. J. Patton, Trans.). New York: Harper & Row. (Original work published 1785)

Kant, I. (1964b). The metaphysical principles of virtue (J. Ellington, Trans.). New York: Bobbs-Merrill. (Original work published 1797)

Kaplan, J. (1988). The use of animals in research. Science, 242, 839-840.

Kazdin, A. E. (1994). Psychotherapy for children and adolescents. In A. E. Bergin & S. L. Garfield (Eds.), Handbook of psychotherapy and behavior change (4th ed., pp. 543-594). New York: Wiley.

Keller, S. A. (1999). Split loyalties: The conflicting demands of individual treatment goals and parental responsibility. Women and Therapy, 22, 117-131.

Kelly, T. A., & Strupp, H. H. (1992). Patient and therapist values in psychotherapy: Perceived changes, assimilation, similarity, and outcome. Journal of Consulting and Clinical Psychology, 60, 34-40.

Keppel, G., Saufley, W. H., Jr., & Tokunaga, H. (1992). Introduction to design and analysis (2nd ed.). New York: W. H. Freeman.

Kitchener, K. S. (1984). Intuition, critical evaluation, and ethical principles: The foundation for ethical decisions in counseling psychology. The Counseling Psychologist, 12(3), 43-55.

Kitchener, R. F. (1980). Ethical relativism and behavior therapy. Journal of Consulting and Clinical Psychology, 48, 1-7.

Kitchener, R. F. (1991). The ethical foundations of behavior therapy. Ethics and Behavior, 1, 221-238.

Klein, K., & Cheuvront, B. (1990). The subject-experimenter contract: A reexamination of subject pool contamination. Teaching of Psychology, 17, 166-169.

Koocher, G. P., & Keith-Spiegel, P. (1998). Ethics in psychology: Professional standards and cases (2nd ed.). New York: Oxford University Press.

Lambert, M. J., & Bergin, A. E. (1994). The effectiveness of psychotherapy. In A. E. Bergin & S. L. Garfield (Eds.), Handbook of psychotherapy and behavior change (4th ed., pp. 143-189). New York: Wiley.

Landrum, R. E., & Chastain, G. (1999). Subject pool policies in undergraduate-only departments: Results from a nationwide survey. In G. Chastain & R. E. Landrum (Eds.), Protecting human subjects: Departmental subject pools and institutional review boards (pp. 25-42). Washington, DC: American Psychological Association.

Laosa, L. M. (1990). Population generalizability, cultural sensitivity, and ethical dilemmas. In I. E. Sigel (Series Ed.), C. B. Fisher & W. W. Tryon (Vol. Eds.), Annual advances in applied developmental psychology: Vol. 4. Ethics in applied developmental psychology: Emerging issues in an emerging field (pp. 227-251). Norwood, NJ: Ablex Publishing.

Lazarus, A. A. (1995). Multimodal therapy. In R. J. Corsini & D. Wedding (Eds.), Current psychotherapies (5th ed., pp. 322-355). Itasca, IL: F.E. Peacock Publishers.

Levine, R. J. (1995a). Adolescents as research subjects without permission of their parents or guardians: Ethical considerations. Journal of Adolescent Health, 17, 287-297.

Levine, R. J. (1995b). Children as research subjects: Ethical and legal considerations. Child and Adolescent Psychiatric Clinics of North America, 4, 853-868.

Lilienfeld, S. O., & Marino, L. (1995). Mental disorder as a Roschian concept: A critique of Wakefield's "harmful dysfunction" analysis. Journal of Abnormal Psychology, 104, 411-420.

Link, B. G. (1987). Understanding labeling effects in the area of mental disorders: An assessment of the effects of expectations of rejection. American Sociological Review, 52, 96-112.

Link, B. G., Cullen, F. T., Frank, J., & Wozniak, J. F. (1987). The social rejection of former mental patients: Understanding why labels matter. American Journal of Sociology, 92, 1461-1500.

Link, B. G., & Steuve, A. (1994). Psychotic symptoms and the violent/illegal behavior of mental patients compared to community controls. In J. Monahan & H. J. Steadman (Eds.), Violence and mental disorder: Developments in risk assessment (pp. 137-159). Chicago: University of Chicago Press.

Litwack, T. R. (1997). Communications regarding risk. American Psychologist, 52, 1245.

Litwack, T. R., & Schlesinger, L. B. (1999). Dangerousness risk assessments: Research, legal, and clinical considerations. In A. K. Hess & I. B. Weiner (Eds.), The handbook of forensic psychology (2nd ed., pp. 171-217). New York: Wiley.

Loftus, E. (1987, June 29). Trials of an expert witness. Newsweek, 109, pp. 10-11.

Loftus, E., & Ketcham, K. (1991). Witness for the defense: The accused, the eyewitness, and the expert who puts memory on trial. New York: St. Martin's Press.

Loftus, E., & Ketcham, K. (1994). The myth of repressed memory. New York: St. Martin's Press.

Luepker, E. T. (1999). Effects of practitioners' sexual misconduct: A follow-up study. Journal of the American Academy of Psychiatry and the Law, 27, 51-63.

Luster, T., & Small, S. A. (1997). Sexual abuse history and problems in adolescence: Exploring the effects of moderating variables. Journal of Marriage and the Family, 59, 131-142.

Lydon, C. (1972, July 26). Eagleton tells of shock therapy on two occasions. The New York Times, pp. A1, A20.

Lymburner, J. A., & Roesch, R. (1999). The insanity defense: Five years of research. International Journal of Law and Psychiatry, 22, 213-240.

MacAndrew, C. (1965). The differentiation of male alcoholic outpatients from nonalcoholic psychiatric outpatients by means of the MMPI. Quarterly Journal of Studies on Alcohol, 26, 238-246.

Maccoby, E. E. (1990). Gender and relationships: A developmental account. American Psychologist, 45, 513-520.

MacKay, E., & O'Neill, P. (1992). What creates the dilemma in ethical dilemmas? Examples from psychological practice. Ethics and Behavior, 2, 227-244.

Macklin, R. (1992). Autonomy, beneficence, and child development. In B. Stanley & J. E. Sieber (Eds.), Social research on children and adolescents: Ethical issues (pp. 88-105). Newbury Park, CA: Sage.

Mann, T. (1994). Informed consent for psychological research: Do subjects comprehend consent forms and understand their legal rights? Psychological Science, 5, 140-143.

Margolin, G. (1998). Ethical issues in marital therapy. In R. M. Anderson, Jr., T. L. Needels, & H. V. Hall (Eds.), Avoiding ethical misconduct in psychology specialty areas (pp. 78-94). Springfield, IL: Charles C. Thomas.

Martin, S. (1999, July/August). Revision of ethics code calls for stronger former client sex rule. APA Monitor, p. 44.

McCarthy, W. C., & Frieze, I. H. (1999). Negative aspects of therapy: Client perceptions of therapists' social influence, burnout, and quality of care. Journal of Social Issues, 55, 33-50.

McFarlane, W. J. G., Bowman, R. G., & MacInnes, M. (1980). Patient access to hospital records: A pilot project. Canadian Journal of Psychiatry, 25, 497-502.

McMahon, M. (1997). Criminalising professional misconduct: Legislative regulation of psychotherapist-patient sex. Psychiatry, Psychology and Law, 4, 177-193.

McMinn, M. R., Ellens, B. M., & Soref, E. (1999). Ethical perspectives and practice behaviors involving computer-based test interpretation. Assessment, 6, 71-77.

McShane, R. H., & Rowe, D. (1994). Access to psychiatric records: Bane or boon? Journal of Mental Health, 3, 301-309.

Meehl, P. E., & Rosen, A. (1955). Antecedent probability and the efficacy of psychometric signs, patterns, or cutting scores. Psychological Bulletin, 52, 194-216.

Megargee, E. I. (1993). Aggression and violence. In P. B. Sutker & H. E. Adams (Eds.), Comprehensive handbook of psychopathology (2nd ed., pp. 617-644). New York: Plenum.

Megargee, E. I. (1995). Assessing and understanding aggressive and violent patients. In J. N. Butcher (Ed.), Clinical personality assessment: Practical considerations (pp. 395-409). New York: Oxford University Press.

Michaels, T. F., & Oetting, E. R. (1979). The informed consent dilemma: An empirical approach. Journal of Social Psychology, 109, 223-230.

Milan, M. A., Chin, C. E., & Nguyen, Q. X. (1999). Practicing psychology in correctional settings: Assessment, treatment, and substance abuse programs. In A. K. Hess & I. B. Weiner (Eds.), The handbook of forensic psychology (2nd ed., pp. 580-602). New York: Wiley.

Milgram, S. (1963). Behavioral study of obedience. Journal of Abnormal and Social Psychology, 67, 371-378.

Mill, J. S. (1910). Utilitarianism. In Utilitarianism, On liberty, and Representative government (pp. 1-60). London: J. M. Dent & Sons. (Original work published 1863)

Miller, L. (1998). Our own medicine: Traumatized psychotherapists and the stresses of doing therapy. Psychotherapy, 35, 137-146.

Mills, L. B., & Huebner, E. S. (1998). A prospective study of personality characteristics, occupational stressors, and burnout among school psychology practitioners. Journal of School Psychology, 36, 103-120.

Mobley, M. J. (1999). Psychotherapy with criminal offenders. In A. K. Hess & I. B. Weiner (Eds.), The handbook of forensic psychology (2nd ed., pp. 603-639). New York: Wiley.

Monahan, J. (1992). Mental disorder and violent behavior: Perceptions and evidence. American Psychologist, 47, 511-521.

Moore, G. E. (1962). Principia ethica. London: Cambridge University Press.

Mordock, J. B. (1995). Institutional review boards in applied settings: Their role in judgments of quality and consumer protection. Psychological Science, 6, 320-321.

Moreland, K. L. (1987). Computer-based test interpretations: Advice to the consumer. Applied Psychology: An International Review, 36, 385-399.

Muller, R. T., & Diamond, T. (1999). Father and mother physical abuse and child aggressive behaviour in two generations. Canadian Journal of Behavioural Science, 31, 221-228.

Mulvey, E. P., & Lidz, C. W. (1998). Clinical prediction of violence as a conditional judgment. Social Psychiatry and Psychiatric Epidemiology, 33(Suppl. 1), S107-S113.

Mumford, G. (1996, Summer). Family privacy protection act. Psychopharmacology Newsletter, 29, p. 3.

Murphy, D. A., O'Keefe, Z. H., & Kaufman, A. H. (1999). Improving comprehension and recall of information for an HIV vaccine trial among women at risk for HIV: Reading level simplification and inclusion of pictures to illustrate key concepts. AIDS Education and Prevention, 11, 389-399.

Murphy, G. E. (1988). The prediction of suicide. In S. Lesse (Ed.), What we know about suicidal behavior and how to treat it (pp. 47-58). Northvale, NJ: Jason Aronson.

Murphy, K. R., & Davidshofer, C. O. (1994). Psychological testing: Principles and applications (3rd ed.). Englewood Cliffs, NJ: Prentice Hall.

National Association of Social Workers. (1982). NASW standards for continuing professional education. Washington, DC: Author.

National Association of Social Workers. (1989). NASW standards for the practice of clinical social work. Washington, DC: Author.

National Association of Social Workers. (1993). Code of ethics of the National Association of Social Workers. Washington, DC: Author.

National Commission for the Protection of Human Subjects of Biomedical and Behavioral Research (NCPHS). (1977). Research involving children: Report and recommendations (DHEW Publication No. [OS] 77-0004. Washington, DC: U. S. Government Printing Office.

National Institutes of Health (1998, March 6). NIH policy and guidelines on the inclusion of children as participants in research involving human subjects. NIH Guide for Grants and Contracts [On-line]. Available: http://grants.nih.gov/grants/ guide/notice-files/not98-024.html

National Institutes of Health, Applied Research Ethics National Association, & Office for Protection from Research Risks. (1992). Institutional animal care and use committee guidebook (NIH Publication No. 92-3415). Bethesda, MD: National Institutes of Health.

National Institutes of Health Guidelines on the Inclusion of Women and Minorities as Subjects in Clinical Research, 59 Fed. Reg. 11146-11151 (1994).

National Research Act of 1974, 42 U.S.C. § 241 et seq. (West 1994).

Naughton, J. M. (1972, August 1). Successor sought: O'Brien and Muskie in running--Dakotan to address nation. The New York Times, pp. A1, A24.

Newman, E., Kaloupek, D. G., Keane, T. M., & Folstein, S. F. (1997). Ethical issues in trauma research: The evolution of an empirical model for decision making. In G. K. Kantor & J. L. Jasinski (Eds.), Out of the darkness: Contemporary perspectives on family violence (pp. 271-281). Thousand Oaks, CA: Sage Publications.

Nimmer, J. G., & Handelsman, M. M. (1992). Effects of subject pool policy on student attitudes toward psychology and psychological research. Teaching of Psychology, 19, 141-144.

Ogloff, J. R. P., & Otto, R. K. (1991). Are research participants truly informed? Readability of informed consent forms used in research. Ethics and Behavior, 1, 239-252.

Oliansky, A. (1991). A confederate's perspective on deception. Ethics and Behavior, 1, 253-258.

Ortmann, A., & Hertwig, R. (1997). Is deception acceptable? American Psychologist, 52, 746-747.

Parrott, J., Strathdee, G., & Brown, P. (1988). Patient access to psychiatric records: The patient's view. Journal of the Royal Society of Medicine, 81, 520-522.

Pearson, B., & Piazza, N. (1997). Classification of dual relationships in the helping professions. Counselor Education and Supervision, 37, 89-99.

Peele, S. (1990). Behavior in a vacuum: Social-psychological theories of addiction that deny the social and psychological meanings of behavior. Journal of Mind and Behavior, 11, 513-529.

Perrone, J. (1997). Open secrets: HHS proposals don't restrict police access to patient records--and some fear this invites abuse. Hospitals and Health Networks, 71(21), 68.

Petersen, A. C., & Leffert, N. (1995). Developmental issues influencing guidelines for adolescent health research: A review. Journal of Adolescent Health, 17, 298-305.

Plaut, S. M. (1997). Boundary violations in professional-client relationships: Overview and guidelines for prevention. Sexual and Marital Therapy, 12, 77-94.

Plous, S. (1996a). Attitudes toward the use of animals in psychological research and education: Results from a national survey of psychologists. American Psychologist, 51, 1167-1180.

Plous, S. (1996b). Attitudes toward the use of animals in psychological research and education: Results from a national survey of psychology majors. Psychological Science, 7, 352-358.

Policy modifies bars to resignations during ethics investigations. (1997, November). APA Monitor, pp. 38-39.

Pollack, D. A., McFarland, B. H., George, R. A., & Angell, R. H. (1994). Prioritization of mental health services in Oregon. The Milbank Quarterly, 72, 515-553.

Pope, K. S. (1989). Therapist-patient sex syndrome: A guide for attorneys and subsequent therapists to assessing damage. In G. Gabbard (Ed.), Sexual exploitation in professional relationships (pp. 39-55). Washington, DC: American Psychiatric Press.

Pope, K. S. (1991). Dual relationships in psychotherapy. Ethics and Behavior, 1, 21-34.

Pope, K. S., & Bouhoutsos, J. C. (1986). Sexual intimacy between therapists and patients. New York: Praeger.

Pope, K. S., Butcher, J. N., & Seelen, J. (2000). The MMPI, MMPI-2, & MMPI-A in court: A practical guide for expert witnesses and attorneys (2nd ed.). Washington, DC: American Psychological Association.

Porter, J. (1996). Regulatory considerations in research involving children and adolescents with mental disorders. In K. Hoagwood, P. S. Jensen, & C. B. Fisher (Eds.), Ethical issues in mental health research with children and adolescents (pp. 15-28). Mahwah, NJ: Lawrence Erlbaum.

Powell, M. P., & Vacha-Haase, T. (1994). Issues related to research with children: What counseling psychologists need to know. The Counseling Psychologist, 22, 444-453.

Protection of Human Subjects, 45 C.F.R. 46 (1991).

Quadrio, C. (1994). Sexual abuse involving therapists, clergy and judiciary: Closed ranks, collusions and conspiracies of silence. Psychiatry, Psychology and Law, 1, 189-198.

Quinn, T. C., Glasser, D., Cannon, R. O., Matuszak, D. L., Dunning, R. W., Kline, R. L., Campbell, C. H., Israel, E., Fauci, A. S., & Hook, E. W., III. (1988). Human immunodeficiency virus infection among patients attending clinics for sexually transmitted diseases. New England Journal of Medicine, 318, 197-203.

Raskin, N. J., & Rogers, C. R. (1995). Person-centered therapy. In R. J. Corsini & D. Wedding (Eds.), Current psychotherapies (5th ed., pp. 128-161). Itasca, IL: F. E. Peacock Publishers.

Reid, S. (1998). Suicide in schizophrenia: A review of the literature. Journal of Mental Health, 7, 345-353.

Remley, T. P., Jr., Herlihy, B., & Herlihy, S. B. (1997). The U. S. Supreme Court decision in Jaffee v. Redmond: Implications for counselors. Journal of Counseling and Development, 75, 213-218.

Renjilian, D. A., Baum, R. E., & Landry, S. L. (1998). Psychotherapist burnout: Can college students see the signs? Journal of College Student Psychotherapy, 13, 39-48.

Rice, M. E., & Harris, G. T. (1995). Violent recidivism: Assessing predictive validity. Journal of Consulting and Clinical Psychology, 63, 737-748.

Richards, P. S., & Davison, M. L. (1989). The effects of theistic and atheistic counselor values on client trust: A multidimensional scaling analysis. Counseling and Values, 33, 109-120.

Roback, H. B., Moore, R. F., Bloch, F. S., & Shelton, M. (1996). Confidentiality in group psychotherapy: Empirical findings and the law. International Journal of Group Psychotherapy, 46, 117-135.

Robiner, W. N., Arbisi, P. A., & Edwall, G. E. (1994). The basis for the doctoral degree for psychology licensure. Clinical Psychology Review, 14, 227-254.

Roesch, R., Zapf, P. A., Golding, S. L., & Skeem, J. L. (1999). Defining and assessing competency to stand trial. In A. K. Hess & I. B. Weiner (Eds.), The handbook of forensic psychology (2nd ed., pp. 327-349). New York: Wiley.

Rogers, C. R. (1961). On becoming a person. Boston: Houghton Mifflin.

Rogers, C. R., & Skinner, B. F. (1956). Some issues concerning the control of human behavior. Science, 124, 1057-1066.

Rosenbaum, M. (1982). Ethical problems of group psychotherapy. In M. Rosenbaum (Ed.), Ethics and values in psychotherapy (pp. 237-257). New York: Free Press.

Rosenthal, R. (1994). Science and ethics in conducting, analyzing, and reporting psychological research. Psychological Science, 5, 127-134.

Roth, L. H., Wolford, J., & Meisel, A. (1980). Patient access to records: Tonic or toxin? American Journal of Psychiatry, 137, 592-596.

Russell, B. (1945). A history of Western philosophy. New York: Simon and Schuster.

Sales, B. D., & Simon, L. (1993). Institutional constraints on the ethics of expert testimony. Ethics and Behavior, 3, 231-249.

Salisbury, W. A., & Kinnier, R. T. (1996). Posttermination friendship between counselors and clients. Journal of Counseling and Development, 74, 495-500.

Sampson, J. P., Kolodinsky, R. W., & Greeno, B. P. (1997). Counseling on the information highway: Future possibilities and potential problems. Journal of Counseling and Development, 75, 203-212.

Sandoval, J. (1998). Critical thinking in test interpretation. In J. Sandoval, C. L. Frisby, K. F. Geisinger, J. D. Scheuneman, & J. R. Grenier (Eds.), Test interpretation and diversity: Achieving equity in assessment (pp. 31-49). Washington, DC: American Psychological Association.

Sarbin, T. R. (1990). Toward the obsolescence of the schizophrenia hypothesis. Journal of Mind and Behavior, 11, 259-283.

Sarbin, T. R. (1997). On the futility of psychiatric diagnostic manuals (DSMs) and the return of personal agency. Applied and Preventive Psychology, 6, 233-243.

Scherer, D. G., & Reppucci, N. D. (1988). Adolescents' capacities to provide voluntary informed consent: The effects of parental influence and medical dilemmas. Law and Human Behavior, 12, 123-141.

Schwehn, J., & Schau, C. G. (1990). Psychotherapy as a process of value stabilization. Counseling and Values, 35, 24-30.

Shadish, W. R. (1994). APA ethics and student authorship on master's theses. American Psychologist, 49, 1096.

Sharkey, J. (1997, September 28). You're not bad, you're sick. It's in the book. The New York Times, pp. 1, 5.

Shergill, S. S., & Szmukler, G. (1998). How predictable is violence and suicide in community psychiatric practice? Journal of Mental Health, 7, 393-401.

Shields, J. M., & Johnson, A. (1992). Collision between law and ethics: Consent for treatment with adolescents. Bulletin of the American Academy of Psychiatry and Law, 20, 309-323.

Shneidman, E. S. (1992). Rational suicide and psychiatric disorders. New England Journal of Medicine, 326, 889-890.

Shope, J. T., Copeland, L. A., & Dielman, T. E. (1994). Measurement of alcohol use and misuse in a cohort of students followed from grade 6 through grade 12. Alcoholism: Clinical and Experimental Research, 18, 726-733.

Sidman, M. (1999). Coercion in educational settings. Behaviour Change, 16, 79-88.

Sieber, J. E. (1999). What makes a subject pool (un)ethical? In G. Chastain & R. E. Landrum (Eds.), Protecting human subjects: Departmental subject pools and institutional review boards (pp. 43-64). Washington, DC: American Psychological Association.

Sieber, J. E., & Saks, M. J. (1989). A census of subject pool characteristics and policies. American Psychologist, 44, 1053-1061.

Singh, S. N., Mishra, S., & Kim, D. (1998). Research-related burnout among faculty in higher education. Psychological Reports, 83, 463-473.

Sireci, S. G., & Geisinger, K. F. (1998). Equity issues in employment testing. In J. Sandoval, C. L. Frisby, K. F. Geisinger, J. D. Scheuneman, & J. R. Grenier (Eds.), Test interpretation and diversity: Achieving equity in assessment (pp. 105-140). Washington, DC: American Psychological Association.

Skorupa, J., & Agresti, A. A. (1993). Ethical beliefs about burnout and continued professional practice. Professional Psychology: Research and Practice, 24, 281-285.

Slovenko, R. (1999). Civil competency. In A. K. Hess & I. B. Weiner (Eds.), The handbook of forensic psychology (2nd ed., pp. 151-167). New York: Wiley.

Smart, J. J. C., & Williams, B. (1973). Utilitarianism: For and against. London: Cambridge University Press.

Smart, R. N. (1958). Negative utilitarianism. Mind, 67, 542-543.

Smith, T. S., McGuire, J., Abbott, D., & Blau, B. (1991). Clinical ethical decision making: An investigation of the rationales used to justify doing less than one believes one should. Professional Psychology: Research and Practice, 22, 235-239.

Smyer, M. A., Balster, R. L., Egli, D., Johnson, D. L., Kilbey, M. M., Leith, N. J., & Puente, A. E. (1993). Summary of the report of the ad hoc task force on psychopharmacology of the American Psychological Association. Professional Psychology: Research and Practice, 24, 394-403.

Society for Industrial and Organizational Psychology. (1987). Principles for the validation and use of personnel selection procedures (3rd ed.). College Park, MD: Author.

Solomon, P. (1996). Research on the coercion of persons with severe mental illness. In D. L. Dennis & J. Monahan (Eds.), Coercion and aggressive community treatment: A new frontier in mental health law (pp. 129-145). New York: Plenum.

Somer, E., & Saadon, M. (1999). Therapist-client sex: Clients' retrospective reports. Professional Psychology: Research and Practice, 30, 504-509.

Stanley, B. H., & Guido, J. R. (1996). Informed consent: Psychological and empirical issues. In B. H. Stanley, J. E. Sieber, & G. B. Melton (Eds.), Research ethics: A psychological approach (pp. 105-128). Lincoln, NE: University of Nebraska Press.

Stanton, A. L., Burker, E. J., & Kershaw, D. (1991). Effects of researcher follow-up of distressed subjects: Tradeoff between validity and ethical responsibility. Ethics and Behavior, 1, 105-112.

Steadman, H. J., McGreevy, M. A., Morissey, J. P., Callahan, L. A., Robbins, P. C., & Cirincione, C. (1993). Before and after Hinckley: Evaluating insanity defense reform. New York: Guilford.

Stein, E. J., Furedy, R. L., Simonton, M. J., & Neuffer, C. H. (1979). Patient access to medical records on a psychiatric inpatient unit. American Journal of Psychiatry, 136, 327-329.

Stevens, J., Yock, T., & Perlman, B. (1979). Comparing master's clinical training with professional responsibilities in community mental health centers. Professional Psychology: Research and Practice, 10, 20-27.

Strom-Gottfried, K. (1999). Professional boundaries: An analysis of violations by social workers. Families in Society, 80, 439-449.

Summers, C. (1992). Militarism, human welfare, and the APA Ethical Principles of Psychologists. Ethics and Behavior, 2, 287-310.

Swenson, C. C., & Hanson, R. F. (1998). Sexual abuse of children: Assessment, research, and treatment. In J. R. Lutzker (Ed.), Handbook of child abuse research and treatment (pp. 475-499). New York: Plenum.

Szasz, T. (1974). The myth of mental illness: Foundations of a theory of personal conduct (Rev. ed.). New York: HarperCollins.

Szasz, T. (1986). The case against suicide prevention. American Psychologist, 41, 806-812.

Szasz, T. (1999). Fatal freedom: The ethics and politics of suicide. Westport, CT: Praeger.

Tallent, N. (1987). Computer-generated psychological reports: A look at the modern psychometric machine. Journal of Personality Assessment, 51, 95-108.

Tarasoff v. Board of Regents of the University of California, 13 Cal.3d 177, 529 P. 2d 533 (1974), vacated, 17 Cal.3d 425, 551 P. 2d 334 (1976).

Texas Family Code, Title 2(A) § 32.004 (West 2000).

Thapar v. Zezulka, 994 S.W.2d 635 (1999).

Thompson, B. (1994). The big picture(s) in deciding authorship order. American Psychologist, 49, 1095-1096.

Thompson, R. A. (1992). Developmental changes in research risk and benefit. In B. Stanley & J. E. Sieber (Eds.), Social research on children and adolescents: Ethical issues (pp. 31-64). Newbury Park, CA: Sage.

Thoreson, R. W., Shaughnessy, P., & Frazier, P. A. (1995). Sexual contact during and after professional relationships: Practices and attitudes of female counselors. Journal of Counseling and Development, 74, 84-89.

Thoreson, R. W., Shaughnessy, P., Heppner, P. P., & Cook, S. W. (1993). Sexual contact during and after the professional relationship: Attitudes and practices of male counselors. Journal of Counseling and Development, 71, 429-434.

Thorndike, E. L. (1911). Animal intelligence. New York: Macmillan.

Thorndike, E. L. (1940). Human nature and the social order. New York: Macmillan.

Tillman, J. G. (1998). Psychodynamic psychotherapy, religious beliefs, and self-disclosure. American Journal of Psychotherapy, 52, 273-286.

Treppa, J. A. (1998). A practitioner's guide to ethical decision-making. In R. M. Anderson, Jr., T. L. Needels, & H. V. Hall (Eds.), Avoiding ethical misconduct in psychology specialty areas (pp. 26-41). Springfield, IL: Charles C. Thomas.

Tsemberis, S., Miller, A. C., & Gartner, D. (1996). Expert judgments of computer-based and clinician-written reports. Computers in Human Behavior, 12, 167-175.

Tseng, H. M., Macleod, H. A., & Wright, P. (1997). Computer anxiety and measurement of mood change. Computers in Human Behavior, 13, 305-316.

Tseng, H. M., Tiplady, B., Macleod, H. A., & Wright, P. (1998). Computer anxiety: A comparison of pen-based personal digital assistants, conventional computer and paper assessment of mood and performance. British Journal of Psychology, 89, 599-610.

Tucker, G. J. (1998). Putting DSM-IV in perspective. American Journal of Psychiatry, 155, 159-161.

Turkheimer, E., & Parry, C. D. H. (1992). Why the gap? Practice and policy in civil commitment hearings. American Psychologist, 47, 646-655.

Tymchuk, A. J. (1981). Ethical decision making and psychological treatment. Journal of Psychiatric Treatment and Evaluation, 3, 507-513.

Tymchuk, A. J. (1986). Guidelines for ethical decision making. Canadian Psychology, 27, 36-43.

Tymchuk, A. J., & Ouslander, J. G. (1990). Optimizing the informed consent process with elderly people. Educational Gerontology, 16, 245-257.

Uniform Guidelines on Employee Selection Procedures, 43 Fed. Reg. 38290 (1978).

Vachon, D. O., & Agresti, A. A. (1992). A training proposal to help mental health professionals clarify and manage implicit values in the counseling process. Professional Psychology: Research and Practice, 6, 509-514.

VandeCreek, L., & Knapp, S. (1993). Tarasoff and beyond: Legal and clinical considerations in the treatment of life-endangering patients (Rev. ed.). Sarasota, FL: Professional Resource Press.

Velasquez, R. J., & Callahan, W. J. (1992). Psychological testing of Hispanic Americans in clinical settings: Overview and issues. In K. F. Geisinger (Ed.), Psychological testing of Hispanics (pp. 253-265). Washington, DC: American Psychological Association.

Vredenburgh, L. D., Carlozzi, A. F., & Stein, L. B. (1999). Burnout in counseling psychologists: Type of practice setting and pertinent demographics. Counselling Psychology Quarterly, 12, 293-302.

Waite, B. M., & Bowman, L. L. (1999). Research participation among general psychology students at a metropolitan comprehensive public university. In G. Chastain & R. E. Landrum (Eds.), Protecting human subjects: Departmental subject pools and institutional review boards (pp. 69-85). Washington, DC: American Psychological Association.

Wallace, J. D. (1988). Moral relevance and moral conflict. Ithaca, NY: Cornell University Press.

Walters, G. D., White, T. W., & Greene, R. L. (1988). Use of the MMPI to identify malingering and exaggeration of psychiatric symptomatology in male prison inmates. Journal of Consulting and Clinical Psychology, 56, 111-117.

Weiner, I. B. (1999). Writing forensic reports. In A. K. Hess & I. B. Weiner (Eds.), The handbook of forensic psychology (2nd ed., pp. 501-520). New York: Wiley.

Whitecotton, S. M., Sanders, D. E., & Norris, K. B. (1998). Improving predictive accuracy with a combination of human intuition and mechanical decision aids. Organizational Behavior and Human Decision Processes, 76, 325-348.

Williams, M. H. (1992). Exploitation and inference: Mapping the damage from therapist-patient sexual involvement. American Psychologist, 47, 412-421.

Wohlberg, J. W., & Reid, E. A. (1996). Helen Bramson: Treatment after sexual abuse by a mental health practitioner. Bulletin of the Menninger Clinic, 60, 52-61.

Wrightsman, L. S., Nietzel, M. T., & Fortune, W. H. (1998). Psychology and the legal system (4th ed.). Pacific Grove, CA: Brooks/Cole.

Wyatt v. Stickney, 325 F. Supp. 781 (M.D. Ala. 1971) and 344 F. Supp. 373 (M.D. Ala. 1972).

Yanagida, E. H. (1998). Ethical dilemmas in the clinical practice of child psychology. In R. M. Anderson, Jr., T. L. Needels, & H. V. Hall (Eds.), Avoiding ethical misconduct in psychology specialty areas (pp. 47-77). Springfield, IL: Charles C. Thomas.

Young, D. R., Hooker, D. T., & Freeberg, F. E. (1990). Informed consent documents: Increasing comprehension by reducing reading level. IRB: A Review of Human Subjects Research, 12(3), 1-5.

Zeiger, M., & Lewis, J. E. (1998). The spiritually responsible therapist: Religious material in the psychotherapeutic setting. Psychotherapy, 35, 415-424.

Zinermon v. Burch, 494 U.S. 113 (1990).

# Appendix A
# "Ethical Principles of Psychologists and Code of Conduct"*

## INTRODUCTION

The American Psychological Association's (APA's) Ethical Principles of Psychologists and Code of Conduct (hereinafter referred to as the Ethics Code) consists of an Introduction, a Preamble, six General Principles (A-F), and specific Ethical Standards. The Introduction discusses the intent, organization, procedural considerations, and scope of application of the Ethics Code. The Preamble and General Principles are *aspirational* goals to guide psychologists toward the highest ideals of psychology. Although the Preamble and General Principles are not themselves enforceable rules, they should be considered by psychologists in arriving at an ethical course of action and may be considered by ethics bodies in interpreting the Ethical Standards. The Ethical Standards set forth *enforceable* rules for conduct as psychologists. Most of the Ethical Standards are written broadly, in order to apply to psychologists in varied roles, although the application of an Ethical Standard may vary depending on the context. The Ethical Standards are not exhaustive. The fact that a given conduct is not specifically addressed by the Ethics Code does not mean that it is necessarily either ethical or unethical.

Membership in the APA commits members to adhere to the APA Ethics Code and to the rules and procedures used to implement it. Psychologists and students, whether or not they are APA members, should be aware that the Ethics Code may be applied to them by state psychology boards, courts, or other public bodies.

This Ethics Code applies only to psychologists' work-related activities, that is, activities that are part of the psychologists' scientific and professional functions or that are psychological in nature. It includes the clinical or counseling practice of psychology, research, teaching, supervision of trainees, development of assessment instruments, conducting assessments, educational counseling, organizational consulting, social intervention, administration, and other activities as well. These work-related activities can be distinguished from the purely private conduct of a psychologist, which ordinarily is not within the purview of the Ethics Code.

The Ethics Code is intended to provide standards of professional conduct that can be applied by the APA and by other bodies that choose to adopt them. Whether or not a psychologist has violated the Ethics Code does not by itself determine whether he or she is legally liable in a court action, whether a contract is enforceable, or whether other legal consequences occur. These results are based on legal rather than ethical rules. However, compliance with or violation of the Ethics Code may be admissible as evidence in some legal proceedings, depending on the circumstances.

In the process of making decisions regarding their professional behavior, psychologists must consider this Ethics Code, in addition to applicable laws and psychology board regulations. If the Ethics Code establishes a higher standard of conduct than is required by law, psychologists must meet the higher ethical standard. If the Ethics Code standard appears to conflict with the requirements of law, then psychologists make known their commitment to the Ethics Code and take steps to resolve the conflict in a responsible manner. If neither law nor the Ethics Code resolves an issue, psychologists should consider other professional materials[1] and the dictates of their own conscience, as well as seek consultation with others within the field when this is practical.

---

[1]Professional materials that are most helpful in this regard are guidelines and standards that have been adopted or endorsed by professional psychological organizations. Such guidelines and standards, whether adopted by the American Psychological Association (APA) or its Divisions, are not enforceable as such by this Ethics Code, but are of educative value to psychologists, courts, and professional bodies. Such materials include, but are not limited to, the APA's *General Guidelines for Providers of Psychological Services* (1987), *Specialty Guidelines for the Delivery of Services by Clinical Psychologists, Counseling Psychologists, Industrial/Organizational Psychologists, and School Psychologists* (1981), *Guidelines for Computer Based Tests and Interpretations* (1987), *Standards for Educational and Psychological Testing* (1985), *Ethical Principles in the Conduct of Research With Human Participants* (1982), *Guidelines for Ethical Conduct in the Care and Use of Animals* (1986), *Guidelines for Providers of Psychological Services to Ethnic, Linguistic, and Culturally Diverse Populations* (1990), and *Publication Manual of the American Psychological Association* (3rd ed., 1983). Materials not adopted by APA as a whole include the APA Division 41 (Forensic Psychology)/American Psychology-Law Society's *Specialty Guidelines for Forensic Psychologists* (1991).

This version of the APA Ethics Code was adopted by the American Psychological Association's Council of Representatives during its meeting, August 13 and 16, 1992, and is effective beginning December 1, 1992. Inquiries concerning the substance or interpretation of the APA Ethics Code should be addressed to the Director, Office of Ethics, American Psychological Association, 750 First Street, NE, Washington, DC 20002-4242.

This Code will be used to adjudicate complaints brought concerning alleged conduct occurring on or after the effective date. Complaints regarding conduct occurring prior to the effective date will be adjudicated on the basis of the version of the Code that was in effect at the time the conduct occurred, except that no provisions repealed in June 1989, will be enforced even if an earlier version contains the provision. The Ethics Code will undergo continuing review and study for future revisions; comments on the Code may be sent to the above address.

The APA has previously published its Ethical Standards as follows:

American Psychological Association. (1953). *Ethical standards of psychologists*. Washington, DC: Author.
American Psychological Association. (1958). Standards of ethical behavior for psychologists. *American Psychologist, 13*, 268–271.
American Psychological Association. (1963). Ethical standards of psychologists. *American Psychologist, 18*, 56–60.
American Psychological Association. (1968). Ethical standards of psychologists. *American Psychologist, 23*, 357–361.
American Psychological Association. (1977, March). Ethical standards of psychologists. *APA Monitor,* pp. 22–23.
American Psychological Association. (1979). *Ethical standards of psychologists*. Washington, DC: Author.
American Psychological Association. (1981). Ethical principles of psychologists. *American Psychologist, 36*, 633–638.
American Psychological Association. (1990). Ethical principles of psychologists (Amended June 2, 1989). *American Psychologist, 45*, 390–395.

Request copies of the APA's Ethical Principles of Psychologists and Code of Conduct from the APA Order Department, 750 First Street, NE, Washington, DC 20002-4242, or phone (202) 336–5510.

The procedures for filing, investigating, and resolving complaints of unethical conduct are described in the current Rules and Procedures of the APA Ethics Committee. The actions that APA may take for violations of the Ethics Code include actions such as reprimand, censure, termination of APA membership, and referral of the matter to other bodies. Complainants who seek remedies such as monetary damages in alleging ethical violations by a psychologist must resort to private negotiation, administrative bodies, or the courts. Actions that violate the Ethics Code may lead to the imposition of sanctions on a psychologist by bodies other than APA, including state psychological associations, other professional groups, psychology boards, other state or federal agencies, and payors for health services. In addition to actions for violation of the Ethics Code, the APA Bylaws provide that APA may take action against a member after his or her conviction of a felony, expulsion or suspension from an affiliated state psychological association, or suspension or loss of licensure.

## PREAMBLE

Psychologists work to develop a valid and reliable body of scientific knowledge based on research. They may apply that knowledge to human behavior in a variety of contexts. In doing so, they perform many roles, such as researcher, educator, diagnostician, therapist, supervisor, consultant, administrator, social interventionist, and expert witness. Their goal is to broaden knowledge of behavior and, where appropriate, to apply it pragmatically to improve the condition of both the individual and society. Psychologists respect the central importance of freedom of inquiry and expression in research, teaching, and publication. They also strive to help the public in developing informed judgments and choices concerning human behavior. This Ethics Code provides a common set of values upon which psychologists build their professional and scientific work.

This Code is intended to provide both the general principles and the decision rules to cover most situations encountered by psychologists. It has as its primary goal the welfare and protection of the individuals and groups with whom psychologists work. It is the individual responsibility of each psychologist to aspire to the highest possible standards of conduct. Psychologists respect and protect human and civil rights, and do not knowingly participate in or condone unfair discriminatory practices.

The development of a dynamic set of ethical standards for a psychologist's work-related conduct requires a personal commitment to a lifelong effort to act ethically; to encourage ethical behavior by students, supervisees, employees, and colleagues, as appropriate; and to consult with others, as needed, concerning ethical problems. Each psychologist supplements, but does not violate, the Ethics Code's values and rules on the basis of guidance drawn from personal values, culture, and experience.

# GENERAL PRINCIPLES

## PRINCIPLE A: COMPETENCE

Psychologists strive to maintain high standards of competence in their work. They recognize the boundaries of their particular competencies and the limitations of their expertise. They provide only those services and use only those techniques for which they are qualified by education, training, or experience. Psychologists are cognizant of the fact that the competencies required in serving, teaching, and/or studying groups of people vary with the distinctive characteristics of those groups. In those areas in which recognized professional standards do not yet exist, psychologists exercise careful judgment and take appropriate precautions to protect the welfare of those with whom they work. They maintain knowledge of relevant scientific and professional information related to the services they render, and they recognize the need for ongoing education. Psychologists make appropriate use of scientific, professional, technical, and administrative resources.

## PRINCIPLE B: INTEGRITY

Psychologists seek to promote integrity in the science, teaching, and practice of psychology. In these activities psychologists are honest, fair, and respectful of others. In describing or reporting their qualifications, services, products, fees, research, or teaching, they do not make statements that are false, misleading, or deceptive. Psychologists strive to be aware of their own belief systems, values, needs, and limitations and the effect of these on their work. To the extent feasible, they attempt to clarify for relevant parties the roles they are performing and to function appropriately in accordance with those roles. Psychologists avoid improper and potentially harmful dual relationships.

## PRINCIPLE C: PROFESSIONAL AND SCIENTIFIC RESPONSIBILITY

Psychologists uphold professional standards of conduct, clarify their professional roles and obligations, accept appropriate responsibility for their behavior, and adapt their methods to the needs of different populations. Psychologists consult with, refer to, or cooperate with other professionals and institutions to the extent needed to serve the best interests of their patients, clients, or other recipients of their services. Psychologists' moral standards and conduct are personal matters to the same degree as is true for any other person, except as psychologists' conduct may compromise their professional responsibilities or reduce the public's trust in psychology and psychologists. Psychologists are concerned about the ethical compliance of their colleagues' scientific and professional conduct. When appropriate, they consult with colleagues in order to prevent or avoid unethical conduct.

## PRINCIPLE D: RESPECT FOR PEOPLE'S RIGHTS AND DIGNITY

Psychologists accord appropriate respect to the fundamental rights, dignity, and worth of all people. They respect the rights of individuals to privacy, confidentiality, self-determination, and autonomy, mindful that legal and other obligations may lead to inconsistency and conflict with the exercise of these rights. Psychologists are aware of cultural, individual, and role differences, including those due to age, gender, race, ethnicity, national origin, religion, sexual orientation, disability, language, and socioeconomic status.

Psychologists try to eliminate the effect on their work of biases based on those factors, and they do not knowingly participate in or condone unfair discriminatory practices.

## PRINCIPLE E: CONCERN FOR OTHERS' WELFARE

Psychologists seek to contribute to the welfare of those with whom they interact professionally. In their professional actions, psychologists weigh the welfare and rights of their patients or clients, students, supervisees, human research participants, and other affected persons, and the welfare of animal subjects of research. When conflicts occur among psychologists' obligations or concerns, they attempt to resolve these conflicts and to perform their roles in a responsible fashion that avoids or minimizes harm. Psychologists are sensitive to real and ascribed differences in power between themselves and others, and they do not exploit or mislead other people during or after professional relationships.

## PRINCIPLE F: SOCIAL RESPONSIBILITY

Psychologists are aware of their professional and scientific responsibilities to the community and the society in which they work and live. They apply and make public their knowledge of psychology in order to contribute to human welfare. Psychologists are concerned about and work to mitigate the causes of human suffering. When undertaking research, they strive to advance human welfare and the science of psychology. Psychologists try to avoid misuse of their work. Psychologists comply with the law and encourage the development of law and social policy that serve the interests of their patients and clients and the public. They are encouraged to contribute a portion of their professional time for little or no personal advantage.

## ETHICAL STANDARDS

### 1. *General Standards*

These General Standards are potentially applicable to the professional and scientific activities of all psychologists.

### 1.01 Applicability of the Ethics Code

The activity of a psychologist subject to the Ethics Code may be reviewed under these Ethical Standards only if the activity is part of his or her work-related functions or the activity is psychological in nature. Personal activities having no connection to or effect on psychological roles are not subject to the Ethics Code.

### 1.02 Relationship of Ethics and Law

If psychologists' ethical responsibilities conflict with law, psychologists make known their commitment to the Ethics Code and take steps to resolve the conflict in a responsible manner.

### 1.03 Professional and Scientific Relationship

Psychologists provide diagnostic, therapeutic, teaching, research, supervisory, consultative, or other psychological services only in the context of a defined professional or scientific relationship or role. (See also Standards 2.01, Evaluation, Diagnosis, and Interventions in Professional Context, and 7.02, Forensic Assessments.)

### 1.04 Boundaries of Competence

(a) Psychologists provide services, teach, and conduct research only within the boundaries of their competence, based on their education, training, supervised experience, or appropriate professional experience.

(b) Psychologists provide services, teach, or conduct research in new areas or involving new techniques only after first undertaking appropriate study, training, supervision, and/or consultation from persons who are competent in those areas or techniques.

(c) In those emerging areas in which generally recognized standards for preparatory training do not yet exist, psychologists nevertheless take reasonable steps to ensure the competence of their work and to protect patients, clients, students, research participants, and others from harm.

### 1.05 Maintaining Expertise

Psychologists who engage in assessment, therapy, teaching, research, organizational consulting, or other professional activities maintain a reasonable level of awareness of current scientific and professional information in their fields of activity, and undertake ongoing efforts to maintain competence in the skills they use.

### 1.06 Basis for Scientific and Professional Judgments

Psychologists rely on scientifically and professionally derived knowledge when making scientific or professional judgments or when engaging in scholarly or professional endeavors.

### 1.07 Describing the Nature and Results of Psychological Services

(a) When psychologists provide assessment, evaluation, treatment, counseling, supervision, teaching, consultation, research, or other psychological services to an individual, a group, or an organization, they provide, using language that is reasonably understandable to the recipient of those services, appropriate information beforehand about the nature of such services and appropriate information later about results and conclusions. (See also Standard 2.09, Explaining Assessment Results.)

(b) If psychologists will be precluded by law or by organizational roles from providing such information to particular individuals or groups, they so inform those individuals or groups at the outset of the service.

### 1.08 Human Differences

Where differences of age, gender, race, ethnicity, national origin, religion, sexual orientation, disability, language, or socioeconomic status significantly affect psychologists' work concerning particular individuals or groups, psychologists obtain the training, experience, consultation, or supervision necessary to ensure the competence of their services, or they make appropriate referrals.

### 1.09 Respecting Others

In their work-related activities, psychologists respect the rights of others to hold values, attitudes, and opinions that differ from their own.

### 1.10 Nondiscrimination

In their work-related activities, psychologists do not engage in unfair discrimination based on age, gender, race, ethnicity, national origin, religion, sexual orientation, disability, socioeconomic status, or any basis proscribed by law.

### 1.11 Sexual Harassment

(a) Psychologists do not engage in sexual harassment. Sexual harassment is sexual solicitation, physical advances, or verbal or nonverbal conduct that is sexual in nature, that occurs in connection with the psychologist's activities or roles as a psychologist, and that either: (1) is unwelcome, is offensive, or creates a hostile workplace environment, and the psychologist knows or is told this; or (2) is sufficiently severe or intense to be abusive to a reasonable person in the context. Sexual harassment can consist of a single intense or severe act or of multiple persistent or pervasive acts.

(b) Psychologists accord sexual-harassment complainants and respondents dignity and respect. Psychologists do not participate in denying a person academic admittance or advancement, employment, tenure, or promotion, based solely upon their having made, or their being the subject of, sexual harassment charges. This does not preclude taking action based upon the outcome of such proceedings or consideration of other appropriate information.

### 1.12 Other Harassment

Psychologists do not knowingly engage in behavior that is harassing or demeaning to persons with whom they interact in their work based on factors such as those persons' age, gender, race, ethnicity, national origin, religion, sexual orientation, disability, language, or socioeconomic status.

### 1.13 Personal Problems and Conflicts

(a) Psychologists recognize that their personal problems and conflicts may interfere with their effectiveness. Accordingly, they refrain from undertaking an activity when they know or should know that their personal problems are likely to lead to harm to a patient, client, colleague, student, research participant, or other person to whom they may owe a professional or scientific obligation.

(b) In addition, psychologists have an obligation to be alert to signs of, and to obtain assistance for, their personal problems at an early stage, in order to prevent significantly impaired performance.

(c) When psychologists become aware of personal problems that may interfere with their performing work-related duties adequately, they take appropriate measures, such as obtaining professional consultation or assistance, and determine whether they should limit, suspend, or terminate their work-related duties.

### 1.14 Avoiding Harm

Psychologists take reasonable steps to avoid harming their patients or clients, research participants, students, and others with whom they work, and to minimize harm where it is foreseeable and unavoidable.

### 1.15 Misuse of Psychologists' Influence

Because psychologists' scientific and professional judgments and actions may affect the lives of others, they are alert to and guard against personal, financial, social, organizational, or political factors that might lead to misuse of their influence.

### 1.16 Misuse of Psychologists' Work

(a) Psychologists do not participate in activities in which it appears likely that their skills or data will be misused by others, unless corrective mechanisms are available. (See also Standard 7.04, Truthfulness and Candor.)

(b) If psychologists learn of misuse or misrepresentation of their work, they take reasonable steps to correct or minimize the misuse or misrepresentation.

### 1.17 Multiple Relationships

(a) In many communities and situations, it may not be feasible or reasonable for psychologists to avoid social or other nonprofessional contacts with persons such as patients, clients, students, supervisees, or research participants. Psychologists must always be sensitive to the potential harmful effects of other contacts on their work and on those persons with whom they deal. A psychologist refrains from entering into or promising another personal, scientific, professional, financial, or other relationship with such persons if it appears likely that such a relationship reasonably might impair the psychologist's objectivity or otherwise interfere with the psychologist's effectively performing his or her functions as a psychologist, or might harm or exploit the other party.

(b) Likewise, whenever feasible, a psychologist refrains from taking on professional or scientific obligations when preexisting relationships would create a risk of such harm.

(c) If a psychologist finds that, due to unforeseen factors, a potentially harmful multiple relationship has arisen, the psychologist attempts to resolve it with due regard for the best interests of the affected person and maximal compliance with the Ethics Code.

### 1.18 Barter (With Patients or Clients)

Psychologists ordinarily refrain from accepting goods, services, or other nonmonetary remuneration from patients or clients in return for psychological services because such arrangements create inherent potential for conflicts, exploitation, and distortion of the professional relationship. A psychologist may participate in bartering *only* if (1) it is not clinically contraindicated, *and* (2) the relationship is not exploitative.

(See also Standards 1.17, Multiple Relationships, and 1.25, Fees and Financial Arrangements.)

### 1.19 Exploitative Relationships

(a) Psychologists do not exploit persons over whom they have supervisory, evaluative, or other authority such as students, supervisees, employees, research participants, and clients or patients. (See also Standards 4.05-4.07 regarding sexual involvement with clients or patients.)

(b) Psychologists do not engage in sexual relationships with students or supervisees in training over whom the psychologist has evaluative or direct authority, because such relationships are so likely to impair judgment or be exploitative.

### 1.20 Consultations and Referrals

(a) Psychologists arrange for appropriate consultations and referrals based principally on the best interests of their patients or clients, with appropriate consent, and subject to other relevant considerations, including applicable law and contractual obligations. (See also Standards 5.01, Discussing the Limits of Confidentiality, and 5.06, Consultations.)

(b) When indicated and professionally appropriate, psychologists cooperate with other professionals in order to serve their patients or clients effectively and appropriately.

(c) Psychologists' referral practices are consistent with law.

### 1.21 Third-Party Requests for Services

(a) When a psychologist agrees to provide services to a person or entity at the request of a third party, the psychologist clarifies to the extent feasible, at the outset of the service, the nature of the relationship with each party. This clarification includes the role of the psychologist (such as therapist, organizational consultant, diagnostician, or expert witness), the probable uses of the services provided or the information obtained, and the fact that there may be limits to confidentiality.

(b) If there is a foreseeable risk of the psychologist's being called upon to perform conflicting roles because of the involvement of a third party, the psychologist clarifies the nature and direction of his or her responsibilities, keeps all parties appropriately informed as matters develop, and resolves the situation in accordance with this Ethics Code.

## 1.22 Delegation to and Supervision of Subordinates

(a) Psychologists delegate to their employees, supervisees, and research assistants only those responsibilities that such persons can reasonably be expected to perform competently, on the basis of their education, training, or experience, either independently or with the level of supervision being provided.

(b) Psychologists provide proper training and supervision to their employees or supervisees and take reasonable steps to see that such persons perform services responsibly, competently, and ethically.

(c) If institutional policies, procedures, or practices prevent fulfillment of this obligation, psychologists attempt to modify their role or to correct the situation to the extent feasible.

## 1.23 Documentation of Professional and Scientific Work

(a) Psychologists appropriately document their professional and scientific work in order to facilitate provision of services later by them or by other professionals, to ensure accountability, and to meet other requirements of institutions or the law.

(b) When psychologists have reason to believe that records of their professional services will be used in legal proceedings involving recipients of or participants in their work, they have a responsibility to create and maintain documentation in the kind of detail and quality that would be consistent with reasonable scrutiny in an adjudicative forum. (See also Standard 7.01, Professionalism, under Forensic Activities.)

## 1.24 Records and Data

Psychologists create, maintain, disseminate, store, retain, and dispose of records and data relating to their research, practice, and other work in accordance with law and in a manner that permits compliance with the requirements of this Ethics Code. (See also Standard 5.04, Maintenance of Records.)

## 1.25 Fees and Financial Arrangements

(a) As early as is feasible in a professional or scientific relationship, the psychologist and the patient, client, or other appropriate recipient of psychological services reach an agreement specifying the compensation and the billing arrangements.

(b) Psychologists do not exploit recipients of services or payors with respect to fees.

(c) Psychologists' fee practices are consistent with law.

(d) Psychologists do not misrepresent their fees.

(e) If limitations to services can be anticipated because of limitations in financing, this is discussed with the patient, client, or other appropriate recipient of services as early as is feasible. (See also Standard 4.08, Interruption of Services.)

(f) If the patient, client, or other recipient of services does not pay for services as agreed, and if the psychologist wishes to use collection agencies or legal measures to collect the fees, the psychologist first informs the person that such measures will be taken and provides that person an opportunity to make prompt payment. (See also Standard 5.11, Withholding Records for Nonpayment.)

## 1.26 Accuracy in Reports to Payors and Funding Sources

In their reports to payors for services or sources of research funding, psychologists accurately state the nature of the research or service provided, the fees or charges, and where applicable, the identity of the provider, the findings, and the diagnosis. (See also Standard 5.05, Disclosures.)

## 1.27 Referrals and Fees

When a psychologist pays, receives payment from, or divides fees with another professional other than in an employer-employee relationship, the payment to each is based on the services (clinical, consultative, administrative, or other) provided and is not based on the referral itself.

## 2. Evaluation, Assessment, or Intervention

## 2.01 Evaluation, Diagnosis, and Interventions in Professional Context

(a) Psychologists perform evaluations, diagnostic services, or interventions only within the context of a defined professional relationship. (See also Standard 1.03, Professional and Scientific Relationship.)

(b) Psychologists' assessments, recommendations, reports, and psychological diagnostic or evaluative statements are based on information and techniques (including personal interviews of the individual when appropriate) sufficient to provide appropriate substantiation for their findings. (See also Standard 7.02, Forensic Assessments.)

### 2.02 Competence and Appropriate Use of Assessments and Interventions

(a) Psychologists who develop, administer, score, interpret, or use psychological assessment techniques, interviews, tests, or instruments do so in a manner and for purposes that are appropriate in light of the research on or evidence of the usefulness and proper application of the techniques.

(b) Psychologists refrain from misuse of assessment techniques, interventions, results, and interpretations and take reasonable steps to prevent others from misusing the information these techniques provide. This includes refraining from releasing raw test results or raw data to persons, other than to patients or clients as appropriate, who are not qualified to use such information. (See also Standards 1.02, Relationship of Ethics and Law, and 1.04, Boundaries of Competence.)

### 2.03 Test Construction

Psychologists who develop and conduct research with tests and other assessment techniques use scientific procedures and current professional knowledge for test design, standardization, validation, reduction or elimination of bias, and recommendations for use.

### 2.04 Use of Assessment in General and With Special Populations

(a) Psychologists who perform interventions or administer, score, interpret, or use assessment techniques are familiar with the reliability, validation, and related standardization or outcome studies of, and proper applications and uses of, the techniques they use.

(b) Psychologists recognize limits to the certainty with which diagnoses, judgments, or predictions can be made about individuals.

(c) Psychologists attempt to identify situations in which particular interventions or assessment techniques or norms may not be applicable or may require adjustment in administration or interpretation because of factors such as individuals' gender, age, race, ethnicity, national origin, religion, sexual orientation, disability, language, or socioeconomic status.

### 2.05 Interpreting Assessment Results

When interpreting assessment results, including automated interpretations, psychologists take into account the various test factors and characteristics of the person being assessed that might affect psychologists' judgments or reduce the accuracy of their interpretations. They indicate any significant reservations they have about the accuracy or limitations of their interpretations.

### 2.06 Unqualified Persons

Psychologists do not promote the use of psychological assessment techniques by unqualified persons. (See also Standard 1.22, Delegation to and Supervision of Subordinates.)

### 2.07 Obsolete Tests and Outdated Test Results

(a) Psychologists do not base their assessment or intervention decisions or recommendations on data or test results that are outdated for the current purpose.

(b) Similarly, psychologists do not base such decisions or recommendations on tests and measures that are obsolete and not useful for the current purpose.

### 2.08 Test Scoring and Interpretation Services

(a) Psychologists who offer assessment or scoring procedures to other professionals accurately describe the purpose, norms, validity, reliability, and applications of the procedures and any special qualifications applicable to their use.

(b) Psychologists select scoring and interpretation services (including automated services) on the basis of evidence of the validity of the program and procedures as well as on other appropriate considerations.

(c) Psychologists retain appropriate responsibility for the appropriate application, interpretation, and use of assessment instruments, whether they score and interpret such tests themselves or use automated or other services.

## 2.09 Explaining Assessment Results

Unless the nature of the relationship is clearly explained to the person being assessed in advance and precludes provision of an explanation of results (such as in some organizational consulting, preemployment or security screenings, and forensic evaluations), psychologists ensure that an explanation of the results is provided using language that is reasonably understandable to the person assessed or to another legally authorized person on behalf of the client. Regardless of whether the scoring and interpretation are done by the psychologist, by assistants, or by automated or other outside services, psychologists take reasonable steps to ensure that appropriate explanations of results are given.

## 2.10 Maintaining Test Security

Psychologists make reasonable efforts to maintain the integrity and security of tests and other assessment techniques consistent with law, contractual obligations, and in a manner that permits compliance with the requirements of this Ethics Code. (See also Standard 1.02, Relationship of Ethics and Law.)

## 3.    Advertising and Other Public Statements

## 3.01 Definition of Public Statements

Psychologists comply with this Ethics Code in public statements relating to their professional services, products, or publications or to the field of psychology. Public statements include but are not limited to paid or unpaid advertising, brochures, printed matter, directory listings, personal resumes or curricula vitae, interviews or comments for use in media, statements in legal proceedings, lectures and public oral presentations, and published materials.

## 3.02 Statements by Others

(a) Psychologists who engage others to create or place public statements that promote their professional practice, products, or activities retain professional responsibility for such statements.

(b) In addition, psychologists make reasonable efforts to prevent others whom they do not control (such as employers, publishers, sponsors, organizational clients, and representatives of the print or broadcast media) from making deceptive statements concerning psychologists' practice or professional or scientific activities.

(c) If psychologists learn of deceptive statements about their work made by others, psychologists make reasonable efforts to correct such statements.

(d) Psychologists do not compensate employees of press, radio, television, or other communication media in return for publicity in a news item.

(e) A paid advertisement relating to the psychologist's activities must be identified as such, unless it is already apparent from the context.

## 3.03 Avoidance of False or Deceptive Statements

(a) Psychologists do not make public statements that are false, deceptive, misleading, or fraudulent, either because of what they state, convey, or suggest or because of what they omit, concerning their research, practice, or other work activities or those of persons or organizations with which they are affiliated. As examples (and not in limitation) of this standard, psychologists do not make false or deceptive statements concerning (1) their training, experience, or competence; (2) their academic degrees; (3) their credentials; (4) their institutional or association affiliations; (5) their services; (6) the scientific or clinical basis for, or results or degree of success of, their services; (7) their fees; or (8) their publications or research findings. (See also Standards 6.15, Deception in Research, and 6.18, Providing Participants With Information About the Study.)

(b) Psychologists claim as credentials for their psychological work, only degrees that (1) were earned from a regionally accredited educational institution or (2) were the basis for psychology licensure by the state in which they practice.

## 3.04 Media Presentations

When psychologists provide advice or comment by means of public lectures, demonstrations, radio or television programs, prerecorded tapes, printed articles, mailed material, or other media, they take reasonable precautions to ensure that (1) the statements are based on appropriate psychological literature and practice, (2) the statements are otherwise consistent with this Ethics Code, and (3) the recipients of the information are not encouraged to infer that a relationship has been established with them personally.

### 3.05 Testimonials

Psychologists do not solicit testimonials from current psychotherapy clients or patients or other persons who because of their particular circumstances are vulnerable to undue influence.

### 3.06 In-Person Solicitation

Psychologists do not engage, directly or through agents, in uninvited in-person solicitation of business from actual or potential psychotherapy patients or clients or other persons who because of their particular circumstances are vulnerable to undue influence. However, this does not preclude attempting to implement appropriate collateral contacts with significant others for the purpose of benefiting an already engaged therapy patient.

### 4.    *Therapy*

### 4.01 Structuring the Relationship

(a) Psychologists discuss with clients or patients as early as is feasible in the therapeutic relationship appropriate issues, such as the nature and anticipated course of therapy, fees, and confidentiality. (See also Standards 1.25, Fees and Financial Arrangements, and 5.01, Discussing the Limits of Confidentiality.)

(b) When the psychologist's work with clients or patients will be supervised, the above discussion includes that fact, and the name of the supervisor, when the supervisor has legal responsibility for the case.

(c) When the therapist is a student intern, the client or patient is informed of that fact.

(d) Psychologists make reasonable efforts to answer patients' questions and to avoid apparent misunderstandings about therapy. Whenever possible, psychologists provide oral and/or written information, using language that is reasonably understandable to the patient or client.

### 4.02 Informed Consent to Therapy

(a) Psychologists obtain appropriate informed consent to therapy or related procedures, using language that is reasonably understandable to participants. The content of informed consent will vary depending on many circumstances; however, informed consent generally implies that the person (1) has the capacity to consent, (2) has been informed of significant information concerning the procedure, (3) has freely and without undue influence expressed consent, and (4) consent has been appropriately documented.

(b) When persons are legally incapable of giving informed consent, psychologists obtain informed permission from a legally authorized person, if such substitute consent is permitted by law.

(c) In addition, psychologists (1) inform those persons who are legally incapable of giving informed consent about the proposed interventions in a manner commensurate with the persons' psychological capacities, (2) seek their assent to those interventions, and (3) consider such persons' preferences and best interests.

### 4.03 Couple and Family Relationships

(a) When a psychologist agrees to provide services to several persons who have a relationship (such as husband and wife or parents and children), the psychologist attempts to clarify at the outset (1) which of the individuals are patients or clients and (2) the relationship the psychologist will have with each person. This clarification includes the role of the psychologist and the probable uses of the services provided or the information obtained. (See also Standard 5.01, Discussing the Limits of Confidentiality.)

(b) As soon as it becomes apparent that the psychologist may be called on to perform potentially conflicting roles (such as marital counselor to husband and wife, and then witness for one party in a divorce proceeding), the psychologist attempts to clarify and adjust, or withdraw from, roles appropriately. (See also Standard 7.03, Clarification of Role, under Forensic Activities.)

### 4.04 Providing Mental Health Services to Those Served by Others

In deciding whether to offer or provide services to those already receiving mental health services elsewhere, psychologists carefully consider the treatment issues and the potential patient's or client's welfare. The psychologist discusses these issues with the patient or client, or another legally authorized person on behalf of the client, in order to minimize the risk of confusion and conflict, consults with the other service providers when appropriate, and proceeds with caution and sensitivity to the therapeutic issues.

### 4.05 Sexual Intimacies With Current Patients or Clients

Psychologists do not engage in sexual intimacies with current patients or clients.

### 4.06 Therapy With Former Sexual Partners

Psychologists do not accept as therapy patients or clients persons with whom they have engaged in sexual intimacies.

### 4.07 Sexual Intimacies With Former Therapy Patients

(a) Psychologists do not engage in sexual intimacies with a former therapy patient or client for at least two years after cessation or termination of professional services.

(b) Because sexual intimacies with a former therapy patient or client are so frequently harmful to the patient or client, and because such intimacies undermine public confidence in the psychology profession and thereby deter the public's use of needed services, psychologists do not engage in sexual intimacies with former therapy patients and clients even after a two-year interval except in the most unusual circumstances. The psychologist who engages in such activity after the two years following cessation or termination of treatment bears the burden of demonstrating that there has been no exploitation, in light of all relevant factors, including (1) the amount of time that has passed since therapy terminated, (2) the nature and duration of the therapy, (3) the circumstances of termination, (4) the patient's or client's personal history, (5) the patient's or client's current mental status, (6) the likelihood of adverse impact on the patient or client and others, and (7) any statements or actions made by the therapist during the course of therapy suggesting or inviting the possibility of a posttermination sexual or romantic relationship with the patient or client. (See also Standard 1.17, Multiple Relationships.)

### 4.08 Interruption of Services

(a) Psychologists make reasonable efforts to plan for facilitating care in the event that psychological services are interrupted by factors such as the psychologist's illness, death, unavailability, or relocation or by the client's

relocation or financial limitations. (See also Standard 5.09, Preserving Records and Data.)

(b) When entering into employment or contractual relationships, psychologists provide for orderly and appropriate resolution of responsibility for patient or client care in the event that the employment or contractual relationship ends, with paramount consideration given to the welfare of the patient or client.

### 4.09 Terminating the Professional Relationship

(a) Psychologists do not abandon patients or clients. (See also Standard 1.25e, under Fees and Financial Arrangements.)

(b) Psychologists terminate a professional relationship when it becomes reasonably clear that the patient or client no longer needs the service, is not benefiting, or is being harmed by continued service.

(c) Prior to termination for whatever reason, except where precluded by the patient's or client's conduct, the psychologist discusses the patient's or client's views and needs, provides appropriate pretermination counseling, suggests alternative service providers as appropriate, and takes other reasonable steps to facilitate transfer of responsibility to another provider if the patient or client needs one immediately.

### 5.    Privacy and Confidentiality

These Standards are potentially applicable to the professional and scientific activities of all psychologists.

### 5.01 Discussing the Limits of Confidentiality

(a) Psychologists discuss with persons and organizations with whom they establish a scientific or professional relationship (including, to the extent feasible, minors and their legal representatives) (1) the relevant limitations on confidentiality, including limitations where applicable in group, marital, and family therapy or in organizational consulting, and (2) the foreseeable uses of the information generated through their services.

(b) Unless it is not feasible or is contraindicated, the discussion of confidentiality occurs at the outset of the relationship and thereafter as new circumstances may warrant.

(c) Permission for electronic recording of interviews is secured from clients and patients.

## 5.02 Maintaining Confidentiality

Psychologists have a primary obligation and take reasonable precautions to respect the confidentiality rights of those with whom they work or consult, recognizing that confidentiality may be established by law, institutional rules, or professional or scientific relationships. (See also Standard 6.26, Professional Reviewers.)

## 5.03 Minimizing Intrusions on Privacy

(a) In order to minimize intrusions on privacy, psychologists include in written and oral reports, consultations, and the like, only information germane to the purpose for which the communication is made.

(b) Psychologists discuss confidential information obtained in clinical or consulting relationships, or evaluative data concerning patients, individual or organizational clients, students, research participants, supervisees, and employees, only for appropriate scientific or professional purposes and only with persons clearly concerned with such matters.

## 5.04 Maintenance of Records

Psychologists maintain appropriate confidentiality in creating, storing, accessing, transferring, and disposing of records under their control, whether these are written, automated, or in any other medium. Psychologists maintain and dispose of records in accordance with law and in a manner that permits compliance with the requirements of this Ethics Code.

## 5.05 Disclosures

(a) Psychologists disclose confidential information without the consent of the individual only as mandated by law, or where permitted by law for a valid purpose, such as (1) to provide needed professional services to the patient or the individual or organizational client, (2) to obtain appropriate professional consultations, (3) to protect the patient or client or others from harm, or (4) to obtain payment for services, in which instance disclosure is limited to the minimum that is necessary to achieve the purpose.

(b) Psychologists also may disclose confidential information with the appropriate consent of the patient or the individual or organizational client (or of another legally authorized person on behalf of the patient or client), unless prohibited by law.

## 5.06 Consultations

When consulting with colleagues, (1) psychologists do not share confidential information that reasonably could lead to the identification of a patient, client, research participant, or other person or organization with whom they have a confidential relationship unless they have obtained the prior consent of the person or organization or the disclosure cannot be avoided, and (2) they share information only to the extent necessary to achieve the purposes of the consultation. (See also Standard 5.02, Maintaining Confidentiality.)

## 5.07 Confidential Information in Databases

(a) If confidential information concerning recipients of psychological services is to be entered into databases or systems of records available to persons whose access has not been consented to by the recipient, then psychologists use coding or other techniques to avoid the inclusion of personal identifiers.

(b) If a research protocol approved by an institutional review board or similar body requires the inclusion of personal identifiers, such identifiers are deleted before the information is made accessible to persons other than those of whom the subject was advised.

(c) If such deletion is not feasible, then before psychologists transfer such data to others or review such data collected by others, they take reasonable steps to determine that appropriate consent of personally identifiable individuals has been obtained.

## 5.08 Use of Confidential Information for Didactic or Other Purposes

(a) Psychologists do not disclose in their writings, lectures, or other public media, confidential, personally identifiable information concerning their patients, individual or organizational clients, students, research participants, or other recipients of their services that they obtained during the course of their work, unless the person or organization has consented in writing or unless there is other ethical or legal authorization for doing so.

(b) Ordinarily, in such scientific and professional presentations, psychologists disguise confidential information concerning such persons or organizations so that they are not individually identifiable to others and so that discussions do not cause harm to subjects who might identify themselves.

### 5.09 Preserving Records and Data

A psychologist makes plans in advance so that confidentiality of records and data is protected in the event of the psychologist's death, incapacity, or withdrawal from the position or practice.

### 5.10 Ownership of Records and Data

Recognizing that ownership of records and data is governed by legal principles, psychologists take reasonable and lawful steps so that records and data remain available to the extent needed to serve the best interests of patients, individual or organizational clients, research participants, or appropriate others.

### 5.11 Withholding Records for Nonpayment

Psychologists may not withhold records under their control that are requested and imminently needed for a patient's or client's treatment solely because payment has not been received, except as otherwise provided by law.

### 6.　Teaching, Training Supervision, Research, and Publishing

### 6.01 Design of Education and Training Programs

Psychologists who are responsible for education and training programs seek to ensure that the programs are competently designed, provide the proper experiences, and meet the requirements for licensure, certification, or other goals for which claims are made by the program.

### 6.02 Descriptions of Education and Training Programs

(a) Psychologists responsible for education and training programs seek to ensure that there is a current and accurate description of the program content, training goals and objectives, and requirements that must be met for satisfactory completion of the program. This information must be made readily available to all interested parties.

(b) Psychologists seek to ensure that statements concerning their course outlines are accurate and not misleading, particularly regarding the subject matter to be covered, bases for evaluating progress, and the nature of course experiences. (See also Standard 3.03, Avoidance of False or Deceptive Statements.)

(c) To the degree to which they exercise control, psychologists responsible for announcements, catalogs, brochures, or advertisements describing workshops, seminars, or other non-degree-granting educational programs ensure that they accurately describe the audience for which the program is intended, the educational objectives, the presenters, and the fees involved.

### 6.03 Accuracy and Objectivity in Teaching

(a) When engaged in teaching or training, psychologists present psychological information accurately and with a reasonable degree of objectivity.

(b) When engaged in teaching or training, psychologists recognize the power they hold over students or supervisees and therefore make reasonable efforts to avoid engaging in conduct that is personally demeaning to students or supervisees. (See also Standards 1.09, Respecting Others, and 1.12, Other Harassment.)

### 6.04 Limitation on Teaching

Psychologists do not teach the use of techniques or procedures that require specialized training, licensure, or expertise, including but not limited to hypnosis, biofeedback, and projective techniques, to individuals who lack the prerequisite training, legal scope of practice, or expertise.

### 6.05 Assessing Student and Supervisee Performance

(a) In academic and supervisory relationships, psychologists establish an appropriate process for providing feedback to students and supervisees.

(b) Psychologists evaluate students and supervisees on the basis of their actual performance on relevant and established program requirements.

### 6.06 Planning Research

(a) Psychologists design, conduct, and report research in accordance with recognized standards of scientific competence and ethical research.

(b) Psychologists plan their research so as to minimize the possibility that results will be misleading.

(c) In planning research, psychologists consider its ethical acceptability under the Ethics Code. If an ethical issue is unclear, psychologists seek to resolve the issue through consultation with institutional review boards, animal care and use committees, peer consultations, or other proper mechanisms.

(d) Psychologists take reasonable steps to implement appropriate protections for the rights and welfare of human participants, other persons affected by the research, and the welfare of animal subjects.

## 6.07 Responsibility

(a) Psychologists conduct research competently and with due concern for the dignity and welfare of the participants.

(b) Psychologists are responsible for the ethical conduct of research conducted by them or by others under their supervision or control.

(c) Researchers and assistants are permitted to perform only those tasks for which they are appropriately trained and prepared.

(d) As part of the process of development and implementation of research projects, psychologists consult those with expertise concerning any special population under investigation or most likely to be affected.

## 6.08 Compliance With Law and Standards

Psychologists plan and conduct research in a manner consistent with federal and state law and regulations, as well as professional standards governing the conduct of research, and particularly those standards governing research with human participants and animal subjects.

## 6.09 Institutional Approval

Psychologists obtain from host institutions or organizations appropriate approval prior to conducting research, and they provide accurate information about their research proposals. They conduct the research in accordance with the approved research protocol.

## 6.10 Research Responsibilities

Prior to conducting research (except research involving only anonymous surveys, naturalistic observations, or similar research), psychologists enter into an agreement with participants that clarifies the nature of the research and the responsibilities of each party.

## 6.11 Informed Consent to Research

(a) Psychologists use language that is reasonably understandable to research participants in obtaining their appropriate informed consent (except as provided in Standard 6.12, Dispensing With Informed Consent). Such informed consent is appropriately documented.

(b) Using language that is reasonably understandable to participants, psychologists inform participants of the nature of the research; they inform participants that they are free to participate or to decline to participate or to withdraw from the research; they explain the foreseeable consequences of declining or withdrawing; they inform participants of significant factors that may be expected to influence their willingness to participate (such as risks, discomfort, adverse effects, or limitations on confidentiality, except as provided in Standard 6.15, Deception in Research); and they explain other aspects about which the prospective participants inquire.

(c) When psychologists conduct research with individuals such as students or subordinates, psychologists take special care to protect the prospective participants from adverse consequences of declining or withdrawing from participation.

(d) When research participation is a course requirement or opportunity for extra credit, the prospective participant is given the choice of equitable alternative activities.

(e) For persons who are legally incapable of giving informed consent, psychologists nevertheless (1) provide an appropriate explanation, (2) obtain the participant's assent, and (3) obtain appropriate permission from a legally authorized person, if such substitute consent is permitted by law.

## 6.12 Dispensing With Informed Consent

Before determining that planned research (such as research involving only anonymous questionnaires, naturalistic observations, or certain kinds of archival research) does not require the informed consent of research participants, psychologists consider applicable regulations and institutional review board requirements, and they consult with colleagues as appropriate.

### 6.13 Informed Consent in Research Filming or Recording

Psychologists obtain informed consent from research participants prior to filming or recording them in any form, unless the research involves simply naturalistic observations in public places and it is not anticipated that the recording will be used in a manner that could cause personal identification or harm.

### 6.14 Offering Inducements for Research Participants

(a) In offering professional services as an inducement to obtain research participants, psychologists make clear the nature of the services, as well as the risks, obligations, and limitations. (See also Standard 1.18, Barter [With Patients or Clients].)

(b) Psychologists do not offer excessive or inappropriate financial or other inducements to obtain research participants, particularly when it might tend to coerce participation.

### 6.15 Deception in Research

(a) Psychologists do not conduct a study involving deception unless they have determined that the use of deceptive techniques is justified by the study's prospective scientific, educational, or applied value and that equally effective alternative procedures that do not use deception are not feasible.

(b) Psychologists never deceive research participants about significant aspects that would affect their willingness to participate, such as physical risks, discomfort, or unpleasant emotional experiences.

(c) Any other deception that is an integral feature of the design and conduct of an experiment must be explained to participants as early as is feasible, preferably at the conclusion of their participation, but no later than at the conclusion of the research. (See also Standard 6.18, Providing Participants With Information About the Study.)

### 6.16 Sharing and Utilizing Data

Psychologists inform research participants of their anticipated sharing or further use of personally identifiable research data and of the possibility of unanticipated future uses.

### 6.17 Minimizing Invasiveness

In conducting research, psychologists interfere with the participants or milieu from which data are collected only in a manner that is warranted by an appropriate research design and that is consistent with psychologists' roles as scientific investigators.

### 6.18 Providing Participants With Information About the Study

(a) Psychologists provide a prompt opportunity for participants to obtain appropriate information about the nature, results, and conclusions of the research, and psychologists attempt to correct any misconceptions that participants may have.

(b) If scientific or humane values justify delaying or withholding this information, psychologists take reasonable measures to reduce the risk of harm.

### 6.19 Honoring Commitments

Psychologists take reasonable measures to honor all commitments they have made to research participants.

### 6.20 Care and Use of Animals in Research

(a) Psychologists who conduct research involving animals treat them humanely.

(b) Psychologists acquire, care for, use, and dispose of animals in compliance with current federal, state, and local laws and regulations, and with professional standards.

(c) Psychologists trained in research methods and experienced in the care of laboratory animals supervise all procedures involving animals and are responsible for ensuring appropriate consideration of their comfort, health, and humane treatment.

(d) Psychologists ensure that all individuals using animals under their supervision have received instruction in research methods and in the care, maintenance, and handling of the species being used, to the extent appropriate to their role.

(e) Responsibilities and activities of individuals assisting in a research project are consistent with their respective competencies.

(f) Psychologists make reasonable efforts to minimize the discomfort, infection, illness, and pain of animal subjects.

(g) A procedure subjecting animals to pain, stress, or privation is used only when an alternative procedure is unavailable and the goal is justified by its prospective scientific, educational, or applied value.

(h) Surgical procedures are performed under appropriate anesthesia; techniques to avoid infection and minimize pain are followed during and after surgery.

(i) When it is appropriate that the animal's life be terminated, it is done rapidly, with an effort to minimize pain, and in accordance with accepted procedures.

### 6.21 Reporting of Results

(a) Psychologists do not fabricate data or falsify results in their publications.

(b) If psychologists discover significant errors in their published data, they take reasonable steps to correct such errors in a correction, retraction, erratum, or other appropriate publication means.

### 6.22 Plagiarism

Psychologists do not present substantial portions or elements of another's work or data as their own, even if the other work or data source is cited occasionally.

### 6.23 Publication Credit

(a) Psychologists take responsibility and credit, including authorship credit, only for work they have actually performed or to which they have contributed.

(b) Principal authorship and other publication credits accurately reflect the relative scientific or professional contributions of the individuals involved, regardless of their relative status. Mere possession of an institutional position, such as Department Chair, does not justify authorship credit. Minor contributions to the research or to the writing for publications are appropriately acknowledged, such as in footnotes or in an introductory statement.

(c) A student is usually listed as principal author on any multiple-authored article that is substantially based on the student's dissertation or thesis.

### 6.24 Duplicate Publication of Data

Psychologists do not publish, as original data, data that have been previously published. This does not preclude republishing data when they are accompanied by proper acknowledgment.

### 6.25 Sharing Data

After research results are published, psychologists do not withhold the data on which their conclusions are based from other competent professionals who seek to verify the substantive claims through reanalysis and who intend to use such data only for that purpose, provided that the confidentiality of the participants can be protected and unless legal rights concerning proprietary data preclude their release.

### 6.26 Professional Reviewers

Psychologists who review material submitted for publication, grant, or other research proposal review respect the confidentiality of and the proprietary rights in such information of those who submitted it.

## 7.   Forensic Activities

### 7.01 Professionalism

Psychologists who perform forensic functions, such as assessments, interviews, consultations, reports, or expert testimony, must comply with all other provisions of this Ethics Code to the extent that they apply to such activities. In addition, psychologists base their forensic work on appropriate knowledge of and competence in the areas underlying such work, including specialized knowledge concerning special populations. (See also Standards 1.06, Basis for Scientific and Professional Judgments; 1.08, Human Differences; 1.15, Misuse of Psychologists' Influence; and 1.23, Documentation of Professional and Scientific Work.)

### 7.02 Forensic Assessments

(a) Psychologists' forensic assessments, recommendations, and reports are based on information and techniques (including personal interviews of the individual, when appropriate) sufficient to provide appropriate substantiation for their findings. (See also Standards 1.03, Professional and Scientific Relationship; 1.23, Documentation of Professional and Scientific Work; 2.01, Evaluation, Diagnosis, and Interventions in Professional Context; and 2.05, Interpreting Assessment Results.)

(b) Except as noted in (c), below, psychologists provide written or oral forensic reports or testimony of the psychological characteristics of an individual only after they have conducted an examination of the individual adequate to support their statements or conclusions.

(c) When, despite reasonable efforts, such an examination is not feasible, psychologists clarify the impact of their limited information on the reliability and validity of their reports and testimony, and they appropriately limit the nature and extent of their conclusions or recommendations.

### 7.03 Clarification of Role

In most circumstances, psychologists avoid performing multiple and potentially conflicting roles in forensic matters. When psychologists may be called on to serve in more than one role in a legal proceeding–for example, as consultant or expert for one party or for the court and as a fact witness–they clarify role expectations and the extent of confidentiality in advance to the extent feasible, and thereafter as changes occur, in order to avoid compromising their professional judgment and objectivity and in order to avoid misleading others regarding their role.

### 7.04 Truthfulness and Candor

(a) In forensic testimony and reports, psychologists testify truthfully, honestly, and candidly and, consistent with applicable legal procedures, describe fairly the bases for their testimony and conclusions.

(b) Whenever necessary to avoid misleading, psychologists acknowledge the limits of their data or conclusions.

### 7.05 Prior Relationships

A prior professional relationship with a party does not preclude psychologists from testifying as fact witnesses or from testifying to their services to the extent permitted by applicable law. Psychologists appropriately take into account ways in which the prior relationship might affect their professional objectivity or opinions and disclose the potential conflict to the relevant parties.

### 7.06 Compliance With Law and Rules

In performing forensic roles, psychologists are reasonably familiar with the rules governing

their roles. Psychologists are aware of the occasionally competing demands placed upon them by these principles and the requirements of the court system, and attempt to resolve these conflicts by making known their commitment to this Ethics Code and taking steps to resolve the conflict in a responsible manner. (See also Standard 1.02, Relationship of Ethics and Law.)

## 8.   *Resolving Ethical Issues*

### 8.01 Familiarity With Ethics Code

Psychologists have an obligation to be familiar with this Ethics Code, other applicable ethics codes, and their application to psychologists' work. Lack of awareness or misunderstanding of an ethical standard is not itself a defense to a charge of unethical conduct.

### 8.02 Confronting Ethical Issues

When a psychologist is uncertain whether a particular situation or course of action would violate this Ethics Code, the psychologist ordinarily consults with other psychologists knowledgeable about ethical issues, with state or national psychology ethics committees, or with other appropriate authorities in order to choose a proper response.

### 8.03 Conflicts Between Ethics and Organizational Demands

If the demands of an organization with which psychologists are affiliated conflict with this Ethics Code, psychologists clarify the nature of the conflict, make known their commitment to the Ethics Code, and to the extent feasible, seek to resolve the conflict in a way that permits the fullest adherence to the Ethics Code.

### 8.04 Informal Resolution of Ethical Violations

When psychologists believe that there may have been an ethical violation by another psychologist, they attempt to resolve the issue by bringing it to the attention of that individual if an informal resolution appears appropriate and the intervention does not violate any confidentiality rights that may be involved.

### 8.05 Reporting Ethical Violations

If an apparent ethical violation is not appropriate for informal resolution under Standard 8.04 or is not resolved properly in that fashion, psychologists take further action appropriate to the situation, unless such action conflicts with confidentiality rights in ways that cannot be resolved. Such action might include referral to state or national committees on professional ethics or to state licensing boards.

## 8.06 Cooperating With Ethics Committees

Psychologists cooperate in ethics investigations, proceedings, and resulting requirements of the APA or any affiliated state psychological association to which they belong. In doing so, they make reasonable efforts to resolve any issues as to confidentiality. Failure to cooperate is itself an ethics violation.

## 8.07 Improper Complaints

Psychologists do not file or encourage the filing of ethics complaints that are frivolous and are intended to harm the respondent rather than to protect the public.

# Appendix B

**AMERICAN
COUNSELING
ASSOCIATION**

# Code of Ethics
# and Standards
# of Practice*

**As Approved by Governing Council
April 1997
Effective July 1, 1997**

## PREAMBLE

The American Counseling Association is an educational, scientific and professional organization whose members are dedicated to the enhancement of human development throughout the life span. Association members recognize diversity in our society and embrace a cross-cultural approach in support of the worth, dignity, potential, and uniqueness of each individual.

The specification of a code of ethics enables the association to clarify to current and future members, and to those served by members, the nature of the ethical responsibilities held in common by its members. As the code of ethics of the association, this document establishes principles that define the ethical behavior of association members. All members of the American Counseling Association are required to adhere to the Code of Ethics and the Standards of Practice. The Code of Ethics will serve as the basis for processing ethical complaints initiated against members of the association.

---

## SECTION A:
## THE COUNSELING RELATIONSHIP

### A.1. CLIENT WELFARE

*a. Primary Responsibility.*

The primary responsibility of counselors is to respect the dignity and to promote the welfare of clients.

*b. Positive Growth and Development.*

Counselors encourage client growth and development in ways that foster the clients' interest and welfare; counselors avoid fostering dependent counseling relationships.

*c. Counseling Plans.*

Counselors and their clients work jointly in devising integrated, individual counseling plans that offer reasonable promise of success and are consistent with abilities and circumstances of clients. Counselors and clients regularly review counseling plans to ensure their continued viability and effectiveness respecting clients' freedom of choice. (See A.3.b.)

*d. Family Involvement.*

Counselors recognize that families are usually important in clients' lives and strive to enlist family understanding and involvement as a positive resource when appropriate.

*e. Career and Employment Needs.*

Counselors work with their clients in considering employment in jobs and circumstances that are consistent with the clients' overall abilities, vocational limitations, physical restrictions, general temperament, interest and aptitude patterns, social skills, education, general qualifications, and other relevant characteristics and needs. Counselors neither place nor participate in placing clients in positions that will result in damaging the interest and the welfare of clients, employers, or the public.

### A.2. Respecting Diversity

*a. Nondiscrimination.*

Counselors do not condone or engage in discrimination based on age, color, culture, disability, ethnic group, gender, race, religion, sexual orientation, marital status, or socioeconomic status. (See C.5.a., C.5.b., and D.1.i.)

*b. Respecting Differences.*

Counselors will actively attempt to understand the diverse cultural background of the clients with whom they work. This includes, but is not limited to, learning how the counselor's own cultural/ethnic/racial identity impacts her/his values and beliefs about the counseling process. (See E.8. and F.2.i.)

### A.3. CLIENT RIGHTS

*a. Disclosure to Clients.*

When counseling is initiated, and throughout the counseling process as necessary, counselors inform clients of the purposes, goals, techniques, procedures, limitations, potential risks and benefits of services to be performed, and other pertinent information. Counselors take steps to ensure that clients understand the implications of diagnosis, the intended use of tests and reports, fees, and billing arrangements. Clients have the right to expect confidentiality and to be provided with an explanation of its limitations, including supervision and/or treatment team professionals; to obtain clear information about their case records; to participate in the ongoing counseling plans; and to refuse any recommended services and be advised of the consequences of such refusal. (See E.5.a. and G.2.)

*b. Freedom of Choice.*

Counselors offer clients the freedom to choose whether to enter into a counseling relationship and to determine which professional(s) will provide counseling. Restrictions that limit choices of clients are fully explained. (See A.1.c.)

*c. Inability to Give Consent.*

When counseling minors or persons unable to give voluntary informed consent, counselors act in these clients' best interests. (See B.3.)

### A.4. CLIENTS SERVED BY OTHERS

If a client is receiving services from another mental health professional, counselors, with client consent, inform the professional persons already involved and develop clear agreements to avoid confusion and conflict for the client. (See C.6.c.)

### A.5. PERSONAL NEEDS AND VALUES

*a. Personal Needs.*

In the counseling relationship, counselors are aware of the intimacy and responsibilities inherent in the counseling relationship, maintain respect for clients, and avoid actions that seek to meet their personal needs at the expense of clients.

*b. Personal Values.*

Counselors are aware of their own values, attitudes, beliefs, and behaviors and how these apply in a diverse society and avoid imposing their values on clients. (See C.5.a.)

### A.6. DUAL RELATIONSHIPS

*a. Avoid When Possible.*

Counselors are aware of their influential positions with respect to clients, and they avoid exploiting the trust and dependency of clients. Counselors make every effort to avoid dual relationships with clients that could impair professional judgment or increase the risk of harm to clients. (Examples of such relationships include, but are not limited to, familial, social, financial, business, or close personal relationships with clients.) When a dual relationship cannot be avoided, counselors take appropriate professional precautions, such as informed consent, consultation, supervision, and documentation, to ensure that judgment is not impaired and no exploitation occurs. (See F.1.b.)

*b. Superior/Subordinate Relationships.*

Counselors do not accept as clients superiors or subordinates with whom they have administrative, supervisory, or evaluative relationships.

### A.7. SEXUAL INTIMACIES WITH CLIENTS

*a. Current Clients.*

Counselors do not have any type of sexual intimacies with clients and do not counsel persons with whom they have had a sexual relationship.

*b. Former Clients.*

Counselors do not engage in sexual intimacies with former clients within a minimum of two years after terminating the counseling relationship. Counselors who engage in such relationship after two years following termination have the responsibility to thoroughly examine and document that such relations did not have an exploitative nature, based on factors, such as duration of counseling, amount of time since counseling, termination circumstances, client's personal history and mental status, adverse impact on the client, and actions by the counselor suggesting a plan to initiate a sexual relationship with the client after termination.

### A.8.  MULTIPLE CLIENTS

When counselors agree to provide counseling services to two or more persons who have a relationship (such as husband and wife, or parents and children), counselors clarify at the outset which person or persons are clients and the nature of the relationships they will have with each involved person. If it becomes apparent that counselors may be called upon to perform potentially conflicting roles, they clarify, adjust, or withdraw from roles appropriately. (See B.2. and B.4.d.)

### A.9.  GROUP WORK

*a.  Screening.*

Counselors screen prospective group counseling/therapy participants. To the extent possible, counselors select members whose needs and goals are compatible with goals of the group, who will not impede the group process, and whose well-being will not be jeopardized by the group experience.

*b.  Protecting Clients.*

In a group setting, counselors take reasonable precautions to protect clients from physical or psychological trauma.

### A.10.  FEES AND BARTERING
### (See D.3.a. and D.3.b.)

*a.  Advance Understanding.*

Counselors clearly explain to clients, prior to entering the counseling relationship, all financial arrangements related to professional services including the use of collection agencies or legal measures for nonpayment. (A.11.c.)

*b.  Establishing Fees.*

In establishing fees for professional counseling services, counselors consider the financial status of clients and locality. In the event that the established fee structure is inappropriate for a client, assistance is provided in attempting to find comparable services of acceptable cost. (See A.10.d., D.3.a., and D.3.b.)

*c.  Bartering Discouraged.*

Counselors ordinarily refrain from accepting goods or services from clients in return for counseling services because such arrangements create inherent potential for conflicts,

exploitation, and distortion of the professional relationship. Counselors may participate in bartering only if the relationship is not exploitive, if the client requests it, if a clear written contract is established, and if such arrangements are an accepted practice among professionals in the community. (See A.6.a.)

*d.  Pro Bono Service.*

Counselors contribute to society by devoting a portion of their professional activity to services for which there is little or no financial return (pro bono).

### A.11.  TERMINATION AND
### REFERRAL

*a.  Abandonment Prohibited.*

Counselors do not abandon or neglect clients in counseling. Counselors assist in making appropriate arrangements for the continuation of treatment, when necessary, during interruptions, such as vacations, and following termination.

*b.  Inability to Assist Clients.*

If counselors determine an inability to be of professional assistance to clients, they avoid entering or immediately terminate a counseling relationship. Counselors are knowledgeable about referral resources and suggest appropriate alternatives. If clients decline the suggested referral, counselors should discontinue the relationship.

*c.  Appropriate Termination.*

Counselors terminate a counseling relationship, securing client agreement when possible, when it is reasonably clear that the client is no longer benefiting, when services are no longer required, when counseling no longer serves the client's needs or interests, when clients do not pay fees charged, or when agency or institution limits do not allow provision of further counseling services. (See A.10.b. and C.2.g.)

### A.12.  COMPUTER TECHNOLOGY

*a.  Use of Computers.*

When computer applications are used in counseling services, counselors ensure that (1) the client is intellectually, emotionally, and physically capable of using the computer application; (2) the computer application is appropriate for the needs of the client; (3) the client understands the purpose and operation of the computer appli-

cations; and (4) a follow-up of client use of a computer application is provided to correct possible misconceptions, discover inappropriate use, and assess subsequent needs.

*b.  Explanation of Limitations.*

Counselors ensure that clients are provided information as a part of the counseling relationship that adequately explains the limitations of computer technology.

*c.  Access to Computer
    Applications.*

Counselors provide for equal access to computer applications in counseling services. (See A.2.a.)

### SECTION B: CONFIDENTIALITY

### B.1.  RIGHT TO PRIVACY

*a.  Respect for Privacy.*

Counselors respect their clients' right to privacy and avoid illegal and unwarranted disclosures of confidential information. (See A.3.a. and B.6.a.)

*b.  Client Waiver.*

The right to privacy may be waived by the client or their legally recognized representative.

*c.  Exceptions.*

The general requirement that counselors keep information confidential does not apply when disclosure is required to prevent clear and imminent danger to the client or others or when legal requirements demand that confidential information be revealed. Counselors consult with other professionals when in doubt as to the validity of an exception.

*d.  Contagious, Fatal Diseases.*

A counselor who receives information confirming that a client has a disease commonly known to be both communicable and fatal is justified in disclosing information to an identifiable third party, who by his or her relationship with the client is at a high risk of contracting the disease. Prior to making a disclosure the counselor should ascertain that the client has not already informed the third party about his or her disease and that the client is not intending to inform the third party in the immediate future. (See B.1.c and B.1.f) *e. Court Ordered Disclosure.*

When court ordered to release confidential information without a client's permission, counselors request to the court that the disclosure not be required due to potential harm to the client or counseling relationship. (See B.1.c.)

*f. Minimal Disclosure.*

When circumstances require the disclosure of confidential information, only essential information is revealed. To the extent possible, clients are informed before confidential information is disclosed.

*g. Explanation of Limitations.*

When counseling is initiated and throughout the counseling process as necessary, counselors inform clients of the limitations of confidentiality and identify foreseeable situations in which confidentiality must be breached. (See G.2.a.)

*h. Subordinates.*

Counselors make every effort to ensure that privacy and confidentiality of clients are maintained by subordinates including employees, supervisees, clerical assistants, and volunteers. (See B.1.a.)

*i. Treatment Teams.*

If client treatment will involve a continued review by a treatment team, the client will be informed of the team's existence and composition.

## B.2. GROUPS AND FAMILIES

*a. Group Work.*

In group work, counselors clearly define confidentiality and the parameters for the specific group being entered, explain its importance, and discuss the difficulties related to confidentiality involved in group work. The fact that confidentiality cannot be guaranteed is clearly communicated to group members.

*b. Family Counseling.*

In family counseling, information about one family member cannot be disclosed to another member without permission. Counselors protect the privacy rights of each family member. (See A.8., B.3., and B.4.d.)

## B.3. MINOR OR INCOMPETENT CLIENTS

When counseling clients who are minors or individuals who are unable

to give voluntary, informed consent, parents or guardians may be included in the counseling process as appropriate. Counselors act in the best interests of clients and take measures to safeguard confidentiality. (See A.3.c.)

## B.4. RECORDS

*a. Requirement of Records.*

Counselors maintain records necessary for rendering professional services to their clients and as required by laws, regulations, or agency or institution procedures.

*b. Confidentiality of Records.*

Counselors are responsible for securing the safety and confidentiality of any counseling records they create, maintain, transfer, or destroy whether the records are written, taped, computerized, or stored in any other medium. (See B.1.a.)

*c. Permission to Record or Observe.*

Counselors obtain permission from clients prior to electronically recording or observing sessions. (See A.3.a.)

*d. Client Access.*

Counselors recognize that counseling records are kept for the benefit of clients and, therefore, provide access to records and copies of records when requested by competent clients unless the records contain information that may be misleading and detrimental to the client. In situations involving multiple clients, access to records is limited to those parts of records that do not include confidential information related to another client. (See A.8., B.1.a., and B.2.b.)

*e. Disclosure or Transfer.*

Counselors obtain written permission from clients to disclose or transfer records to legitimate third parties unless exceptions to confidentiality exist as listed in Section B.1. Steps are taken to ensure that receivers of counseling records are sensitive to their confidential nature.

## B.5. RESEARCH AND TRAINING

*a. Data Disguise Required.*

Use of data derived from counseling relationships for purposes of training, research, or publication is confined to content that is disguised to ensure the anonymity of the individuals involved. (See B.1.g. and G.3.d.)

*b. Agreement for Identification.*

Identification of a client in a presentation or publication is permissible only when the client has reviewed the material and has agreed to its presentation or publication. (See G.3.d.)

## B.6. CONSULTATION

*a. Respect for Privacy.*

Information obtained in a consulting relationship is discussed for professional purposes only with persons clearly concerned with the case. Written and oral reports present data germane to the purposes of the consultation, and every effort is made to protect client identity and avoid undue invasion of privacy.

*b. Cooperating Agencies.*

Before sharing information, counselors make efforts to ensure that there are defined policies in other agencies serving the counselor's clients that effectively protect the confidentiality of information.

## Section C: Professional Responsibility

### C.1. STANDARDS KNOWLEDGE

Counselors have a responsibility to read, understand, and follow the Code of Ethics and the Standards of Practice.

### C.2. PROFESSIONAL COMPETENCE

*a. Boundaries of Competence.*

Counselors practice only within the boundaries of their competence, based on their education, training, supervised experience, state and national professional credentials, and appropriate professional experience. Counselors will demonstrate a commitment to gain knowledge, personal awareness, sensitivity, and skills pertinent to working with a diverse client population.

*b. New Specialty Areas of Practice.*

Counselors practice in specialty areas new to them only after appropriate education, training, and supervised experience. While developing skills in new specialty areas, counselors take steps to ensure the competence of their work and to protect others from possible harm.

*c.   Qualified for Employment.*

Counselors accept employment only for positions for which they are qualified by education, training, supervised experience, state and national professional credentials, and appropriate professional experience. Counselors hire for professional counseling positions only individuals who are qualified and competent.

*d.   Monitor Effectiveness.*

Counselors continually monitor their effectiveness as professionals and take steps to improve when necessary. Counselors in private practice take reasonable steps to seek out peer supervision to evaluate their efficacy as counselors.

*e.   Ethical Issues Consultation.*

Counselors take reasonable steps to consult with other counselors or related professionals when they have questions regarding their ethical obligations or professional practice. (See H.1)

*f.   Continuing Education.*

Counselors recognize the need for continuing education to maintain a reasonable level of awareness of current scientific and professional information in their fields of activity. They take steps to maintain competence in the skills they use, are open to new procedures, and keep current with the diverse and/or special populations with whom they work.

*g.   Impairment.*

Counselors refrain from offering or accepting professional services when their physical, mental or emotional problems are likely to harm a client or others. They are alert to the signs of impairment, seek assistance for problems, and, if necessary, limit, suspend, or terminate their professional responsibilities. (See A.ll.c.)

## C.3.   ADVERTISING AND SOLICITING CLIENTS

*a.   Accurate Advertising.*

There are no restrictions on advertising by counselors except those that can be specifically justified to protect the public from deceptive practices. Counselors advertise or represent their services to the public by identifying their credentials in an accurate manner that is not false, misleading, deceptive, or fraudulent. Counselors may only advertise the highest degree earned which is in counseling or a

closely related field from a college or university that was accredited when the degree was awarded by one of the regional accrediting bodies recognized by the Council on Postsecondary Accreditation.

*b.   Testimonials.*

Counselors who use testimonials do not solicit them from clients or other persons who, because of their particular circumstances, may be vulnerable to undue influence.

*c.   Statements by Others.*

Counselors make reasonable efforts to ensure that statements made by others about them or the profession of counseling are accurate.

*d.   Recruiting Through Employment.*

Counselors do not use their places of employment or institutional affiliation to recruit or gain clients, supervisees, or consultees for their private practices. (See C.5.e.)

*e.   Products and Training Advertisements.*

Counselors who develop products related to their profession or conduct workshops or training events ensure that the advertisements concerning these products or events are accurate and disclose adequate information for consumers to make informed choices.

*f.   Promoting to Those Served.*

Counselors do not use counseling, teaching, training, or supervisory relationships to promote their products or training events in a manner that is deceptive or would exert undue influence on individuals who may be vulnerable. Counselors may adopt textbooks they have authored for instruction purposes.

*g.   Professional Association Involvement.*

Counselors actively participate in local, state, and national associations that foster the development and improvement of counseling.

## C.4.   CREDENTIALS

*a.   Credentials Claimed.*

Counselors claim or imply only professional credentials possessed and are responsible for correcting any known misrepresentations of their credentials by others. Professional credentials include graduate degrees in counseling or closely related mental health fields,

accreditation of graduate programs, national voluntary certifications, government-issued certifications or licenses, ACA professional membership, or any other credential that might indicate to the public specialized knowledge or expertise in counseling.

*b.   ACA Professional Membership.*

ACA professional members may announce to the public their membership status. Regular members may not announce their ACA membership in a manner that might imply they are credentialed counselors.

*c.   Credential Guidelines.*

Counselors follow the guidelines for use of credentials that have been established by the entities that issue the credentials.

*d.   Misrepresentation of Credentials.*

Counselors do not attribute more to their credentials than the credentials represent and do not imply that other counselors are not qualified because they do not possess certain credentials.

*e.   Doctoral Degrees From Other Fields.*

Counselors who hold a master's degree in counseling or a closely related mental health field but hold a doctoral degree from other than counseling or a closely related field do not use the title, "Dr.," in their practices and do not announce to the public in relation to their practice or status as a counselor that they hold a doctorate.

## C.5.   PUBLIC RESPONSIBILITY

*a.   Nondiscrimination.*

Counselors do not discriminate against clients, students, or supervisees in a manner that has a negative impact based on their age, color, culture, disability, ethnic group, gender, race, religion, sexual orientation, or socioeconomic status, or for any other reason. (See A.2.a.)

*b.   Sexual Harassment.*

Counselors do not engage in sexual harassment. Sexual harassment is defined as sexual solicitation, physical advances, or verbal or nonverbal conduct that is sexual in nature, that occurs in connection with professional activities or roles, and that either (1) is unwelcome, is offensive, or creates a hostile workplace environment, and counselors know or are told this; or (2) is sufficiently severe or intense to be perceived as harassment to a reasonable person in the context. Sexual harassment can consist of a single intense or severe act or multiple persistent or pervasive acts.

### c. Reports to Third Parties.

Counselors are accurate, honest, and unbiased in reporting their professional activities and judgments to appropriate third parties including courts, health insurance companies, those who are the recipients of evaluation reports, and others. (See B.1.g.)

### d. Media Presentations.

When counselors provide advice or comment by means of public lectures, demonstrations, radio or television programs, prerecorded tapes, printed articles, mailed material, or other media, they take reasonable precautions to ensure that (1) the statements are based on appropriate professional counseling literature and practice; (2) the statements are otherwise consistent with the Code of Ethics and the Standards of Practice; and (3) the recipients of the information are not encouraged to infer that a professional counseling relationship has been established. (See C.6.b.)

### e. Unjustified Gains.

Counselors do not use their professional positions to seek or receive unjustified personal gains, sexual favors, unfair advantage, or unearned goods or services. (See C.3.d.)

### C.6. RESPONSIBILITY TO OTHER PROFESSIONALS

### a. Different Approaches.

Counselors are respectful of approaches to professional counseling that differ from their own. Counselors know and take into account the traditions and practices of other professional groups with which they work.

### b. Personal Public Statements.

When making personal statements in a public context, counselors clarify that they are speaking from their personal perspectives and that they are not speaking on behalf of all counselors or the profession. (See C.5.d.)

### c. Clients Served by Others.

When counselors learn that their clients are in a professional relationship with another mental health professional, they request release from cli-

ents to inform the other professionals and strive to establish positive and collaborative professional relationships. (See A.4.)

### SECTION D: RELATIONSHIPS WITH OTHER PROFESSIONALS

### D.1. RELATIONSHIPS WITH EMPLOYERS AND EMPLOYEES

### a. Role Definition.

Counselors define and describe for their employers and employees the parameters and levels of their professional roles.

### b. Agreements.

Counselors establish working agreements with supervisors, colleagues, and subordinates regarding counseling or clinical relationships, confidentiality, adherence to professional standards, distinction between public and private material, maintenance and dissemination of recorded information, workload, and accountability. Working agreements in each instance are specified and made known to those concerned.

### c. Negative Conditions.

Counselors alert their employers to conditions that may be potentially disruptive or damaging to the counselor's professional responsibilities or that may limit their effectiveness.

### d. Evaluation.

Counselors submit regularly to professional review and evaluation by their supervisor or the appropriate representative of the employer.

### e. In-Service.

Counselors are responsible for in-service development of self and staff.

### f. Goals.

Counselors inform their staff of goals and programs.

### g. Practices.

Counselors provide personnel and agency practices that respect and enhance the rights and welfare of each employee and recipient of agency services. Counselors strive to maintain the highest levels of professional services.

### h. Personnel Selection and Assignment.

Counselors select competent staff and assign responsibilities compatible with their skills and experiences.

### i. Discrimination.

Counselors, as either employers or employees, do not engage in or condone practices that are inhumane, illegal, or unjustifiable (such as considerations based on age, color, culture, disability, ethnic group, gender, race, religion, sexual orientation, or socioeconomic status) in hiring, promotion, or training. (See A.2.a. and C.5.b.)

### j. Professional Conduct.

Counselors have a responsibility both to clients and to the agency or institution within which services are performed to maintain high standards of professional conduct.

### k. Exploitive Relationships.

Counselors do not engage in exploitive relationships with individuals over whom they have supervisory, evaluative, or instructional control or authority.

### l. Employer Policies.

The acceptance of employment in an agency or institution implies that counselors are in agreement with its general policies and principles. Counselors strive to reach agreement with employers as to acceptable standards of conduct that allow for changes in institutional policy conducive to the growth and development of clients.

### D.2. CONSULTATION (See B.6.)

### a. Consultation as an Option.

Counselors may choose to consult with any other professionally competent persons about their clients. In choosing consultants, counselors avoid placing the consultant in a conflict of interest situation that would preclude the consultant being a proper party to the counselor's efforts to help the client. Should counselors be engaged in a work setting that compromises this consultation standard, they consult with other professionals whenever possible to consider justifiable alternatives.

### b. Consultant Competency.

Counselors are reasonably certain that they have or the organization represented has the necessary competencies and resources for giving the kind of consulting services needed and that appropriate referral resources are available.

### c.  Understanding with Clients.

When providing consultation, counselors attempt to develop with their clients a clear understanding of problem definition, goals for change, and predicted consequences of interventions selected.

### d.  Consultant Goals.

The consulting relationship is one in which client adaptability and growth toward self-direction are consistently encouraged and cultivated. (See A.1.b.)

### D.3.  FEES FOR REFERRAL

### a.  Accepting Fees from Agency Clients.

Counselors refuse a private fee or other remuneration for rendering services to persons who are entitled to such services through the counselor's employing agency or institution. The policies of a particular agency may make explicit provisions for agency clients to receive counseling services from members of its staff in private practice. In such instances, the clients must be informed of other options open to them should they seek private counseling services. (See A.10.a., A.ll.b., and C.3.d.)

### b.  Referral Fees.

Counselors do not accept a referral fee from other professionals.

### D.4.  SUBCONTRACTOR ARRANGEMENTS

When counselors work as subcontractors for counseling services for a third party, they have a duty to inform clients of the limitations of confidentiality that the organization may place on counselors in providing counseling services to clients. The limits of such confidentiality ordinarily are discussed as part of the intake session. (See B.l.e. and B.l.f.)

### SECTION E: EVALUATION, ASSESSMENT, AND INTERPRETATION

### E.1.  GENERAL

### a.  Appraisal Techniques.

The primary purpose of educational and psychological assessment is to provide measures that are objective and interpretable in either comparative or absolute terms. Counselors recognize the need to interpret the

statements in this section as applying to the whole range of appraisal techniques including test and nontest data.

### b.  Client Welfare.

Counselors promote the welfare and best interests of the client in the development, publication, and utilization of educational and psychological assessment techniques. They do not misuse assessment results and interpretations and take reasonable steps to prevent others from misusing the information these techniques provide. They respect the client's right to know the results, the interpretations made, and the basis for their conclusions and recommendations.

### E.2.  COMPETENCE TO USE AND INTERPRET TESTS

### a.  Limits of Competence.

Counselors recognize the limits of their competence and perform only those testing and assessment services for which they have been trained. They are familiar with reliability, validity, related standardization, error of measurement, and proper application of any technique utilized. Counselors using computer-based test interpretations are trained in the construct being measured and the specific instrument being used prior to using this type of computer application. Counselors take reasonable measures to ensure the proper use of psychological assessment techniques by persons under their supervision.

### b.  Appropriate Use.

Counselors are responsible for the appropriate application, scoring, interpretation, and use of assessment instruments whether they score and interpret such tests themselves or use computerized or other services.

### c.  Decisions Based on Results.

Counselors responsible for decisions involving individuals or policies that are based on assessment results have a thorough understanding of educational and psychological measurement including validation criteria, test research, and guidelines for test development and use.

### d.  Accurate Information.

Counselors provide accurate information and avoid false claims or misconceptions when making statements about assessment instruments or techniques. Special efforts are made to avoid unwarranted connotations of

such terms as IQ and grade equivalent scores. (See C.5.c.)

### E.3.  INFORMED CONSENT

### a.  Explanation to Clients.

Prior to assessment, counselors explain the nature and purposes of assessment and the specific use of results in language the client (or other legally authorized person on behalf of the client) can understand unless an explicit exception to this right has been agreed upon in advance. Regardless of whether scoring and interpretation are completed by counselors, by assistants, or by computer or other outside services, counselors take reasonable steps to ensure that appropriate explanations are given to the client.

### b.  Recipients of Results.

The examinee's welfare, explicit understanding, and prior agreement determine the recipients of test results. Counselors include accurate and appropriate interpretations with any release of individual or group test results. (See B.1.a. and C.5.c.)

### E.4.  RELEASEOFINFORMATION TO COMPETENT PROFESSIONALS

### a.  Misuse of Results.

Counselors do not misuse assessment results, including test results, and interpretations and take reasonable steps to prevent the misuse of such by others. (See C.5.c.)

### b.  Release of Raw Data.

Counselors ordinarily release data (e.g., protocols, counseling or interview notes, or questionnaires) in which the client is identified only with the consent of the client or the client's legal representative. Such data are usually released only to persons recognized by counselors as competent to interpret the data. (See B.1.a.)

### E.5.  PROPER DIAGNOSIS OF MENTAL DISORDERS

### a.  Proper Diagnosis.

Counselors take special care to provide proper diagnosis of mental disorders. Assessment techniques (including personal interview) used to determine client care (e.g., locus of treatment, type of treatment, or recommended follow-up) are carefully selected and appropriately used. (See A.3.a. and C.5.c.)

### b. Cultural Sensitivity.

Counselors recognize that culture affects the manner in which clients' problems are defined. Clients' socioeconomic and cultural experience is considered when diagnosing mental disorders.

### E.6. TEST SELECTION

### a. Appropriateness of Instruments.

Counselors carefully consider the validity, reliability, psychometric limitations, and appropriateness of instruments when selecting tests for use in a given situation or with a particular client.

### b. Culturally Diverse Populations.

Counselors are cautious when selecting tests for culturally diverse populations to avoid inappropriateness of testing that may be outside of socialized behavioral or cognitive patterns.

### E.7. CONDITIONS OF TEST ADMINISTRATION

### a. Administration Conditions.

Counselors administer tests under the same conditions that were established in their standardization. When tests are not administered under standard conditions or when unusual behavior or irregularities occur during the testing session, those conditions are noted in interpretation, and the results may be designated as invalid or of questionable validity.

### b. Computer Administration.

Counselors are responsible for ensuring that administration programs function properly to provide clients with accurate results when a computer or other electronic methods are used for test administration. (See A.12.b.)

### c. Unsupervised Test-Taking.

Counselors do not permit unsupervised or inadequately supervised use of tests or assessments unless the tests or assessments are designed, intended, and validated for self-administration and/or scoring.

### d. Disclosure of Favorable Conditions.

Prior to test administration, conditions that produce most favorable test results are made known to the examinee.

### E.8. DIVERSITY IN TESTING

Counselors are cautious in using assessment techniques, making evaluations, and interpreting the performance of populations not represented in the norm group on which an instrument was standardized. They recognize the effects of age, color, culture, disability, ethnic group, gender, race, religion, sexual orientation, and socioeconomic status on test administration and interpretation and place test results in proper perspective with other relevant factors. (See A.2.a.)

### E.9. TEST SCORING AND INTERPRETATION

### a. Reporting Reservations.

In reporting assessment results, counselors indicate any reservations that exist regarding validity or reliability because of the circumstances of the assessment or the inappropriateness of the norms for the person tested.

### b. Research Instruments.

Counselors exercise caution when interpreting the results of research instruments possessing insufficient technical data to support respondent results. The specific purposes for the use of such instruments are stated explicitly to the examinee.

### c. Testing Services.

Counselors who provide test scoring and test interpretation services to support the assessment process confirm the validity of such interpretations. They accurately describe the purpose, norms, validity, reliability, and applications of the procedures and any special qualifications applicable to their use. The public offering of an automated test interpretations service is considered a professional-to-professional consultation. The formal responsibility of the consultant is to the consultee, but the ultimate and overriding responsibility is to the client.

### E.10. TEST SECURITY

Counselors maintain the integrity and security of tests and other assessment techniques consistent with legal and contractual obligations. Counselors do not appropriate, reproduce, or modify published tests or parts thereof without acknowledgment and permission from the publisher.

### E.11. OBSOLETE TESTS AND OUTDATED TEST RESULTS

Counselors do not use data or test results that are obsolete or outdated for the current purpose. Counselors make every effort to prevent the misuse of obsolete measures and test data by others.

### E.12. TEST CONSTRUCTION

Counselors use established scientific procedures, relevant standards, and current professional knowledge for test design in the development, publication, and utilization of educational and psychological assessment techniques.

### SECTION F: TEACHING, TRAINING, AND SUPERVISION

### F.1. COUNSELOR EDUCATORS AND TRAINERS

### a. Educators as Teachers and Practitioners.

Counselors who are responsible for developing, implementing, and supervising educational programs are skilled as teachers and practitioners. They are knowledgeable regarding the ethical, legal, and regulatory aspects of the profession, are skilled in applying that knowledge, and make students and supervisees aware of their responsibilities. Counselors conduct counselor education and training programs in an ethical manner and serve as role models for professional behavior. Counselor educators should make an effort to infuse material related to human diversity into all courses and/or workshops that are designed to promote the development of professional counselors.

### b. Relationship Boundaries with Students and Supervisees.

Counselors clearly define and maintain ethical, professional, and social relationship boundaries with their students and supervisees. They are aware of the differential in power that exists and the student's or supervisee's possible incomprehension of that power differential. Counselors explain to students and supervisees the potential for the relationship to become exploitive.

### c. Sexual Relationships.

Counselors do not engage in sexual relationships with students or supervisees and do not subject them to sexual harassment. (See A.6. and C.5.b)

### d.  Contributions to Research.

Counselors give credit to students or supervisees for their contributions to research and scholarly projects. Credit is given through co-authorship, acknowledgment, footnote statement, or other appropriate means in accordance with such contributions. (See G.4.b. and G.4.c.)

### e.  Close Relatives.

Counselors do not accept close relatives as students or supervisees.

### f.  Supervision Preparation.

Counselors who offer clinical supervision services are adequately prepared in supervision methods and techniques. Counselors who are doctoral students serving as practicum or internship supervisors to master's level students are adequately prepared and supervised by the training program.

### g.  Responsibility for Services to Clients.

Counselors who supervise the counseling services of others take reasonable measures to ensure that counseling services provided to clients are professional.

### h.  Endorsement.

Counselors do not endorse students or supervisees for certification, licensure, employment, or completion of an academic or training program if they believe students or supervisees are not qualified for the endorsement. Counselors take reasonable steps to assist students or supervisees who are not qualified for endorsement to become qualified.

### F.2.  COUNSELOR EDUCATION AND TRAINING PROGRAMS

### a.  Orientation.

Prior to admission, counselors orient prospective students to the counselor education or training program's expectations including but not limited to the following: (1) the type and level of skill acquisition required for successful completion of the training, (2) subject matter to be covered, (3) basis for evaluation, (4) training components that encourage self-growth or self-disclosure as part of the training process, (5) the type of supervision settings and requirements of the sites for required clinical field experiences, (6) student and supervisee evaluation and dismissal policies and procedures, and (7) up-to-date employment prospects for graduates.

### b.  Integration of Study and Practice.

Counselors establish counselor education and training programs that integrate academic study and supervised practice.

### c.  Evaluation.

Counselors clearly state to students and supervisees, in advance of training, the levels of competency expected, appraisal methods, and timing of evaluations for both didactic and experiential components. Counselors provide students and supervisees with periodic performance appraisal and evaluation feedback throughout the training program.

### d.  Teaching Ethics.

Counselors make students and supervisees aware of the ethical responsibilities and standards of the profession and the students' and supervisees' ethical responsibilities to the profession. (See C.1. and F.3.e.)

### e.  Peer Relationships.

When students or supervisees are assigned to lead counseling groups or provide clinical supervision for their peers, counselors take steps to ensure that students and supervisees placed in these roles do not have personal or adverse relationships with peers and that they understand they have the same ethical obligations as counselor educators, trainers, and supervisors. Counselors make every effort to ensure that the rights of peers are not compromised when students or supervisees are assigned to lead counseling groups or provide clinical supervision.

### f.  Varied Theoretical Positions.

Counselors present varied theoretical positions so that students and supervisees may make comparisons and have opportunities to develop their own positions. Counselors provide information concerning the scientific basis of professional practice. (See C.6.a.)

### g.  Field Placements.

Counselors develop clear policies within their training program regarding field placement and other clinical experiences. Counselors provide clearly stated roles and responsibilities for the student or supervisee, the site supervisor, and the program supervisor. They confirm that site supervisors are qualified to provide supervision and are informed of their professional and ethical responsibilities in this role.

### h.  Dual Relationships as Supervisors.

Counselors avoid dual relationships, such as performing the role of site supervisor and training program supervisor in the student's or supervisee's training program. Counselors do not accept any form of professional services, fees, commissions, reimbursement, or remuneration from a site for student or supervisee placement.

### i.  Diversity in Programs.

Counselors are responsive to their institution's and program's recruitment and retention needs for training program administrators, faculty, and students with diverse backgrounds and special needs. (See A.2.a.)

### F.3.  STUDENTS AND SUPERVISEES

### a.  Limitations.

Counselors, through ongoing evaluation and appraisal, are aware of the academic and personal limitations of students and supervisees that might impede performance. Counselors assist students and supervisees in securing remedial assistance when needed and dismiss from the training program supervisees who are unable to provide competent service due to academic or personal limitations. Counselors seek professional consultation and document their decision to dismiss or refer students or supervisees for assistance. Counselors assure that students and supervisees have recourse to address decisions made, to require them to seek assistance, or to dismiss them.

### b.  Self-Growth Experiences.

Counselors use professional judgment when designing training experiences conducted by the counselors themselves that require student and supervisee self-growth or self-disclosure. Safeguards are provided so that students and supervisees are aware of the ramifications their self-disclosure may have on counselors whose primary role as teacher, trainer, or supervisor requires acting on ethical obligations to the profession. Evaluative components of experiential training experiences explicitly delineate predetermined academic standards that are separate and not dependent on the student's level of self-disclosure. (See A.6.)

c. *Counseling for Students and Supervisees.*

If students or supervisees request counseling, supervisors or counselor educators provide them with acceptable referrals. Supervisors or counselor educators do not serve as counselor to students or supervisees over whom they hold administrative, teaching, or evaluative roles unless this is a brief role associated with a training experience. (See A.6.b.)

d. *Clients of Students and Supervisees.*

Counselors make every effort to ensure that the clients at field placements are aware of the services rendered and the qualifications of the students and supervisees rendering those services. Clients receive professional disclosure information and are informed of the limits of confidentiality. Client permission is obtained in order for the students and supervisees to use any information concerning the counseling relationship in the training process. (See B.1.e.)

e. *Standards for Students and Supervisees.*

Students and supervisees preparing to become counselors adhere to the Code of Ethics and the Standards of Practice. Students and supervisees have the same obligations to clients as those required of counselors. (See H.1.)

**SECTION G: RESEARCH AND PUBLICATION**

G.1. RESEARCH RESPONSIBILITIES

a. *Use of Human Subjects.*

Counselors plan, design, conduct, and report research in a manner consistent with pertinent ethical principles, federal and state laws, host institutional regulations, and scientific standards governing research with human subjects. Counselors design and conduct research that reflects cultural sensitivity appropriateness.

b. *Deviation from Standard Practices.*

Counselors seek consultation and observe stringent safeguards to protect the rights of research participants when a research problem suggests a deviation from standard acceptable practices. (See B.6.)

c. *Precautions to Avoid Injury.*

Counselors who conduct research with human subjects are responsible for the subjects' welfare throughout the experiment and take reasonable precautions to avoid causing injurious psychological, physical, or social effects to their subjects.

d. *Principal Researcher Responsibility.*

The ultimate responsibility for ethical research practice lies with the principal researcher. All others involved in the research activities share ethical obligations and full responsibility for their own actions.

e. *Minimal Interference.*

Counselors take reasonable precautions to avoid causing disruptions in subjects' lives due to participation in research.

f. *Diversity.*

Counselors are sensitive to diversity and research issues with special populations. They seek consultation when appropriate. (See A.2.a. and B.6.)

G.2. INFORMED CONSENT

a. *Topics Disclosed.*

In obtaining informed consent for research, counselors use language that is understandable to research participants and that (1) accurately explains the purpose and procedures to be followed; (2) identifies any procedures that are experimental or relatively untried; (3) describes the attendant discomforts and risks; (4) describes the benefits or changes in individuals or organizations that might be reasonably expected; (5) discloses appropriate alternative procedures that would be advantageous for subjects; (6) offers to answer any inquiries concerning the procedures; (7) describes any limitations on confidentiality; and (8) instructs that subjects are free to withdraw their consent and to discontinue participation in the project at any time. (See B.1.f.)

b. *Deception.*

Counselors do not conduct research involving deception unless alternative procedures are not feasible and the prospective value of the research justifies the deception. When the methodological requirements of a study necessitate concealment or deception, the investigator is required

to explain clearly the reasons for this action as soon as possible.

c. *Voluntary Participation.*

Participation in research is typically voluntary and without any penalty for refusal to participate. Involuntary participation is appropriate only when it can be demonstrated that participation will have no harmful effects on subjects and is essential to the investigation.

d. *Confidentiality of Information.*

Information obtained about research participants during the course of an investigation is confidential. When the possibility exists that others may obtain access to such information, ethical research practice requires that the possibility, together with the plans for protecting confidentiality, be explained to participants as a part of the procedure for obtaining informed consent. (See B.1.e.)

e. *Persons Incapable of Giving Informed Consent.*

When a person is incapable of giving informed consent, counselors provide an appropriate explanation, obtain agreement for participation and obtain appropriate consent from a legally authorized person.

f. *Commitments to Participants.*

Counselors take reasonable measures to honor all commitments to research participants.

g. *Explanations After Data Collection.*

After data are collected, counselors provide participants with full clarification of the nature of the study to remove any misconceptions. Where scientific or human values justify delaying or withholding information, counselors take reasonable measures to avoid causing harm.

h. *Agreements to Cooperate.*

Counselors who agree to cooperate with another individual in research or publication incur an obligation to cooperate as promised in terms of punctuality of performance and with regard to the completeness and accuracy of the information required.

i. *Informed Consent for Sponsors.*

In the pursuit of research, counselors give sponsors, institutions, and publication channels the same respect and opportunity for giving informed consent that they accord to individual research participants. Counselors are aware of their obligation to future research workers and ensure that host institutions are given feedback information and proper acknowledgment.

## G.3.  REPORTING RESULTS

### a.  *Information Affecting Outcome.*

When reporting research results, counselors explicitly mention all variables and conditions known to the investigator that may have affected the outcome of a study or the interpretation of data.

### b.  *Accurate Results.*

Counselors plan, conduct, and report research accurately and in a manner that minimizes the possibility that results will be misleading. They provide thorough discussions of the limitations of their data and alternative hypotheses. Counselors do not engage in fraudulent research, distort data, misrepresent data, or deliberately bias their results.

### c.  *Obligation to Report Unfavorable Results.*

Counselors communicate to other counselors the results of any research judged to be of professional value. Results that reflect unfavorably on institutions, programs, services, prevailing opinions, or vested interests are not withheld.

### d.  *Identity of Subjects.*

Counselors who supply data, aid in the research of another person, report research results, or make original data available take due care to disguise the identity of respective subjects in the absence of specific authorization from the subjects to do otherwise. (See B.1.g. and B.5.a.)

### e.  *Replication Studies.*

Counselors are obligated to make available sufficient original research data to qualified professionals who may wish to replicate the study.

## G.4.  PUBLICATION

### a.  *Recognition of Others.*

When conducting and reporting research, counselors are familiar with and give recognition to previous work on the topic, observe copyright laws, and give full credit to those to whom credit is due. (See F.1.d. and G.4.c.)

### b.  *Contributors.*

Counselors give credit through joint authorship, acknowledgment, footnote statements, or other appropriate means to those who have contributed significantly to research or concept development in accordance with such contributions. The principal contributor is listed first and minor technical or professional contributions are acknowledged in notes or introductory statements.

### c.  *Student Research.*

For an article that is substantially based on a student's dissertation or thesis, the student is listed as the principal author. (See F.1.d. and G.4.a.)

### d.  *Duplicate Submission.*

Counselors submit manuscripts for consideration to only one journal at a time. Manuscripts that are published in whole or in substantial part in another journal or published work are not submitted for publication without acknowledgment and permission from the previous publication.

### e.  *Professional Review.*

Counselors who review material submitted for publication, research, or other scholarly purposes respect the confidentiality and proprietary rights of those who submitted it.

## Section H: Resolving Ethical Issues

### H.1.  KNOWLEDGE OF STANDARDS

Counselors are familiar with the Code of Ethics and the Standards of Practice and other applicable ethics codes from other professional organizations of which they are members or from certification and licensure bodies. Lack of knowledge or misunderstanding of an ethical responsibility is not a defense against a charge of unethical conduct. (See F.3.e.)

### H.2.  SUSPECTED VIOLATIONS

### a.  *Ethical Behavior Expected.*

Counselors expect professional associates to adhere to Code of Ethics. When counselors possess reasonable cause that raises doubts as to whether a counselor is acting in an ethical manner, they take appropriate action. (See H.2.d. and H.2.e.)

### b.  *Consultation.*

When uncertain as to whether a particular situation or course of action may be in violation of Code of Ethics, counselors consult with other counselors who are knowledgeable about ethics, with colleagues, or with appropriate authorities.

### c.  *Organization Conflicts.*

If the demands of an organization with which counselors are affiliated pose a conflict with Code of Ethics, counselors specify the nature of such conflicts and express to their supervisors or other responsible officials their commitment to Code of Ethics. When possible, counselors work toward change within the organization to allow full adherence to Code of Ethics.

### d.  *Informal Resolution.*

When counselors have reasonable cause to believe that another counselor is violating an ethical standard, they attempt to first resolve the issue informally with the other counselor if feasible providing that such action does not violate confidentiality rights that may be involved.

### e.  *Reporting Suspected Violations.*

When an informal resolution is not appropriate or feasible, counselors, upon reasonable cause, take action, such as reporting the suspected ethical violation to state or national ethics committees, unless this action conflicts with confidentiality rights that cannot be resolved.

### f.  *Unwarranted Complaints.*

Counselors do not initiate, participate in, or encourage the filing of ethics complaints that are unwarranted or intend to harm a counselor rather than to protect clients or the public.

### H.3.  COOPERATION WITH ETHICS COMMITTEES

Counselors assist in the process of enforcing Code of Ethics. Counselors cooperate with investigations, proceedings, and requirements of the ACA Ethics Committee or ethics committees of other duly constituted associations or boards having jurisdiction over those charged with a violation. Counselors are familiar with the ACA Policies and Procedures and use it as a reference in assisting the enforcement of the Code of Ethics.

# STANDARDS OF PRACTICE

All members of the American Counseling Association (ACA) are required to adhere to the Standards of Practice and the Code of Ethics. The Standards of Practice represent minimal behavioral statements of the Code of Ethics. Members should refer to the applicable section of the Code of Ethics for further interpretation and amplification of the applicable Standard of Practice.

## SECTION A: THE COUNSELING RELATIONSHIP

### STANDARD OF PRACTICE ONE (SP-1) NONDISCRIMINATION

Counselors respect diversity and must not discriminate against clients because of age, color, culture, disability, ethnic group, gender, race, religion, sexual orientation, marital status, or socioeconomic status. (See A.2.a.)

### STANDARD OF PRACTICE TWO (SP-2) DISCLOSURE TO CLIENTS

Counselors must adequately inform clients, preferably in writing, regarding the counseling process and counseling relationship at or before the time it begins and throughout the relationship. (See A.3.a.)

### STANDARD OF PRACTICE THREE (SP-3) DUAL RELATIONSHIPS

Counselors must make every effort to avoid dual relationships with clients that could impair their professional judgment or increase the risk of harm to clients. When a dual relationship cannot be avoided, counselors must take appropriate steps to ensure that judgment is not impaired and that no exploitation occurs. (See A.6.a. and A.6.b.)

### STANDARD OF PRACTICE FOUR (SP-4) SEXUAL INTIMACIES WITH CLIENTS

Counselors must not engage in any type of sexual intimacies with current clients and must not engage in sexual intimacies with former clients within a minimum of two years after terminating the counseling relationship. Counselors who engage in such relationship after two years following termination have the responsibility to thoroughly examine and document that such relations did not have an exploitative nature.

### STANDARD OF PRACTICE FIVE (SP-5) PROTECTING CLIENTS DURING GROUP WORK

Counselors must take steps to protect clients from physical or psychological trauma resulting from interactions during group work. (See A.9.b.)

### STANDARD OF PRACTICE SIX (SP-6) ADVANCE UNDERSTANDING OF FEES

Counselors must explain to clients, prior to their entering the counseling relationship, financial arrangements related to professional services. (See A.10. a-d. and A.11.c.)

### STANDARD OF PRACTICE SEVEN (SP-7) TERMINATION

Counselors must assist in making appropriate arrangements for the continuation of treatment of clients, when necessary, following termination of counseling relationships. (See A.11.a.)

### STANDARD OF PRACTICE EIGHT (SP-8) INABILITY TO ASSIST CLIENTS

Counselors must avoid entering or immediately terminate a counseling relationship if it is determined that they are unable to be of professional assistance to a client. The counselor may assist in making an appropriate referral for the client. (See A.11.b.)

## SECTION B: CONFIDENTIALITY

### STANDARD OF PRACTICE NINE (SP-9) CONFIDENTIALITY REQUIREMENT

Counselors must keep information related to counseling services confidential unless disclosure is in the best interest of clients, is required for the welfare of others, or is required by law. When disclosure is required, only information that is essential is revealed and the client is informed of such disclosure. (See B.1.a-f.)

### STANDARD OF PRACTICE TEN (SP-10) CONFIDENTIALITY REQUIREMENTS FOR SUBORDINATES

Counselors must take measures to ensure that privacy and confidentiality of clients are maintained by subordinates. (See B.1.h.)

### STANDARD OF PRACTICE ELEVEN (SP-11) CONFIDENTIALITY IN GROUP WORK

Counselors must clearly communicate to group members that confidentiality cannot be guaranteed in group work. (See B.2.a.)

### STANDARD OF PRACTICE TWELVE (SP-12) CONFIDENTIALITY IN FAMILY COUNSELING

Counselors must not disclose information about one family member in counseling to another family member without prior consent. (See B.2.b.)

### STANDARD OF PRACTICE THIRTEEN (SP-13) CONFIDENTIALITY OF RECORDS

Counselors must maintain appropriate confidentiality in creating, storing, accessing, transferring, and disposing of counseling records. (See B.4.b.)

### STANDARD OF PRACTICE FOURTEEN (SP-14) PERMISSION TO RECORD OR OBSERVE

Counselors must obtain prior consent from clients in order to electronically record or observe sessions. (See B.4.c.)

### STANDARD OF PRACTICE FIFTEEN (SP-15) DISCLOSURE OR TRANSFER OF RECORDS

Counselors must obtain client consent to disclose or transfer records to third parties unless exceptions listed in SP-9 exist. (See B.4.e.)

### STANDARD OF PRACTICE SIXTEEN (SP-16) DATA DISGUISE REQUIRED

Counselors must disguise the identity of the client when using data for training, research, or publication. (See B.5.a.)

## SECTION C: PROFESSIONAL RESPONSIBILITY

### STANDARD OF PRACTICE SEVENTEEN (SP-17) BOUNDARIES OF COMPETENCE

Counselors must practice only within the boundaries of their competence. (See C.2.a.)

### STANDARD OF PRACTICE EIGHTEEN (SP-18) CONTINUING EDUCATION

Counselors must engage in continuing education to maintain their professional competence. (See C.2.f.)

## STANDARD OF PRACTICE NINETEEN (SP-19) IMPAIRMENT OF PROFESSIONALS

Counselors must refrain from offering professional services when their personal problems or conflicts may cause harm to a client or others. (See C.2.g.)

## STANDARD OF PRACTICE TWENTY (SP-20) ACCURATE ADVERTISING

Counselors must accurately represent their credentials and services when advertising. (See C.3.a.)

## STANDARD OF PRACTICE TWENTY-ONE (SP-21) RECRUITING THROUGH EMPLOYMENT

Counselors must not use their place of employment or institutional affiliation to recruit clients for their private practices. (See C.3.d.)

## STANDARD OF PRACTICE TWENTY-TWO (SP-22) CREDENTIALS CLAIMED

Counselors must claim or imply only professional credentials possessed and must correct any known misrepresentations of their credentials by others. (See C.4.a.)

## STANDARD OF PRACTICE TWENTY-THREE (SP-23) SEXUAL HARASSMENT

Counselors must not engage in sexual harassment. (See C.5.b.)

## STANDARD OF PRACTICE TWENTY-FOUR (SP-24) UNJUSTIFIED GAINS

Counselors must not use their professional positions to seek or receive unjustified personal gains, sexual favors, unfair advantage, or unearned goods or services. (See C.5.e.)

## STANDARD OF PRACTICE TWENTY-FIVE (SP-25) CLIENTS SERVED BY OTHERS

With the consent of the client, counselors must inform other mental health professionals serving the same client that a counseling relationship between the counselor and client exists. (See C.6.c.)

## STANDARD OF PRACTICE TWENTY-SIX (SP-26) NEGATIVE EMPLOYMENT CONDITIONS

Counselors must alert their employers to institutional policy or conditions that may be potentially disruptive or damaging to the counselor's

professional responsibilities or that may limit their effectiveness or deny clients' rights. (See D.l.c.)

## STANDARD OF PRACTICE TWENTY-SEVEN (SP-27) PERSONNEL SELECTION AND ASSIGNMENT

Counselors must select competent staff and must assign responsibilities compatible with staff skills and experiences. (See D.1.h.)

## STANDARD OF PRACTICE TWENTY-EIGHT (SP-28) EXPLOITIVE RELATIONSHIPS WITH SUBORDINATES

Counselors must not engage in exploitive relationships with individuals over whom they have supervisory, evaluative, or instructional control or authority. (See D.1.k.)

## SECTION D: RELATIONSHIP WITH OTHER PROFESSIONALS

## STANDARD OF PRACTICE TWENTY-NINE (SP-29) ACCEPTING FEES FROM AGENCY CLIENTS

Counselors must not accept fees or other remuneration for consultation with persons entitled to such services through the counselor's employing agency or institution. (See D.3.a.)

## STANDARD OF PRACTICE THIRTY (SP-30) REFERRAL FEES

Counselors must not accept referral fees. (See D.3.b.)

## SECTION E: EVALUATION, ASSESSMENT, AND INTERPRETATION

## STANDARD OF PRACTICE THIRTY-ONE (SP-31) LIMITS OF COMPETENCE

Counselors must perform only testing and assessment services for which they are competent. Counselors must not allow the use of psychological assessment techniques by unqualified persons under their supervision. (See E.2.a.)

## STANDARD OF PRACTICE THIRTY-TWO (SP-32) APPROPRIATE USE OF ASSESSMENT INSTRUMENTS

Counselors must use assessment instruments in the manner for which they were intended. (See E.2.b.)

## STANDARD OF PRACTICE THIRTY-THREE (SP-33) ASSESSMENT EXPLANATIONS TO CLIENTS

Counselors must provide explanations to clients prior to assessment about the nature and purposes of assessment and the specific uses of results. (See E.3.a.)

## STANDARD OF PRACTICE THIRTY-FOUR (SP-34) RECIPIENTS OF TEST RESULTS

Counselors must ensure that accurate and appropriate interpretations accompany any release of testing and assessment information. (See E.3.b.)

## STANDARD OF PRACTICE THIRTY-FIVE (SP-35) OBSOLETE TESTS AND OUTDATED TEST RESULTS

Counselors must not base their assessment or intervention decisions or recommendations on data or test results that are obsolete or outdated for the current purpose. (See E.11.)

## SECTION F: TEACHING, TRAINING, AND SUPERVISION

## STANDARD OF PRACTICE THIRTY-SIX (SP-36) SEXUAL RELATIONSHIPS WITH STUDENTS OR SUPERVISEES

Counselors must not engage in sexual relationships with their students and supervisees. (See F.l.c.)

## STANDARD OF PRACTICE THIRTY-SEVEN (SP-37) CREDIT FOR CONTRIBUTIONS TO RESEARCH

Counselors must give credit to students or supervisees for their contributions to research and scholarly projects. (See F.1.d.)

## STANDARD OF PRACTICE THIRTY-EIGHT (SP-38) SUPERVISION PREPARATION

Counselors who offer clinical supervision services must be trained and prepared in supervision methods and techniques. (See F.l.f.)

## STANDARD OF PRACTICE THIRTY-NINE (SP-39) EVALUATION INFORMATION

Counselors must clearly state to students and supervisees, in advance of training, the levels of competency expected, appraisal methods, and timing of evaluations. Counselors must provide students and supervisees with periodic performance appraisal and evaluation feedback throughout the training program. (See F.2.c.)

## STANDARD OF PRACTICE FORTY (SP-40) PEER RELATIONSHIPS IN TRAINING

Counselors must make every effort to ensure that the rights of peers are not violated when students and supervisees are assigned to lead counseling groups or provide clinical supervision. (See F.2.e.)

## STANDARD OF PRACTICE FORTY-ONE (SP-41) LIMITATIONS OF STUDENTS AND SUPERVISEES

Counselors must assist students and supervisees in securing remedial assistance, when needed, and must dismiss from the training program students and supervisees who are unable to provide competent service due to academic or personal limitations. (See F.3.a.)

## STANDARD OF PRACTICE FORTY-TWO (SP-42) SELF-GROWTH EXPERIENCES

Counselors who conduct experiences for students or supervisees that include self-growth or self disclosure must inform participants of counselors' ethical obligations to the profession and must not grade participants based on their nonacademic performance. (See F.3.b.)

## STANDARD OF PRACTICE FORTY-THREE (SP-43) STANDARDS FOR STUDENTS AND SUPERVISEES

Students and supervisees preparing to become counselors must adhere to the Code of Ethics and the Standards of Practice of counselors. (See F.3.e.)

## Section G: Research and Publication

## STANDARD OF PRACTICE FORTY-FOUR (SP-44) PRECAUTIONS TO AVOID INJURY IN RESEARCH

Counselors must avoid causing physical, social, or psychological harm or injury to subjects in research. (See G.l.c.)

## STANDARD OF PRACTICE FORTY-FIVE (SP-45) CONFIDENTIALITY OF RESEARCH INFORMATION

Counselors must keep confidential information obtained about research participants. (See G.2.d.)

## STANDARD OF PRACTICE FORTY-SIX (SP-46) INFORMATION AFFECTING RESEARCH OUTCOME

Counselors must report all variables and conditions known to the investigator that may have affected research data or outcomes. (See G.3.a.)

## STANDARD OF PRACTICE FORTY-SEVEN (SP-47) ACCURATE RESEARCH RESULTS

Counselors must not distort or misrepresent research data nor fabricate or intentionally bias research results. (See G.3.b.)

## STANDARD OF PRACTICE FORTY-EIGHT (SP-48) PUBLICATION CONTRIBUTORS

Counselors must give appropriate credit to those who have contributed to research. (See G.4.a. and G.4.b.)

## Section H: Resolving Ethical Issues

## STANDARD OF PRACTICE FORTY-NINE (SP-49) ETHICAL BEHAVIOR EXPECTED

Counselors must take appropriate action when they possess reasonable cause that raises doubts as to whether counselors or other mental health professionals are acting in an ethical manner. (See H.2.a.)

## STANDARD OF PRACTICE FIFTY (SP-50) UNWARRANTED COMPLAINTS

Counselors must not initiate, participate in, or encourage the filing of ethics complaints that are unwarranted or intended to harm a mental health professional rather than to protect clients or the public. (See H.2.f.)

## STANDARD OF PRACTICE FIFTY-ONE (SP-51) COOPERATION WITH ETHICS COMMITTEES

Counselors must cooperate with investigations, proceedings, and requirements of the ACA Ethics Committee or ethics committees of other duly constituted associations or boards having jurisdiction over those charged with a violation. (See H.3.)

## References

The following documents are available to counselors as resources to guide them in their practices. These resources are not a part of the Code of Ethics and the Standards of Practice.

**American Association for Counseling and Development/Association for Measurement and Evaluation in Counseling and Development.** (1989). The responsibilities of users of standardized tests (revised). Washington, DC: Author.

**American Counseling Association.** (1988). American Counseling Association Ethical Standards. Alexandria, VA: Author.

**American Psychological Association.** (1985). Standards for educational and psychological testing (revised). Washington, DC: Author.

**American Rehabilitation Counseling Association, Commission on Rehabilitation Counselor Certification, and National Rehabilitation Counseling Association.** (1995). Code of professional ethics for rehabilitation counselors. Chicago, IL: Author.

**American School Counselor Association.** (1992). Ethical standards for school counselors. Alexandria, VA: Author.

**Joint Committee on Testing Practices.** (1988). Code of fair testing practices in education. Washington, DC: Author.

**National Board for Certified Counselors.** (1989). National Board for Certified Counselors Code of Ethics. Alexandria, VA: Author.

Prediger, D. J. (Ed.). (1993, March). Multicultural assessment standards. Alexandria, VA: Association for Assessment in Counseling.

# Notes

1. The differences in the humanistic and behavioral viewpoints regarding the nature of human behavior and their implications for behavior change were illustrated very clearly in Carl Rogers's and B. F. Skinner's classic debate regarding control of human behavior (Rogers & Skinner, 1956).
2. The specific issues addressed by the Federal Trade Commission and their implications for the "Ethical Principles" will be discussed in Chapter 2.
3. Critics of APA have argued that this concern with "educating" the public has been misapplied as a justification for APA's many political statements. For example, in 1991, APA withdrew its plans to hold its 1997 annual convention in New Orleans, Louisiana, "because of Louisiana's strict new anti-abortion law" (DeAngelis, 1991, p. 1). The distinction between ethical and political positions will be discussed in Chapter 12.
4. The authority of APA to restrict several other aspects of members' advertisements was removed in 1992 under a consent agreement signed with the Federal Trade Commission. Under the terms of the agreement, APA can no longer place restrictions on members' nondeceptive advertising that presents their services as comparatively more desirable, implies unique or one-of-a-kind abilities, presents testimonials regarding the quality of services, or includes statements "likely to appeal to people's emotions, fears or anxieties" about the consequences of obtaining services (DeAngelis, 1993, p. 7). Furthermore, APA cannot prevent psychologists from paying referral services as a means of obtaining clients.
5. Clients' self-evaluation of their improvement in psychotherapy was demonstrated in one study to be related significantly to their acquisition of the therapist's values (Beutler, Pollack, & Jobe, 1978).
6. Prosenjit Poddar was convicted of second-degree murder, but the conviction was overturned on appeal because of errors in the instructions given to the jury by the trial judge. After Poddar was released, he returned to India (VandeCreek & Knapp, 1993).
7. The *ideal* utilitarian would add the point that one should not only be concerned with producing the greatest *amount* of pleasure, but also that the pleasure produced be of the highest *quality* (Smart & Williams, 1973).
8. Utilitarians who believe that minimizing suffering is a more pressing concern than maximizing happiness, referred to as "negative utilitarians" (Smart, 1958), are not subject to this criticism. However, this viewpoint has never been very popular among utilitarians.
9. Kant's theory is also referred to as *deontological* (from the Greek *deon*, meaning "that which is obligatory") because ethical duties are justified independent of any theory of value. Conversely, in utilitarianism, moral duties are justified by reference to the "good" (i.e., pleasurable) results that such actions bring about (based upon the theory of value called hedonism). Utilitarianism is therefore a teleological, or *axiological* (from the Greek *axios*, meaning "worth"), theory of moral obligation.
10. Even in everyday life, ethical issues, however subtle, are present. For example, when I moved to Texas to take a university position, there was a restaurant in town that featured a W.O.P. burger (i.e., a hamburger topped with tomato sauce and mozzarella cheese) on its menu. "W. O. P." is a derogatory term used in the United States to refer to Italians. Immigrant laborers in the early 1900s, many of whom were Italian, often did not have the work permits required by the government to engage in various occupations. Thus, Italians were referred to as people WithOut Permit (i.e., as "W. O. P. s"). Is there an ethical issue involved in ordering the W.O.P. burger? Also, is there an ethical issue involved in eating at the restaurant?

11. One could certainly argue that there are additional duties represented in this situation. In the interest of clarity and length, the present discussion is limited to the three duties stated.

12. Fletcher (1966) makes the interesting point that, from a legal standpoint, acting in accordance with the ethical principle of honesty in such a circumstance, as Kant suggests one ought, could cause one to become an accessory before the fact to murder.

13. Obviously, the ethical implications of this or any other scenario will vary in different contexts. If the question were asked during an initial psychotherapy interview, the client might be viewed as requesting information relevant to his or her decision as to whether to proceed with psychotherapy with the therapist. The issue of the potential influence of therapist values on clients will be discussed in Chapter 7.

14. The existence of a legal statute addressing the situation may or may not eliminate the *ethical* conflict. In some instances, a law may be incompatible with a professional's ethical duty. This type of situation will be addressed in Chapter 12.

15. The role of professional values in therapy will be addressed in Chapter 7. A training model for dealing more effectively with personal values in ethical decision making will be presented in Chapter 10.

16. Unprotected sexual behavior is the primary source of concern because available evidence indicates that living with an infected person does not place one at significant risk (VandeCreek & Knapp, 1993).

17. In some cases, it is neither possible, nor ethically necessary, to discover a solution that reflects all of the competing considerations because one duty clearly takes precedence. For example, a Tarasoff-type "duty to warn" scenario, in which a client clearly expresses the intention to kill an identifiable person, creates a situation in which the threat to human life obviously takes priority over a client's confidentiality.

18. In the *Diagnostic and Statistical Manual of Mental Disorders* (DSM-IV; American Psychiatric Association, 1994), life situations that may be the focus of treatment but do not involve clinically significant maladaptive reactions on the part of the client (e.g., Partner Relational Problem, Bereavement) are referred to as "V-codes." They are found in the section "Other Conditions That May Be a Focus of Clinical Attention" in the *DSM-IV.*

19. Informed consent and confidentiality issues concerning the treatment of children are discussed in greater detail in Chapter 8.

20. If the marital therapist did maintain the woman's confidentiality by keeping his knowledge of an illegal extramarital affair secret, he could be setting himself up for a charge of criminal conspiracy or "alienation of affection" (Cottone, Mannis, & Lewis, 1996).

21. The practice of "bartering" one's professional services (e.g., a therapist agreeing to treat an individual in exchange for the client repairing the therapist's roof) is strongly discouraged. The "Ethical Principles" points out the "inherent potential for conflicts, exploitation, and distortion of the professional relationship" in such an arrangement (APA, 1992, 1.18). Bartering should be avoided; in rare cases where it might be permissible, the arrangement should be handled with extreme care. Such arrangements are fertile ground for ethics complaints.

22. Because of the potential for sampling bias in the studies that have been conducted, it is difficult to evaluate the validity or prevalence of the "therapist-patient sex syndrome," and whether it is a causal factor or a result of the sexual relationship with a therapist (Williams, 1992). Nevertheless, there is strong agreement that clients can and have suffered considerable harm as a result of the unethical sexual behavior of therapists.

23. These topics are discussed in Chapter 12.

24. Paradoxical intention does have many useful applications that do not involve deceiving a client, such as encouraging the client to exaggerate a compulsive symptom in order to recognize his voluntary control of the behavior (Frankl, 1963).

25. Ethical issues pertaining to involuntary commitment procedures are discussed in Chapter 12.

26. There are serious ethical questions about using such a program with involuntarily committed clients, for whom treatment already involves a degree of coercion. These clients should receive all privileges for which they are eligible in light of their psychiatric condition.

27. Mental health professionals with specialized knowledge and experience in issues pertaining to child abuse may also conduct child protection evaluations. This and other types of forensic evaluations (e.g., child custody assessments) are discussed in Chapter 12.

28. In the professional ethics course I completed as a graduate student, a child clinical professor said that he makes a judgment regarding whether the abusive situation can be managed effectively in family therapy or requires reporting. I was shocked by the therapist's willingness to stake a child's life on the accuracy of his professional judgment (besides encouraging students in training to consider disobeying the law). No therapist should set herself in the position of being above the law in her ability to make an omnipotent judgment regarding what is truly in the best interest of the child. Also, reporting suspected abuse is simply abiding by the terms of the informed consent agreement a therapist should make with the client before therapy begins. If a client observes that his therapist can be manipulated to disobey the law, what kind of model is she of good citizenship and the unbiased protection of children's welfare? There is no guarantee that reporting will produce positive results, of course, but neither is there a guarantee with illegal failure to report, which will quite possibly lead to disastrous consequences for both the therapist and the child.

29. McMinn, Ellens, and Soref (1999) suggested that a professional might also need to inform clients prior to testing if he intends to use a computer-based test interpretation as the final test report because this practice is inconsistent with standards of professional practice.

30. Ethical issues pertaining to suicide prevention are discussed in Chapter 12.

31. Most tests are also protected by copyright, which would make it a violation of copyright law, as well as an ethical violation, to publish or reveal the content of tests.

32. Clinicians using computer-based test interpretation software should clarify whether the program's interpretations are based on data from computerized, rather than paper-and-pencil, administration of the test.

33. Ethical issues pertaining to forensic assessment are discussed in Chapter 12.

34. As discussed in Chapter 8, these issues can also arise when a clinician is working for an MCO that rewards efforts to contain costs.

35. The following journals are among those devoted to teaching issues in higher education: *Active Learning in Higher Education, College Teaching, Journal of Excellence in College Teaching, Teaching in Higher Education,* and *Teaching of Sociology.*

36. Supervisors must remember that e-mail communication is not an acceptable substitute for face-to-face interaction with supervisees in a supervised training experience.

37. The issue of the age at which children ought to be allowed to provide self-consent for research participation has been somewhat controversial. Shields and Johnson (1992) reported that children have cognitive capacities equal to those of adults for making consent decisions. It should be noted, however, that although the cognitive capacity to make competent decisions may exist at this age, experience in actually making decisions, which is a vital part of competent decision making, is usually lacking (Croxton, Churchill, & Fellin, 1988; Petersen & Leffert, 1995). In addition, even 14- or 15-year-old children may not possess the social competence to be able to act autonomously and give *voluntary* consent because of the influence the researcher, parent, or other authority figure might have over them (Scherer & Reppucci, 1988). Children are much more vulnerable to coercion than adults, though this changes as children reach adolescence (Thompson, 1992). Levine (1995a) suggested that adolescents should be permitted to provide self-consent for anonymous survey research and other studies involving no risk to participants.

38. Holmes (1976) referred to this debriefing process as "dehoaxing." He pointed out that when a researcher tells participants the truth about a study, they often do not believe him. They assume that, since he lied before, he is probably doing so now as another part of the study.

39. As mentioned earlier, debriefing subject pool participants can create problems for the validity of the research because subsequent participants are "contaminated" by their contact with debriefed classmates (Klein & Cheuvront, 1990). Delaying debriefing can prevent this problem, but it presents the ethical complications discussed earlier in the chapter.

40. If she could know the outcome in advance, the study would definitely be a waste of the participants' time and effort because the outcome would already be an established fact.

41. Removing an irreversibly comatose patient from life support is obviously not relevant to the issue of suicide because the person is not capable of making a choice. Arguably, such situations are also not potentially cases of murder because the person's life has, to some extent, already ended. Medical technology can keep a person's body alive when he is no longer capable of performing any of the functions we associate with living (e.g., interacting, thinking, feeling). These capacities of living persons are what makes the preservation of life so precious to humankind. Since these capacities are no longer present, and there is no hope that they will be regained in the future, the person is really already dead in terms of human functioning (Jamison, 1999).

42. On the other hand, suicide as self-sacrifice, which is intended to preserve the lives of others, may be permissible for Kant.

43. The procedures described in this section are those adopted by the APA Ethics Committee (1996). The policies of the ACA Ethics Committee (1997b) are very similar and address the same issues.

44. These categories and percentages of ethical violations are roughly comparable to those received by state boards, although a large proportion of the disciplinary actions taken by state boards in recent years concern failure of licensees to meet continuing education requirements ("Fiscal Year 1998 Enforcement Statistics," 1999). APA does not impose a continuing education requirement of its own for members.

45. APA rules prevent a member from resigning during an ethics investigation. This rule ensures that the APA Ethics Committee will retain jurisdiction over the complaint until it has been resolved ("Policy Modifies Bars to Resignation," 1997).

# Index

## A

Abortion, 155
  rights, 30
  on demand, 75
  opposition to on religious grounds, 135
Abuse, *see also* specific types
  evidence of, 158
  suspicion of, 29
ACA, *see* American Counseling Association
Academic probation, 197
Active parental consent, 218
Act utilitarianism, 57
ADA, *see* Americans with Disabilities Act
Addiction, disease model of, 150
Adult authority, children's trust in, 225
Advertisement of service, 41
Agape, 74
Aggression, 157
AIDS, developing symptoms of, 99
Alcohol Dependence, 143
Alcoholism, 243
ALI, *see* American Law Institute
Alzheimer's disease, 11
American Association of Applied and Preventive
      Psychology, 18
American Civil Liberties Union, 268
American Counseling Association (ACA), 5, 8,
      282
American Educational Research Association, 171
American Law Institute (ALI), 258
American Psychological Association (APA), 5,
      11, 171, 282
Americans with Disabilities Act (ADA), 45
Anger, 157
Animal Welfare Act (AWA), 236
Antidepressants, 137
Antipsychotic medication, 22
Antisocial behavior, 222
Antisocial Personality Disorders, 76, 92
Antisuggestion, 131
Anxiety
  chronic, intense, 220
  interpersonal, 34
APA, *see* American Psychological Association
Aspirational goals, 13
Assessment
  feedback, 173

report, 181
Assessment and testing, ethical issues in, 167–188
  college orientation testing, 186–187
  diversity issues in psychological assessment,
      175–177
  ethics and test validity, 177–178
  industrial/organizational assessment, 182–186
  practice case involving model of ethical
      decision making, 187–188
  psychological and educational assessment and
      testing, 171–175
    client feedback, 173
    competence in psychological assessment,
      175
    confidentiality issues in psychological
      assessment, 174
    informed consent issues in psychological
      testing, 171–172
    informed consent issues when testing
      children, 172–173
  report writing, 180–182
  use of computerized test administration,
      scoring, and interpretation, 178–180
  value and ethical implications of psychiatric
      diagnoses, 167–171
    prediction of low base rate behaviors,
      169–171
    pros and cons of labeling clients, 168–169
    values underlying DSM diagnostic
      scheme, 167–168
At-risk research participants, 218
Attitudes, 224
Avoidant Personality Disorder, 187
AWA, *see* Animal Welfare Act

## B

Bait and switch tactic, advertising free
      consultation as, 21
Bank robbery, 276
Bartering, 117, 138
Base rate behaviors, 169, 170
Bate-and-switch, among confidence tricksters,
      105
Beck Depression Inventory-II, 177
Behavioral disorders, 123, 167
Behaviors, 224

Milton Keynes UK
Ingram Content Group UK Ltd.
UKHW031127141024
449569UK00006B/393